JOURNEY TO THE BEGINNING

Edgar Snow

JOURNEY TO
THE BEGINNING

*To know that Heaven and Earth are
but as a tare-seed, and that the tip of
the hair is a mountain: this is the
expression of relativity . . . Beginning
and end are like a circle. Growth and
decay are the succession of transformations.
Where there is end there is the beginning.*

The *Chuang-tzu*

Vintage Books

A Division of Random House   *New York*

FIRST VINTAGE BOOKS EDITION, November 1972
Copyright © 1958 by Edgar Snow

All rights reserved under International
and Pan-American Copyright Conventions.
Published in the United States by Random House, Inc.,
New York, and simultaneously in Canada by
Random House of Canada Limited, Toronto.
Originally published by Random House, Inc., in 1958.

Library of Congress Cataloging in Publication Data

Snow, Edgar, 1905–1972
Journey to the beginning.

1. World politics—20th century.   1. Title.
[D443.S588 1972]   909.82   72-4257
ISBN 0-394-71847-X

Manufactured in the United States of America

For Lois, Chris and Sian — and Pete and Saxe

CONTENTS

PART ONE : THE NOMAD

PART TWO : TO BLOW THE FIRE

PART THREE: THE OTHER SIDE OF THE RIVER

PART FOUR : LA GUERRE FROIDE

PART ONE

THE NOMAD

*A man is a bundle of relations,
a knot of roots, whose flower and
fruitage is the world.*

EMERSON

CHAPTER 1

Into China

WHEN I FIRST reached Shanghai I was every youth, full of curiosity and wide open to the world. I could have been anyone of my generation of America moved westward, like my forebears, by the pull of some frontier dream, some nameless beckoning freedom, seeking fortune or following knowledge "like a sinking star" beyond the sunset.

I was twenty-two and I had picked up a few dollars in Wall Street speculation which gave me just enough of a stake, I thought, to finance a year of parsimonious traveling and adventuring around the world. I planned to return to New York after the year, make a fortune before I was thirty, and devote the rest of my life to leisurely study and writing. It really looked that easy in 1928.

I set out for the Pacific by way of the Panama Canal, spent three months in Hawaii and Japan, and went on to Shanghai. I had, on my itinerary, allotted six weeks to China. I was not to see America again for thirteen years.

At the end of my first year abroad I was about as far from home as I could get. I was in the baking city of Saratsi, south of the Gobi Desert. There in the Northwest I saw children dying by the thousands in a famine which eventually took more than five million lives. It was an awakening point in my life and remained the most shocking of all my experiences with war, poverty, violence and revolution until, fifteen years later, I saw the furnaces and gas chambers in which the Nazis, too impatient to wait for mere starvation, exterminated six to seven million people.

At Shanghai I presented a letter of introduction from Walter Williams, dean of the School of Journalism of the University of Missouri, to John Benjamin Powell, editor of the *China Weekly Review,* and correspondent of the *Chicago Tribune.* It was Powell who was to send me to the Northwest, where seven years later I would write a basic story about one of the great revolutions of human history, and the men and women who made it.

"Why don't you stay in Shanghai and help me put out the *Review*?" Powell asked. "I'm publishing a special edition in a few months—

a 'New China' edition to show the diehards that the Nationalists are here to stay. China is about to become really independent and we have to face it. I want somebody with a fresh outlook to put this edition together for me."

My outlook was fresh enough, if fresh meant green. "But I know nothing about China," I answered. "Besides, my schedule says six weeks in China, no more."

"Well, Shanghai is China, even though there are plenty of people here who don't know it," he laughed. "Spend your six weeks here and then leave. My guess is that you'll like it and stay."

I thought otherwise; Shanghai looked anything but appetizing to me after the beauty of Hawaii and the charm and order of Japan. But I liked something about Powell: his warm friendliness, his imported corncob pipe, his wonderful knack of story-telling. I decided I could learn something from him.

"All right," I said, "let's get started. Where does New China begin?"

It took me and my Chinese assistants three months to fill up the two hundred pages of that special edition with copy and advertising. I got little co-operation from the American business men in Shanghai or from the Consulate. They mostly considered Chiang Kai-shek a Communist and looked at the *Review* askance for defending him. I crammed prodigiously from Powell's big library of Orientalia and shamelessly cribbed background for my reporting. The more I read the more enamored I became. I discovered what antiquity meant and the dramatic contradictions it posed for the very young China I saw struggling to find its place in the modern world. Before my first task was completed Powell offered me a job as assistant editor of the *Review* and I accepted.

Then I did a series of article-supplements describing the tourist attractions of towns and cities along the Chinese railways. Powell wanted to persuade Americans that it was safe to travel in China again, and Sun Fo, minister of communications, enthusiastically endorsed his idea. Minister Sun promised me all possible help.

"Now that the Reds are suppressed," he told me, "there's no more antiforeignism. The revolution is over, the country is unified, and you'll see how peaceful and friendly the people are. Just publish the facts."

During the next four months I did the grand tour of China, in so far as it was accessible to an 8,000-mile railway system, in the best of style and comfort available. My trip took in every railway town of any importance and I came to know the look of the land from Ningpo to Hankow, from Nanking to Harbin, and from Peking to the Great Wall and beyond, to Manchuria, and to Korea. For weeks I filled the *Review* with travel articles, which were later made into "literature" used by the Chinese Tourist Bureau. Before my travels were over I also saw that the country was far from unified, and began to doubt that the real revolution had begun.

Vastly edifying and almost wholly pleasant days led up to my macabre journey into the land of death west of Peking. I saw all the storied places in the lower Yangtze and along the Grand Canal: Lake Taihu's islands and the mulberry trees and silk filatures around its green shores; the temples and the pagodas of West Lake at Hangchow; Yangchow's graceful bridges and Marco Polo's image in that town where he governed for three years under Kubilai Khan; Soochow, the Venice of China veined with canals and celebrated for its pleasure boats and exquisite singing girls; the great Ming walls of Nanking, and the majestic Purple Mountain where Sun Yat-sen is entombed; and then all the wonders of the north: the sacred mountain of Tai Shan, the birthplace and temple of Confucius, and the native town of Mencius. Finally Peking, which I was later to call "home," city of golden roofs and marble altars, of wine-colored walls and shaded temples and palaces, of magnificent acacia trees and perfect vistas. Beyond the Great Wall I traveled in streamlined comfort on the Japanese-owned South Manchuria Railway and at Mukden interviewed the young ruler of Manchuria, Marshal Chang Hsueh-liang. I saw Tsarist-built and Russian-populated Harbin, and in colonial Korea first met a people living under foreign conquerors.

For these travels Dr. Sun Fo loaned me the services of a diminutive companion named (something like) C. T. Washington Wu. He was an American-returned "student," aged forty-one, and his card announced him as a "technical expert" of the Ministry. It was the custom then for Chinese who studied abroad to adopt a Christian name for use in Sino-foreign society, and Mr. Wu had chosen to honor the father of our country. I soon discovered that he knew nothing about railways; he had not traveled much in China beyond Shanghai and Nanking. He was one of thousands of the hangers-on with whom high officials always seemed encumbered and had to place in some sinecure, for various family or personal reasons. But if Wu took little interest in temples, folklore or locomotives, he thoroughly enjoyed the sharks fins provided at their own expense by underpaid minor officials along the way, awed by Wu's ambiguous title.

At the end of a hard day of sightseeing Washington would reach his room in a Chinese hotel and shout for the *lao-kuan-ti,* or "old-fix-it." That omnipresent factotum would appear bearing steaming water and hot towels. While Washington was still wiping the dust from his face and hands he would give sharp instructions to the porter, who would *shih-shih* (yes, yes) him and leave. In a few minutes there would be a knock at the door and in would come a young girl or maybe two or three together. Washington would look them over, pinching a behind or two, and make a city-man's joke. As a rule he would then reject the first offering. "Old-Fix-It" would be recalled and rebuked for sending in a flower-face (pock-marked) girl. Eventually, a rosy-cheeked lass would be found satisfactory. Washington would do her the honor, and a few minutes later he would be ready, a technical expert, for the evening banquet.

A veritable army of prostitutes swarmed over the cities of China. The sale of women was a major industry. Vast numbers of boys as well as girls were sold to brokers for indentured labor of various kinds, including apprentices, factory operatives and domestic servants. Pretty girls were selected for distribution to metropolitan markets where buyers were always waiting for concubines, singing girls or tea-house waitresses. The most talented and strongest of the singing girls sometimes managed to surmount the conditions of the trade and emerge as independent "house-mothers." But the great multitude fell into the category of cheap prostitutes who were simply slaves of their owners and procurers.

In 1929 the Shanghai International Settlement and French Concession together held 48,000 *"piao-tzu."* There were in addition fifty to a hundred thousand unlicensed women operating on the streets and sidewalks, accompanied by voracious amahs whom you could see dragging still-bargaining customers into back-lane lairs. There were other thousands of women in the teahouses and brothels of the Chinese-administered part of Shanghai. And these were to increase still more during the years of famine, flood and war that lay ahead.

All over China the poorer peasants were being steadily driven from the land by confiscatory taxes and excessive rents. In the regions of prolonged drought millions were completely destitute and the sale of children was common. Foreigners in Shanghai would say, "These Chinese are heartless; they think no more of selling a child than a pig." But in a Settlement where a public burial detail was continuously on duty and in the year 1930 reported that it had "buried or otherwise disposed of" more than 28,000 corpses found on the streets or floating on the canals—mostly victims of infanticide—and where the figure thereafter never dropped below that, there were worse fates than living to be sold into service.

CHAPTER 2

I Meet the Dead

IN THAT TIME of the great famine throughout Northwest China, an area larger than Texas, political power was in fact or in theory in the hands of Marshal Yen Hsi-shan, yclept the "Model Governor." He held the title of Pacification Commissioner from the central government at Nanking and his ally was another old warlord, Feng Yu-hsiang, the so-called "Christian-General," who had helped Chiang Kai-shek during the counter-revolution in 1927. But the Generalissimo did not trust either of them now and the famine was looked upon as a useful weapon with which to bring them into line. Nanking sent no food to the starving. The International Famine Relief Commission even had great difficulty getting government rolling stock or other transportation for the little grain it purchased with privately contributed funds.

Beyond Kalgan, only skeleton trains shuttled back and forth from Suiyuan and trade had stagnated. Washington Wu wanted to end the trip over the Peking-Suiyuan Railway at Kalgan. Tourists couldn't go farther, he argued. I contended that I had been ordered to see *all* the railways, and insisted on continuing into Suiyuan. After much debate the assistant traffic manager of the line finally put a special car on a freight train going west and stocked it with provisions and bodyguards. He said he would take me if Wu would not. Washington went.

Not far out of Kalgan we came to a small station on a hot dusty plain and drew up beside a gasping locomotive pulling a few broken-down cars going in the opposite direction. A couple of goods wagons in it were packed with wan, half-naked, hungry children, nearly all girls, who seemed to be under the general care of a few old women and men. From the traffic manager I learned that they were going to work in the shops or in brothels.

Kalgan was the chief entrepot in this trade along the border of the famine area. Sometimes the children fared well when apprenticed by honest artisans or taken into orderly homes; it was at least a way of keeping alive. But everything depended upon the purpose and character or whim of the purchaser. At this time I heard other details of slavery in China from Rewi Alley, a New Zealander whose red head suddenly flamed out of a crowd of black-topped Chinese debouched from one of the cars on our train at a wayside station.

Alley was then employed as factory inspector by the Shanghai International Settlement. He had chosen to spend his annual vacation in the famine region, working with a handful of foreigners who ran a few soup kitchens and were building the Sa Tao Chu irrigation canal. Here I began a friendship that ripened several years later when Alley and I worked together to start Chinese Industrial Co-operatives. Now I simply thought of him as a queer duck, but interesting. I asked Washington to let the red-head sleep in one of the unoccupied bunks of the private car and share our food. The technical expert haughtily refused. He didn't like "imperialists," especially "missionaries," and he had an idea that Alley was one of them. They were "always talking about China's backwardness." They made the country "lose face," he thought.

Alley took it good-naturedly. "I've met dozens of the type around Shanghai and Nanking," he said. "The lousy peasants are better company." And back to them he went, waving cheerfully from an open gondola.

I felt like leaving the car and joining the better company. But I had my job to do and I was also beginning to like traveling in comfort. "Washington" had become Mr. Wu to me again when we pulled into Kueihua a day later. I went into the city with Alley to explore its misery and next day we rode on to Saratsi, the end of the line, where tens of thousands of refugees had crawled up from the stricken plains below.

To Wu's disgust I insisted on spending several days riding into the ghost towns and across deserts which had once been fertile farmlands. The technical expert hotly contended that this had nothing to do with railways and at first retired to the special car and said he would go back without me. He changed his mind when some local elders called him *ta-jen* (great man), mistook him for a high official and asked him for help.

We went with O. J. Todd, an American engineer in charge of the Famine Commission's canal project, and with Dr. Robert Ingram, a medical missionary whose special task was to keep the labor gangs and the refugee camps deloused to prevent the spread of typhus and plague. It was a weird landscape swept of every growing thing as if by volcanic ash from a newly erupted earth. Even the trees had been stripped of their bark and were dying. In the villages most of the mud-brick houses were collapsing. Their few timbers had been pulled out and sold for the coppers they would bring.

Here and there last-ditchers still sat or lay on their doorsteps, scarcely conscious. In one place I saw a naked twig-armed child, his belly a balloon from a diet of leaves and sawdust. He was trying to shake back to life his naked father who had just died on the road. We picked up the lad and carried him off to a soup kitchen in town. Again we came upon a couple of young women as thin as the dried baked ducks dangling before a Chinese meat shop. They were the same color and just as naked, with their withered breasts hanging like deflated paper sacks. They had fainted on a village street where those who could still walk dragged past, not noticing them. Our party took that pair on to a camp. So many thousands were doomed that the salvation of a few lives seemed meaningless. As much as half the population had perished within the year in two towns we visited. The dead were so numerous that they were buried in shallow trenches outside the walls, and it was difficult to find men physically able to do the digging. Corpses frequently disappeared before they could be interred and human flesh was openly sold in some villages.

People in Saratsi were relatively better off than those hundreds of miles from the railhead and any hope of help. Everywhere the tenants as well as farmowners had gambled for the third spring and again no rain had fallen. Now they had mortgaged their last land and labor to buy seed which never sprouted, and they had nothing left. Having planted or eaten all their seed grain they faced early extinction. But the wealthiest landlords could survive and even grow richer. This was a time when a sack of grain would buy a farm. Even around Saratsi, where the canal was being cut to tap the Yellow River and flood 400,000 acres, a dismal fate awaited those who would live to see the soil yield again. The small farmers, tenants and laborers were bankrupt, and money-lenders and grain merchants were foreclosing rapidly. Their profits swollen through hoarding and speculation on grain, a few rich families were taking over the land for a fraction of its normal value. Their homes and granaries were protected by well-fed private police, loyal to their rice bowls, while millions starved.

Of course the problem was too enormous for any extant foreign relief agency to handle. It needed state or world intervention on a huge scale; at least twenty million people were seriously affected. "We haven't the money or the means to reach one in a hundred!" said Dr. Ingram. "It's shameful that the officials do nothing. They're too busy passing resolutions and making new jobs for their friends."

In the winter of 1929-30 and in the equally terrible year that followed before the drought finally ended, vast acreage passed into the hands of usurers and absentee owners, from the Great Wall southward to the Yellow River. During my next dozen years in China there would never be a year when famine or flood did not strike some area of that sprawling, ravaged land. In every case I would see the same confiscatory economics at work, the same exploitation of human tragedy going unchecked, the same abasement of the farmer and degradation of sex, the constant growth of the landless peasantry, and the making of recruits for rebellion. By the mid-Forties the deterioration would be so far advanced that starvation and rebellion would be simultaneous in Western China. Graham Peck would see swarms of Chiang Kai-shek's own troops falling upon the countryside and murdering starving peasants, in the midst of the war against Japan. But few Americans would trouble to read Peck's graphic book about it, called *Two Kinds of Time,* which clearly told why Communist revolution was inevitable in China.

More Americans read Graham Peck, however, than read my report on the Northwest famine in the New York *Herald Tribune* in 1929. And whereas America would pour billions into the Chiang Kai-shek government by 1945, not for famine relief but for a military alliance, the only response to my 5,000-word story came from an American schoolboy who sent me a letter and a dollar bill to help feed his starving Chinese "brothers."

"The victims of the Yellow River floods in China amount to hundreds of thousands," says Ivanov in Koestler's *Darkness at Noon.* "Nature is generous in her senseless experiments on mankind. Why should mankind not have the right to experiment with itself?" That was the question I was bound to ask more and more in the years ahead.

But that year, as we rolled southward from Peking through the yellow fields of ripening kaoliang and the verdant wet green of the rice, I was still a long way from realizing that the Nationalists did not have much time left in which to redeem their promises. Washington Wu may have been reflecting about that more than I supposed. He was sobered and chastened by our visit.

"Terrible! Terrible!" he suddenly muttered one day when we discussed what we had seen. "I had been in America so many years I forgot about things like this. What a miserable, miserable country our China is!"

I felt a bond of sympathy with Wu when at last I heard him concede some evil in China apart from the sins of the white imperialists. His facade of arrogance and false pride cracked. There was a new spirit of protest against injustice in his voice, a new sense of humility and personal responsibility.

"We must, we *must* do something to save China—quickly," he said. "But *how?*"

"There you sit, with thirty centuries of experience behind you," said I. "As an American, I can trace my origins a few generations. How can I answer that question for China!"

"There has to be a new birth," he said thoughtfully. "It can only come out of our own body—the body of our own history."

Why did I begin to share a sense of concern about the process? Why did China begin to mean something to me? I could not help thinking how different a childhood I had had, and how vastly greater my opportunities as the child of a rich, open, frontier civilization, where nature laid its bounty before man, asking only that he work to enjoy it, as compared to the problems of survival in old China, where the struggle had to go on in a society encrusted with thousands of years of traditional exploitation of man by man on the harshest predatory level.

Wu was silent for a long time, locked by his own thoughts, as I was by mine.

CHAPTER 3

Up from Kentucky

MY PATERNAL GRANDFATHER was the member of my family most likely to have understood the kind of urge that had pushed me toward China and which held me in the East.

Horace Parks Snow would be more than one hundred years old if he were alive today. He was born on his father's place in Clinton County, Kentucky, near Cainey Gap in the Cumberlands. His own great-grandfather, William Snow, had been the first to settle in the region, coming up from North Carolina late in the eighteenth century, to break new land given to his father "for services rendered" during the revolution.

By the time my grandfather arrived, the Kentucky farm had become "one of the most beautiful in the state," according to a Kentucky writer, J. W. Hall; but in all the fields, the blue grass pastures, the stables and the orchards, there was no slave to be found. The Snows were anti-secessionists. My great-great-grandfather, Samuel Frost Snow, freed his slaves before the Civil War. All Cainey Gap, though it bordered right on the deep South, was solidly pro-Union. During my father's early boyhood in Kentucky his grandmother once told him that there had been only one open Confederate sympathizer in Cainey Gap. He had tried to join the rebellion one morning but by evening his neighbors brought him back home and propped him up on his own porch "to stay there and protect his womenfolk during the war," as they said. "He was deader than a doornail," my great-grandmother Snow added.

Many Snows of Kentucky had moved west with the frontier, and before the 1870's "H.P." had himself ranged into the plains and found good farmland and pasture in Kansas territory. He had married Louisa Frances Kella from Petersburg, Virginia, grand-daughter of a celebrated circuit rider inspired by John Wesley. He was one of the sources of the Snows' firm anti-Papism. In the Eighties my grandfather took Louisa and their three sons and four daughters to settle near Winfield, Kansas, where he invested his patrimony in farming and what they used to call "the mercantile business"—a general store. "H.P." boasted that he "never worked a day in his life for another man." After surviving the "panic" of the Nineties he acquired extensive land holdings in Missouri, Kansas and Texas and eventually made a modest fortune.

My father, James Edgar, appeared on the scene about the time Lenin and Sun Yat-Sen were born and a decade after the Taiping Rebellion was crushed in China, at a cost of forty million lives. Years later all three events were to have a deep personal impact on me. At that time, however, so remote were Americans from a sense of membership in the Pacific community that a holocaust involving the loss of forty million lives in China went virtually unnoticed.

What happened in Asia was of little consequence to my father. He grew up in Kentucky and Kansas unaware of a seething world across the Pacific. He courted and married Anna Catherine Edelmann, a Columbus, Ohio, girl of mixed Irish-German descent. Her mother was a native of Menagh, Tipperary, and her father was the child of

German immigrants from Silesia who had brought him to America when he was two years old.

The Snows were somewhat shocked when they learned that Anna was a "Papist"; she was the first Catholic to marry one of the Snows "up from Kentucky." What was more, there were priests on both sides of her family. My father finally agreed to study Catholic doctrine with a view to becoming a convert in order to make it possible for the beautiful red-haired Anna to marry him. He also conceded that the children should be baptized in and receive instruction in the faith— a compromise he soon regretted.

My father took a job with a cattle-buying concern, after he left Southwestern College, and moved to Chicago with Anna. He soon made a bit of capital and returned to Kansas City, where he bought a cattlemen's paper and a small publishing and printing business. By the time the Snow Printing Company's best customer was the *Kansas City Star,* James and Anna had two sons and a daughter. As if "Edgar" were not bad enough for the youngest I was given the middle moniker "Parks," which was all right for Grandfather but not for me. I dropped it; in fact I never picked it up.

We children were duly catechised through Catholic communion and then brought up to confirmation and membership. But my father insisted that we be educated in public schools. If the local priests had not made our rejection of the parochial school a sin on mother's conscience, and persuaded her to persist in her duty to save my father's soul by getting him into the Church, "J.E." might not have become so hostile to Catholicism.

As it was, he had agreed to study, and study he did—too much for a good Catholic layman. He even read the Douay Bible, and pointed out its inconsistencies. He ended by being better informed, particularly on the "bad sides" of the Church, than the true believers around us. He did not interfere with my indoctrination, but when I was old enough to understand I had to listen, on Sunday afternoons, to well-chosen lines from Ingersoll or Brand or others on the Index. My brother and sister were happily spared most of this but by the time I arrived my father was convinced that it was his duty to keep me "open-minded about God."

In the end I lost faith not because of Robert Ingersoll's arguments, but because one day I went with an older altar boy to collect the host, or communion wafers, from a nearby convent. It struck me as strange when I saw that the wafers were baked in ordinary coal stoves. On the way back the older boy opened one of the tins and consumed, on the spot, a handful of "the body and blood of Christ." I expected to see him knocked flat, but nothing happened.

Bill laughed. "They ain't been blessed yet. They don't become the blessed *sakament* till they been blessed!"

I thought of dear old Father Joseph Walsh, our parish priest, and all at once I didn't believe he could turn those flour and water wafers into the body and blood of Jesus Christ. I derived no particular joy from this realization. "Easily may a man become an infidel but hardly can he be converted to another faith."

For my mother's sake I continued to attend mass while I remained at home. By the time I entered college I was indifferent to sectarian religion of any kind. Much later I became interested in Buddhism and Taoism as philosophies, but not in institutionalized worship and cults.

The skepticism driven into me by my father made me a rationalist in most things and caused me to shy away from dogma and absolutism in any form. Yet Church teaching of my youthful mind had penetrated enough to set up a dichotomy between faith and reason which would persist for many years. The yearning to believe in an external and personal savior, once inculcated in the child, rather than to accept personal responsibility, with all its agony mixed with its satisfactions, is not easily put aside.

My father would have agreed with Einstein's idea of God as "the presence of a superior reasoning power which is revealed in the incomprehensible universe" but his methods of opposing Catholicism were not good for our family unity. Doubtless he won his campaign, intellectually; he lost it somewhere in the heart. I knew that Mother was good, unselfish and full of loving kindness. That was enough to prevent me from becoming a militant anti-Catholic.

In a far strange land now, with Mr. C. T. Washington Wu still beside me, I thought of Mother with love and gratitude and of the letters I would soon be writing to her. It never occurred to me that I would not see her again. The letter from home which would within a few weeks report her illness to me did not reach me until two weeks after a cable which told me of her death.

It is hard to believe that so recently as that it was physically impossible for me or anyone else to get home from the Orient in much less than a month. China seemed as remote as the moon is now. In terms of current rocket time it was more so. But the time-space lag between us was already closing up miraculously compared to the clipper voyage of another Snow who had preceded me when President

Madison commissioned stern-visaged Captain Samuel Snow to serve as our first resident consul at Canton. I was one day to fall unexpected heir to Captain Snow's portrait, his papers, and the leather-bound journal in which he described his long voyage around the Cape to India and China in 1795.

CHAPTER 4

Shanghai!

J. B. POWELL had wired me, when I was still in Peking with Washington Wu, to return to Shanghai at once. The *Chicago Tribune* had ordered him to Manchuria to cover hostilities there following Marshal Chang Hsueh-liang's brash attempt to expel the Russians from their offices, jobs and homes along the Chinese Eastern Railway, in north Manchuria. Encouraged by the Nationalist hero, Chiang Kai-shek, the young Marshal had tried forcibly to cancel the agreement which made that railway a joint Sino-Soviet enterprise, inherited from Tsarist days, when Russian funds and engineers had built it. The adventure proved disastrous; Soviet troops invaded Manchuria and restored the former status quo. Having done that, the Soviet Government invited the Chinese to Moscow to negotiate a settlement, after which, rather to everybody's surprise, they retired their troops to Siberia.

Powell had already left when I got back. I read his letter and found myself acting editor of the *Review,* as well as South China correspondent for the *Chicago Tribune.* From Manchuria, Powell was to go on to Moscow and remain there for months. It was thus that I became a foreign correspondent—and really got acquainted with Shanghai.

In the Nineteen Thirties it took John Gunther only a few days in foreign-ruled Shanghai to decide that it was "a political ulcer on the face of China." Shanghai had waxed fat and corrupt and was soon to pay a dismaying price for the past its Western heirs had forgotten. History always collects, and the Chinese had waited a hundred years.

But Western business men who lived there when I arrived in 1928 acted as if the Settlement were real and would last forever. In their euphoria they felt that they were the continent and the four hundred

million Chinese beyond were a kind of suburb put there by God for
trading purposes. And yet it was a fascinating old Sodom and Gomor-
rah, at that, while it lasted!

At first I too mistook Shanghai for China. The bizarre contrasts of
very old and very new, the sublime ugliness of the place, its kind of
polyglot glamor (all nations poised for crisis there), and its frank
money-is-all vulgarity held me in puzzled wonder. Initially I also felt
vaguely oppressed by its sheer physical weight of "mass." I never saw
so very many people (ruled by so very few) and to me they all looked
alike, an agglomerate seeming to lack individual shapes, but consisting of color, movement and contrariness. They read from right to
left, put surnames first and given names last, waved you away when
wishing to beckon, put their hands in their sleeves instead of shaking
yours to say good-bye, pared an apple away from them instead of
toward them, pulled to saw a piece of wood instead of pushing, dealt
cards from right to left, drank soup at the end of the meal, and said
"no" when they meant "yes"! It was hard for a young American to see
at once that these ways had nothing to do with the basic human proposition that "within the four seas all men are brothers."

The streets of downtown Shanghai likewise seemed a continuous
freak circus at first, unbelievably *alive* with all manner of people per-
forming almost every physical and social function in public: yelling,
gesturing, always acting, crushing throngs spilling through every kind
of traffic, precariously amidst old cars and new ones and between
coolies racing wildly to compete for ricksha fares, gingerly past "honey-
carts" filled with excrement dragged down Bubbling Well Road, sar-
donically past perfumed, exquisitely gowned, mid-thigh-exposed Chinese ladies, jestingly past the Herculean bare-backed coolie trundling
his taxi-wheelbarrow load of six giggling servant girls en route to home
or work, carefully before singing peddlers bearing portable kitchens
ready with delicious noodles on the spot, lovingly under gold-lettered
shops overflowing with fine silks and brocades, dead-panning past
village women staring wide-eyed at frightening Indian policemen,
gravely past gambling mah-jongg ivories clicking and jai alai and pari-
mutuel betting, slyly through streets hung with the heavy-sweet acrid
smell of opium, sniffingly past southern restaurants and brightly-lighted
sing-song houses, indifferently past scrubbed, aloof young Englishmen
in their Austins popping off to cricket on the Race Course, snickeringly
around elderly white gentlemen in carriages with their wives or Russian mistresses out for the cool air along the Bund, and hastily past
sailors looking for beer and women—from noisy dawn to plangent

night the endless hawking and spitting, the baby's urine stream on the curb, the amah's scolding, the high falsetto of opera at Wing On Gardens where a dozen plays went on at once and hotel rooms next door filled up with plump virgins procured for wealthy merchants in from the provinces for business and debauch, the wail of dance bands moaning for slender be-jewelled Chinese taxi dancers, the whine of innumerable beggars and their naked unwashed infants, the glamor of the Whangpoo with its white fleets of foreign warships, its shaggy freighters, its fan-sailed junks, its thousand lantern-lit sampans darting fireflies on the moon-silvered water filled with deadly pollution.

Shanghai!

But there were large, quiet areas of the Settlement and the French Concession much like the best residential parts of our Eastern Seaboard or French provincial towns. Wide streets of stately homes and broad lawns were sheltered behind high walls topped by broken glass, and foreign drinking and eating clubs and country clubs and the longest bar in the world and modern apartment houses were all intended for the superior race only, no Chinese allowed except as servants. It was just at the end of that time when the Chinese, who paid most of the taxes, were excluded even from the city parks and the Bund gardens. And Shanghai was well policed, by Europeans and by long-haired Sikh traffic cops who terrorized the ricksha coolies by beating them with their sticks or—worse!—confiscating the cushioned seats of their rickshas. The Settlement was still so "secure" then that creaking wheelbarrow loads of solid gold and silver bars were openly rolled from bank to bank, often only a pompous Chinese clerk as escort, by muscled coolies grunting and grinning proudly under their rich-man's burden.

(In 1949 Chiang Ching-kuo, the Generalissimo's son, would make the final days of the Kuomintang's subsequent brief rule in Shanghai memorable by the wholesale arrest, torture or murder of alleged Chinese "traitors"—rich men, not Communists—to extract from them the last of the hidden gold, to carry off to the new democracy in Formosa.)

Soon after I decided to stay for awhile in this vast, unkempt, exciting, primitive and sophisticated village, then Asia's largest city, I took a small apartment on Seymour Road with John Allison, an American my own age. John was one day to be our Ambassador to Japan, but as a clerk at the Consulate in Shanghai he earned no more than I—six hundred Chinese dollars a month. Yet we both had quite enough to keep up the white man's prestige. Our rent was negligible, transportation was cheap, you could go anywhere in a taxi for a flat fee of one Chinese dollar or about thirty cents, and the best American meal at the American club or "Jimmy's" cost little more. Hand-tailored clothes were half the price of ready-made at home. We could easily afford a cook-houseboy and soon found ourselves with an "apprentice" as well, whom we had to hire to save I-Sung's face; for no Chinese wanted to work in a one-servant household.

It was indubitably an easy life. So easy, in fact, that it would soon pall. All the leg work, and often most of the brain work, in foreign business offices was done by Chinese assistants, and office hours were short. Lunch was called tiffin, and it went on for two or three hours. After an hour or two back at the office the average American or Englishman or Frenchman was ready to call it a day and go home or drop in at his club for a swim or shower and a "peg" or two before his valet dressed him for dinner. Life was a round of parties, food and liquor were very cheap even for the very best, and credit was unlimited. Any European or American resident could sign a "chit" for purchases in any shop, bar, restaurant or hotel without any identification beyond his business card.

How had that now vanished way of life come to be? The answer need not long detain us, for this is personal history. Yet each of us is a piece of any history that affects our lives, and in this sense Shanghai became part of the perishable words I was to write about it. The spirit of Settlement life embodied the essence of our intercourse with China everywhere for a century and all Americans are heirs to it, albeit unwitting. Today the legacy lives on in the posture of our fleet, Ajax five thousand miles from home astride China's seas.

The moral basis of Shanghai society was traceable to Britain's victories in the so-called opium wars of the Eighteen Forties and Fifties which first fully exposed China to major intervention. Originally, British traders had simply won the right to reside on a smudge of mud-flat waterfront along the Whangpoo. This they took from the Manchu rulers, who might have yielded nothing more but for the Taiping revolution. For two decades the Manchus, themselves alien conquerors from Manchuria, were continuously engaged in that war of suppression and counter-revolution which altogether dwarfed the death and pillage of the greatest Western catastrophe of the period, the American Civil War. Taking a toll of between forty and sixty million lives, the Taiping-Manchu conflict surpassed in savagery even the twenty years of violent struggle between the Nationalists and the Communists which we were to see in our own time.

The Taipings? *Tai-p'ing* meant "Great Peace." Their leader, Hung Hsiu-chuan, having been converted to Christianity, with characteristic Chinese political sense declared himself a "younger brother" of Jesus Christ. His followers sought not only to Christianize the nation, the Manchus having suborned and corrupted and discredited Buddhism, Confucianism and Taoism, but to achieve clear and popular aims. They sought to destroy the Manchus and their puppets, restore full Chinese sovereignty, curtail foreign privilege, equalize land owner-ship, limit the opium trade, elevate the status of women, abolish foot-binding, and enforce certain other "Christian" reforms. In their social aspirations the Taipings were ahead of their Asian, as well as many European, contemporaries, and their means were no more barbarous.

By mid-century the Manchus had been driven from southernmost China to far above the Yangtze and Peking itself was in danger. Pressed by the British and the French without and the Taipings within, the Manchu throne would have toppled from a combined push of the two. But after a series of stinging defeats at the hands of the Westerners in 1858 and 1860 the Manchus chose the lesser evil. They fully le-galized the opium traffic, gave the British control of their customs stations, granted new treaty port concessions, including enlargement of the Shanghai Settlement, and conceded extraterritoriality, which made foreigners immune to processes of native law. They also fully legalized Christian propaganda and travel rights for the missionaries who, with a few exceptions, now in turn opposed the Taiping version of Christianity as a heresy worse than paganism.

At this time "the West" made its Christian decision in defense of foreign interests, justice, civilization, free institutions and free trade. The latter then meant chiefly the unrestricted importation and sale of narcotics in China. Franco-British land and naval forces now made an informal alliance with the Manchus which gradually drove the rebels back from key positions on the seacoast and the rivers. Manchu-Ameri-can forces under the Yankee adventurer Frederick Townsend Ward, organized and armed in Shanghai, advanced southward, scoring nota-ble successes. A Franco-Manchu army cleared the Chekiang coast and, with the help of British and French warships, bombarded, pil-laged and reduced many a Taiping garrison to ruins and killed thou-sands of Chinese civilians as well as soldiers. When Ward himself was killed in 1862 the Manchus commissioned a British officer, General Charles George Gordon, to command greatly enlarged mixed forces which undertook a decisive offensive up the Yangtze Valley. Town after town, though stubbornly defended, fell to the British commander.

The American Government, absorbed with civil war at home, never officially participated in the intervention, but Parliament legalized the loan of regular British officers and soldiers, as well as the traffic in opium, arms and ships on a large scale. Many individual Americans joined for the high rewards offered. Foreign guns were vastly superior to Chinese native weapons, and this equipment, together with foreign training and leadership, resulted in heavier and heavier Taiping defeats. Soochow fell. General Gordon captured most of the Taiping imperial family, who surrendered on his personal promise of sanctuary. Gordon reluctantly turned them over to the Manchu prime minister, Li Hung-chang, who beheaded them forthwith, along with hundreds of their followers. At first miffed by Li's unseemly haste, Gordon was soon reconciled and resumed his march at the head of the victorious allies. They thoroughly shattered the Taiping hold on the lower Yangtze Valley and completed the encirclement of the capital at Nanking. Alarmed at the potential threat of the loot-laden freebooting foreign army to the Manchu power itself, if Gordon occupied Nanking, Li Hung-chang now insisted that Gordon disband his forces. When he faithfully did so they were richly rewarded and Gordon returned to England, covered with honors, to await his later destiny as the hero of Khartoum. With the conquest of Nanking by the foreign-trained and foreign-equipped Manchu forces, now under Manchu command, the "Heavenly Peace Emperor" committed suicide, the "Christian Rebellion" collapsed, and final breakup of the Taipings everywhere soon followed.

Thus "the West" preserved and enlarged its civilizing influence in China, for the Manchu Dynasty never afterward could redeem full independence from its saviors. And thus was the first Chinese national revolution postponed for more than a half century. Is this ancient history with no bearing on China's present policies? Perhaps the West did rob and murder a few people in Asia, but that is all past now and forgotten. Times have changed, this is the atomic age, imperialism is dead.

But the past is father and mother of the present. One generation feeds upon the carrion of dead fears and hates which yesterday were live enough. That is the great factor of subjectivity in history which at all times and places is the unwritten part of the "objective" report of the present, and the unseen element of fantasy in every foreign policy. Neither the expropriated master nor the liberated slave forgets what recently lay between them, and it is that which they fight about more often than living questions or the future. No doubt we now understand something besides force; perhaps we even believe that the Oriental understands something besides force, but should we be surprised if the West's most successful students of might makes right have been slow to believe that we have now abandoned it?

Every Chinese nationalist from Sun Yat-sen to Chiang Kai-shek to Mao Tse-tung relived the Taiping revolution, and the counter-revolution. As a correspondent in China I discovered that, particularly among those Chinese revolutionists who were finally to emerge triumphant, the Taiping revolution never ended. Its martyrs were childhood heroes of Chu Teh, P'eng Teh-huai, Mao Tse-tung and Chou En-lai, the enemies of the Taipings became their enemies, and in place of a Christianity discredited by Christian interventionists they were to seize upon and glorify a new "universal faith" of the West called Marxist Communism.

Seventy years after the last of the Taipings were surrounded and massacred on the Ta Tu Ho, in Western Szechuan, Chinese Communists who fought and won a decisive battle of survival there against the forces of Chiang Kai-shek (the Methodist) would shout, in the same breath, *"Shih Ta-k'ai, wan sui!"* and *"Chung-kuo kê-ming, wan sui!"* "Long live Shih Ta-k'ai" (the Taiping hero who perished on the Ta Tu) and "Long live the Chinese revolution!"

A few years before that, by the early Thirties, the pretensions of Shanghai were destined to be first punctured by the Japanese, revealing to everyone that the myths of racial superiority were no more substantial than the momentary superiority in technique on which they rested. But for the present the Shanghai taipans were still in charge. Shanghai means "above the sea," and economically and politically it was then above the nation. Through its portals poured half the entire imports and a third of the exports of the whole country. The heart of the city was the International Settlement and the French Concession, only 10,000 acres in area, yet here lived three million Chinese and more than half the skilled industrial workers of China. All real power was in the hands of a few thousand British, French, American and Japanese residents and their consuls.

The French Concession was run as a closed monopoly by a handful of French *propriétaires* and the Settlement by an equally narrow oligarchy. Though Chinese paid nearly all the taxes they could not own land in their own names and had to hire foreigners to serve as dummies in the land register. Even among the few thousand foreigners only substantial property owners could vote—never more than three thousand. Only toward the very end were the Chinese "ratepayers" given some representation on the Settlement Council. Before the Japanese period the Council was always controlled by the British land-lords, banks, insurance firms, oil and shipping companies, textile mills and their brokers, and to a lesser extent by American counterparts.

Of course it was the admirable British law, order and protection of property backed by foreign diplomacy and foreign troops, and war-ships lying in the Whangpoo, that had made Shanghai stable and at-tractive to Chinese and foreign capital. When this was undermined by Japanese attack, first in 1932, again in 1937, finally in 1941, the sanctuary itself was doomed. But always implicit, beyond that, had been the knowledge by all that whenever any Chinese government succeeded in effectively uniting the entire country, the day of the foreign interventionist and the taipan would be over.

Long before that could happen I would realize that the Nationalist Government was not likely to complete that task. For its Kuomintang leaders were not so much dissatisfied with the way people in Shanghai were being "eaten" as by the fact that it was the foreign devil who was doing the eating. A mere change of masters would not suffice to appease the pent-up energies of the revolution. For the sons of the Taipings, whose doctrines had been proclaimed by a Chinese the brother and equal of Jesus Christ, no less than the founder of an Eastern branch of a new religion was required. And with that fact my own fate was to be knotted, when I came to meet and know the new messiah, whose name was Mao Tse-tung.

But still ahead of me lay a long apprenticeship which, as editor of the *Review,* I was only now beginning.

CHAPTER 5

Editing the Review

A TALL, OPEN-FACED, long-jawed intelligence officer in the fourth regiment, U.S. Marines, dropped in once a week to exchange informa-tion with me at the *Review.* His name was Evans Fordyce Carlson. Increasingly I found myself anticipating his visits. This was a man who would three times win the Navy Cross, cover himself with glory during World War II, and die of wounds suffered at Saipan—leaving behind him that unique contribution in combat training and organization, the Marine Raider battalions.

Carlson was a rare combination of idealism and practical ability, as warm-hearted as General Joseph Stilwell, whom he admired, and an equally tough soldier. (It was characteristic that Carlson temporarily resigned from the Marine Corps in 1938 in order to protest America's continued arming of the Japanese after they began their conquest of China, and that he then went to work for Chinese Industrial Co-operatives.) The basis for our mutual confidence was laid in the *Review* office, probably on the day he showed me a copy of a dossier about myself prepared by Pat Givens, an Irishman who was chief of the political department of the Shanghai International Settlement police.

According to the dossier my real name was something like "Lavinsky"—some ex-convict wanted by the Los Angeles police. This "Snow" was a dangerous agitator who'd served a jail term for some alleged connection with the Tom Mooney case. Now I was said to be traveling on a bogus passport and "believed to be an agent of the Third International."

"Very funny," I said, handing back the papers to Evans. "The picture is flattering but it so happens I was a twelve-year-old Boy Scout in Kansas City during the Tom Mooney affair. As for the Third International, I'm just studying the Second."

"I know," he grinned. "All the same it would be a good idea to provide Givens with the facts. These things circulate, you know."

I was young and naive and too proud to think it mattered. When not long afterward I wrote an article for *Current History* about Chinese communism, I went to the Irish cop for information. Givens questioned me briefly about myself and I answered laconically. My replies evidently made little impression, for I would hear about that dossier, embellished by further lies, for many years and in far places. We found out that the source was a White Russian informer paid on a piece basis who had been hanging around the *Review*. J. B. Powell literally kicked the Russian out of the office after he admitted that he had concocted the entire fable "as a joke on Pat."

Givens was undoubtedly responsible for the arrest of more Chinese students and workers in Shanghai than any other officer. Many thousands of them picked up as Communist suspects by the Settlement police were turned over to the Chinese garrison at Lunghwa, where the rate of executions was high. Givens eventually retired with a good pension from the Shanghai Settlement Council and the Order of Brilliant Jade and other rewards from Chiang Kai-shek.

Review policy was strongly anti-Communist and anti-imperialist in the best liberal tradition. It supported Chinese Nationalist demands for an end to unequal treaties, peaceful return of the International Settlement and other foreign concessions, and abolition of extraterritoriality. J. B. Powell was a warm admirer of Chiang Kai-shek and from the start he supported him as a leader of the Nationalist revolution against the old Peking Government. Shanghai's elite balefully dismissed his views as "pro-Chinese," a cardinal sin in pukka British eyes. I was soon found guilty by association.

Most American business men also thought Powell "too radical." Before the Nationalist revolution he had been the popular young secretary of the Shanghai Chamber of Commerce. After the *Review* came out for Chiang Kai-shek, "J.B." was fired. Our then Ambassador, John Von Antwerp MacMurray, and American business leaders preferred the corrupt and weak old Northern warlords. Powell was considered "a traitor to his class and color." Although the *Review* was easily the most influential American journal of fact and opinion in China, it could not have survived except for Chinese advertising and subscriptions. Foreign business men saw little difference between Chiang Kai-shek and the Communists; many were genuinely convinced that Chiang *was* a Communist. They hadn't seen anything yet! They didn't begin to until the Japanese invasion, when the more astute conceded that Chiang might be the "lesser evil."

"J.B." was the most generous of men and editors. His readily extended friendship was an invaluable asset to a novice. Though we later differed about China I fell in with his opinions initially because of his manifest integrity, because his decade of experience was impressive, and perhaps simply because we were both from Missouri. He was more patriotic about China than many Chinese. Once he was kidnapped from the Blue Express by bandits and held for ransom for many days in the Shantung mountains, along with Miss Lucy Aldrich, sister-in-law of John D. Rockefeller, Jr., a story told in his autobiography, *Twenty-five Years in China*. But, characteristic of his modesty, he did not mention that he was offered decorations and a sizeable solatium by the Chinese Government and refused both. He was destined, in fact, to die for China. As a result of cruel punishment inflicted on him by the Japanese in retaliation for his "pro-Chinese" policy he contracted a fatal infection in a Shanghai prison during World War II.

"J.B." was himself the protégé of a rather more sophisticated Missourian who also took me under his wing: Thomas Fairfax Millard, a senior correspondent of the *New York Herald Tribune* and for years the best-informed newspaper man in the Far East. Millard also happened to be a Beta Theta Pi fraternity brother of mine. Powell and Millard doubtless found in me some sentiments latent in many Midwesterners, among which was an easy identification with the underdog in any struggle with the still mighty British Empire. My estimate of the English was to be modified as I came to appreciate the contribution to orderly progress toward world unity which British political genius has made, along with certain evil done. My education in that respect properly began with a friendship with Sir Archibald Clark-Kerr; but in the years before Pearl Harbor British virtues were obscured by consistently retrogressive policies in Asia, as the best Britons were quick to admit. It occurs to me also that the harsh talk about British imperialism I heard in childhood from Irish relatives, strong sympathizers with the Sinn Feiners, must have helped prepare me to believe that morality always lay on the side of rebellion, and divinity as well, where Britain was the overlord.

The *Review* likewise fought social discrimination against the Chinese, particularly in their own country, and ridiculed the Colonel Blimps of the Superior Race. It was partly responsible for ending the exclusion policy in the clubs, the parks and the Bund gardens. Some office buildings even required Chinese to use separate entrances, as in the Cable Building where the *Review* was located. One day while I was acting editor a Chinese official visitor was denied passage on the front elevator, reserved for white men. I wrote a satirical editorial about it and the British owners of the building changed their elevator policy. But when the *Review*'s lease expired Powell couldn't get a renewal and had to move. Although he knew the reason, he never uttered a word of admonition to me.

No one was more amused by such crusading than our copy editor. He was an eccentric American individualist named George Missemer, who had taught himself Chinese and half a dozen other languages. He had been all over the world, paying his way by taking along either a small cargo of old newspapers or some used printing machinery, items he claimed could instantly be sold at a profit anywhere. George was an entertaining and ambulating encyclopedia of information and could have been a business success, but he preferred his kind of semi-hobo existence, rejecting all serious responsibility. Although I could not have run the *Review* without him, he would have nothing to do with editorial tasks beyond a few hours a day devoted to make-up and copy reading, after which he would go off to quarrel happily with his Russian mistress.

It was mystifying to me how Chinese typographers who did not know a word of English could set up the paper, much less read Missemer's scrawling corrections, but while he was there the *Review* had few typos. When there was a bloomer it was often sensational. There was the time Mmes. Darling, Estes and Wolfe, who ran the de-luxe American brothel on Soochow Road, sent out a discreet announcement of a reopening, after a holiday and redecorating. Somehow the Chinese typographer got hold of it and it slipped into the society column. No great damage was done to Shanghai's morals but several missionaries cancelled their subscriptions.

Missemer was completely cynical about the Kuomintang (the Nationalist party), which he called "the same old set of gangsters with new titles." He first pointed out to me that Tu Yueh-sheng, a leader of the Shanghai underworld's most powerful secret society (the *Ch'ing pang*), which controlled the opium traffic, had worked for the Northern warlord, Chang Tsung-chang, before transferring his affections to Chiang Kai-shek.

From our Chinese editor I also learned how Tu Yueh-sheng had saved Shanghai from the Communists. In March, 1927, before the Nationalist-Communist split, the Nationalist revolution leftist organizers staged an insurrection and forced the Northern warlords to retreat from the Chinese-ruled parts of Shanghai before revolutionary troops reached the city. The workers had only 300 rifles but nearly the whole working class was organized and ready to welcome Chiang Kai-shek. Upriver, however, Chiang was about to expel the Communists from the Kuomintang and civil war threatened. At this point Sterling Fesseden, an American city manager hired by the Settlement Council, secretly conferred with Tu Yueh-sheng at his headquarters in the French Concession. He offered him 5,000 rifles, armored cars and safe conduct through the Settlement, to attack and destroy the "commune" that had taken over the surrounding area. Chiang Kai-shek's supporters among the Chinese bankers in Shanghai financed the operation, which was highly successful. Escorted by foreign police, Tu's gunmen poured into the workers' homes and factories in a surprise night attack. Between five and ten thousand youths were slain, including many Communists and Socialists (Left-Wing Nationalists). It would be more than twenty years before Chou En-lai, who escaped death in that Shanghai massacre by sheer luck, returned to settle accounts. By that time Mr. Tu was safe in Hongkong and the Generalissimo safe in Formosa.

The Chinese are not without a sly sense of irony. I think it was

Lin Yu-tang who first pointed out to me the humor of the situation when Chiang Kai-shek made Tu Yueh-sheng, who held a virtual monopoly of the opium business in the lower Yangtze area, his "chief of the bureau of opium suppression," and decorated him with the Order of the Brilliant Jade.

Tu Yueh-sheng and his gangsters ran the underworld in both foreign and Chinese parts of Shanghai so closely that not a brothel could solicit trade, not an opium smoker could dream in peace, not a shopkeeper could turn an honest profit, without the *pang* collecting tribute. By the mid-Thirties, kidnapping, assassination and procurement each had its price. These gang leaders sat on boards of directors and were prominent in charitable activities. Mr. Tu was also a patriot. During the war against Japan he went to the interior after Shanghai was lost, leaving behind him a lieutenant who worked for the Japanese; thus tribute could be collected on both sides of the smuggling trade conducted between Free and Occupied China.

In the Thirties we foreigners and respectable Chinese alike felt that Mr. Tu and Mr. Chiang had saved China from "the mob." Talking it over with business men and with J. B. Powell, I concluded that the sacrifice had been necessary, and that the *Review*'s policy was right. Powell believed that this one quick firm action had "saved China from the Communists." By China we meant, of course, Shanghai.

Alas, it turned out that it had been saved only momentarily and for the Japanese. I was then as convinced as Mr. Dulles was thirty years later that morality lay on the side of Chiang Kai-shek. I had yet to learn that in politics as in medicine one must diagnose before prescribing, that the patient here was China, not the Outsiders, and that a nation's political behavior is not finally determined by moral judgments from abroad so much as by practical demands of the deepest internal hungers which motivate it from within.

CHAPTER 6

Missouri Days

I KNEW ONLY one Chinese in my boyhood in Kansas City. He owned a tiny laundry near our local grocery store. We children would creep up and yell a ditty we had learned from Crazy Mary, our Negro washwoman, who disliked her slant-eyed competitor:

> Chinaman, Chinaman,
> Eat dead rats!
> Chew them up
> Like gingersnaps!

If we could get the poor fellow to come dashing out, his queue swinging, and hurl inhuman curses at us, we were successful. When he learned to ignore us the game lost its zest. Years later I would think of him when, in the village streets of China, small boys would sometimes run after me to shout, "Foreign devil! Foreign devil! Big, big big-nose!" It rhymed better in Chinese and had the same effect on the small braves who thus challenged the different and the terrifying.

That laundryman probably played no part in my going to China, but two experiences I had when I was fourteen seem to link me to that certainty. I left home that summer, to go to California; and I read *Les Misérables*.

My father believed in making my brother and me work, on Saturdays and during vacations, "to learn that money represents labor." When I was nine I began to help carry packages from the Snow Printing Company to the *Kansas City Star*, a glamorous building with a great living heart in its pressroom. There I worshipped the editors from afar: George B. Longan, Henry Haskell, Earl McCullum, and Roy Roberts. McCullum said I "carried my load better than most newspaper men." I stopped working for Dad when I was offered higher wages, twelve and a half cents an hour, as a soda boy in Worthman's Drug Store. The next summer I was an office boy for the "Katy" Line, where I acquired week-end passes for trips to the Ozarks, and became interested in "travel."

The summer I was fourteen I worked for several weeks shocking wheat in the Kansas harvest fields and used the money I made to go to California. My schoolmates, Robert Long and Charlie White, were driving there in Bob's new Model T touring car, an adventure of which I managed to keep my parents in the dark until we were well along the way. It took us two weeks, as I remember it. For most of the trip we followed the then unpaved Santa Fe trail, which over long stretches disappeared altogether in the sand and the boulders. Bob joined his parents in Santa Monica; Charlie and I, having spent all our money, had to bum our way home. If I had not seen the Pacific that summer I might never have fixed so firmly in my mind the ambition to sail across it. And if I had not bummed my way on freight trains up the coast of California, and through the Feather River Canyon and the Royal Gorge of Colorado, I would not have known, so early, the taste of rough adventure, the infinite variety of nature and man, and the kindness of strangers to an adolescent just discovering that he had the muscle, if not the brains, to do a man's job in the world.

I learned something else: the importance of luck—and mental and physical co-ordination—in the miracle of human survival. How many lives some of us are given! Standing on a moving train I straddled a coupling between freight cars, holding onto the two iron ladders, and fell asleep. When I awoke I was wet with sweat and lying under the wheel of a car where I must have fallen when the train stopped. On a dark night I was chased from the blinds of a passenger express at a railway station. I came out after it again as it started off but it moved so swiftly that I was just able to latch onto the rear platform of the tail car. Immediately afterward we shot across a high trestle and I looked down into a deep abyss where in another moment my run would have tumbled me to extinction. Then I was in Kansas again, asleep on a pile of scrap iron on a flat car, when I was prodded awake. Two guns were held on me by "harvest bandits." They robbed me of only fifty cents (I had five dollars in my shoe!) but looted more than a hundred migratory workers on the train of their entire summer's earnings. To me they were the meanest kind of thieves, robbing the poor. I realized that under these circumstances I would shoot a man if I could.

Jack London had been my hero. That autumn when I went back to high school I discovered in *Les Misérables* some "foreign" characters who reminded me of some of the workers and unemployed—just "bums" to respectable people—whom I had met and come to like during my summer's adventure. Hugo opened up a strange new world of ideas and great moral and political issues for me and involved me in history in a faraway and stirring time. Before this, books like *Robinson*

Crusoe, The Swiss Family Robinson and *Treasure Island* had probably infected me with an itch to see strange lands. It was only now that reading became vicarious travel for me and the second best thing to action. My early *Wanderjahr* and its consequences probably did more to shape my life than all my formal education. "A man's life," says the Chinese proverb, "is a candle in the wind."

CHAPTER 7

Roving Correspondent

WHILE POWELL was in Manchuria and Russia I was the *Chicago Tribune* in China. This wasn't as disastrous as it might have been, in spite of my extreme youth for the job, because I had the constant advice of Tom Millard, and frequent help from Morris Harris, bureau chief of the Associated Press, and Frank Oliver of Reuters, next door. Their kindness to me as a beginner was part of a newspaper man's tradition in the Far East.

Besides giving the *Tribune* daily spot news coverage I wrote "mailers," which were seldom used. The paper was not interested in background material that would help make sense out of the laconic cabled dispatch. Its dish was strictly of the after-birth category, the cataclysm itself but never the causes. What I chiefly learned from my brief *Tribune* experience was that any correspondent could make a living by specializing in reporting the worst about a foreign country for newspapers which wouldn't dream of publishing the worst about ourselves.

The approach of the "world's greatest newspaper" to China during that period of vast awakening was illustrated by a message from Colonel McCormick to Powell during the Nationalist revolution. "Send us a few sticks," he wrote, "about this laundryman Chiang Kai-shek." His contemptuous attitude would persist down to Pearl Harbor. Only a few months before that blow he decided that his important but capriciously managed newspaper, which millions of Midwesterners read as gospel truth, was getting clogged up with too much "pro-Chinese propaganda." He closed down the China bureau entirely and thereafter depended solely on his correspondent in Japan, a Japanese, to cover the events leading up to the attack on Hawaii. After more than fifteen years of distinguished service Powell found himself without an outlet for his abundant knowledge and without even a thank-you from that ridiculous flag-waving buffoon who hated King George but mistook himself for "one of the kings of the earth." Doubtless that wouldn't happen today on the *Tribune,* which displays far more sense of responsibility toward both its staff and its readers than during Bertie's reign.

While I was still filing to Chicago I found a place for more informative reports in the New York *Herald Tribune*'s weekly magazine, which published fairly long, serious articles on foreign countries. I contributed to it for years. The *Herald Tribune* daily then had a broad, liberal interest in Asia and favored recognition of the Kuomintang regime long before our own ambassador of the time had given up hope of restoring the Northern warlords to power. Tom Millard, its chief correspondent in Asia since the Russo-Japanese war, had a major influence on his paper's editorial policy.

Millard founded the *Review* and the *China Press,* for long the best American daily in Asia. He also became mentor to a host of Missouri School of Journalism products in the Far East, both American and Chinese. They were so numerous that competitors used to complain of "the Missouri news monopoly." For years representatives of the chief wire services and many American newspapers, as well as the editors of the principal English-language newspapers and magazines from Tokyo to Bangkok, were Missourians. Most of them also reflected Millard's vigorously expressed views: anti-colonial, anti-imperialist, pro-independence, pro-equality-of-nations, pro-republican, pro-self-determination—and pro-American. Any resemblance between his opinions and my own is not, therefore, purely coincidental.

One night as I was finishing an editorial for the *Review* Millard dropped in. He pulled one of his books off the library shelf and said, "Listen a minute." He read a passage aloud. Then he smiled and said, "I wasn't much older than you when I wrote that. I wouldn't say it just that way today but it was right at the time. Nothing is true forever but anything that was true once has a seed in it that finds life again in another truth."

I nodded, remembered it, and went back to typing.

"Still thinking about going to Madras or wherever it was?"

"Madagascar. Eventually. I'd like to see what's in between, first. Central Asia, India, Persia."

"Wouldn't a job as foreign correspondent keep you here?"

"The *Tribune?* 'J.B.' will be back from Russia next month."

"I'm talking about the New York *Tribune*—the *Herald Tribune*."

I stopped typing. Was Tom offering me a job as his legman? That would be all right.

"I've got a cable here from the boss," he went on, "authorizing me to pick my own successor. You can begin as soon as 'J.B.' gets back." He folded up the cable and smiled as if the matter were settled.

"What do you mean, *successor?* You aren't quitting?"

I looked at him closely now: immaculately tailored, silver-haired, wise, worldly, and, I noted for the first time, old. Suddenly I realized he must be nearing seventy. I had always thought of him as much younger because basically he was, and remained, a *modern* man. But take *his* place? How could I?

"I'm getting along and I've seen too many of my colleagues hang on after they've lost their reporter's legs," he said. "I had been thinking of retiring; I'd like to travel in Europe for a while; but C. T. Wang has helped make up my mind for me. He's offered me a post as his adviser in the Ministry of Foreign Affairs and I've taken it. I've been watching your work. You'll learn. So the job is yours. The only condition is that you'll have to agree to stay here *at least three years*."

Three years! It seemed a lifetime. I asked for two days to think it over, and for two nights I did not sleep. Aside from the fact that I wasn't qualified I *had* to have freedom to move, to see the world, to write about whatever interested me. After two years in Shanghai and mostly on the *Review* desk, I knew that I had to travel more, study more, feel more, sense more, get inside the picture somehow. I could not do all this by rooting myself in Shanghai. And that's what it meant in those days because that's where the cables were.

"I think you're making a mistake," Tom said, after he'd heard me out patiently. "What happens in China in the next twenty years will be the most important story in the world. But if you've still got the wanderlust in you, go ahead and good luck. You'll be back."

I would be back, and back with the *Herald Tribune* eventually, too. But now I had no idea what I was going to do next. I did not have time to regret my decision; in a few weeks an offer of another job came unexpectedly, and tailored to my needs.

Drew Pearson and David Lawrence cabled to ask J. B. Powell to find a Far Eastern representative for the Consolidated Press Association, a new foreign service set up to serve a dozen metropolitan newspapers. Its chief backers were the New York *Sun* and the Chicago *Daily News*. They wanted an unmarried man, somebody free to roam Asia, ignoring routine spot news and cabling about events of magnitude only when he happened to be near them. They wanted, in other words, a roving correspondent. They wanted me, I decided. The pay was small compared to the *Herald Tribune* job, but it promised time for study, freedom to travel, and release from hours wasted reading handouts, propaganda and agency material. I read the cable and wired Powell (he was still in Moscow) to recommend me. I got the "appointment." At the same time my friend Edward Hunter became the Consolidated Press representative in Peking and thus began his eventful career as a correspondent.

The new job went well. After Powell's return I traveled around central China for several months, covering a few skirmishes. Then I planned an ambitious trip to Russian Turkestan. The home office gave approval; I lacked only a Soviet visa. As diplomatic relations between Nanking and Moscow were still severed, I had to go to Tokyo. The Russian Ambassador welcomed me cordially, questioned me two hours about Chinese affairs, took my twenty dollars to cover cable costs to Moscow, and promised me a speedy answer. He kept his word; that was the promptest reply I would ever get from a Soviet embassy. Within a week my application was refused: mainly, because of my association with the *Review* when we published Powell's extremely anti-Soviet reports after his return from Moscow.

Thwarted by Mr. Stalin, I turned south and mapped out an itinerary covering Formosa, the China coast, Indo-China and Yunnan. I hoped to *walk* from China to Burma, cross the Mekong and the Salween Rivers, see the eaves of Tibet, and go down the Irrawaddy into Burma. Then, to India, and on, and on. The New York *Sun* and the Chicago *Daily News* again approved. They had a long feature called "The World Today" which was syndicated widely through the Consolidated Press. My "expedition" was to fill that column for many months.

Just before I left Shanghai I was standing on Bubbling Well Road with a young Shanghai-born American girl, waiting for a taxi. There came a loud clamor from a side lane and we ran over to look. Chinese poured out of a building, followed by big puffs of smoke. Suddenly a burning wheel shot out and I saw it was a man on fire. He collapsed almost at my feet. Immobilized by horror or curiosity, nobody in the crowd made a move.

There was nothing to do but wrap my new camel hair coat around him quickly, and that I did, mourning it but having no choice. Soon the fire was out but he still smouldered. *"Shui! Shui!"* I yelled; finally a coolie appeared with a bucket. I splashed the water over the ruins. The crowd closed in and there was excited talk. Fire engines roared up and an ambulance at last carried off the still breathing body.

My hands were only slightly blistered but the coat lay in black shreds. When a ricksha coolie asked for it I threw it to him. Then the coolie who had brought the water tugged at my sleeve. "You pay me watah, mastah, you pay me watah!" Disgusted, I wrenched myself free. Money—for water to put out a burning man! Half a dozen others tagged after me yelling *"Kumsha!"* for alms. Among them was the man who had the charred tatters of my camel hair coat. He so annoyed me that I grabbed the rag back, cursed him and cursed them all. They laughed and turned away and I went on but not in peace. They had lost face but so had humanity, I thought, and I was part of it and at that moment hated it.

Back on the corner I found the American girl withdrawn, waiting, with a slightly bored expression on her pretty face. "What a miserable, miserable country China is!" I exclaimed, before I realized they were the exact words of Washington Wu.

"I could have told you that and saved you the trouble," said the girl, conditioned to such lack of feeling from childhood in Shanghai. "That's what always happens when an outsider tries to interfere with fate in China," she added good-humoredly. "They let you burn your fingers, take your coat, and then want to be paid for it."

"Very smart," I said in fury, "but I hope that I never get that cynical." I never saw her after that night.

Of course what angered me was that she made me feel like a sentimental fool and I suppose I had expected to be a hero. I had not been in the East long enough to know that anyone can become so inured to commonplace suffering in others that he no longer feels it. Part of the white Shanghailander's defense was his conviction that the two races didn't belong to the same species.

Later I thought of the obvious answer. It didn't matter what others felt. What mattered was how I would have felt if I had let that neighbor burn. And this feeling of concern for one's neighbor was not, I would yet discover, any monopoly of the Christian white man.

CHAPTER 8

The Banker's Daughters

I CROSSED OVER from Shanghai to Formosa on a small but well-run Japanese ship of the O.S.K. Line. Among the passengers was a Japanese business man and his wife, accompanied by their rather attractive daughter. She was in her teens, very demure and modest, and invariably kept her eyes cast down or averted, as was expected of a properly brought-up young Japanese woman of the time.

The purser, noticing me eyeing her one day, grinned and said, "She not like Japanese *modan garu, sodesu-ka, ne?* Not looking at any man."

"No, she certainly is not. But she's very pretty."

"You know any *modan garu* in Japan?"

"Know any? Why, yes." I surprised him by saying. "I met some on my first visit to Japan two years ago. They were banker's daughters."

"Sa-a-h?" He looked skeptical and waited for more. I said, "Yes, they were very nice girls," and left him wondering . . .

It was Larry J. who had introduced me to the banker's daughters. He was a newspaper man I'd met soon after my arrival in Japan.

"Have you ever had a date with a Japanese girl?" Larry asked. "I mean a nice girl, a family girl?"

"I haven't had a date with any kind of Japanese girl," I replied. "How do you start?"

"I know a couple who will knock your eye out. They're daughters of a respectable banker. One speaks very good English."

"I've always heard family girls here are much too strictly watched to permit any running around with foreigners." (They generally were, too, in those days.)

"You don't know there's a rebellion on? It's led by what they call the *modan garu*. That means 'modern girl' to you, son. Different article. Emancipated. Bobs her hair, wears rouge and lipstick, crazy about jazz and dancing. Got the old folks up in arms. What do you say, shall I call them up?"

"Why not?" I listened, awed, as Larry spread considerable *hai-hai moshi-moshi* over the telephone. He was about five years older than I and had been in Japan several years, long enough to know his way around and to enjoy impressing a novice to the Orient.

"It's okay," he said after he hung up the phone. "I'll get them and bring them over here. Wait for me." He drove off and an hour later returned to his apartment with Chiyeko and Seiko.

They were all Larry had promised: exquisite doll-like creatures whose gorgeous kimonos, flashing obis and enameled hair-do's were indeed style such as only a banker could afford. We had tea and then danced to some obsolete American records. Seiko's English proved to be sharply limited but she made astonishingly expressive use of it. I had never seen girls who could so easily and so charmingly cover confusion with laughter.

Late in the afternoon Seiko invited us to her home for supper. We got into Larry's car and drove out of Yokohama along a road that skirted a rugged coast fringed with Japanese evergreens and alternately dipped back into a countryside gay with iris in full bloom. Toward dusk the car turned into a copse of cedars and cryptomeria trees beyond which I glimpsed a white beach.

"Come into my house, please," said Seiko, bowing. "Now you are my guest."

We followed her and Chiyeko up a lanterned way that led through a hedge and into a well-kept garden in the center of which lay a small sunken pool where golden carp darted among wide lotus leaves. On the tatami of a paper-windowed cottage within sound of the surf we ate dinner served by a neisan who giggled at my awkward use of chopsticks. At the end of the meal Larry spoke to her in Japanese to which she said *"Hai"* and looked at me and once more giggled politely. Then Larry excused himself, saying that he and Chiyeko were going for a walk. He never did come back.

Left alone with Seiko and some sake cups in whose tiny chambers floated flakes of real gold I made desperate use of my pocket dictionary, as I tried to interest her in the wonders of America. But who wished to discuss America now? For the neisan had returned, touched her head to the floor, and deposited two thin cotton kimonos there.

"Ofuro wo kudasai, suki desuka?" she said, and Seiko added sweetly, *"Basu* ready now."

After we had changed to the light kimonos and straw sandals Seiko led me into the garden again. We followed another lantern-lit path that opened onto a red pavilion wherein stood a large glassed-in tiled pool within sight and sound of the surf. Half a dozen high-piled shining black coifs dotted the pool, crowning the heads of dignified-looking young Japanese women who steamed contentedly while chatting with Japanese gentlemen immersed beside them. I wondered if Seiko's father was one of them. But she made no move to introduce me.

Instead, she dropped her kimono and sat on a low wooden stool while a bath boy poured water over her and vigorously scrubbed her back. As she rose and entered the pool she beckoned me to follow. Then did I conform to the customs of the land, submitting to the scrub and the cold douche before solemnly committing myself to the deep. After a suitable period of pleasant parboiling Seiko led me back into the enchanted night. We walked in silence through the fragrant woods and then down to the rocky beach, where we stood and tossed pebbles into the restless Pacific. The night air grew chill and soon we hurried up to the rustic cottage where we had dined. Padded comforters were now spread upon the tatami and a teapot simmered cheerily over a glowing hibachi.

And all that too was like a dream of a far land which would never again be the same, but only for this once was real.

The next morning I saw that there were a half dozen other cottages discreetly hidden along the artfully landscaped waterfront. Larry had handled all the details in a conspiracy in order to sustain in me the illusion of his practical joke, so that I might appreciate the Japanese courtesan at her best, an artist in an ancient profession recognized there as worthy of a glorious setting. Seiko and Chiyeko were bankers' daughters, not of any banker in particular, but of what was then a celebrated and novel geisha garden. Of course the difference between them and the Twelfth Street bordellos of Kansas City was merely a matter of time, space and culture, the fundamental laws of economics remaining the same. That thought did not trouble me at the time.

CHAPTER 9

South China

WHEN I FIRST visited Formosa (Taiwan) it had been in Japanese hands for thirty-five years. It was a colony, of course, but the administration seemed free of graft and people seemed secure in their homes and property as long as they obeyed the law. The land was clean and prosperous, beggars were rare, public services including sanitation and health were good, there were numerous schools, and Formosa had a higher standard of living and a higher percentage of literacy than any province of China.

I have seldom seen a more tranquil, pastoral country than the low hills of sugar cane in central Formosa through which our train crept up to Lake Jitsugetsutan, surrounded by rainbow-shrouded peaks quite like the beautiful Igorot mountains of Northern Luzon. In fact the aborigines thereabouts were close relatives of the Igorots but more primitive. They offered me a weird concert with what surely must be one of the earliest of man's attempts at orchestral music, their instruments consisting simply of poles of different weights and lengths held by players who dropped them alternately, *ensemble,* on flat stones of varying sizes placed over holes in the ground.

Yet that very peaceful frontier town on the edge of the reservations in which the Japanese had confined those wild men of the mountains would, within a week of my visit, be the scene of the bloodiest aboriginal uprising of a decade. Nearly every Japanese in Jitsugetsutan was murdered in his sleep. Appearances are on brief acquaintance with a land deceptive.

From Formosa I proceeded leisurely along the South China coast toward Canton.

The Nationalist regime at Nanking was three years old, but the city of Canton and Kwantung province had been under Kuomintang rule much longer. "In Canton," Dr. Sun Fo had told me, "you will see how a progressive and modern city can be run by our party." Sun's father, Sun Yat-sen, had seized power there in 1920. From Canton Chiang Kai-shek had launched the Northern expedition in alliance with native Communist, and Russian, support. But the Communists had long since been driven to the mountains and the Kuomintang flag now flew across most of China. I knew that much of the central government authority was fictitious but I had yet to learn to what extent the "revolution" had ended in compromises with old and new warlords and gangsters by means of which the Generalissimo held recognition as chief of state.

In brief stops at Foochow, Amoy and Swatow I listened to our consuls and other foreigners talk of bribery, corrupt officials, illegal confiscations, imprisonment and executions without trial, the suppression of labor unions, and officially fostered xenophobia, as routine matters. But I told myself that my informants were prejudiced against a government pledged to end their special privileges. In Canton, birthplace of the Nationalist revolution, I would stay longer, and get a different story, I thought.

In that great clamorous port at the mouth of the Pearl River I was met by Kan Teh-yuan, a Honolulu-born Chinese who had known Sun Yat-sen and Sun Fo in Hawaii. Now he was publishing a paper called *China Truth,* subsidized by the Kuomintang through Dr. C. T: Wang, Minister of Foreign Affairs at Nanking.

"Dr. Wang," he explained at a dinner after many cups of wine, "told me to write against foreign aggression and imperialism but not about our own government. Sometimes the journalist in me takes over and I get into hot water. They have had arrest warrants out for me four times."

"Three protections" saved him. First, he could appeal to Dr. Wang to intervene. Second, he could seek asylum on the tiny island of Shameen, then a foreign concession connected to the Canton waterfront by a bridge. In a really serious situation he could always take an overnight trip by river steamer to Hongkong, to live under the British imperialists for awhile. Now in a quiescent period, Mr. Kan inwardly seethed against the corruption in Cantonese politics and insisted on giving me facts to expose it.

"Every official here is getting rich off the tax racket," he complained. "It hasn't improved a bit since Sun Fo was mayor."

"Sun Fo? I thought his was the 'model administration'?"

"Model for get-rich-quick! He disgraced all Honolulu-born Chinese, don't you know? His own father removed him from office for bribery and embezzlement. Why, he even managed to make money out of the anti-superstition campaign! Had temples confiscated and torn down and then sold the land and kept the money! He arrived penniless and left a millionaire."

I was disappointed, for in a minor way Sun Fo had been my sponsor. But Mr. Kan's facts, I learned from our consul, Mr. Joseph Ballantine, were all too true.

Kan educated me concerning the devious tax system in a city where the collectors' duties were taken over by private syndicates consisting of officials, merchants, bankers and gangsters. Concessions for taxes on land, transportation, salt, tobacco, wine, prostitution, and other amusements, were all farmed out. Among the more lucrative was the restaurant tax. Kan showed me published reports that it had sold for $600,000 a year, but now the restaurant owners association was protesting that the syndicate was making a two-hundred-percent profit.

There was also a novel monopoly granted for what the British euphemistically called "night-soil"—as if bowels moved only in the dark. The government sold the collection privilege to *hongs* which made good profits out of marketing the product to surrounding truck gardens where it was in demand as fertilizer.

"A man can't even have a *ta-pien** here," as Mr. Kan put it, "without some official making graft out of it."

This information was confirmed by a young American, G. Edward Lyon, the only foreign attorney recognized by the Canton bar association. He spoke fluent Cantonese and knew Canton inside out. According to Lyon the bidding for the syndicates was not even competitive. Officials and militarists first had to be bribed to make sure of a successful bid.

"Of course the tax monopolists get back the bribe-money by squeezing as much as they can from the taxpayers."

"Don't people ever contest assessments in court?"

"You might, if a collector gets too greedy or if you have influence. Otherwise it costs you more in the end. Most disputes are simply settled by the police. And the police are paid by the collectors."

I then supposed that the system was unique to Canton, but in later travels found that variants existed throughout China. In most *hsien* (county) governments payment of the land tax and other levies was traditionally a matter of bargaining between the peasants and the collector, and Kuomintang rule did not change that. Keeping a generous share for himself, the collector split another part with the *hsien* magistrate and other officials. By general agreement the balance was recorded as the official tax.

Delinquent taxpayers were often re-arrested and kept in jail even after being acquitted, and still more were held without formal charges, I discovered. Lyon was friendly with the city's high officials, who permitted us to visit the Hon Sao-so, a lower court "model prison" for women, where we questioned inmates. Three prisoners there were accused of soliciting without a license, several were wives jailed on *complaints* of infidelity, one was a concubine who had run away from a man twenty years her elder, three were alleged Communists, and the rest were in for defaulting payment of taxes. The "Communists" had been there three years but had not been brought to court trial. Only two of a dozen women we personally questioned had ever appeared in any court. The rest had been jailed without any hearing.

For all that, Canton was a very interesting, lively city bustling with energy, its shops filled with gorgeous silks, its little lanes of craftsmen making exquisite things embellished with jade, ivory and semi-precious

* Literally, "great relief."

stones and marvelous carved blackwood furniture, its crowded water-front by day a bewildering bedlam of rickshas, trams, smoking buses, wheelbarrows, human beasts of burden carrying prodigious loads on their wet brown patient backs, and by night transformed into a picture from an old Chinese screen, with thousands of lights bobbing on myriad sampans dotting the pale river, the colored lanterns of pleasure boats strung like a necklace along the quay, the gay laughter and the high voices of singing girls exciting, and the odor of opium mingling with fragrance of camellias on the flower boats, and the garlic and soya sauce and food smells everywhere rising from thousands of charcoal fires glowing in the warm, fecund, charming Southern night.

After Canton I could not be properly indignant about the little Portuguese colony of Macao. When I went to see the governor's secretary he frankly conceded that the bulk of the colony's revenues came from gambling, opium and prostitution.

"*Mais, monsieur,*" he earnestly insisted, "understand that we permit zees business because it ees what zee people want. We cannot go against ze popular will, *n'est-ce pas?* Zat would be ze imperialism. As for us, ze Portuguese, all zat ees *défendu.* Any Portuguese gambling, smoking opium or whoring, 'e ees deported for home at once."

In this poor man's Monte Carlo the most important Chinese family was named Loo. For three generations it had controlled the opium and gambling concessions. The Loos paid handsome fees to high Portuguese officials, who pocketed certain sums for themselves and remitted the balance to Lisbon, as tribute from Portugal's tiny empire. Loo Chook-sum, then head of the great family, was a mild-mannered gentleman with an extraordinary love of flowers. I had tea with him one day. As we walked through the most beautiful garden in South China he spoke to me of his many charitable interests and benefactions. Among those was a home for the cure of opium addicts.

Loo's father had boasted a harem of six wives who produced twenty-eight sons for him. Just before he died he became a Catholic and had all his children baptised, but the new religion did not hamper the family's business activity in any way. Their opium and gambling monopolies alone brought in up to a million American dollars annually. But a large slice of it, Loo complained, had to be spent on "gifts" for state officials. He said he probably did not clear much more than a third of it . . .

Such were the weird sinews of administrative life in Canton, China's third largest city, and its environs, and I was never to find any great improvement on subsequent visits. I believe opium smoking was eventually almost suppressed, as it was briefly in many places before the Japanese brought it back again. But Canton was never any show-case for Kuomintang democracy, where no official was ever elected to office before World War II. But despite that, money was made, people were born, they suffered, they lived and they loved. Canton thrived in the midst of its corruption, proving that it is true that "Chinese can live under almost any conditions except outright hanging." And life for the have-gots really was relatively good. There was worse to come.

At least Canton was run by Cantonese. And that, I was now to discover in Indo-China, made a difference.

CHAPTER 10

Civilisatrice

SHEEP, RICE and Chinese deck passengers were the main cargo in the thousand-ton French vessel that tossed me over the 450 miles from Hongkong to Haiphong, where I was to take a train through Tonkin, Northern Indo-China, to Yunnanfu. A French parfumeur who was selling airplanes as a side line, and an English woman with a beautiful red-haired child, were the other cabin passengers. For three days we ate together at one round table in the tiny saloon. Coudray, the Frenchman, did most of the talking. He spoke fluent English.

"You will see, when you get to Tonkin," said Coudray, "why it is that France is a successful colonizer. We treat the natives like people, we don't interfere with their culture, we have no prejudices. *Civilisatrice,* that is our mission. We civilize them, then we marry them. *Voilà!* The natives remain happy and contented."

Although Coudray was making his first trip to Indo-China he had read about benevolent French colonial policy and the gratitude of the natives. As for me, I was content to wait and see.

At Haiphong a swarm of natives overran the boat, eager for the few coppers to be earned for carrying our luggage ashore. Hot and infuriated, the French customs guards used long corded whips to keep the coolies back, yelling, *"Canailles! Cochons!"* Though they seldom actually hit anybody it seemed to me an undignified method of *civilisatrice.*

We became aware of a disturbance up the quay, centering around a French mail liner. Important officials and army officers in wedding-cake hats moved down the gangway into a knot of gesticulating Europeans, wearing white topees. Beyond, a large crowd was being dispersed by soldiers and guards with whips. As the agile brown people scurried from the scene many were laughing—enigmatically, for it was a rare thing to see any Tonkinese even smile in those days.

It turned out that the liner had been ready to leave, with its distinguished passenger none other than M. Pasquier, Governor-General of Indo-China. Bands played, hats and handkerchiefs waved, friends shouted *bon voyage*. Then the captain gave his commands and nothing happened. Amazed engineers came up to report that vital machinery had been smashed.

"*Sabotage!*" muttered the Frenchmen among themselves. "*Les rebelles! La sédition!*"

"So, you have a revolution on your hands?" I asked.

"Impossible!" exclaimed Coudray. "There is no trouble here or I would have heard of it."

But there was. I spent a fortnight in Haiphong and Hanoi to get the story, of which I learned more as I traveled back up to China's mountainous southern frontier at Yunnan.

In outer aspect Hanoi was the most European city in East Asia, with few reminders that it had been under Chinese suzerainty for centuries before the war of 1885. Its wide, tree-lined boulevards and avenues, modern shops and couturiers, the opera house and public buildings and fine homes set in fragrant gardens and parks, might have been part of Neuilly, in Paris, except for the intrusion of the mouselike natives, with their disconcerting habit of surreptitiously spitting long streams of scarlet betel juice from under their wide mushroom hats across every inviting target of white walk or wall.

Both Haiphong and Hanoi gave the impression of stable and confident power. The natives were so meek and demoralized that it seemed "impossible" for revolution to be on their minds. The three or four great cities were the thin shallow European show-cases of a country which, though larger than France and potentially just as rich, was more backward than China, quite undeveloped compared to Japan, and as yet lacked even a single trans-national railway. In the thousands of squalid, crowded villages buried in the mud and steeped in poverty, disease and ignorance, twenty million natives waited for the *mission civilisatrice,* after a half century of French power.

Of course the French were beginning to educate the Annamites and choosing a few for higher study in France whom they did, indeed, accept as social equals. But this loyal veneer spread around the puppet princes was ever so thin and did not touch the lives of the masses. Nor could the French produce Eurasians fast enough to compete with native fecundity, as the Dutch methodically tried (and failed) to do in Java. Those who wished to marry Annamites did so. But for the most part Franco-Annamite biology was outside matrimony, in places such as the French Madame's where a chance bar-room acquaintance took me in Hanoi. There Eurasian girls, dressed in native silk trousers only, served opium and/or ether to the guests. A newspaper man's duty and prerogative is to see everything (and write a tenth of it) but that evening I was thwarted. I had tried Shanghai opium once, in an overdose that made me deathly ill, and the smell of ether revived my worst trauma from a tonsilectomy in childhood. I had to leave the place without waiting to hear Madame's report on Franco-Annamite "miscegenation"—a subject on which, my acquaintance had assured me, she was an authority.

The Metropole was called the "little capital" of Hanoi, just as Hanoi itself was the "little capital" of Indo-China. The big capital was Saigon. In the hotel you saw the colony's officers and officials and salesmen with their French wives or Eurasian mistresses. At night it was gay with laughter and champagne while an orchestra played nostalgic songs from Paris. How bizarre and strangely unreal the brilliance and opulence seemed in contrast to the bedraggled villages we had just driven through on our way up from the coastal plain, when Coudray and I walked in the first night! A clerk from Marseilles registered us and shouted to a couple of gray-haired Annamite "boys," who wore gold-braided uniforms but no shoes. They did not move at once; perhaps they misunderstood his rapid French.

"Dépêchez! Imbéciles!" he shrieked. He came from behind the counter and took the little men by their collars. He shook them, pulled their hair and ended by knocking their heads together. Then he sent them sprawling toward our luggage which they picked up with what remained of their dignity.

Coudray gave me an embarrassed look and asked the clerk whether that had been necessary. Surprised, the man lifted his hands and shoulders high. "Messieurs, vous ne connaissez pas les indigènes," he said. "It is not possible to reason with them. Les enfants! They are simply children, stupid children!"

Later I concluded that it was the triumph of the method and the system over the human personality that was degrading about colonial doctrine; few men could resist it. In Tonkin I saw it when an exasperated little Frenchman, a conductor on a train, went through the car slapping the cheeks of natives now and then who were too slow to produce their tickets. The victims were women, occasionally, as well as men. They took it with closed faces, and yet these "children" would not forget it, nor would their children's children.

Perhaps there was more sullen meanness of that kind just then because of the rebellion, which infuriated the French—to them an unnecessary act of impertinent disobedience—more than it yet alarmed them.

"It is necessary to teach them a lesson, *monsieur; regrettable, oui, mais ils sont enfants,*" said the Governor-General when I interviewed him while he still awaited transportation to France. *La sédition,* he said, had begun with the mutiny at Yen Bay, near the China frontier, where Annamite troops disarmed their French officers and took over the garrison. They lost their nerve when Foreign Legion reinforcements arrived; they surrendered without firing a shot. Monsieur Pasquier admitted that they had been "a little too harsh" in retaliating. About sixty Annamites were executed there. Then followed a whole series of uprisings and outbreaks, all very minor, "but, one comprehended, an inconvenience." And now arrests and interrogations had uncovered a widespread but infantile plot to organize a revolution which promised "independence." Ridiculous? Of course! But one could not blame the people too much. They were being utilized by a few clever Communists and possibly even by some French traitors on the spot.

But did one have to be a Communist, I wondered, to love one's country and liberty and hate being pushed around by outsiders?

The heart of the rebellion was in the richest rice-growing area of Annam (Viet-nam), where the revolutionists had seized a number of districts and set up a so-called "republic." At a student demonstration in Dalat the French had fired on and killed a number of unarmed people. Exaggerated accounts were carried into the villages and the students organized an unarmed procession to march to Dalat with a petition of grievances to the puppet child king, Bao Dai. The French lost their heads again and sent out airplanes to bomb and machine-gun the procession and a lot more Annamites were killed. Now they would have to bring in more troops.

Through a Chinese merchant I met some French-educated Annamites who got me copies of the "terms" presented by the rebels to Hanoi. Their "highest demand" was for a constitutional government and a popularly elected assembly with legislative powers subject to the French Governor-General's veto. Other "demands" included abolition of serfdom (still a legal institution), abolition of polygamy, reduction of land rents, and liquidation of the puppet monarchy in favor of a republican form of government.

In response the French suspended what civil rights existed and made any kind of political talk or gathering a crime. The guillotine was freely used. Heads of rebels or alleged rebels were publicly displayed around Dalat, Hué, Touraine and other centers of disaffection. There were more than 700 decapitations. The French justified this harsh measure on the supposition that it aroused unholy terror in the superstitious natives because, while they might care little for this life, they could not easily face the next as headless ghosts.

This first great rebellion, quixotic, premature, poorly armed and poorly organized, inevitably was crushed by the might of France. News of it was strictly censored. My own meagre reports had to be smuggled out through Hongkong, and I believe they were the only coverage in America. I myself did not see much and yet it was enough to make me doubt that France had much time left to carry out the *mission civilisatrice,* in terms of *liberté, égalité, fraternité,* if her brown "children" were to become true brothers.

New heads would grow from the torsos of the fallen leaders. They would always be waiting, I wrote, "waiting for French vigilance to weaken, waiting for France to be involved in major troubles elsewhere, waiting for arms, for the next world war, tirelessly waiting . . ."

CHAPTER 11

The Stone Collector

I WAS EXCITED about the effect on our policy which I imagined my revelations on Indo-China must have when they hit the papers at home. Just before I left Hanoi for Yunnan an amusing encounter restored my sense of proportion. In the Metropole lobby I met a Texas oilman on a leisurely trip around the world. He was visiting his company's agents here and there, but his real passion was stones. He was a collector not of jewels but of big hunks of rock, rocks of a very special kind. In earlier travels he had picked up pieces of the Sphinx, Cheops, the Parthenon, Gibraltar, Stonehenge and the Colosseum. Now he had added slabs from Fujiyama and the Great Wall to his treasures and he was on his way to Cambodia to bribe a guide to get him a piece of Angkor Wat.

"And what will you do with Angkor Wat?" I asked.

"I'll make a seat out of it. A nice stone seat."

"I don't get it."

"Back in Texas we've got a lahge tehhace 'n' bahbecue grill," he explained. "When I invite the boys in for a feed of good old Texas steer I sit 'em down and I say, 'Bill, yall know what that big fat behind a yuahs is sittin' on? That is Kee-ops under you, man—*Kee*-ops!' I say to anothah, 'Jim, yall're sittin' on the ruins a *Pom*-pay!' "

I still didn't get the point.

"Why, Jesus Christ's long lost elder brothah, man, y'oughta see their faces when they know they're *sittin' on history!*"

In those dreamy years of lingering isolationism we Americans thought of both Asia and Europe as a museum of inanimate ruins. The history I was then witnessing could not be brought home "to sit on." The living humanity in the old world was far more important than its relics and its problems would affect the lives and fortunes of our own sons for many years to come.

CHAPTER 12

Raw-Meat Country

A CHALLENGING JOURNEY lay ahead of me.

Yunnan, which was to become our principal air base in East Asia a decade later, was during my first visit still directly accessible to the rest of China only by horse or by foot. A remote plateau as large as Germany and Poland combined, its single modern connection with the outside world was the French-built railway that rose from Hanoi to Yunnanfu, the capital. Even by that roundabout route it took a week to get there from Hongkong. Tourists seldom ventured even as far as the railhead, for trains were frequently attacked by bandits.

Part of my assignment was to "have adventures" and the name

"Yün-nan," which means "South of the Clouds," seemed promising. I liked the look of Yunnan on the map, wedged between Tibet, India, Burma and Indo-China. This was the frontier over which the Mongol cavalry of Kubilai Khan once carried the yak-tailed banner in triumph to the Bay of Bengal. That much I knew from Marco Polo's travels. It was his account of his own trip across this high mountainous Tibetan periphery, centuries earlier, that really started in me an ambition to follow in his footsteps and enter Burma that way.

"Let me tell you that the people of that country (Yunnan) eat their meat raw," reported Marco. "Raw, just as we eat meat that is dressed."

Marco was probably speaking of the tribal peoples, so numerous in Yunnan, which is indeed their homeland. It was for many centuries largely a kind of Southern Siberia for China, to which disgraced officials were exiled. That partly explains why its people spoke Mandarin, the language of the North, instead of some Southern Chinese dialect. Yunnan's eating habits had changed, since Marco's time, but little else, it seemed, except perhaps for the worse.

One improvement was the railway itself, an early miracle of the enterprise and engineering skill which France had imposed on China against her will. Peking had rightly feared the political consequences, after France had detached Indo-China itself from the Middle Kingdom. It took three days and more than two hundred tunnels to reach Yunnanfu, at 6,400 feet above the sea. Beyond the capital all traffic moved over imperial stone-paved caravan "roads" which hadn't been rebuilt since the Great Khan's day and aptly fitted the Chinese aphorism about roads in general: "Good for ten years, bad for ten thousand."

In Yunnanfu, also known as Kunming and Tien, I quickly learned that the four-hundred-mile trip across the mountains and rivers to Upper Burma was no engagement lightly to be undertaken by an amateur. I had neither the money nor the scientific education for such an expedition. All I had was curiosity and a need for unusual copy. Our consul in Yunnanfu, Harry Stevens, hospitably put me up for weeks and did his best to get me to abandon the quixotic expedition. He was afraid he would have another "incident" on his hands when those raw-meat-eating bandits got hold of me. And he was not the only one.

"Yes, you'll be murdered, ha! ha!" roared Mr. Kuo Ping-kan, the massive Commissioner for the Chinese salt monopoly in the capital, when I told him of my plans. "Last week three of our students on their way from Burma were captured by bandits, robbed and killed on the road. One of our salt caravans was held up near She-tze; it turned out their own guards were bandits, ha! Now my landlord comes to me this morning and says he has just lost his caravan at Lufeng. That's only three days from here."

Mr. Kuo was a Shantung man, himself, and assessed the local Chinese as a poor copy of the real thing. He combined a Rotarian's conviction of the superiority of his own province to any part of the world with fluency in French and colloquial American; yet he had never been out of China. He had learned foreign languages in missionary schools "back East." Of course his Shantung province had bandits of its own; as we have seen, they made guests of Powell and Mlle. Aldrich; but in Kuo's opinion there was simply no comparison between Yunnan bandits and those of Shantung.

"Here," he bellowed, handing me a box of Havana Havanas, "have a cigar, just smuggled in, ha!" He put one in the corner of his own grin and lighted up. "Why shouldn't I smoke them? I work for the salt monopoly, not the customs. Besides, they're a present from the Governor!"

In Yunnan, he explained, the only difference between a bandit and an official was that the official was a successful bandit. He himself, as an official of a monopoly, still partly under foreign control, owed his appointment not to local influence but to Shanghai.

"We have an old Chinese saying, 'Big fish eat little fish, little fish eat shrimps, shrimps eat mud!' That's sure true here, my friend, but don't quote me, ha! The peasants are the shrimps, the little fish are the bandits, the big fish are the officials!"

"Hasn't the revolution changed that?"

"Revolution? The Kuomintang? I'm a member, mind you, but here it's just a new flag under old warlords. Take that Yunnan expedition to support Chiang Kai-shek's campaign against Kuangsi.* Know what that was all about? Yunnan generals were sore at Kuangsi for blocking the opium road to Canton, so they impressed an army and began this expedition for the People's Three Principles, and took along 2500 mule loads of opium to sell down there! As soon as they got rid of the opium they came back to Yunnan and bought French piastres with the proceeds. Then they disbanded half their troops without pay. So now we have more bandits. You see?"

Mr. Kuo was nevertheless a good politician. A few nights later I was his guest at a banquet in honor of Chang Fêng-chung, local garrison

* Pai Chung-hsi and Chang Fa-kuei, "leftist" Kuomintang generals in the southwest, were in one of their periodic moods of opposition to the Generalissimo, who never quite got control of Kuangsi province.

commander and deputy chairman of the Kuomintang. The meal ran into twenty-four courses washed down with French wines and champagne. Afterward we were invited to the theatre by General Chang. He had brought his protégé from Shanghai, an actor named Hu Hanling. The theatre was in a garden filled with magnolia trees, where painted lanterns were strung along a fairy lake. The entrancing spectacle was marred only by a cluster of unarmed soldiers who wore tattered uniforms that did not match. They hung around the gate to watch the players and neo-mandarins arrive. As we went in, the general's personal bodyguards pushed them aside.

Seats were divided into sections by raised platforms used by peddlers who sold hot meat rolls, oranges, peanuts and watermelon seeds. They trotted back and forth throughout the performance, as usual, accompanied by small boys who expertly sailed steaming towels over your head, to anybody who wanted them. The play was an old classic known by heart to everybody except the foreigners, but Hu Hanling, impersonating a courtesan hotly pursued by a Taoist god, introduced one innovation. When it came to the ballet the lights were turned out and Hu did some fancy juggling with a pair of magic wands loaded with flashlights. In the middle of that business a great commotion broke out in back of the theatre. Lights blinked on again and the proprietor came up to appeal to General Chang Fêng-chung. Then I saw the commander of his bodyguard rush out with several men.

"Those ex-soldiers we saw hanging around outside are trying to crash the gate," Kuo explained in his surprising idiomatic English. "Chang ordered them dispersed." Soon we heard machine guns bark for a few minutes, above the high falsetto screams on the stage, the crashing of cymbals and the whine of the Chinese violins. When we came out after the show the street was completely emptied of the disbanded soldiers, but three crumpled figures lay in the shadow of a wall.

General Chang was locally known as "Pock-Mark Ten Wives" and "Thirty-Six Horse Chang," the nicknames referring to his personal stables in each respect. He was still expanding both, apparently, for while I was there he tried to annex a young Christian girl. When her parents declined he sent his bodyguard to kidnap her but she escaped by climbing over the compound wall and hiding in the Anglican mission. There she was protected until Dr. John Watson, head of the mission, personally escorted her by rail to Indo-China and safety.

"Pock-Mark Ten Wives" believed in swift justice to the wicked. Consul Harry Stevens told me that just before I arrived Chang had publicly executed fifty-three "counter-revolutionaries," including several women, none of whom had had a public trial. Chang invited the American and other consuls to witness it, for two reasons of state. Some of the consuls had received anti-foreign literature and threatening letters through the mails. Chang wished them to know that his regime had had nothing to do with that and believed in law, order, and the protection of private property. Secondly, the former American consul had protested against the old-fashioned beheadings as too barbarous. Chang wanted it noted that modern civilized and humane methods had been adopted. This time the malcontents were shot in the back of the head.

CHAPTER 13

Life under Dragon Cloud

CHANG FÊNG-CHUNG was one of the three "big fish" in Yunnan. The other two were Governor Lung Yun, whose name meant "Dragon Cloud," and his cousin, General Lu Han, "pacification commissioner." The big fish had all begun life as shrimp, and then become "little fish." They had been denounced as bandits by earlier rulers before they triumphed as regional leaders of the Kuomintang. Lung Yun was also known as "Caged Tiger" because he had once been captured by a rival, put in a cage, and paraded through the streets so that plebeians could throw stones and spit at him—a practice I had thought extinct but which I later learned was often repeated during the Communist-Kuomintang civil war. Lung was rescued and escaped death. He was one day again to be betrayed, and by Cousin Lu Han, whom Chiang Kai-shek supported in another coup. That internecine operation so angered Lung Yun that he helped the Communists against Chiang.

But just now the three big fish were working well together, and getting rich. A principal source of easy spoils, I learned from Consul Stevens and others, was their firm grip on the semi-state bank, called the Fu Tien Yin-hong. Not so many years earlier Yunnan had very good silver money, but now it had all been converted to paper, except in the far west, where they still used old imperial coins, the most beautiful in China. The paper no longer had anything behind it but force, so that it was accepted only where the militarists were able to offer the alternative of death to "counter-revolutionaries." Somewhat the same situation would eventually prevail nearly everywhere in the latter part of the Kuomintang era. So would the following practice which developed as a fine art in Yunnan:

The big fish were all directors of the state bank and also engaged in private business as merchants, landlords and speculators. They controlled the output of the tin and opium monopolies, for example, which they bought with loans from the bank and then resold without having put out a penny of their own. Just before each new fall in paper money value, which they knew was inevitable, they would buy up other commodities or foreign exchange. During the temporary stabilization they would sell out. Later, they would unload their paper money once more, buy up other real values, sell at big profits, and put aside more "savings" in foreign money. This simple process would become enormously popular in the Central Government during the Sino-Japanese and World Wars, when the United States attempted to shore up the wildly inflated Kuomintang yuan by giving it a false exchange rate in American dollars. In such ways millions of dollars of American money were to be banked abroad by the ruling families and their satellites.

Yunnanfu smelled of opium everywhere; pipes and lamps were sold in all the markets; the drug was as easy to buy as rice. On the streets you could see mothers give their tiny children sugar cane smeared with opium in lieu of a pacifier. Demoralization and impoverishment were especially apparent in the abuse of children, who were exploited all over China but nowhere quite so unconscionably as in Yunnan.

"There are probably half a million slaves in the whole province," to quote from an interview I had with Richard Lankester, English headmaster of a mission school run by the Church of Christ. "Twenty thousand would be a conservative estimate for the capital alone. They do all the drudgery in the stores, workshops and homes. Their masters and mistresses do as they please with them. They really are *ya-t'ou* or 'yoke-heads,' as they are called, just cattle. Our missionary ladies opened a home for the runaways and tried to get some prominent Chinese women to help manage it, but it turned out that even the Chinese Christian families all had slave girls themselves!"

In that home for slave girls I talked to about a dozen children from eight to sixteen years old. I remember how proudly they displayed their personal possessions. It enormously improved their morale to know that they actually owned things like toothbrushes, chopsticks, bowls and the cheap clothes given to them. Before they had escaped to the home, or been bought out of slavery by it, even the rags on their backs had belonged to their owners. One child of nine had been paralyzed from the hips down by a beating delivered with an iron rod. Another was nearly deaf from a blow on the head. A girl of fifteen had been bought and sold four times. Her last master had starved her for a week and then hung her up by her thumbs to punish her for "laziness."

The pauperization of the peasantry was accelerated by forced production of opium and its widespread use. Alienation of the land to absentee owners proceeded apace; at that time fewer than one-third of the peasants on the Yunnan plain owned their farms. A girl sold outright on the local market then brought the equivalent of only five to ten dollars, but that was more than a farm laborer, working for four cents (U.S.) a day, could save in a year. Poverty in other parts of China also obliged the very poor to sell their surplus daughters, as we have seen, but except in deep famine conditions they rarely sold their sons. In Yunnan large numbers of boys were in servitude.

One of the most criminal uses of them was in the primitive tin mines at Kochiu, a semi-government enterprise. Once there, the boys often developed rickets, scabies and beri-beri. The shafts and tunnels in the mines were very small, hardly big enough for a boy to crawl in and out on his hands and knees, with the ore basket strapped to his back. As a result many became permanently deformed and were cast aside. An American missionary named Baker specialized in salvaging the little wrecks, and he and his wife nursed scores back to health and taught them useful trades or handicrafts.

Even if Yunnanfu was revolting humanly, its natural surroundings were beautiful and the historic old walled city had all the color and excitement of a wild frontier town, the end of railway and roads, and the beginning of the caravan. Horses and mules stumbled in and out of the stone gates; the narrow crowded streets were a confusion of sly merchants and outland Chinese and of sun-browned men and women of a dozen different tribes, wearing distinctive bright costumes often beautifully embroidered. Tall bare-shouldered Tibetans, as shaggy as their dogs, wandered around gazing open-mouthed at the shoddy wares of lowland civilization and such wonders as electric lights, so dim they were lost in the brilliance of kerosene lamps, a movie house, and steam locomotives. Always in the distance lay the blue-rimmed mountains of a region magnificently endowed with potential wealth and natural scenery, where every prospect pleased and only man seemed vile.

In spite of the bandit menace I did go on to Burma. I might never have done so if I had not met Dr. Joseph F. Rock, the naturalist and explorer. Rock had made Yunnan famous among botanists, proving its unmapped western territories to be among the true Edens of the world and the source of hundreds of varieties of plants unknown abroad. One of a handful of non-missionary Americans in Yunnan, he was just getting ready to leave on another expedition sponsored by the National Geographic Association. He had six or seven well-armed Nashi (Nosu) tribesmen in his personal entourage. When he invited me to go with him, Consul Stevens' objections lost all effect. After I accepted I got myself a pony, hired some mules, and bought supplies. Then I hunted for a weapon and finally found a Browning automatic which I bought from, of all people, a missionary.

"So, you're going, after all!" yelled Mr. Kuo when I went to ask him to transfer some silver to me through the office of the salt monopoly at Talifu, in Western Yunnan. "Don't worry, I'll see that your ransom is paid if the bandits get you, ha! ha!" He asked me to send him copies of any photographs I might take along the road, and gave me some last-minute advice as he escorted me to my horse at the door.

"Don't forget," he said, "bandits are just people in business for money. Don't argue, give them your money, and they won't hurt you." Then he pulled a carton of Capstan cigarettes out of his long gown and said, "Here, take this along. They like to smoke, too! *I-p'ing hao-lu* [Peaceful good road], as we say in Chinese. Good luck. Ha! Ha!"

Quite a character, Mr. Kuo. I liked him.

CHAPTER 14

Caravan Tales

TWO WEEKS of bandits and hacking over broken trails lay between us and the glory of the white-capped Ts'ang Mountain that rises beyond the lake of Talifu, a crossroads of Yunnan, Tibet and Burma.

It was a rewarding experience to travel with Dr. Joseph F. Rock. He had an unsurpassed knowledge of Far China and Eastern Tibet, where he had been collecting and exploring for many years. He was now on another plant-hunting expedition. The first person to measure China's tallest mountain, Minya Konka (an eternally snow-crowned peer of Everest and Katchenchunga), Rock was a botanist, explorer, cartographer, ethnologist, writer and photographer. The shrubs and trees we passed were friends he knew by their Latin names, which he had in some instances bestowed on them. He had "discovered" dozens of new varieties of flowers and plants, among them many rhododendrons new to the Western world. Near Xiengmai he had gathered the seeds of the chaulmoogra tree, which he carried back to Hawaii and tenderly brought to life for the first time outside Asia. Chaulmoogra nuts produce an oil that was for long the only known cure for leprosy, a disease as common as goiter, which was quite common indeed in Yunnan. Rock always had with him a complete kit of medicines and a bag of medical instruments, and he was also an itinerant dentist. An agnostic, he held evangelists in the utmost contempt, but he was a missionary in spite of himself.

"What's the use of wasting money sending soul-savers here if they only add one kind of ignorance to another?" he would say. "Some of them shouldn't be turned loose even at home, much less be allowed to come out to 'save' Chinese. Take that fellow Joseph Brown. Christians haven't got enough denominations, he had to form one of his own. Had his letterheads printed in Chinese for Brown's Salvationists, and who do you suppose the officers were? President, God; Vice-president, Jesus Christ; Treasurer, Joseph Brown! What a disgrace!"

"Even so," I would argue, "it's a harmless kind of banditry for Yunnan."

"Harmless? Such people are worse than bandits. A man and his wife came up to Likiang once, for the Holy Rollers. This couple had been in bible school together when they had a vision and an angel told them to come out here and 'save' the Chinese and Tibetans. They believed prayer heals all and would have nothing to do with medicine or surgery. 'Have faith,' they would preach, 'and your faith will cure anything.' Think of treating people with tuberculosis, syphilis and leprosy that way! The Tibetans can do just as well with their own joss men and lamas. They didn't make any converts, anyway, though the beggars went around for free soup."

"Well," said I, "faith is a miracle in itself, doesn't it help cure mental illness, at least?"

"It didn't cure their baby boy. One day I heard he was very sick and I went over to see him even though I knew they wouldn't listen to me.

The child had amoebic dysentery and already looked like a skeleton. I told them I had some emetine which would cure him, but they wouldn't let me treat him. I lost my temper. 'You're criminals!' I shouted as I left. 'You're deliberate killers.' They said, 'If it's the Lord's will he will live. The Lord will hear our prayers.'

"All I can say is that if they prayed in *their* Chinese you couldn't blame the Lord for not understanding them. Ten days later they did finally send for me. When I arrived they said, 'We've been thinking, maybe the Lord wouldn't mind if you helped with His work.' But it was too late for that. Their child died in an hour. They didn't even cry. 'It's the Lord's will,' they kept saying. 'The Lord wanted him and He has His reasons.' How can a man be conceited enough to think God has made him His spokesman? As if God couldn't talk for Himself!"

"What about Dr. Watson back at the Anglican mission in Yunnanfu? He looks to me like a missionary doing good."

"Oh, he's a doctor, that's different. I'm talking about soul-savers. Take those young evangelists we saw in Yunnanfu going out with their bags of *grapenuts!*" He snorted. "They're just crazy." He meant the two Seventh Day Adventists we had met just as they began their first tour of the province. Except for some homemade "grapenuts" they had taken no food with them, and no bedding. They said they would just "live off the country, like the people."

"Do you think Chinese will listen to them? They say 'Look what these foreign-devils eat. This Christianity can't be much good if its priests eat stuff we feed our pigs!'" He snorted again. "Those boys will be lucky to get back alive." Alas, his prescience of tragedy proved correct. Although the "boys" themselves returned safely, they found that during their absence their wives had been murdered in Yunnanfu. Their cook, drunk on opium and wine, had slit their throats one night as they slept—a rare thing to happen to foreigners in China in those days.

Rock wouldn't go near a Chinese inn but always camped in the woods or temples. He carried along everything Abercrombie and Fitch could provide, including a folding bathtub and a complete kitchen. During the march his tribal retainers divided into a vanguard and rear guard. The advance party, led by a cook, an assistant cook, and a butler, would spot a sheltered place with a good view, unfold the table and chairs on a leopard-skin rug, and lay out clean linen cloth, china, silver and napkins. By the time we arrived our meal would be almost ready. At night it was several courses ending with tea and liqueurs. If we stopped in a settled place the whole village would crouch down and look on from a distance. When we chose a temple, a matter easily arranged by a small tip to the priests, Rock's Nashi retainers would first give the God of War or Goddess of Mercy a thorough dusting and end by washing down the floors, before putting our cots beneath the idols.

"You've got to make people believe you're someone of importance if you want to live in these wilds," Rock would say. It seemed to work —for him—though it was expensive. Natives who knew him called him "the foreign prince."

At Laoyakuan we met a caravan of Tibetans who had been attacked by bandits the day before and lost a few loads of furs. The Tibetans claimed they had driven off the bandits after killing four. They were annoyed because they were on their way to see Dragon Cloud (Governor Lung Yun) and present him with gifts from the Dalai Lama. Farther on we passed a big salt caravan which had also been held up. Every settled place we saw had either just been liberated from "Iron Watch," the leading brigand, or lived in fear of him. Once the village we were stopping in was attacked at four o'clock in the morning and the next day we followed the provincial troops on the road as they gave half-hearted chase.

"Going out to get their share of the loot," said Rock contemptuously.

Local magistrates supplied the "foreign prince" and me with between twenty and fifty soldiers as bodyguards, and we took the precaution of paying them well in *ya-p'ien ch'ien,* or opium money. Our own small company had a sizeable arsenal, too. Rock didn't believe in the kindness of bandits, and when I got right down to it I didn't believe in it, either. The truth was that Rock's caravan of sixty mules and horses would have been a rich prize. He carried a vast amount of supplies and valuable scientific equipment as well as ten thousand dollars in silver, I learned after we were on the road. He expected to be "in the wilds," as he put it, for at least a year. This responsibility tended to make him calculate each day's risk very carefully. More than once, after a conference with his Nashi "staff" about the security situation, he was ready to halt or turn back. But then we would take on more bodyguards and go ahead.

The local bandits were not "Red-bandits," as Chiang Kai-shek then called the Communists, but were what the Reds called "white-bandits": ruined peasants or out-of-work soldiers without any special ideology except to rob to live. If their leaders could not be killed and grew powerful they would be bought off and given provincial commands. Later on many bandit chieftains like these joined the Kuomintang in other provinces, and some were "converted" and joined the

Communists. Armies had been built up in this way in times of trouble in China for ages past. Four years after I rode over these trails Yunnan would become the scene of great battles of survival for the Chinese Reds as they fought rear-guard actions against Central Government troops pursuing them during their 5,000-mile Long March.

Yunnanese had a saying that "The Chinese own the plains, the tribesmen own the mountains, the bandits own the road." But it was the poppy that really ruled Yunnan. On the plains between Yunnanfu and Tali about half the acreage was planted for opium. For years afterward opium taxes of various kinds provided the chief source of revenue. Local magistrates usually fixed the amount of land to be devoted to poppies, the ratio depending on how much they had paid for their appointments. Often peasant tillers could *avoid* planting poppies only by paying a "fine"—to the Opium Suppression Bureau.

All our muleteers smoked themselves to sleep every night, but Rock wouldn't let his Nashis touch opium. The heaviest addicts with us were the Szechuanese chairbearers. Rock had taken them on when he developed recurrent malaria and could not ride his horse. The chair was a bamboo and wicker affair built on a framework of four shafts, two to a bearer, with the seat in between, covered by an oilskin. It was roadless China's most comfortable means of travel—for the passengers.

For some reason the Yunnanese, who would do anything else for money, would not stoop to carry a chair, and it was a Szechuanese monopoly. Rock's bearers were four, or two teams, who alternated on the road. They had calluses an inch thick on their bare shoulders and their sole personal "valuables" were the opium pipes that hung at their cotton girdles. At night they ate little but some sticky rice before they smoked off into the dreamland of Coleridge. Yet they had amazing, tireless strength and grace as they loped along hour after hour. During the day they infuriated Rock by spitting against the wind, but he couldn't help laughing at the songs they improvised.

"The Yunnanese are dogs," the lead man would cry. "They scratch their lice with their feet."

"Not human," the rear man would echo, "they talk but their language is not human."

"Move to one side," the first would sing out, "a great man is coming."

"Why, it's only a turtle-son official! Rape his grandmother!" the second would shout back.

Or one would simply wail, "Ai, ai, ai, ai, ya, ya, yah"—and the other would answer, "To be—in bed—with—little—sis-ter." For "little sister" and "elder brother" were also terms of warm endearment in Chinese.

When not otherwise engaged some of the muleteers sang opera arias picked up in Yunnanfu. But they couldn't remember the words and they would substitute the single oath *ma-ti* throughout the song, much as Elliot Paul's L'Oursin (in *The Last Time I saw Paris*) sang "Silent Night" in its entirety by using the one word *merde*. *Ma-ti* is the commonest oath in China. The full expression is *wo ts'ao ni ma-ti p'i* which literally means, "I have ravished your mother." But it can also be applied forward or backward in time, to all relations and ranks, and to all things. Its variations and abbreviations are more complex, yet simpler, more elegant, yet more vulgar, than the Anglo-Saxon equivalent. But I need not pursue this fascinating subject because Lu Hsun, China's most famous modern writer, devoted a classic essay to the history, prevalence and virtuosity of *ma-ti*. Anyone interested in Chinese sociology will find it in a book* of translations of Lu Hsun's work which I later compiled when we became friends.

Gradually I felt somewhat embarrassed by our luxury and guarded possessions in contrast to the surrounding poverty, and I was relieved when Rock's fever declined and he no longer needed the chairbearers. What made me think they were as wretched as they looked? Didn't Taoism teach the beggar to rationalize his mind, or fate, and accept it as entirely logical? And should I ignore the fact that these chair coolies were convinced that as Szechuanese they were the Superior Race compared to Yunnanese, not to mention mere foreign-devils like myself who could not speak the "human" language at all? What more reassurance did a man need?

"Of course, there'll be a revolution in this country," said Rock. "It's bound to come some day and it will be the bloodiest in history. I don't want to be around then but I won't blame them. Look at that lad with us we're taking back to Likiang! He was only fourteen but he was impressed into the army to replace another fellow whose mother could bribe the officers. They led him off with a rope around his neck and gave him a gun and now he's back from Kuangsi with that crippled arm. Had to crawl back to Yunnanfu by himself, and when he came to me his arm was full of maggots! Look at the other case I told you about yesterday—the old lady who jumped into the lake after General Chang Fêng-chung hauled off both her sons with ropes around their necks— and left her to starve! How long will people put up with that kind of business?"

* *Living China*, New York, 1936.

CHAPTER 15

On to Burma

THE COUNTRY GREW lovelier and more peaceful as we drew farther away from the capital. On the twelfth day we rode toward the historic town of Hungai, where the immortal Chuko Liang arrived with his arguments and his army to subdue the Shan Kingdom, seventeen centuries ago. All morning we climbed through torrential rain, until at noon we halted at the crest of a pass nine thousand feet high. Then our caravan sloshed down the always twisting, ankle-breaking road, now become the bed of a sludgy flood pouring over what was once Kubilai Khan's highway.

Sometimes a mule sank with his load and a puller cursed and yanked him back to his feet. Yellow oilskins covered the loads and the muleteers wore wide straw hats bound with the same stuff, looking like giant sunflowers in the rain. Only the chairbearers went hatless, near-naked and barefoot, their melancholy chants heard above the tinkling bells of the be-ribboned lead mule. A long drop of three thousand feet brought us onto the Hungai plain, where smoke curled from straw-roofed huts and early-lighted lamps winked through the paper windows. Errant winds traced their fingers in zig-zag lines across lake-fields of rice. We slid below the dark green shoulders of the mountains and ended at a Buddhist temple where we watched a young monk make a new god out of wet clay.

Next day we rode out upon the Tali plain and I saw the peaks of the Ts'ang Shan loom up. They were awesome and beautiful in their white-hooded symmetry, a brooding stillness above the ancient walled city. Girdling the lower slopes were tens of thousands of graves, many of them elaborate marble sarcophagi with their portals facing the blue lake and its fringe of eucalyptus trees. Shan, Arabic, Mongol, Manchu, Tibetan and Chinese inscriptions covered these tombs, which were quite unlike the earth-mounds of Eastern China. They were among the few records left of notables before and after Tali's age of greatness as an independent kingdom, a thousand years ago.

In the ancient capital's newly cleaned cobbled streets we met a monstrous green and red dragon a hundred feet long. Chinese New Year had just begun, shops were closed, cup cakes and sweet rice were served as debts were settled, and incense burned before the kitchen gods. Sallow-faced merchants in black silk gowns and jackets and soft felt shoes wore round hats and bowed to one another, hands rubbing pieces of polished jade inside their long sleeves, as they smiled, smelling faintly of wine and opium. Red-cheeked urchins wrapped in padded jackets and slit trousers that left cold bottoms bare, sailed kites and yelled with delight. Women in embroidered robes, their bound feet crammed exquisitely into shoes smaller than your hand, stood gossiping as their wide-eyed infants sucked scarlet candied apples or rice balls, and old men sucked brass or silver water pipes while they squatted in the sun. Drunk Tibetans, naked to the waist and yelling like cowboys, rode their wild horses through the throngs, and muleteers clung desperately to their frightened animals to keep them from dumping their saddle packs, as they cursed the delay that kept them from the noisy celebration. And through it all twisted the cavorting dragon, up from his legendary home in Tali Lake for this annual carnival visit, his frail *papier-mâché* head and the long body carried on the backs of the townspeople.

Tali's shops sold jade, jadeite and amber at a fraction of their cost in the world beyond. They were famous also for *Tali-shih,* a locally quarried marble very beautifully veined, which when cut into plaques was highly prized all over the East for its natural resemblance to fanciful landscapes or human figures. But it was with difficulty that I found a merchant willing to sell me even a few souvenirs of *Tali-shih.* Jade and amber, of which I bought several necklaces farther south, were hidden away during this holiday season and not to be seen or bought.

From Tali onward I was on my own, for here Rock's path was to the north and west and mine was to the south. Fortunately the road to Burma was, except for two or three days beyond Tali, free of bandits. I had my own "cook," a mission-trained boy who spoke a bit of English, and we got together our four mules, a couple of ponies, and a pair of muleteers, who attached us to a well-guarded merchant caravan bound for Tengyueh. While Tali slept off its New Year hangover I shook hands with Rock, whom I thought I might never see again (but did). Then I said *Tsou!* the word I had learned for "March"! Off we went, down toward what Marco Polo called the country of the "gold-teeth people," who in his day apparently had their teeth capped purely for aesthetic effect.

I would like to be able to describe in detail the wild, grand beauty of the land that lies around the great divides of the lordly Mekong and the Salween Rivers over which I crept for the next two weeks: the thick green forest canvas splashed with crimson flame trees, the mile-deep malarious gorges, the twilit paths under sky-high bamboos that make a weird music of their own, and the brilliant parakeets and monkeys chattering fiercely in the lowland jungle as we neared Burma. I could tell something of the techniques and economy of caravan travel, the comradeship of the road, the dirty, Elizabethan-like inns which now, without Rock, I began to frequent, and of the pre-dawn peace— the pleasant smells of wood-smoke and leather and sweat and charcoal fires. I could mention the old gentleman I saw taking his breakfast from a wet nurse near Yungchang, of lepers who came to beg medicine at Yungpi, of the muleteer who "cured" his syphilis by tying a piece of string around his leg, of the innkeeper at Kanai who hospitably offered me his daughter, and of the Chinese Arabs and Jews I met and how they came to be there. All that country south of the Mekong day by day became more verdant, richer by nature, its aboriginal peoples more picturesque, and its valleys fatter with rice and wealth.

By the end of the trip I was determined to go back to this anthropological wonderland some day and learn more about the tribal men and women whose ancient homelands we skirted: the industrious Miaos, the rebellious Kachins (who worship *Nats,* and whose Jehovah holds each man's life by an invisible string), the Nungs, whose handsome women went naked above the waist, and those gentle cousins of the Siamese, the Shans—all tribal remnants of three distinct culture and language groups who have here resisted Chinese absorption for many centuries.

But all that would fill another book—a book about Yunnan that I began and never finished.

The Southwest was in some ways unique; yet much the same political facts prevailed over most of the West and Northwest provinces, as I would learn. Within the next few years opium production was curtailed as the problem of food became more serious; a few miles of dirt roads were built; and squeeze was more equitably distributed between the officials and the bandits, as most of the latter were assimilated by the army. Otherwise, things altered little up to the time Yunnanfu became an American air base during World War II.

As I left the grassy jungle lane on the outskirts of Bhamo, with the Irrawaddy gleaming in the distance, I never thought that in a few years I would cover all that turbulent land of river heads and toilsome trails in two hours, by army plane, which it had just taken me more than a month to traverse by caravan. But the riches of travel are not paid to the swift, and I was satisfied then to be simply one of the very few Americans or Europeans who had ever walked from China to Burma.

One last mishap marred the completion of my journey, but a mishap with a reward of hidden splendor.

Batalá

As WE GROW older a casual amour of youth may no longer seem much more significant than the remembered glory of a day. But occasionally a purely sentimental encounter may endear a whole people to you, and that is a different matter. Batalá was a different matter.

One morning I woke up between clean sheets in a real bed again and with a sharp hot pain in my knee. I had fever; but something wonderful seemed to be happening, too. A flower-like apparition in a crisp white organdie blouse above an azure silk *longyi* wrapped snugly around a figure too exquisite to be real sat beside me. It was topped by a coil of thick black glossy hair, pinned with a spray of jasmine and a green jade dragon clasp. Her oval face had a smile fresh and sweet.

"Thakin," she said, "you are feeling better now? How is your knee? Shall I get more compresses?"

"Who are you?" I expected her to vanish at my whisper.

"I am your nurse, Batalá. Do you forget?"

Gradually my head cleared. I was in the government circuit house in Bhamo beside the Irrawaddy River, where the British commissioner had kindly put me up. Back on the border of Yunnan a mule, goaded by my pony's habit of nibbling the behind of any animal in front of him, had suddenly let go with both hooves. He had missed the head of his tormentor but made a perfect landing on my knee. The pain and swelling had begun the day my trip ended and I had feared it was a cracked knee cap. A young English official staying at the house called in an Indian doctor. He ordered cold compresses—and Batalá, an itinerant nurse and his assistant.

Out of touch with my editor for months, I should have been anxious to get on to Rangoon. And so I had been. But after seeing Batalá I had begun to fear that the knee would heal too soon. The blessed fever had come to my aid. I had a bad case of malaria.

"I must have been delirious," I said.

"You were, Thakin. Your fever was one hundred four half an hour ago." The vision of cool loveliness put a quiet hand on my forehead. She looked at her gold watch proudly and fed me quinine.

"What did I say?"

"You talked a lot," she said, "about Betty. Who is Betty? Your wife?"

"Oh, no, no! I'm not married. Betty's just—somebody I knew at home—a friend."

I said it much too emphatically. She laughed and I felt myself blushing. What was wrong with me? I remembered how when I shaved off my beard and looked in a mirror after my arrival it had left me with a strange misplaced feeling. After seeing nothing but Mongolian faces for so long, and particularly in recent weeks among the gentle, comely Shan people, I could understand why Europeans looked so absurd. Our big noses, our pasty faces, our jutting chins, our heavy-browed eyes! The small regular features of these round-faced people, their satiny smooth, hairless and odorless skin, now seemed the plausible way for men and women to be made.

I felt huge and crude, a Yahoo among the Houyhnhnms, as Batalá lifted the cold packs from my swollen hairy knee. "It's much better," she noted expertly and far too impersonally.

"It still hurts a great deal."

"You will be well in a few days," she said, "a strong one like you." She gave a tinker-bell laugh and flexed the muscles of her slender bare arm. And I was strong, too, after weeks of riding and climbing. But what did she mean? Could this poem of color and silk be leaving me?

"You—" I made a fool of myself. "You'll stay until the fever is gone, won't you?"

"I have other patients, Thakin." Her white teeth flashed in a mischievous smile. "But I shall be here every day, as long as you need me."

Batalá kept her word.

In a week my fever was gone and I was walking again. She was a total surprise to me. Why was it no one had ever told me about Burma's women, among the most charming and emancipated in the world? I discovered that they possessed a degree of social grace and freedom then unknown in China or India or anywhere in the Asia I had seen. A variety of explanations for this went back to vestiges of matriarchy from their own Tibetan ancestors. Their social prestige derived also from a relatively pure form of caste-free Hinayana Buddhism which prevailed among Burman peoples for centuries. Burmese women could even divorce their husbands, and no odium was attached to re-marriage of the divorcée. They had had the voting privilege in village councils from ancient times. Under Buddhist law they had equal rights in nearly everything, including inheritance. They shared in all the tasks of labor. They were as literate and cultured as their men and they ran as many shops and businesses.

Batalá took me to a *pwé,* a riotous festival of dancing and acrobatics, and afterward I met her mother. She was half-Chinese, a semi-invalid who smoked long cheroots. Batalá had two younger brothers whom she was seeing through school. They were all originally from a village near Mandalay where they had once owned a farm. But Batalá's father had lost it, some years before, in a week-long gambling spree. After that he disappeared, as Burmese husbands had a way of doing. An uncle had helped Batalá through school, English, and nursing. And now at twenty-two she was a philosopher, a Buddhist philosopher.

"My father's weakness was gambling, but he was a good man," she said. "He was pure in his heart. All humans have some weakness, but weakness is not evil unless it hurts other living creatures. My father hurt us somewhat, but he will suffer more when he is reborn. That is a pity. We all travel in the same boat and some must go over the same journey many times. But some overcome weakness and need not be reborn again. The important thing is not to injure people but to help them. That is why I like nursing."

She seemed to have no envy in her and coveted nothing. She said something I could not forget. "The jade and the rubies of life are your strong body and strong mind, not in the goods of the market. Many are born with goods that can be taken away but have not those riches that can be kept, and they are the poor."

Batalá enchanted me. I had been a lonely stranger and she comforted me. I had been sick and weary and she made me whole again. In a fine clear voice she sang plaintive folksongs to me as a yellow moon rose over the Himalayas. One afternoon we sat in the shade of some bamboos on the ferny banks of the Irrawaddy. She translated some ancient Burmese poetry, full of quaint images of dragons, thunder and nature gods. I read some sonnets to her from Richard Le Galliene's anthology that I had carried across Yunnan with me and she was moved by their beauty.

"I like 'thee' and 'thou,' " she suddenly said. "Now I shall call you 'thee.' " When she did so it was like a blessing.

But the day came when I had to leave Bhamo for Rangoon. Yes, we promised to write to each other.

CHAPTER 17

Theebaw's Realm

BELOW BHAMO we dropped through the "defiles" of the Irrawaddy down to Mandalay, with many stops at the market towns where the arrival of the SS *Taping* was the event of the week. The colorful docks were filled with happy, laughter-loving people dressed in their best silks for boat day. Along the jungled banks were frequent clusters of well-kept white pagodas banded in gold, with glittering jeweled spires reaching into the warm, friendly sky that brought abundant rainfall in its season to a land rich with many things. We passed huge rafts of teak logs floating on their two-months' trip to Rangoon. Each had its little rush hut from which spilled the raftsman's sun-clad children, to shout and wave to us, and to rock gleefully in our wake.

A fellow passenger was Douglas Parmentier, an ex-editor of *Harper's,* who had wearied of worldly success and had come out to seek wisdom in the East. His hunch was that he would find it somewhere in the Buddhist countries. Oddly enough an American missionary on board was half converted himself.

"Three years ago I arrived to preach the word of God to these people," he said. "But first I had to study their language and their own religion, to find the flaws in their teaching. Well, I have studied it and now I am about convinced that Gautama Buddha and Christ had the same message, different tongues of the same basic faith. I am going home and I think I shall not return. Not as a missionary, anyway."

But not everybody on board was satisfied to meditate on God, the tranquil beauty of the river and the green mystery of its fecund shores. An Indian passenger who was agent for the Singer Sewing Machine Company stayed in his cabin during most of the journey and marred the air with noises emanating from his portable phonograph bought on a recent visit to America. His collection of records was extremely limited and it was *The Maine Stein Song* that thumped most of the time.

"I wish for a change," I said one day as every loyal Maine man sang for the hundredth time, "that he'd play his Singer Sewing Machine."

Meanwhile, Burma unfolded around us, serene and rich, as we lowered through immense stands of fine timber down into the fertile rice fields that were one of Asia's great granaries. Generously endowed by nature, with enough land to feed twice its population, Burma lay before us, a prosperous realm where the British raj seemed to have made a genuine contribution, with a higher conception of law, to replace Queen Supiyalat's mad misgovernment with peace and unity that had lasted fifty years. The Burmese liked the British as individuals, especially the Scots, and British civil servants got along with them better than with the Indians; and yet it was the rigid British "law and order" which was to bring about the downfall of the power that implanted it.

At Rangoon I found the same discontent with alien rule and among youths the same rebellious spirit and yearning for national freedom that were rapidly infecting every Eastern colony. Burmese intellectuals openly clamored for self-government, for separation from India, and for recovery of their national resources. They had begun to plot for complete independence. At Rangoon University students such as U Nu, later to be independent Burma's first prime minister, were organizing the Thakin party. The name itself was subversively nationalistic because *thakin* (sir) had been a respectful term reserved for Europeans, and now in derision every Burman could call himself and his friends *thakin*.

U Nu, Aung San, U Kyaw Nein and others were soon to form the nucleus of a Socialist movement which began with discussions in an English bookshop owned by the beloved J. S. Furnivall, friend of Burmans and Burmese freedom. Years later, when Furnivall had become my friend and the young republic's first foreign adviser, he would tell me how he had helped those rebellious students to organize a book club which affiliated itself with the then influential Left Book Club of England, run by Victor Gollancz, Harold Laski and John Strachey. Without that influence the Burmese revolution might have followed the course of the Chinese Communist revolution rather than the road of Fabian gradualism it was eventually to choose.

But during my first visit I could not know that, nor faintly have imagined that my own books would in a few years be hotly debated in that yet unborn Rangoon book club. Nor could the British then believe that those young students could ever threaten their dividends. How secure British ownership of the country's tin, timber, oil, transportation and other monopolies still seemed! Nowhere else could one see returns pile up at a rate which not uncommonly paid back investors (as in Arabia today) more than two hundred percent in a single year. But it was not such industrial enterprises, which (again, as in Arabia) often represented distinct gains for Burmese labor despite their exorbitant profits, that foredoomed the British raj. It was their *laws* which ruined the agrarian stability of the country.

Britain's grave mistake was to permit a horde of usurers (chiefly Indian immigrants) to get control of the best rice-growing lands and create a large new class of Burmese tenant farmers. In pre-British times all land was under nominal ownership of the throne, but in practice was collectively held by each village. The tiller was thus secure in his home and the product of his labor; no outsider could buy or sell him out. Subdivision and individual ownership were first established under British law. Easygoing Burmese farmers suddenly found themselves with the illusion of new wealth and soon yielded *en masse* to the temptation to mortgage their land to buy imported luxuries or gamble and win face with expensive feasts. Great numbers lost their farms to money-lenders who descended by thousands and made quick fortunes. By the Thirties, Indian landlords already owned well over half the best paddy land in Lower Burma and the native farmers found themselves working for foreigners on soil immemorially their own.

It was from this newly created landless mass of peasants that Saya San drew his fanatical followers to stage Burma's first agrarian revolt in 1930, which shocked the complacent British more with its ferocity than its omens. When it came to rebellion the Burmese did not, as did the Indians, believe in non-violence. As I was there when the uprising began I stayed on for a month, to write the only detailed reports of it published in America. Even the British press did not cover it. A London *Times* correspondent in Rangoon told me with disgust that when he attempted to report it his editors wired him curtly, "Not interested in sideshows." Gandhi, in India, was enough. But that rebellion and its meaning early convinced me that expropriation and a return to nationalization were bound to come, and that Saya San, who was eventually killed, was part of a pattern rapidly spreading all over an Asia on the edge of social revolution.

In the face of these sanguinary events I found the stuffiness of the

British at my hotel irritating. I liked the British and made friends among the hard-working civil service men in the hills, but the Rangoon get-rich-quick English business men were too like their Shanghai counterparts. It seemed to me indecent for the management to insist upon guests dressing for its insipid dinners, but the others welcomed it. "It doesn't do to let down, old chap," they would say when I turned up in mufti. "Dressing holds up white prestige, you know."

Inevitably I did succumb to form, simply because I couldn't let any middle-class English snob think an American couldn't afford to buy silk lapels. But at the table I often found myself longing for the clean air of Yunnan's mountains and the campfires left behind me.

It was in part a relief, therefore, when that excruciating pain returned in my knee. I had an excuse to have the bearer serve meals in my room. An X-ray showed that there was no broken bone, but a displaced internal ligament was causing severe inflammation. Again I had to stay off my feet for more than a week, and again I had malaria. One evening I lay in a world of pain and delirium while the fever rode little horses beating tracks in the blood and images of white and gold and red traced through my head. I slept and woke up soaking wet under the punka and there was the illusion of Batalá smiling. I opened my eyes, not dreaming. And now the rustle of silk and scent of jasmine were real.

"Your letter came," she said. "I knew you would be needing me again."

Rangoon became a different place. When I was better Batalá took me to her aunt's thatched cottage and served delicious curried food. At night we went to Burmese theatres and temples. By day she showed me where to find the finest silks, and we bought *longyis* and Burmese sandals. I saw how the ivory tusks of the elephants were exquisitely carved and where the purest jade and rubies were sold. It was the time of the water festival and a carnival spirit prevailed. We were continually being drenched by pitchers of water poured from balconies, a not unpleasant experience in the dry dusty season just before the monsoon strikes Rangoon.

One night when my knee was strong enough we climbed to the top of the Shwe Dagon pagoda. We watched pious pilgrims burn incense or put leaves of gold on the tall graceful shaft, its brilliant *hti* flashing with rubies, emeralds and diamonds under a soft southern sky. I did not see another European there. Burmese Buddhist law required that you show respect for the shrine by removing your footwear. But when

I was there the custom had been set for Europeans by Edward, then Prince of Wales, who had declined to comply, saying, "No Englishman removes his shoes for man or god."

But he would, in time, for trade. Fifteen years later a British prime minister, Clement Attlee, would docilely follow the rule.

Britishers I knew in Rangoon frowned in envious disapproval at Batalá and called me a freak but since I was an American it did not matter. White men might go abroad with native women in the villages and in early days British governors had been known to marry them; but now Rangoon was pukka, as pukka as India. To be seen in the company of a Burmese woman was to invite social quarantine: enough to send a young Englishman packing home, and to exclude an American from the Gymkhana Club. George Orwell, in his own day in Burma, called England "the most class conscious land under the sun," full of "snobbery and privilege, ruled largely by the old and the silly." A little harsh of England but true enough of Rangoon.

"We don't rule here by force but by prestige and we can rule only so long as the natives regard us as their betters."

My young Bloomsbury friend who said that was perhaps right. But what was British prestige to me compared to Batalá's gay company? As for "bloomin' idols made o' mud," they of course had nothing to do with it.

All the same I left Rangoon in accordance with the new schedule I had sent my editors. Batalá and I had shared an hour or two "saved from that eternal silence" and that was enough. Henry Adams, in a moment of nostalgia for the East brought on by a first reading of "Mandalay," confessed that he "knew the poetry before he knew the poem—like millions of other wanderers who had felt the world exactly as it is."

I had known the poem first but now I knew the poetry, and it was true, all true.

CHAPTER 18

First Look at India

I WAS IN INDIA more than four months on this initial visit, and considering the immensity and variety of that fabulous realm of realms I saw a great deal. I traveled from one extremity to the other, from steaming Calcutta to the rough Khyber pass, from cool Simla to busy Bombay, and from princely Rajputana to the very old temples of Madras and Madura, and then across the channel to Ceylon and back. I was to return for stays of greater or lesser duration, and yet remain a tourist, and not really a well-traveled tourist, at that. For no country is more varied, more complex, more heterogenous, more exclusive to the outsider, and more rewarding as a study in the history of human travail.

"He that traveleth into a strange country before he hath some entrance into the language," said Francis Bacon, "goeth to school and not to travel." The information sent abroad about India could be measured more in degrees of ignorance than of knowledge. Only the fact that the British had imposed English as the *lingua franca* among educated Indians—one of the benefits left as the legacy of British imperialism in that vast multi-lingual community—made it possible for the outsider to understand India at all.

I had the advantage, over the tourist freshly arrived from the West, of having lived in China. This provided at least "some entrance" into the emotional and intellectual or social-political life of India in terms of problems the two countries shared. Yet I soon saw that India and China were not just fellow Asians, together nearly half of mankind, but separate worlds, largely independent in their history and development. Although China had at times been immensely influenced by Indian religious thought and art (much more so than the reverse) their contacts had been established by a few travelers only; as nations they remained strangers.

The lordly Himalayas, the forbidding forests and jungles, the deserts of Turkestan, the dark torrential headwaters of great rivers that divide China and India, were as formidable a barrier to close contact as any ocean. In the rise of modern nationalism, India and China were contemporaries, but there was no real contact between them. I remember my dismay on first speaking with Mahatma Gandhi about China to discover that he knew little of recent events there and had only the most detached kind of interest. China faced East while India's gaze seemed fixed on the West. By mid-century the focus would veer somewhat, in proportion to the declining power of the West, the renewal of ancient drives that brought the two main cultural streams of Asia into a subtle struggle for dominance in Southeast Asia, and the rapid shrinkage of the atomic-age earth, making every land today its neighbor's keeper.

India was a religious country, living by religion and divided by it. China was not. China was united, except for its fringe peoples, by a single script and written language. India had eleven principal languages and used many scripts, not to mention 225 dialects. China's population is all Mongolian and shares a common anthropology. To the Hindu a Mongolian is an outsider. I recall my astonishment at a remark by Sarojini Naidu, for years a member of Gandhi's working committee, after seeing Mme. Chiang Kai-shek and failing to be impressed by her beauty. "Why, she looked like any little common Nepalese girl." And that, she seemed to say, settled it. The Nepalese, a fringe people of India, are Mongolians.

Although for the most part Caucasian and of the same racial type as Europeans, "Indians" are of much more mixed descent than Chinese. India was a land of perpetual contrast and often of conflict of cultures, dress and speech; in China the blue-clad Taoist-Confucianist peasant of the North had his brother in the blue-clad Taoist-Confucianist peasant of the South. And India, despite its highest snow peaks in the world, deserts without rainfall, and the wettest spots on earth, is mainly a "hot country" where a loincloth or a cotton sari suffices most of the time. China's almost uniformly temperate climate and distribution of rainfall, again, make for greater natural homogeneity.

What these two countries did have in common, and that which was to make them together the greatest challenge in history to the continued dominance of the West, was not Communism or any ideology or religion, but their huge, underfed, illiterate peasant majorities, their backward, greedy, landlord-owner classes, their intellectuals' wounded pride as heirs of ancient civilizations branded inferior because they had fallen a century behind in scientific techniques and the modernization of agrarian and industrial economies, their joint search for short cuts to close this alarming gap, and a determination amounting to national paranoia to toss European imperialism out of their houses forever.

India helped me to understand China, and to complete for me the whole panorama of insurgent Asia. At first the process was more assimilative than the result of methodical study. Judging from my diary notes my reading at the time was haphazard if not chaotic. It included translations of the *Bhagavad Gita* and the *Upanishads,* Abbé Du Bois' classic on Hindu behavior patterns, a history of Benares, Gandhi's *My Experiments with Truth,* Andrews' *Mahatma Gandhi,* and another "life" by Romain Rolland, an assortment of socio-political books by foreigners embracing such diverse views as Katherine Mayo and Fenner Brockway, Nehru's speeches in pamphlet form, and an inscribed book of Sarojini Naidu's poems.

I note that I also read, while in India or shortly after leaving, *The Essentials of Marx,* Lenin's *The Proletarian Revolution,* Engels on the Family—and the *Ananga Ranga* and the *Kama Sudra Vatsyayana!* My interest in man as a political animal evidently did not exclude my curiosity about his twin brother, the angel of sex, "chaos of thought and passion, all confused." I was very far from accepting the abstinence of *brahmacharya* when I first listened to Mr. Gandhi. The Greek ideal of moderation in all things, and the Chinese "golden mean," seemed to me more attainable adult social aims than complete renunciation. They still seem so. But for Gandhi *brahmacharya* was part of a dedication quite beyond ordinary mortal aspirations. I need not have troubled myself as much as I did to try to reconcile Gandhi's sex views with his politics. He was, as Nehru said, "India's greatest paradox."

As an American I readily found friends among young Indians. Fortunately, we had not yet replaced Britain as the chief rich-man sinner in the eyes of the "oppressed peoples" and Americans were still held in good-natured esteem. Our promises of freedom to the Filipinos had impressed many Indian intellectuals in contrast to the adamant imperialism of Europe. Asians thought of us as young and somewhat crude, but we had once fought for independence from Britain. That made us spiritual allies.

Soon after I arrived I went to see Rabindranath Tagore. At his home, "Santiniketan," I met a gifted young Indian poet named Sundaram, who became my first guide through the maze of Indian politics. He was secretary to Pandit Modan Malaviya, president of Benares Hindu University, and head of the controversial but powerful Hindu Mahasabha. Malaviya, always ready to answer any question, and always hospitable, enchanted me with his learning and generosity. He was clearly not only the intellectual superior of most of the rulers of the country but one of the handsomest of men. Sundaram himself proffered a warmth of friendship that almost overwhelmed me until I realized that a certain extravagance of language was quite common among sensitive Indian youths in a sympathetic relationship. What may have been a little extraordinary was that Sundaram was a brahman: so much so that when he invited me to stay in his home I was served alone at meals and apart from him and his wife. I never did meet her. He kept his religious orthodoxy completely partitioned from the cosmic spirit of his love for mankind.

Few brahmans would be that strict today, of course. But Indian women were only beginning to emerge in public, led by Nehru's lovely wife and sisters, by Mrs. Gandhi, by Sarojini Naidu and others. I remember my amazement, upon going to a mass meeting of nationalists for the first time, to see that an immense wall of black cotton cloth was used to segregate the women and girls in the audience, including Moslems still in purdah, from the evil eyes of men.

While I was in Benares, Pandit Malaviya invited me to travel to Simla with him and Sundaram to be present while Gandhi negotiated with Lord Irwin in the hope of reaching an agreement that would end the great civil disobedience campaign of 1930. I was delighted to go but I soon discovered that it was considered practically subversive for "Europeans" to travel with Indians as equals. Jim Crow was not the law, but in practice "Europeans" demanded separate accommodations. Conductors would not put an Indian with a European even if there were no seats in other compartments. Besides that, Malaviya was classed as a "reb," despite his conservatism; he did, of course, support Gandhi. By the time we reached Simla I was already an object for special observation on the part of the C.I.D., or Criminal Investigation Department, which handled political cases.

At Malaviya's headquarters in the summer capital I met many Indian nationalist leaders and their supporters. Youth League members spoke rapturously of Gandhi and what they would do with freedom. I took long walks with them over the hills where monkeys scampered in the cedars. Above us the frosty peaks of the Himalayas stood godlike and in the distance the bells of Tibetan caravans tinkled as they descended from the pale, windy passes.

"Our country is the most beautiful on earth," Sundaram exclaimed, "but we can never make a race of men fit to live in it as long as we are slaves. The British must go!"

When we returned to town I would think how much better the brave, new world would be than Simla's caste-bound society, English as well as Hindu, for at its top sat the white suprabrahmans, the sahibs and memsahibs in the Viceregal circle. In truth the economic facts of the empire were simple. A few thousand British coupon clippers were drawing enormous dividends from a small original investment and a few thousand others lived in easy luxury as business men and administrators. You had only to see their pomp and circumstance, together with their corrupt and wasteful native princes, in contrast to the naked misery of the vast majority of the population who never got enough to eat, to realize that the anachronism could not stand much longer.

Yet would "independence" bring any real improvement in the lot of the wretched humanity held underfoot? The Indians themselves, the Moslems and the Hindus, the bourgeoisie and the intellectuals, disagreed about that. Communism was not the problem but an "extra syllable" had to be added, as Nehru said—"communalism." Religious differences provided the poison ground in which British power held on by the ancient techniques of divide and rule. Against them Gandhi had nothing but "truth," "love," and the adoration of the unarmed Hindu masses to whom he denied the weapon of violence.

I had to meet and talk to him.

CHAPTER 19

Gandhi and Nehru

PANDIT MALAVIYA introduced me to the Mahatma. He was having important meetings with the Viceroy, Lord Irwin, who was later Lord Halifax. As Gandhi was much too busy to suffer the presence of young greenhorns I had no formal interviews with him at that time. Instead, I had to be content to trot along on his visits to his associates or to the Viceregal Lodge.

Gandhi was already over sixty but on principle he refused to ride in a ricksha. He walked everywhere, taking the steep hills of Simla with strong, agile strides that had carried him across India to the sea, where in symbolic defiance he had led the peasants to appropriate the waters and take from them the Lord's salt over which the British *raj* claimed sole proprietorship. That ingenious tactic had shaken the whole nation and mobilized it as never before in a civil disobedience movement with no less than *swaraj,* independence, as its goal. Gandhi was imprisoned along with tens of thousands of his followers. And now he and Nehru, together with Malaviya and a few others, had been released in order to discuss terms of a "settlement."

I did not get much out of our fragmentary talks, held on the fly, to enable me to grasp the essence of Gandhi's method, his "strange mixture" of religion and politics. That was to come much later. The fact that he derived his political inspiration and his personal authority over the masses from his conception of the Vedantic *ahimsa,* or the identity of love and non-violence as aspects of the ultimate truth, was quite beyond my understanding and my semantics. It did not seem to me really pertinent to the hard facts of the Indian revolution. I did not see how he could "get anywhere" by negotiating what looked to me like surrender on the edge of success.

"La politique," said Talleyrand, *"c'est l'art du possible"* and Gandhi was unnecessarily confusing it with religion, the art of the impossible. What I did not understand was that the one aphorism applies to the politics of the *status quo* but that revolutionary politics indeed demanded an artist of the impossible. Gandhi's attempt to combine the two, in his honest search for truth, was the nexus of his genius.

When I asked Gandhi a question which revealed my doubts along these lines he gently advised me to "study some more." Jawaharlal Nehru himself felt some of the same skepticism about Gandhi's decision, at this time, to drop the demand for independence and call off civil disobedience in exchange for British promises to discuss limited constitutional government.

"Was it for this," Nehru remembers, in his autobiography, that he asked himself, "that our people had behaved so gallantly for a year? Were all our brave words and deeds to end in this? The independence resolution of the Congress, the pledge so often repeated? In my heart there was a great emptiness . . ."

But in the end, "not without great mental conflict and physical distress," Nehru bowed to that strange power, "that something unknown about Gandhi," as he was so often to do in the future. "While we might be more logical, Gandhiji knew India far better than we did, and a man who could command such tremendous devotion and loyalty must have something in him that corresponded to the needs and aspirations of the masses." Somehow Gandhi knew, by his mysterious political intuition, that India was not yet ready for *swaraj.* He still had some teaching to do, of both the British and the Indians.

To me, however, Nehru seemed the more realistic leader, the "practical" politician. I liked his dynamic approach, his directness, his haste to get on with independence in order to tackle the real problems of his agonizingly backward land. I heartily agreed when he said he "could not accept, as Gandhi seemed to do, the present social order, which was based on violence and conflict." That basic "paradox" in the Mahatma was to puzzle him to the end and leave its permanent impression on the Indian revolution.

Nehru's desire for speedy Socialist solutions to all of India's problems, and his sharp rejection of Gandhi's idealization of poverty and fetishes like cow worship and the preservation of the temple and its institutions, fitted in with my own growing awareness of the inevitability of quick and fundamental change.

"I would totally abolish the caste system, remove the feudal princes, curtail or end landlordism, and industrialize and rebuild India's economy from the ground up," Nehru told me in our first interview at Bombay. "As for Hinduism, its evils far outweigh its good points. I want nothing to do with any religion concerned with keeping the masses satisfied to live in hunger, filth and ignorance. I want nothing to do with any order, religious or otherwise, which does not teach people that they are capable of becoming happier and more civilized, on this earth, capable of becoming true *man*, master of his fate and captain of his soul. To attain this I would put priests to work, also, and turn the temples into schools. The sooner people are given education and knowledge in place of superstition and meaningless consolations from the *Gita* the better off they will be."

Real events and deep human and historical forces were to make Gandhi and Nehru—two very contradictory personalities—more and more indispensable to each other. And I was to learn that Nehru's words, like Gandhi's, meant both more and less than they said to me. From this time on, at any rate, the knowledge and passion of Nehru's opinions influenced my own thinking.

The sum total of what I heard and saw in Simla and Delhi convinced me of the justice of the Indian cause, and I became its partisan. The British had done their job, which would in due course be acknowledged as not without its hour of greatness in history, but now any sane observer could see that their duty was to bow out. The idea that a vast, rich subcontinent, an ancient civilization embracing more people than lived in Europe, could be held down much longer by a handful of white men who had happened to get an early monopoly on new weapons and inventions, was as preposterous as it is today to suppose that any power can permanently hold dominion over an unwilling neighbor nation.

I kept these opinions largely to myself and to Jim Mills and Bill Shirer, the only other American correspondents around. I thought they were of no concern or consequence to anyone else. I was soon to learn differently.

CHAPTER 20

Adventures in Bombay

I FOLLOWED GANDHI to Bombay by second-class coach. When an Indian opened the door and diffidently asked to share the compartment I invited him in. He seemed an amiable soul and we were soon on a free-and-easy basis of conversation. He was the only Indian I had met who would stay off the "Indian question" long enough to allow me to boast about my trip from Yunnan to Burma. He even looked at my pictures of the tribesmen. When he got up to leave the train at Agra I was disappointed.

"I thought you were going to Bombay," I said.

"So I was, but I've changed my plans. To tell you the truth, I was supposed to put you under arrest if you were the man we were looking for."

"Arrest *me?*"

"Yes," he said, showing me his credentials. "I'm with the C.I.D. But I'm sure there's a mistake. You're not the man."

"How do you know I'm not?"

"The man we want is an ex-convict and an opium smuggler. You're too young." He grinned. "Too young and too talkative. *Salaam, sahib.*" The train was leaving. He shook hands and jumped off.

Probably what he meant was that no criminal could be so naive. But thinking it over I had to admit that I had a few things to explain. I had never gone through Indian immigration; there had simply been none on the Yunnan frontier. Burma was then an administrative part of India and once I was inside no one had asked to see my passport. My visa had no entry stamp on it. As for opium? Perhaps that was a little additional information invented by that old White Russian informer in Shanghai.

In Bombay I saw Sarojini Naidu again, and almost daily, as we were both staying in the Taj Mahal Hotel. She was shrewd and witty and even then was Gal Friday to Gandhi, to whom she irreverently referred as "Mickey Mouse." She liked to call herself "India's greatest public woman" as she had once been unhappily introduced by an over-zealous speaker at a Congress rally. Sarojini was one of the remarkable Chattopadyaya family, which included her brother Harindranath, a poet like herself, a sister who ran the first modern (Montessori system) girls' school in India, and Dr. Chatty Chattopadyaya, the distinguished scientist who had been Agnes Smedley's husband in Germany. Both her father and grandfather had been official alchemists at the court of Hyderabad. She told me that the old Nizam, then reputed to be the richest individual in the world, was still absorbed in a search for the secrets of synthetic gold.

Sarojini brought me into the company of such Bombay nationalists as were out of jail. With some difficulty she also located for me her "underground" younger sister, Suhasini, who was, according to Sarojini, "even more of an alchemist than her grandfather."

Suhasini was the first Communist I met in India. She was, as far as I am aware, the first I met in Asia. A young person of amazing vitality, intellect and ability, Suhasini was a one-woman revolutionary movement in herself. Although she later left the party, she had at this time completely turned her back on bourgeois life, rejected all Gandhi's teachings as pious hypocrisy, considered her sister a lost cause, and predicted speedy victory for the forces of light. When I failed to thaw sufficiently under the persuasion of her burning convictions she called me "Mr. Iceberg" and said she would soon melt me. She took me to districts of the mill workers and there I saw what she meant.

Bombay's thousands of workers lived in tiny, airless cells with open latrines running through the dark corridors and naked children playing in them. They were miserably paid, underfed, illiterate, full of tuberculosis and other diseases, and exploited in the true classical manner of early machine "civilization" on which Marx based his observations in *Kapital*. Conditions were as bad in the Indian as in British barracks, and whether the inmates worked for Indian or British factories made little difference. Only a few highly skilled workers could afford even one room per family. Single workers lived in rooms of tiered bunks and for solace patronized the Indian girl slaves who sat beckoning behind barred cages in the sunless alleys of commercial sin.

My other guide for a time was "Adi" Adhikari, who was secretary of a Young Communist Workers League and became an important figure in the party, which he would also later leave. He always carried a worn matchbox marked "Made in the U.S.S.R." from which the original contents had probably long since been passed out, like Buddha's teeth, to devoted comrades. The lettering was almost illegible from many handlings, but the box was a sacred relic. It helped convince the Indian poor, "Adi" said, that the story he told about a land where workers owned and managed their own factories was not just a myth but the literal truth. I wondered how Adhikari could be so sure about that, even though he could read, for he had never seen Russia himself. I had yet to comprehend that Russia was an act of faith; one had to believe, and wishing made it so. For the Chinese more of a system of ethics and a philosophy, Marxism was for the Indians a religion. For the young brahmans, who were to become its priests and potential bureaucrats, the more belief rested on dogma the better they liked it. One who had not seen an Indian Communist had not seen "historical necessity" dance on the head of a needle.

And yet those Indian Communists, too, would learn "the art of the possible" from experience. Suhasini and Adhikari did make me realize that there were two revolutions, not one, struggling for birth and power over men, in India as in China.

No doubt the C.I.D. had been watching me on these excursions but I was somewhat stunned to learn about it. One evening I was sitting at the bar of the Taj Mahal with Sir Percy Phillips when a young English army officer, Jimmy Parker, rushed up and drew me aside for a word in private. It so happened that Jimmy was a friend of my brother, whom he had met in New York. Because of that he had looked me up when he read in the newspaper that I was in Bombay. He had taken me to "the club" a few times and he was a nice chap, totally uninterested in politics but a tidy gentleman with the ladies.

"Guess what, old boy, they've got you down as a dangerous Red!" he whispered, very agitated.

"How's that again?"

"The chief of police is a friend of mine. He saw me with you the other day and called me in today to warn me about it. Said I would be up for questioning if it continued. It seems they've been baiting you for weeks and now think they're about to catch a big fish. Tell me you're an ex-convict and an opium smuggler, travel under an assumed name, have two false passports, entered the country illegally, and an agent of the Comintern! By God!"

"But Jimmy, you know that's rubbish!"

"Of course *I* do. That's what I told the chief. I told them I know your brother very well, you look like twins. Their story's fantastic.

By Jove, he thinks I'm a fool. Don't know how clever you are by half! Tells me that at the very least you'll be deported. I say, it's a bit thick."

I told Jimmy the story of the faked dossier in Shanghai, and of my entry into Burma. "But they must know I've been filing stories to the Consolidated Press under my own name, and have credentials from their own press bureau."

"They believe nothing but their bloody dossiers. Now you go down there and see the chief before this goes any further. He tells me they've actually got out an order for your arrest. It might even get *me* into trouble!"

I refused to go to the police. Why should I? But to placate Jimmy I agreed to tell our consul-general the whole story the next day. I did so.

"You may have saved us a lot of embarrassment," said that gentleman stiffly. "After all, as you say, you have some things to explain. But let me take care of it from here on." I heard no more about it, but I'll bet that highly imaginative dossier is still gathering dust in the files of every British colony left in the world—and perhaps even with the F.B.I.

Just before a cable came from my editor, ordering me to return to Shanghai, an unprecedented thing happened. With Gandhi in Bombay, a "radical" group calling themselves "Young Europeans" invited him to appear before them at the Taj and explain what position he intended to adopt at the coming Round Table Conference. In Sarojini's tow, Gandhi arrived, wearing his usual diaper. He sat down on a table, cool and relaxed, and proceeded to tell the Young Europeans, formal in dinner jackets and starched shirts, that complete and utter independence, and "Socialism," was his fixed goal. Most of them were shocked. Until then they had not taken "these Reds" seriously.

Among the British correspondents who boycotted that meeting with a "traitor" was the former American, Sir Percival Phillips, correspondent for the London *Daily Mail*. "I've got a job of work to do here," he kept telling me. "The *Mail* is for the protection of British interests, first, last and always. We can't do business with this blackguard Gandhi."

Nevertheless, Phillips' pride as a journalist got the better of his dignity as a knight of the realm. "I couldn't resist having a look at the little leper," he admitted "I stood on a chair outside the door and heard every word through the transom." That was as near as most of us would ever get to listening to Gandhi while he was alive.

My first trip across Southeast Asia had taken more than a year. All my experiences were going to shape my life and work beyond any

capacity of mine as yet to appreciate. I was losing my good prime
ignorance and beginning to know a little something about "not-knowing." That was all right as long as I could keep the discovery hidden
from my editors.

I now returned to China by the conventional sea route around
Singapore on the N.Y.K. liner *Chichibu Maru*.

CHAPTER 21

"Exquisite Fragment"

BACK IN CHINA I was no longer a tourist. Tom Millard was right:
China was going to be the "great story" of my generation. I wished to
see it happen and to know a little about it in advance of its happening,
if possible. The Manchurian "crisis" and the subsequent Japanese conquest were my immediate assignments on my return, but the physical
activities involved in reporting those "first shots of World War II"
were to give me less prescience of coming events than personal encounters of the same period. Foremost among these was a friendship
with Mme. Sun Yat-sen.

I had already met the Generalissimo and Mme. Chiang at press conferences when I sought out Soong Ching-ling. Mrs. William Brown
Meloney, editor of the *Herald Tribune* magazine, wanted me to do a
profile of her. I knew that she had been Dr. Sun's "child wife" but I
was not prepared for her youthfulness and beauty. She was in her mid-
thirties but she looked ten years younger: still the pale, slender "exquisite fragment of humanity" Jimmy Sheean had described a few
years earlier. Like Sheean, I found "the contrast between her appearance and her destiny" startling. Mme. Sun was the conscience and the
constant heart of a "still unfinished revolution."

There was nothing formidable about her. She was a modest and
naturally self-effacing person. It required great moral and physical
courage for her to resist the pressures put upon her to compromise
with her own conception of the role assigned to her by history. She
was not grandiose; she was simplicity itself with genuine people, but
she kept a scalpel sharp for hypocrites. People who did not know what

a superb actress she was often missed the subtlety and suppleness of her mind and mistook her talent at dissimulation for naiveté. She spoke fluent English and some French and German learned at Wesleyan College in Georgia and she belonged to that select company Marty Sommers chose to call "true lady."

Ching-ling was not easy to meet. It was not convenient for her to see many strangers; for one thing, her home was constantly guarded and watched by Kuomintang plain-clothesmen and French police. Ostensibly that was for her protection. Was she not the saint's widow and continuing spokesman, as well as the sister-in-law of Elder-Born Chiang himself? Her seclusiveness was also a protection against all kinds of people with doubtful claims on her time. For that reason when she first agreed to meet me she chose as a rendezvous (of all spots!) the Chocolate Shop on Bubbling Well Road in the International Settlement. We had lunch and stayed on for tea. By dinner time I thought I had begun to understand her. A few days later I first visited her modest two-storey foreign house on Rue Molière in the French Concession. It was, with its excellent English and Chinese library, about all the property Dr. Sun Yat-sen had left to her. Many millions had passed through his hands in the cause of revolution, but he had died a poor man.

The China Ching-ling believed in was also a poor man's China, a China where the lowliest coolie would walk like a man, and yet a China of the world, not the shut-in China of the Great Wall outside, each home a wall against its neighbor, and every man for himself and the devil take the hindmost. And it wasn't foreign rights but the interests of what we used to call the four hundred millions (the Communists were to discover six hundred millions) which concerned her. That seemed to me also the legitimate first consideration among all people for whom China was home.

It used to be fashionable in limited but influential American quarters to believe that no matter how long you lived abroad you should never learn that American interests, "hard interests," in banal journalese, were not paramount everywhere to the interests of the local people, who presumably had only "soft interests." In working overseas you were bound to notice that fifteen of every sixteen people on earth were not Americans. Those fifteen were likely to behave as if their interests were more important than any of ours which conflicted with them. And this in turn taught you that nothing could ever happen in the way that 100 percent Americans, or 100 percent Chinese or

Russians or Frenchmen, thought it ought to happen. Instead, it would always happen in the way history chose to synthesize these rivalries in its own elusive design.

The attempt to discover what the "soft interests" of other people really are, how they feel and think about their own problems and their place in the world, seemed to me mandatory if we were to have any notion of the direction history was taking toward that compromise which we call world society, not to say peace.

Soong Ching-ling taught me a little about not-knowing. Through her I met the thought and sentiment of China at its best. Over the years she would introduce me to young writers and artists and fighters who were to make history. I would later work with her to organize co-operatives among thousands of refugees, to provide homes for orphans of war and famine, to equip hospitals and to help young people learn to serve their old land in new and useful ways. Ching-ling contributed to my education about the Kuomintang, about Sun Yat-sen and his unwritten hopes, about her own family, the Soongs, and why she refused to share their role in Chiang's rule, and many other facts I could never have learned from books.

Knowing Ching-ling early made me comprehend that the Chinese people were capable of radically changing their country and quickly lifting it from bottom place to the rank its history and multitudes merited in the world. For years she could not express her opinions openly nor permit me to quote them abroad. We planned to collaborate on her biography and I made notes for private reference. Once she had given me her confidence I had no doubt where she stood and why.

Now that her position is clear a few things can be said without abusing her trust.

CHAPTER 22

Christian and Communist

WHAT IS A CHRISTIAN? Opinions differ, especially in China, as we have noticed in the case of the Taipings. Tom Millard used to say, in paraphrase of Carlyle, that if Jesus Christ came to Shanghai he wouldn't be crucified and he wouldn't be asked to dinner; people would simply stand him a drink, listen to his story, and then turn him in to the Settlement police. But when I wrote to that effect for Mr. Mencken's old *American Mercury* the town elders sent letters to the press to insist that Christianity had made Shanghai what it was. Personally, I would never have gone that far.

"You are China's Mrs. George Washington," I said to Ching-ling one day, "but the question people ask is whether you are also a Christian."

"I am Christian by birth and baptism—and a Wesleyan Methodist to boot! I don't go to church and the missionaries don't think I am a Christian, I'm told. But they say the Generalissimo is." She always put a slight satirical emphasis on the word: Gen-eral-*issi*mo.

"And you do not?"

"I hear he reads his Bible every day. Doesn't that prove it?"

"I understand your mother made him promise to study the Bible before she consented to the marriage?"

"That's true," said Ching-ling. "He would have agreed to be a Holy Roller to marry Mei-ling. He needed her to build a dynasty."

Ching-ling knew about Holy Rollers from her Georgia days and she knew Chiang from having worked with him. Chiang had first proposed to her, after Dr. Sun's death in 1925, through a Chinese middleman. She thought it was politics, not love, and declined. Three years later Chiang took her younger sister Mei-ling into wedlock and her suspicions were confirmed. Chiang had a wife and a legal concubine before he married Mei-ling. Ching-ling did not blame Chiang for that. She had herself married a divorced man and the father of a son about her own age. What she never forgave was Chiang's "betrayal of the revolution" in 1927 and her sister's "betrayal" in lending the Soong name to it.

"He has set China back years," she said, "and made the revolution much more costly and terrible than it need have been. In the end he will be defeated just the same."

Ching-ling was in exile in Russia at the time of the wedding. When she returned to China two years later she did not congratulate the bridegroom or bride. Chiang had by then killed so many youthful revolutionaries whom Ching-ling believed closest to her late husband's ideals that she considered him a murderer. Mei-ling's action was also a personal slap in the face. When I first met Ching-ling she said the marriage was opportunism on both sides, with no love involved. And yet some others saw a similarity of pattern in the sisters' marriages. Could it not have been that Mei-ling, a sincere conservative, was quite as convinced that she was marrying China's saviour as Ching-ling, a sincere radical, was convinced of the same when she married Dr. Sun? Sibling rivalry between the two "first ladies" of China was always very strong. Today, as Mme. Sun sits as vice-chairman of a government in Peking which still honors Dr. Sun as "founder of the republic," her sister is an exile in Formosa and their roles seem dramatically reversed.

For years after Mme. Sun's return to China the sisters rarely met. It was not until the Sino-Japanese war that they had a partial reconciliation, and Mme. Sun somewhat changed her mind about Mei-ling's marriage.

"It wasn't love in the beginning," Ching-ling said to me in Hongkong one day in 1940, "but I think it is now. Mei-ling is sincerely in love with Chiang and he with her. Without Mei-ling he might have been much worse." She still had no use for the Generalissimo and continued to regard him as a national tragedy.

Before that, during the Thirties when Mme. Sun lived in Shanghai, she supported whatever opposition existed to Chiang's dictatorship. This once included her stepson, Sun Fo, who openly denounced Chiang as a "usurper" who had "ruined the party." He said that under Chiang "every local government, every provincial and municipal government is rotten to the core." Sun Fo accused Chiang of "betraying all the party's principles" and ridiculed claims that he was Dr. Sun's "chosen heir," adding that his father "never trusted him." But Sun Fo patched things up and took office under Chiang again and Ching-ling broke with her stepson also.

I do not know whether Mme. Sun was then a member of the Communist party. Perhaps she worked under the discipline of the party but remained outside it because as Dr. Sun's widow she had a first duty to him. By retaining her membership in the central executive committee of the Kuomintang she felt she personified that fraternal collaboration between the two parties which Dr. Sun had decisively affirmed in the last years of his life. That may have been what she wished to express when I asked her what achievement of her own meant most to her. "The fact that I was loyal to Dr. Sun from the day I met him until his death," she answered without hesitation. "I still am." I never heard her refer to her late husband as anything but Dr. Sun.

As long as there was a "Left Kuomintang" underground alive (it was Socialist, not Communist) Mme. Sun adhered to it, along with many of Dr. Sun's former comrades. After its leader, Teng Yen-ta, was caught and executed by Chiang early in the Thirties, it virtually disappeared. Dr. Sun had considered Teng one of his favorite young disciples, and Mme. Sun was deeply grieved by Teng's death.

Not long afterward another warm friend of hers, Dr. Yang Ch'uan, was assassinated by Kuomintang gunmen on the streets of Shanghai. A Western-educated scientist, Yang was secretary of the Academia Sinica, whose members included Dr. Hu Shih, Dr. Lin Yu-tang and other outstanding scholars, writers and scientists. Yang, Hu and Lin had all been members of a civil rights league in Shanghai headed by the Kuomintang veteran, Tsai Yuan-pei, and chaired by Mme. Sun. Its purpose was to get fair trials for some of the "50,000 political prisoners" then alleged to be held in various cities. Lin Yu-tang discovered that Tu Yueh-sheng's gangsters had shot Yang Ch'uan on Chiang Kai-shek's orders and then he himself was threatened. Lin resigned, as did most of the others, and the league soon dissolved.

The time was not yet for civil rights in China.

Thereafter Ching-ling was almost alone in her protests against continued assassinations, arrests and executions. She embraced all revolutionaries as her own and through her personal intervention saved many lives. Among her failures the one that most saddened her was the immolation of six young Chinese writers in 1932. They were members of a league of left writers—historians, novelists, short-story-writers and poets led by Lu Hsun, China's greatest contemporary writer. One of those executed was the talented woman novelist, Feng Kung. Shanghai's foreign police had arrested twenty-four young men and women accused of membership in the organization and turned them over to the Kuomintang garrison at Lunghwa. Six of the best known were made to dig their own graves. Then they were bound, thrown into the pits, and buried alive, an old Chinese punishment for subversives.

These details were well authenticated and appeared in foreign papers although suppressed in Chinese. Nothing was done about it by us foreign Christians in Shanghai, however. Some of the victims were probably Communists, and weren't they—"red-bandits"—killing people in the interior? But I knew Lu Hsun and Yang Ch'uan very well; they were no more Communists than Lin Yu-tang. They were all merely Western-oriented liberal individualists—anachronisms in China then as today.

Not long after these killings I discussed them with Mme. Sun when I was compiling *Living China,* in which I included stories by some of the executed writers. "That," said Ching-ling bitterly, "is our Christian Generalissimo—burying our best young people alive. Evidently in his Bible studies he has not yet reached the Corinthians."

"You think he personally knew about it?" I asked.

"He is responsible for all the killings. He began it with the counter-revolution. That's why I'll never take a seat in any Kuomintang government as long as he is dictator. And that's why if he's a Christian I am not."

Whether he was or was not "responsible," there is of course no church canon that says a "counter-revolutionary" cannot be a Christian. Consider Franco, and hundreds before him. But as far as Chingling was concerned no "counter-revolutionary" would ever get through the pearly gates—not while Dr. Sun was guarding them.

"If Dr. Sun were alive today," she said, "he would disown and dissolve the Kuomintang rather than see it used to sanctify the murder of writers and patriots."

No, it was not for that, she said, that she had fled comfort and security years before, to join Sun Yat-sen in exile in Japan.

"How, exactly, did you happen to fall in love with Dr. Sun?" I asked her after some years of friendship.

"I didn't fall in love," she said slowly. "It was hero-worship from afar. It was a romantic girl's idea when I ran away to work for him— but a good one. I wanted to help save China and Dr. Sun was the one man who could do it, so I wanted to help him On my way home from Wesleyan College I went to see him, in exile in Tokyo, and volunteered my services. He soon sent me word in Shanghai that he needed me in Japan. My parents would never consent and tried to lock me up. I climbed out of the window and escaped with the help of my amah."

That was a daring thing for a young Chinese girl of good family to do then, a transgression not only against filial piety but against the basic code of family first, country last. Dr. Sun himself, realizing that an ambiguous relationship would be misconstrued, had made all preparations for a wedding.

"I had no knowledge that he had gone through a divorce proceeding and that he intended to marry me," she said, "until I arrived. When he explained his fear that I would otherwise be called his concubine and that the scandal would harm the revolution, I agreed. I never regretted it."

They were quietly married the day after her arrival. She was barely twenty, he about forty-eight, with ten years to live. The next day she became his private secretary, began to learn cryptography, and was soon doing all his secret coding and decoding.

Sun's rather vague divorce had been intended primarily to still opposition among the Soongs and other Christian families, but it did not have the desired effect. Ching-ling's father had for years supported Sun Yat-sen. Now he felt that his favorite daughter had been stolen by his best friend.

"My father came to Japan and bitterly attacked Dr. Sun," she said. "He tried to annul the marriage on grounds that I was under age and lacked my parents' consent. When he failed he broke all relations with Dr. Sun and disowned me!"

The Christian following in China was less than one percent of the populace, but it was important to Sun, who had been educated by British Christians and had a mind half Chinese and half Christian-Western. But Ching-ling was never warmly received as Mme. Sun in Christian circles. "They called me an adventuress," she said, scornfully. Whether she was snubbed by Dr. Sun's old missionary friends because of the Soong family attitude, or whether it was the spontaneous reaction of the puritanical missionary community at the time, the effect embittered Dr. Sun and probably made it easier for him later to accept atheistic Communists as comrades. When Mei-ling's marriage under similar circumstances was blessed in a Christian ceremony, and applauded by the missionaries who attended the lavish wedding reception, Mme. Sun was inclined to write off her erstwhile missionary friends as hypocrites. She thought their new attitude was due to Chiang's reactionary politics more than to their genuine conversion to liberal views on divorce.

CHAPTER 23

Ching-ling and History

THERE NEVER WAS a complete reconciliation between Dr. and Mme. Sun and the Soong family. After Sun's agreement with the Russians, in 1923, T. V. Soong went south to join forces with the reorganized rebel government, which then held only one Southern province, under the new Kuomintang-Communist coalition. For some time T. V. Soong, Ching-ling's younger brother, an economist recently graduated from Harvard, was the only Soong who saw her. After Chiang's break with the Communists T.V. wavered and then supported Chiang but he remained Ching-ling's one devoted friend in the family.

He managed a small pension fund for her and once in a while sided with her politically.

Chiang never could get Mme. Sun to accept office under his government, but he brought all the rest of the family into it, until it became known humorously as the "Soong Dynasty." He always kept the state treasury in the hands of his brothers-in-law, T. V. Soong and H. H. Kung. Dr. Kung, a former Y.M.C.A. secretary, had married Mme. Sun's elder sister, Ai-ling, the most church-going Christian in the family. The Soongs, Kungs and Chiangs, with the exception of Ching-ling, soon became very rich. Mme. Kung herself was a financier and industrialist of importance even before the days of the large American grants of World War II, after which the tasks of "capital formation" were to be greatly simplified for all friends of the dynasty.

Ching-ling told me details of Ai-ling's manipulations on the currency exchange with a mixture of contempt and admiration. "She's very clever, Ai-ling," Ching-ling would say. "She never gambles. She buys and sells only when she gets advance information from confederates in the ministry of finance about changes in government fiscal policy. It's a pity she can't do it for the people instead of against them." Increasingly she felt the irony of a situation in which her relatives traded on the nation's reverence for her husband's name for personal enrichment and the enrichment of their friends while her countrymen starved.

"America may be able to afford rich men," she would say, "but China cannot. It is impossible to amass a fortune here except through criminal dishonesty and misuse of political power backed by military force. Every dollar comes right out of the blood of our poor people who seldom have enough to eat. One day the people will rise and take it back."

Charity is a Buddhist as well as a Christian virtue, but Confucianist emphasis on the family first tended to make its practice in the abstract relatively rare in China. Ching-ling had no illusion that the spreading of alms would solve the problem of poverty. For her the poor were "the people" and because the people were poor and weak so was China; "the people" had to be made prosperous and strong before China could be recognized as an equal in the world. The relative ease of her own youth perhaps gave her a guilt complex in this respect that was more Methodist than Chinese. She was repelled by rich Chinese who felt no sense of shame at the degradation of "the people" and their ostentatious displays of wealth seemed to her vulgar insults to the nation. It was characteristic that she sold or gave away, in the interest of "causes," most of her share of a rich legacy of her mother's jewels.

But Ching-ling liked beautiful things and chose the few external furnishings of her life with unerring taste. Her home was always immaculate, with an effect of warmth and simplicity. She had a few treasured paintings and scrolls and her rooms were usually bright with exotic flowers. She dressed in subdued colors in gowns of youthful style and she was always perfectly groomed, her jet hair caught severely back and ending in a bun, leaving her delicately boned features in fine cameo relief. Except for a jade hairpin or a clasp she seldom wore any ornament.

Ching-ling liked Western opera and had a fine collection of records. She liked to dance and occasionally gave parties for young people and thoroughly relaxed and enjoyed herself. She firmly believed in equality of the sexes. A sense of devotion to Dr. Sun's memory gave her an awareness that her historical role transcended her personal life, and prevented her from re-marrying.

In her schooldays Ching-ling had been greatly moved by the story of Jeanne d'Arc. Though she was not a mystic who could see herself as the Maid, her identification with what she considered the true liberating forces in an oppressed China was probably her main compensation for an often lonely life. She was a gentle and tender person, who missed not having children and lavished affection on those who fell under her care in the orphanages she was always sponsoring. The savageries of the whole Chinese catastrophe must have hardened her soul, but the lowest estimate that could be placed on her personal answerability for the revolution, past and present, is what she said of her sister Mei-ling's influence on Chiang Kai-shek. Without her, the excesses "might have been much worse."

"Dr. Sun was never against anyone who was for the poor," she said firmly, "and never for anyone who was for the rich. He was a very poor boy himself and never owned a pair of shoes before he was fourteen. He never forgot that eighty percent of our people were the same. My ancestors were very poor people, too, you know. My relatives never talk about it but some of our forebears were Hakkas (tribesmen) from Hainan Island, who came to China as penniless coolies a few generations back."

There was nothing tribal-looking about Ching-ling, however. She had fine, satiny skin, pale ivory in shade, and beautifully shaped hands. Perhaps because of this she had not personally suffered from the color bias which dark or "yellow" Cantonese often felt in America. She seldom referred to her Wesleyan days and I can think of only one suggestion of any sentimentalism in her about them. Her Christian name was

Rosamund and she still liked friends to call her by her schoolgirl nickname, "Suzy," which always seemed to me incongruous beside the musical Ching-ling.

Unfortunately, one thing she remembered deeply about America was the discrimination against Orientals and the degradation of Negroes in the South. This was an experience spared to her Wellesley-educated sister, Mei-ling, who became much more Americanized. In Ching-ling's eyes these were profound flaws in Christian practice. She equated them with foreigners' arrogance and contempt for the Chinese on their native soil, even though she herself used their enclaves of power for political sanctuary.

"The Russians don't treat colored people as racial inferiors," she said when I asked what she liked about her stay in the Soviet Union. "Americans won't let colored boys and girls go to school with their children, and yet they call themselves Christians. That's one of the reasons Dr. Sun came to feel closer to Russia than America."

"But Dr. Sun died a Christian, did he not? And did you not arrange a Christian burial for him?"

"Yes, that was his wish. He had many good Christian friends and so have I. He never felt any contradiction between the teachings of Jesus and his own. Social revolution to him was Christianity in action."

"Then he never did really believe in Communism?"

"Oh, yes! But not at first. He thought our revolution should follow a different path from Russia's. After 1923, however, he believed we could travel the same road."

"Plenty of statements in his works seem to deny that flatly."

"Oh, you're talking about those lectures!" Ching-ling smiled and threw back her head. "He made it all up on the spur of the moment. It all depended on the political situation and the audience. I would be nervous as a cat, sitting next to him on the platform and wondering what was coming next. But he was always a Socialist. He read Marx and accepted him about the same time Lenin did. He had very clear objectives in his mind—land to the tillers, social ownership of production, industrial modernization, equality of education and work opportunities for all, and an end to foreign imperialism, of course."

"But the dictatorship of the proletariat?"

"He thought it would come, eventually, though you won't read it in his books. But he spoke conservatively to those whose help he needed, and his books were edited so as not to divide his followers. 'We have to be very careful how we go at things,' he was always warning me. 'Do it the Chinese way—roundabout—never directly at the goal.'"

Was the great Sun, then, merely an accomplished artist in compromise? From Ching-ling I got an impression of an idealist who muddied his hands in politics and war but never let power take precedence over his dreams. He seems to have been one of those cases Dostoevsky's policeman calls "really dreadful people" who are not simply atheists and revolutionaries but far worse: "Socialists who also believe in Christianity."

"Just think of the China Dr. Sun had to work with," Chingling would exclaim, "a country everybody has been using for a doormat for a hundred years. Even little states like Portugal and Holland treat us as inferiors. Part of it was due to the ridiculous pride and ignorance of the Manchus, but foreigners used them to keep us down. After the republic was set up the foreign powers still ran China like a colony. Dr. Sun tried again and again to get aid in London, Washington and Paris to carry out his plans for the international development of China. He was always treated contemptuously, laughed at and turned away."

"Russia was his last chance?"

"You might say his last choice."

It is true that even after Dr. Sun reached an agreement with the Russians he made a final appeal to the American Minister in China, Jacob Gould Schurman, to ask for international intervention on a scale which even Russia never attempted. He proposed that Britain, France and the United States occupy China for five years, eliminate the warlords, and jointly with the Kuomintang set up an honest adminstration, industrialize and modernize the country, and prepare the people for democratic elections.

Mr. Schurman did not take his wild dream seriously. The Russians did. In 1923 the Bolsheviks became Sun's ally. They helped finance, reorganize, retrain and re-equip his party and his army, and backed the Nationalist revolution—until Chiang Kai-shek threw them out.

"Is it any wonder that Dr. Sun was overjoyed with his agreement? Russia was the first power to recognize China as an equal," said Chingling. Russia was, indeed, the first country to give up its concessions, renounce extraterritoriality, and make an "equal treaty" with China. She is to this day collecting dividends from Lenin's investment in the Chinese revolution.

"Dr. Sun believed that the Russians honestly wanted to see China completely independent, with a government of, by and for the people," said Ching-ling. "He believed that till his death. The last message he signed was to the Russians pledging that we would always work together for the final liberation of China."

"So you think there is no doubt where Dr. Sun would have stood toward Chiang Kai-shek?"

"No doubt at all. From the time the Communists came to his help he saw that they were for the poor. The rest were not."

Is this a good example of history "objectively" summarized? Probably not. But it was the essence of history as Ching-ling saw it, and "truth" for which millions of Chinese would die. Who was I to teach China's Mrs. George Washington history as a professor might see it? What was "true" in the American time-space system of understanding might not be true in China. Hui Shih, one of China's famous dialecticians, "demonstrated"—2,000 years ago—that time is not absolute. One cannot always be quite sure, in judging countries far removed from one's own, what *time* history really is.

In leaning to the side of the Communists and Russia, Ching-ling unquestionably thought she was acting as Dr. Sun, the Christian Socialist, would have acted. But she was not without reservations in her acceptance of the party line. Once when I made some criticism of Trotsky she suddenly smiled and went to her bookshelves. She pulled out Trotsky's newly published *The Revolution Betrayed.* "There's a lot of truth in this," she said, handing it to me. "Read it."

In 1936 the Generalissimo was seized and held captive for two weeks by Marshal Chang Hsueh-liang, in a mutiny in which Chang allied himself with the Chinese Reds. Unexpectedly, Moscow denounced the seizure as a "pro-Japanese plot" (!) and demanded Chiang's immediate release. Ching-ling told me that during Chiang's captivity her brother-in-law, H. H. Kung, came to ask her—now that Stalin had expressed his wishes—to sign a statement denouncing Marshal Chang and demanding that he liberate the Generalissimo.

"What Chang Hsueh-liang did was right," Ching-ling told me she answered Dr. Kung. "I would have done the same thing if I had been in his place. *Only I would have gone farther!*" Obviously little Wesleyan compassion had survived in her as far as Chiang Kai-shek was concerned.

Coupled with this kind of toughness and independence in Chingling was an unexpected pixie quality which made her like to see pomp reduced to ridicule and to poke fun at anybody smug, complacent, chauvinistic or self-important. She was an accomplished mimic and loved to quote silly remarks by Chinese and foreign diplomats and politicians and their wives. When the benign Dr. Kung, who had the same surname as Confucius (Kung Fu-tzu), announced that he was, in fact, the old gentleman's "direct descendant," Ching-ling henceforth referred to him as The Sage. If she was for the Chinese Communists it was not because her sense of humor was inactive about their foibles but because she thought they worked "for the good of the people" rather than for personal enrichment.

Once she said, "I have never trusted any Chinese politician except Dr. Sun Yat-sen. And he didn't have a Chinese mind. He had a world mind."

"You don't trust a single Chinese politician today?" I asked, astonished.

She shook her head. Then she added: "I distrust Mao Tse-tung less than the others."

CHAPTER 24

Footnote on a Forgotten Battle

IT WAS DARK midnight, January 28, 1932.

Suddenly Japanese rifle and machine-gun fire laced Jukong Road up which I hurried from the Shanghai North Station. I saw a figure stop and fall. Beyond, a Chinese soldier dropped to his knees, crawled inside a doorway, and commenced firing. The street emptied like a drain; iron shutters closed as if clams lived inside, and the last light disappeared. As the *p'ing-p'ing* heated up the air I slid along the walls, with nothing to guide me but the general direction in which the Settlement and safety lay, and how-to-take-cover dimly remembered from my brief inglorious days as a National Guardsman.

Turning a corner into a narrow lane I lay down swearing and asked myself, "Why get yourself knocked off in a war that isn't yours? What good is a story you don't live to send out?"

For this was "real" war, at last, not the mere chase and occupation which I had witnessed as a correspondent covering the Japanese conquest of Manchuria. I had returned from there only a few weeks before. I had thought, as others had, that the Chinese would never fight.

But now, in that stinking alley, the "greatest" battle fought since World War I was beginning.

What I wondered was whether Cheng Pao-chen, traffic manager of the Shanghai-Nanking Railway, had moved his people, as well as his rolling stock, out of the North Station, now under open attack. I had gone there to see what was happening and had found everything normal. Hunting up the head man who had turned out to be Mr. Cheng, I told him that I had just come from Admiral Shiozawa's headquarters, where I had learned that he was moving his Japanese marines into Chapei. That was the heart of the Chinese-ruled part of Shanghai, the big industrial and business section just north of Soochow Creek and the International Settlement.

Around us the station was still crowded with the usual chaos of peace: men and women under cumbersome loads of baggage and bedding, baskets of fresh fruit and fish in wicker baskets, high tiers of pots and pans, wet infants, and old men with fighting crickets and pet birds in their cages. While those hundreds innocently waited I had argued with Cheng, an American-educated Chinese who had never seen me before I showed him my credentials.

"You've got to get these people out of here," I said. "The Japanese are on their way. I saw the marines begin their march."

He smiled. Didn't I know that General Wu Teh-chen, mayor of the Chinese city, had accepted all Japan's demands that afternoon? Chinese troops had already begun their withdrawal. Then I pulled out a copy of the laconic declaration which Admiral Kenkichi Shiozawa had, a few minutes earlier, dispatched to Mayor Wu. A Japanese correspondent had given it to me. It announced simply that Japanese troops would immediately occupy Chapei and other Chinese territory to supervise Chinese withdrawal and "protect law and order."

"That inevitably means a clash. They want to 'teach the anti-Japanese Nineteenth Route Army a lesson,' as they put it. So what about moving your people?"

"*People?*" Plainly Cheng was worried now. "What about our *rolling* stock? We've got the best locomotives of the line in these yards. That's my first duty: to save them. But what if you're wrong?"

"It's true, I tell you. But that's for you to decide."

"If I act, and it's a false alarm, I'll have my head cut off," said the excited man. "If I don't act, and you're right, I'll lose the rolling stock *and* my head!"

I left him trying to reach Mayor Wu by telephone, vainly, for the line was cut. I next located the regimental commander of the Chinese station guard. He too had heard nothing of the Japanese plans. As I visited his troops still in position on the edge of Hongkew in Settlement territory, I heard the noise of many bells and steam whistles. Was the rolling stock moving? And what about the people? But I had fled down Jukong road without knowing . . .

Now, it took half an hour to work my way back to the Soochow Canal and into the Western world of the Settlement. Then I got off the first eyewitness story of the "war" which was to hold front pages for weeks.

Inevitably my tale began, "The streets of Shanghai are red with blood tonight." A merciful cable editor provided a new lead. My scoop was a triumph. It won me warm "congratulations" from editors of our important papers, from Keats Speed of the N. Y. *Sun* and Hal O'Flaherty of the Chicago *Daily News*. At first that seemed to me the most significant thing that happened in that strange and stupid battle.

Later I wrote a book about the great "undeclared war" in Shanghai and Manchuria called *Far Eastern Front.** Today the details seem as meaningless as those of battles which were to follow, up to and through World War II. What remains is the memory of people dying simply because, as Pascal said, they lived "on the other side of the river." I would grow inured to the obscenities of war glimpsed on other rivers, but these first pictures would always haunt me.

There was the fresh corpse of a fallen Japanese aviator I saw right after a Chinese soldier pulled out his smoking heart (perhaps to broil it, thought J. B. Powell, who was with me), leaving behind a deep dark wound the shape of a perfect cross, cut by bayonet; and the smell of smoking flesh slapped against the steel sides of a bombed troop train around which naked youths, their clothes blown off and their bodies roasted whole, were plumper than ever in their meagrely-fed lives. I remember, too, the surrealist rag-doll men in their rough cotton-padded blue gowns hanging where the Japanese had left them after using them for bayonet practice; and the heat of skies of a city that the great arsonist burned for a month, to "maintain law and order," while dancing as usual went on in the Settlement sanctuary.

Foreign intelligence officers cabled home the grave discovery that a single bomb, dropped by that sad Chinese aviator who near-missed the Japanese flagship and hit the Settlement, could kill a *thousand* helpless people. That bomb made Nanking Road look like the refuse-laden Whangpoo River suddenly drained dry, or something by Picasso in his Guernica period. Then there was the sick gut when machine-

* N. Y., 1933.

gun bullets burned holes through a wooden fence, two inches above my head, and when a little Chinese girl whom I heard shrieking in some ruins, proved strangely light as I lifted her from a blood-soaked quilt, to find that her legs had been torn off. And now I know why Floyd Gibbons, who arrived and put up at the Cathay Hotel to cover the war from its well-stocked bar, told me that that was the best place to see a war. Gibbons had already seen that little girl, in a previous incarnation, when I was still wet behind the ears.

Thus, war disgusted me with war and yet raised questions to which it was not easy to find any answer except more war.

If the maneuvers of last season's battles are as dead as their corpses, surely the political issues remain? Yes. What were they? What Japan thought she was fighting for, what the heroic Nineteenth Route Army died for, and what the Western powers thought, were quite different concepts. The result was something else again. Not only did wars fail to accomplish the aims for which men began and fought them; they gave unexpected issue to unforeseen wars of the future. If war was "philosophy teaching by example" the trouble was that the method always required bigger and bigger examples. Each war became the generator of the next.

And yet that is quite different from saying that the battle changes nothing. It changes everything. But never in the way aggressors plan it, and usually in ways quite the opposite.

Consider the "example" of the Manchurian-Shanghai "war," often called the real beginning of World War II. On September 18, 1931, a few feet of track allegedly were blown up on the South Manchuria Railway conveniently near the Japanese garrison at Mukden. An express train shortly afterward passed over the spot without damage, but the "incident" was the excuse for punitive action which ended with Japanese conquest of Manchuria, the richest part of China. But the "Mukden Incident" was not a beginning so much as the end-product of a half dozen earlier wars and "unexpected" results and "issues" created by them. Protean social and political forces which exploded in Japan's aggression were mixed with the moral and political convictions of a sense of divine mission to correct ancient wrongs. Their deep roots in political sentiments shared by all Asians were little understood in America of 1931—or 1941.

Japan was out for self-aggrandizement, but historically was also the spearhead of Asian nationalism against European imperialism. By the time she had become Asia's most advanced industrial nation the avenues of easy expansion as a substitute for solving Japan's difficult internal problems had been closed. India, Burma, Indo-China, Malaya and the Philippines were still held by white rulers who, with the exception of the U. S., showed no sign of budging unless removed by force. Vast underdeveloped Sumatra, the Celebes and Borneo were absurdly the legacy of a tiny faraway nation of Dutchmen, clearly no equal of Japanese power, while the whole Australasian world had been seized by the British. Oriental immigrants were excluded.

By 1931 Japan was strong enough to challenge all the colonial powers, but its leaders saw that complete hegemony over China was the necessary preliminary. They correctly understood how morally weak and divided the West really was. They realized also that France and Britain dreaded "communism" more than any rival operating within accepted rules of imperialism. Sedulously they exploited Western illusions that their own incursions on the mainland were intended to encircle Russia and begin a holy war rather than aimed at liquidating European colonialism.

Except for the United States, Japan might have had everything her own way much earlier in East Asia. She had waited years to see what choice America would finally make: to renounce her part in the European overlord position in China, leaving the colonial powers to find their own way out of Asia; or to accept the role of leading overlord and herself become the outright surviving champion of colonialism; or to conciliate and support Japan as the last best hope of imperialist leadership and countervailing power against the "menace of Russia." Japan's conquest of Manchuria was the big test. With that the United States had to put up or shut up about the future of the Western Pacific.

The Generalissimo also waited. In the past we had enjoyed "the luxury of constantly denouncing British imperialism while steadily participating in its benefits," as Prof. John Fairbank wrote.* We could not now act on principle against its Japanese counterpart. America vacillated, never did make up its mind, not then, and not up to the eve of Pearl Harbor. When America did little but moralize against Japan in 1931 Chiang also did nothing. Non-resistance and "reliance on the League of Nations" became his policy. Marshal Chang Hsueh-liang, ruler of Manchuria, obeyed Chiang's orders and withdrew his large army below the Great Wall, letting his rich domain fall to Japan without a struggle. The League also did nothing. From then on the League

* *The United States and China,* Cambridge, Mass., 1948, p. 313.

Covenant and the Kellogg-Briand Pact were ignored. Italy and Germany, rising new aggressor states of the West, now took their cue from the East.

Left as carrion for the eagle to gorge upon at leisure, China and the Chinese people did not, however, play quite the role assigned to them. Despite Chiang Kai-shek's policy, spontaneous anti-Japanese societies and popular Chinese boycott movements began to hurt Japan's trade. Tokyo demanded that Chiang suppress all such activity, especially at Shanghai, the focus of her mainland interests. The Generalissimo agreed. Japan then insisted that Chinese troops in that vicinity, the Nineteenth Route Army, were too anti-Japanese. Japan demanded their withdrawal, and the "demilitarization" of wide areas around Shanghai. Again, the Generalissimo yielded. And yet the Japanese, not satisfied with an easy victory, precipitately involved themselves in the Shanghai battle, with moral and political consequences nobody foresaw.

"The Chinese," said Admiral Shiozawa, "respect nothing but force." A few thousand of his naval bluejackets could end China's "anti-Japanese attitude" without any help from the army, already arrogant with glory in Manchuria. The navy would now get more ships and more men and more power for the ultimate showdown with the West. Shiozawa took everything into consideration except the Nineteenth Route Army. Who would have believed that it was led by brave and proud men who would not run away when attacked—not even after Chiang Kai-shek fled from Nanking to Loyang with his government?

The "Nineteenth" was the best army in the lower Yangtze Valley, a "new" army, the product of the Nationalist revolution. Its commanders had sided with the Generalissimo against the Communists but they had their own system of left-wing nationalism, political indoctrination and morale. Although officers and men were alike indignant when Chiang capitulated to the Shanghai ultimatum, they were good soldiers and began obeying orders to withdraw. When the Japanese attacked, however, they turned in their tracks in passionate self-defense. Within a day or two the whole country offered them unprecedented moral support. Thousands of youths flocked to volunteer. The battle was fought over every street and block of the metropolis. Only after thirty-four days of operations which involved a large part of the Japanese fleet, scores of naval bombers, 65,000 Japanese troops, and extensive operations far on the flanks of the city, did the Nineteenth Army retreat— with about half of its original force of approximately 45,000.

To the Chinese this military defeat was an incredible spiritual victory. Most astounding, it was accomplished mainly by a single army, for Chiang Kai-shek himself never entered the battle. Indeed the "Nineteenth" was later liquidated by the Generalissimo after the shattered remnants had retired southward, to Fukien province. There Chiang kept it bottled up, refusing to make good its human and material losses, and carefully watching for an opening. In a few months its disgruntled commanders rebelled and organized a "reformed" and "revolutionary" Kuomintang. They even sought an anti-Japanese alliance with the Chinese Red Army which, in neighboring Kiangsi, had already formally "declared war" on Japan.

But the Communists blundered and thereby saved Chiang. Divided by doctrinaire arguments over whether they could trust such an alliance, they lost valuable time. Swiftly gathering his best forces, which he had never committed in Shanghai, Chiang Kai-shek attacked by surprise and broke up the Nineteenth before it could re-arm, expand its depleted forces, and unite with the Reds. He was then able to turn all his energy to the suppression of the Reds whom he now described as his "first and worst enemy."

And yet the Shanghai war had its permanent and irreversible effect on the thinking of China. It convinced great numbers of Chinese youths that China could become invincible if united in patriotic struggle. Chinese troops could, when led by selfless, honest men, properly trained and adequately equipped, fight for freedom as well as anybody. This "discovery" revived waning morale and eventually created a political climate in which Chiang Kai-shek would finally have no choice but to compromise with his "first and worst enemy" and join it against Japan. It was that fact, rather than any overt result of the battle, which was to change the history of Asia in a most decisive way.

After the battle I kept wondering what had really happened to Mr. Cheng at the Shanghai North Station. One day my friend Robert Ward, an American consul, telephoned to say that a Chinese acquaintance wanted to honor me with a banquet—"for services rendered." Curious, I went to Ward's, and there was Cheng Pao-chen. He had acted on my word, he said, and saved millions in equipment that night. And the people? Yes, he had dispersed most of them, too, before the station was shelled and burned. Cheng had received a promotion, a cash award, and a decoration for "exceptional initiative under fire."

CHAPTER 25

Nym

GEORGE BERNARD SHAW said that "all autobiographies are lies." That did not prevent him from writing his own *Self-Sketches*. "No man is bad enough to tell the truth about himself during his lifetime," he said, "involving, as it must, the truth about his family and his friends and colleagues." This inhibition applies with special force where a spouse is concerned, and more poignantly to an ex-wife.

If I cannot tell all the truth about myself, and about Nym Wales, having in common with Mr. Shaw "the further difficulty that I have not yet ascertained the truth about myself," I should at least give some account of my life with the very unusual woman who was to be my frequently tormenting, often stimulating, and always energetically creative and faithful co-worker, consort and critic during my next eight years in Asia.

The trouble with Nym was that she did not want to get married. At least that's what she said when I first met her, not that I had mentioned the subject, but as a kind of general warning. Certainly a nomad should know that he travels fastest who travels alone. And I was still, at twenty-six, working on the theory that if you made it clear you were the man who "woo'd in haste and means to wed in leisure" the burden of the defense rested on the other party. A callow young man was I, who had yet to learn that a woman finds you in her own choice of time and place and creates her own conditions.

Helen Foster was her real name; she was the daughter of an attorney in Utah, and no Mormon. She had studied China at home until she just decided one day, as she put it, to come out and "become Empress of Asia." Momentarily she was detained in government service with the American consulate-general in Shanghai.

"It takes an emperor to make an empress," said I. "What's that again about not getting married?"

"The empress part," she laughed, "is only a manner of speaking."

But she acted like one, I noticed, as she brushed off potential conversationalists on the subject who crowded around her. She seemed, in short, a Greek goddess in that town, and lovely to look at anywhere.

She was twenty-two, with a trim, healthy body and dancing blue eyes, a surprising combination of beauty and brains to find adrift on Bubbling Well Road. Adrift was not the word; she was more purposeful than I. She had read prodigiously and that had fired her curiosity and imagination and an intense interest in learning. She passionately wished to be a writer, she said, but couldn't.

"Why not?" I asked. "Anybody can write something. Look at me."

"I haven't a writer's name to my name, that's why."

"We'll soon fix that," I said. And we did. We found her a *nom de plume* half out of Shakespeare—Nym—and the rest from her parents' native land. And she signed her first published work and her first book Nym Wales and has used it ever since.

"How would you like to see Soochow?" I suggested soon after we met.

"If that's a decent proposal I'd love it," she agreed.

As it turned out it was entirely decorous—the first of the trips we made to neighboring ancient cities. At Yangchow and Hangchow and Wusih and elsewhere that summer and autumn we ate rapturous food under green willows and in tranquil temple pavilions; we took long walks across the rice field pathways and through mulberry groves in the silk country, down to the water's edge; and we sailed the blue lakes on dragon junks and rode sampans under arched bridges along the Grand Canal in the moonlight. Then, exhausted from a day's excursion, we would fall asleep in the nearest Chinese inn, and there were then fair inns in such towns.

"*Ting hao!*" a grinning street coolie in Hangchow shouted from under his heavy burden, raising a brown thumb in Nym's direction. "*Hao k'an-ti t'ai-t'ai!*" And we waved back, amused because she wasn't my "beautiful wife," as the friendly well-wisher assumed. We were lovers but at her quaint insistence still Platonic lovers.

The romance waxed above that hidden duel. In a hundred places we talked about large abstract questions such as what is truth, where do the senses end and reason begin, what is reality and what is illusion, Socrates versus Kant, Marx and dialectical materialism versus metaphysics, and my own "experience" versus her "pure ideas" and ideals. Beneath all this non-functional exploration of our innocence and ignorance the furious battle went on over the satisfaction of old *yin* and *yang* (the male and female principles), nature's only interest in our affair.

I don't know how long this endurance contest might have lasted or how it would have ended if Nym had not discovered and produced

Dr. Victor Frene. He was an eccentric German professor who had lived entirely with Chinese for a couple of decades, the last one presiding over a private school for promising Chinese boys sponsored by old Yen Hsi-shan, the "model governor" of Shansi. Stout, somewhat unkempt, partly bald, with a peculiar gait acquired from walking in Chinese cloth shoes, Frene was a mad genius stocked with enough Sinological information to more than qualify him for the chair at Oxford which he had reportedly turned down. Half monk and half messiah, he wrote and preached a "new education" which would combine "the sense power of the West," its vigor developed by the repressive teachings and ideas of sin inherent in Judeo-Christianity, with the "brain power of China," its senses atrophied, according to Frene, by over-indulgence in sex. Out of this East-West heterosis he expected to get the universal "highest man," dedicated solely to the perfection of the human intelligence, beauty over the beast, mind over matter.

"No, not superman," he would insist. "Just *man*. He is still an idea."

"What's wrong with China?" Dr. Frene demanded of me almost immediately, after Nym introduced us. "Why were the Chinese able to invent everything and develop nothing? Why did Chinese civilization undergo a menopause? What happened to China's *creative* power?"

"Maybe China atrophied because of lack of competition," I suggested weakly.

"Nonsense!" he screamed mildly. "China is a case of stability achieved at the expense of stifling the individual. The society lives but the creative personality dies. Taoistic passivism and fatalism on the one hand, bastard-Confucianism on the other: ancestor-worship, adoration of the male offspring, worship of the phallus! Regimentation of the mind by the classics on the one hand, dissipation of sense power and early and constant cohabitation on the other hand. The mind becomes a perfect mechanical instrument but remains a blank because the senses are dead which should serve and stimulate it!"

Frene himself was, naturally, a confirmed celibate, and he was out to recruit teachers of a like disposition to help him put his ideas into force. It became obvious that he considered Nym his ideal helpmate. She was "a genius of unspoiled sense-power," said he, whom he was determined to save from the couch, and me. What he had in mind for her was a marriage like Shaw's, in which "sex had no part" except as a secondary stimulus to work.

"That," I said to Nym after our first encounter, "is a dirty trick."

"What do you mean?"

"Inventing a character like Frene. It's witchcraft, that's what it is! I don't think you can make him appear again."

But she did. For weeks we argued in three-cornered conversations conducted on several levels simultaneously. In recollection the details would sound distinctly fey, but at the time we were all in dead earnest. "We must treat men and women," said Emerson, "as if they were real. Perhaps they are." Love is full of senses, of course, but has no sense of humor. I was myself at first overwhelmed by Frene's erudition, especially when in a moment of generosity he offered to recruit even me for his ashram. While I was not yet ready to be a monk I could not help noticing that I had little to offer Nym if she wished to become a nun. Her intellectual hunger was insatiable and here was the one-man "learned society" capable of indefinitely satisfying it. Who was I to deter her?

And yet on continued exposure to the challenge I felt an overriding compulsion to refute Frene's theories—particularly his sex-and-sense-power fanaticism. He was the subtlest and most tenacious of all my rivals, with his unique approach, and perhaps the only one who could have aroused my altruism to the perilous point of matrimony.

" 'He that hath wife and children,' " my Mephistopheles would intone from Bacon when the debate hit the lower level, " 'hath given hostages to fortune; for they are impediments to great enterprise.' Bacon meant marriage only in the sexual sense, you see," Frene would add in case I missed the point.

"What about Bach and his *twenty* children?" I countered, appalled at the thought of such chaos and yet determined to upset Frene.

"Yes," he retorted, "and do you know who destroyed most of Bach's great works? His own sons."

"All the same, would we ever have had a Bach, or a Bacon, if it weren't for old man Adam?"

I spent hours hunting up obvious examples from Alexander to Cellini to Pushkin. I cited that it was odd that Gandhi had postponed his own celibacy until after he had produced a large family. I plunged headily into Freud and Huxley, Russell, Dorsey, Robinson and such people of that day, hoping to trip up the professor on his home territory, for he was a neo-behaviorist.

In the process I did discover that nobody knew exactly how the endocrine glands and the autonomic nervous system functioned in the ultimate organization of imaginative or creative thought operating in the cortex of the brain. Nor could anyone prove that copulation undertaken in moderation had any more harmful effects on those frontal lobes than did any other kind of musculation. Still less could it be shown that unnatural repression of gonadic activity had contributed to the painting of great pictures or the invention of the microscope.

It was a strange courtship, passion and reason all confused. And in the end the citadel did not fall to any scientific arguments—when does it?—but to the invincible musk of life. For never did clever maid more skillfully permit her adversary to win his argument and lose his heart to the ancient true needs of a man and a maid for organic— but lawful—unity.

One fine day of enchantment I found the gates suddenly unbarred and we decided to finish the course together. Among the first friends I told about it was Soong Ching-ling, who gave us a Cantonese banquet in the grand manner and presented us with a silver electric percolator, made in America. We could never make it work on Chinese current.

Nym and I escaped from Dr. Frene and ended in Tokyo, where we were married on Christmas Day. Nothing could have been more absolute, for we went through three ceremonies. My former Shanghai roommate, John Allison, found us a preacher for one; we were locked again at the Embassy; and finally at the Japanese registry—all good and legal wardens of man's freedom.

As for Dr. Frene, after our marriage I never heard Nym mention him again.

CHAPTER 26

The Southern Seas

MY BOSS, Horace Epes, had authorized my visit to Japan to do a few interviews, but I neglected to inform him that a newly acquired colleague and I had also planned a two months' trip from there through the Southern Seas—the Sulu, the Celebes, the Java and the Flores— down to Bali and back by way of Singapore. I wrote Mr. Epes a prospectus of the rich lodes of mail copy I claimed were only waiting to be exploited along that glamorous but notoriously un-newsworthy route. In a mere postscript I said, "Incidentally, I am getting married on Christmas Day." One reason I could never have left the Consolidated Press while it lasted was Epes' characteristic reply. He cabled me at once: "Trip approved, sounds like marvelous story. P. S. Incidentally, happy honeymoon!"

Greater understanding hath no editor.

We traveled with the Japanese O. S. K. Line, which operated a string of freighters through these out-of-the-way places. Our first ship was the *Canada Maru,* which had such limited passenger accommodations that we were given the first mate's cabin, the *Canada* apparently being quite able to get along without a first mate. We thus had half the captain's deck to ourselves as we sailed in good season at the year's end through ideal weather. After Formosa the air was soft and warm, the sea a sheet of shimmering silk, and the sunsets prolonged symphonies of glory. At night the porpoises flashed patterns of white lace around us and the Southern Cross rose higher and higher.

"If all men were astronomers," said Nym, watching the stars come nearer, "there would be no wars."

"Mr. Wells is making a philosopher of you," said I. We read to each other from his *Outline of World History.* We also read James Harvey Robinson's *Why We Behave Like Human Beings* before we returned to China. These books, together with Wells' *The Work, Wealth and Happiness of Mankind,* and Shaw's *Intelligent Woman's Guide to Capitalism and Socialism,* helped turn Nym from idealism to realism in philosophy. Our observations on this journey also confirmed in her the anti-colonial sentiments which most young Americans then felt as part of their natural heritage.

We sensed something else, being the only white passengers among Japanese with whom we daily shared meals and conversation. As first-class Asians who considered themselves our peers—hadn't they just outbluffed us in Manchuria?—the Japanese did not conceal the immense scorn and dissatisfaction they felt at the way the richest under-populated parts of Asia had been "maldistributed" and were being misused or not used by the white masters. The captain politely but constantly reminded me of the progress and prosperity of Formosa under Japanese rule contrasted with the vast empty spaces and dormant riches of the southern seas. I noted his resentment, too, at the thought that American civilization had made little impression on the primitive economic level of the average inhabitant of the southern islands of the Philippines. Their enormous potential farm production and industrial possibilities lay hardly touched, while the industrious Japanese scrounged for an existence confined to their tidy but tiny parcels of land to the north.

If the Philippines could have supported five times their population,

Borneo and the Celebes could have provided a livelihood for a hundred times theirs. Island continents which would make twenty Hollands, they were still primeval, beyond the seacoast and the forest fringe, with backward populations and almost wholly undeveloped resources held down, like American Indians on reservation, by a few thousand foreign riflemen.

Part of Northern Borneo had until recently been administered and owned outright, including all its dyak inhabitants, by a single British corporation. It skimmed off only the ready-nature crops like coconuts, timber and rubber, which paid huge annual returns to distant London stockholders. The greater part of Borneo was still kept in a Dutch strongbox, its immense potential wealth above and below the land lying idle. Meanwhile the owners leisurely waited for the exploitation of native labor elsewhere to carry on the slow and wasteful process of what was called "capital formation" for coupon-clippers abroad who knew little about how the profits were made.

"One thing seems clear," I said to a British rugger enthusiast with whom I sat, under his public-school photographs, in a bungalow where he presided as assistant "resident" in Tawao, North Borneo, "Asia is moving a lot faster than this island. It's an economic vacuum that can't last. The Japanese or the Chinese or Javanese will soon be here and push you out."

"Don't you believe it!" he answered. "This place would go back to the *orang-utans* tomorrow if we left. The Oriental is a long way from mastering our civilization—*a hundred years away*." Within a decade I would hear exactly the same words from the mouth of Britain's next-to-last viceroy in India.

"Why," the young official chuckled over his whisky soda, "these people are closer to the apes than they are to us. Do you know what *orang-utan* means? It means 'man of the forest' in Malay. The other day I asked a clever Malay chap who works for us, did he really think these apes were men? Yes, he said, they're our cousins. 'Your cousins, not mine, laddie,' I said. 'If they are men, why don't they speak?' 'Oh, *orang-utan* can speak, sir,' he came back. 'Then why don't they?' I asked. 'Too smart,' said he. 'If they speak they got to pay head tax.' "

If this were a comparative study of imperialisms it might be interesting to report how miserably low the Javanese standard of living was in the 1930's, when the Dutch claimed superiority as the "world's best colonial administrators." But all that need be said now in passing is that even in Java the Dutch "modernization" had gone just far enough to break down the fabric of the old feudalism and the old production system and self-sufficiency. It merely excited, in the tenant peasantry and the small native intellectual and bourgeois class that emerged from the wreckage, the foci of inevitable rebellion.

The Dutch were thriftier housekeepers than the British and the French and were drawing even more enormous dividends from the tiny stake their pirates placed on the original colonial gamble. But for the native there was little to choose between imperialisms. The Dutch too were fond of saying, "Zees peoples, zey are jildrens, we must rule zem for zeir own gud." But I learned enough, even on the brief tourist run along the coast of Borneo and the Celebes, and in a longer stay in Java, to realize that the "jildren" held another opinion. It took no prophet to see that they were going to throw out the Dutch at the first opportunity, and that Japan was about ready, unwittingly, to create it for them.*

But the island of Bali was different.

For various reasons, including the proud and independent character of the Balinese, a highly profitable tourist trade, and a monopoly of Balinese exports, the Dutch held down their exploitation and inter-ference with local ownership, law, customs and agrarian economy to a minimum. No outsiders were permitted to purchase land, and foreign investment was negligible. Bali remained wholly agrarian and pastoral except for the mercantilism centered chiefly around Buleleng. The contradictions of white men's profits extracted at the expense of the degradation of an old society without the formation of a new one were not in overt evidence. Dutch suzerainty was gentler and more subtle than in the rest of Indonesia and under it the ancient culture of this homogenous society remained an anomaly in the colonial world.

Here alone in all the East was something close to the "good society" of the Buddhistic golden age, something probably as rarely achieved in practice as the legendary "good society" of the Middle Ages in Europe.

* So I wrote in *The Saturday Evening Post*, Aug. 26, 1933.

CHAPTER 27

On Not Eating Your Neighbor

I AWOKE EARLY one January morning in 1933 in Den Pesar, on the farther side of Bali, and gradually became aware of a dark young man at the end of the bed gently pulling my big toe.

"Sir or madame, the tea," he said softly as he put the tray on the bed table.

He had a large gold ring in his long nose, his hair was wrapped in a twist on his handsome head, he wore no shoes, and he was naked except for a *kain* of yellow batik. He was a Papuan savage from New Guinea.

"Thanks, Matté. What time is it?"

"Seven o'clock. Wish reminding you go with Captain Karsen today seeing jangar dance."

"You are a remarkable gentleman, Matté. Do you wake up everybody with orders of the day?"

"All as like."

"How many languages do you use on them?"

"Oh, speaking Javanese, Balinese and German very good. French some little and English only some. But waking up somebody only pulling toe, not speaking." He smiled, showing strong white teeth, bowed and left the room on silent padded feet.

"I wonder," said I, "if you could eat people in English as easily as Papuan."

"I don't see why not," answered Nym. "As far as I have seen, English is not essentially a vegetarian language."

I might have heard that a dozen times and not believed it if I had not met Matté and, later on, in the hills of Northern Luzon, met an Igorot named Dr. Clapp, whose father was a headhunter. He had, as a child, been exhibited with the wild man from Borneo at the St. Louis world's fair, whence a missionary had rescued him, given him his name and an education. Dr. Clapp became a first-rate surgeon and went back and ran a hospital in his native village.

According to Captain Karsen, Matté had eaten human flesh but had not personally killed anyone for that purpose. He had not had a chance.

Karsen was his German master. He had picked the boy up in the jungles of New Guinea and had adopted him after Matté's father, who had eaten a good many people in his day, was finally killed and boiled by his enemies. And now Matté was chief clerk of Karsen's little *pension*, the Satrya, in Den Pesar. Matté's wife, an attractive Javanese, was his deputy. At night he put on a white jacket and white trousers and became head waiter, all dignity despite his big black splay feet, always bare.

This gentle Papuan and Dr. Clapp gave me visual evidence that civilization is not merely skin deep but only one generation deep. This is not to say that there is nothing to genetics; but a primitive child apparently can be taught everything man knows. One could also make a cannibal out of the son of a Nobel prize winner if one caught him early enough.

Matté was highly respected by the Balinese. One day Prince Karem of Asam came to call on him and they sat together in the kitchen having refreshments. Karsen introduced us, explaining that Karem was the last survivor of Balinese royalty. The other families had deliberately committed suicide by walking into Dutch machine-gun fire, *en masse,* during the final conquest of their island in 1911. Karem's easy democracy with Matté was typical of the difference between Balinese caste and Indian.

Bali was the first planned society I saw and the only colony I knew where people were genuinely happy. With a civilization founded on a complex religious-philosophical ideology which all understood and accepted, it seemed an almost perfect communal state. Its economic and cultural expressions of group activity were closely integrated and often literally put to music, individual behavior being broadly predetermined by arrangements for the common good and harmony and unity of the whole.

Bali seemed like one big co-operative. Group collaboration made every task light, with a minimum of tension, frustration, neurosis and conflict. Bell-like music of the *gamelon* filled the air all day and much of the night and seemed part of the flower-decked beauty and fruitful opulence that poured down the green hills and valleys to the silver beaches and the bountiful turquoise sea. Here a million people of mixed racial origins dwelt in an Eden twice the size of Rhode Island and made living a work of art.

In Bali I learned that it is just as "natural" for people to work together as it is for them to be mutually predatory. And that was a great lesson to learn in 1933. Herbert Spencer was wrong.

Bali was not a primitive idyllic society of island Polynesians such as collapsed before the onslaughts of the white man's opium, machines and syphilis. It was a highly advanced and complex organism protected by geography long enough to evolve and adapt itself over many generations. Buddhism probably arrived there no more than a thousand years ago and Hinduism came later. Both penetrations were peaceful and both were merely assimilated by the much older Balinese culture, which kept its unique *esprit humaine* intact. Basic concepts such as One God (Tintya) and a 210-day calendar, used as a kind of masterplan which determined every event of importance in the community, survived as its living heart.

In all the villages we saw there was the same kind of order everywhere without any obtrusive system of "orders." Even the tourist for a day could not fail to be impressed by the absence of violent quarreling, the courtesy and easy grace among people, the lovely, grave, naked, happy children, the clean, perfectly proportioned houses and the clean, beautiful people who lived in them with their unbelievably clean pigs, the only clean pigs I ever saw.

Balinese Buddhist-Hinduism divided society into four castes but not, as in Indian practice, as marks of social discrimination and segregation. Castes were a functional convenience in organizing and classifying community work to be done, not unlike the medieval guilds of Europe.

There were no untouchables, no pariahs, no begging "holy men" and no outcasts. Unlike India, with its endless tabus, intermarriage between castes was common, most arts and crafts were open to all, and both men and women could be priests or elders. Although priests were in charge of the charming temples there was a clear division between worship and temporal affairs. A council of elders in every village regulated the economy, deciding questions of the tenure of farmers on the village land, the training and performance of artists and musicians, the purchase and care of orchestral instruments also held in common, and so on.

Our days in Bali were all too brief, but thanks to Karsen and other friends we saw that the Balinese "calendar plan" really worked smoothly and effortlessly, governing planting, harvesting, building, festivals, worship, dances and dramatic performances, symphonies, marriages, celebrations, and the cremations which are gay and extremely elaborate excursions for everybody. All this was part of a Buddhist concept of life as a cycle of endless rebirth and death, the timeless process of transition in man's upward climb toward "becoming" God.

"You won't ever see a child beaten or struck in Bali," said Karsen. "It has never happened. To strike a child might mean striking your grandfather, for you never know what stage of evolution a spirit is in."

Education in Bali was philosophical and practical rather than mystical and began at infancy with definite social duties. Treated as adults almost as soon as they could talk, children quickly learned to assume their assigned tasks with grace and dignity.

"A boy of five or six here is already a busy fellow," as Karsen put it. "If you look into it you will see that each one has a job that will hold him to his village. A few years later he learns how to draw or paint or carve or play a *gamelon* or be a farmer. It's the village as a whole, with a place for everybody and everybody in his place, that counts. The individual is secondary."

We saw girl children as young as three or four already being trained in the intricate movements of Balinese dancing. Gradually they were taught how to manipulate all parts of the body with unbelievable control and discipline to express the basic ideas of unity and harmony underlying all Balinese art. Only virgins could take part in sacred dances, but there were others in which the whole community, boys and girls together, joined in. Inter-village dancing and symphonic musical exhibitions were part of the calendar.

The Balinese attitude toward sex was different from anything else in Asia and sharply at variance with Western practice. Tabus on promiscuity were strict; formerly adultery had been punishable by death, but the Dutch had put a stop to that, along with the practice of *suttee*. There was no child marriage among the Balinese. Women matured young and as a rule married by fifteen or sixteen, often as a result of courtship and romance but nearly always depending on group approval of the match. From puberty on, girls slept apart and under the guardianship of an elder until their marriage.

In their daily tasks Balinese women and girls went naked above the waist and bathed every day in the temple or forest pools or grottos. On the beautiful Koeta beach near Den Pesar, with its three miles of coral sand, the loveliest in the tropics, men and women merely dropped their *kains* behind them and walked in as they were born. In such a land there were no "sex secrets" kept from children, to whom knowledge came early, naturally and unashamedly. The practice of segregation of women during menstruation and pregnancy as unclean, which was prevalent in primitive Asian societies and even in parts of India, was unknown in Bali. Boys and girls could watch the swelling womb of the mother and count the days before a baby brother or sister would arrive, just as they could reckon, by the Balinese calendar, when they would be ready for the life cycle themselves.

The Balinese are small, comely and well formed. After the initial surprise of the frank mammary display in all sizes, shapes and color shades, from rosebud swellings of puberty to dark lacteal nipples of voluptuous young mothers and the withered bags of the matriarchs, the very multiplicity and universality of the custom made it non-erotic even to the outsider.

"Once the Dutch sent a new governor here," Karsen told me, "who had a kind of prude for a wife. She was shocked by the naked breasts and demanded that her burgomeister forbid it at once. To pacify her he ordered that women must cover their uppers. The next Sunday when they drove out in their carriage to church hundreds of Balinese women lined the road to wait for them. In each village as the carriage drew up the women lifted their *kains* high above their heads and covered their breasts—but exposed their bare bottoms."

I laughed appreciatively.

"Oh, yes, they have plenty of humor. They made up a play about the whole thing. The governor became such a laughingstock the Dutch had to withdraw him. They never tried to enforce his order again."

Balinese children had a wonderful sense of fun both in their work and play. At ten or twelve they were often good artists whose productions were exhibited and praised with those of their elders. It seemed to us that nearly everyone was a musician. After the day's labor the farmers and craftsmen would gather together in the villages and take turns playing *gamelons* and drums far into the night, repeating old themes and forever inventing new ones.

"Notice that everybody is doing something, not trying to get the best of somebody," said Karsen as we drove out one day. "Nobody is in a hurry. I couldn't stand living anywhere else now." He was an expert at leisure himself, but mostly by leaving everything to Matté.

In the fields you commonly saw young girls carry fruit and cocomilk to the male workers, who always had time to pause for refreshments or a quiet smoke in the shade. Though nobody seemed driven, nobody, not even the old ones, was often idle. Their calendar was more a general direction than a target. Balinese had no sense of punctuality and nothing ever started on time. Like the Quakers, they waited for everybody to get into the proper spirit before acting. We heard that a thatched house was to be moved, in one village, and went to watch. It took all day to get them started, but once they began, all families helping, it was quickly and efficiently done.

There was one great cremation for which we waited on and on as it was postponed day after day. Slowly the great pylon arose until it was forty or fifty feet high, everyone from tiny children to elders contributing something. When all was ready baskets of fruit, flowers, nuts, wine, roast pigs and rice and other food were carried up on the heads of girls and young women beautifully dressed in golden and silver bodices above long formal trailing *kains* of batik. Around them a whole galaxy of *gamelons* played their sweet plaintive rhythms. It took ten days to complete the construction and decoration of that magnificent pylon of bamboo and flowers, painted art and sculpture. Then they burned it all in a few hours of dancing, feasting and song, and saw the spirits of their dead happily on their journey. They created not for permanence but each for the joy of creation.

"That little show probably cost more than a pair of Mercedes-Benzes," said Karsen, "but it's a lot better entertainment for a lot more people."

"Do they ever want to leave their paradise?"

"Practically never," he answered. "Once a troupe of Balinese dancers and musicians were induced to go to Europe and were a great success. But not one of them wanted to stay. They got so homesick they canceled half their tour and came back. They couldn't wait to take off their clothes and be comfortable. 'What's wrong with Europe?' I asked them. 'Everybody is angry all the time,' they said."

A Dutchman got permission to open a cinema in Bali. For a week great crowds went to see the pictures, but nobody ever went more than once. Soon nobody came. The owner went around to ask what was the matter. They all gave the same reply. "We have seen the foreign shadow play and it is not as good as our own. Why should we pay to see bad foreign shadows when we ourselves can *make* better plays with music, and at the same time enjoy ourselves, *for nothing?*"

For the same reason Balinese took no interest in foreign-made cloth, shoes, radios and gadgets.

No wonder they had civilized Matté! Nobody could live very long among the Balinese without realizing that there are more rewarding things to do with your neighbor than eat him.

But it was too late to export Bali to the white-skinned people, even those on the warm and bounteous islands. It was perhaps even too late for Bali itself to survive much longer except as an idea. If hard national interests require it now, Bali may be wiped out with a mere whiff of fall-out if the wind veers to the south.

I have not personally seen Bali for twenty years, but I have heard that during the Japanese occupation women were finally obliged to wear shirts, a number of *free* cinemas were opened and prostitution began to flourish. Heaven knows what other improvements have since been introduced by the Javanese suzerains.

But I am content to have known Bali as it was, and just as my days as a nomad had ended.

PART TWO

TO BLOW THE FIRE

"I, though I brought noe fuell, had desire
With these articulate blasts to blow the fire."

JOHN DONNE

CHAPTER 1

At Home in Peking

WE RETURNED to China in the early spring and went to Peking. Ed
Hunter had left for Europe and I took over Consolidated Press for all
China. Peking was to be our home for the next five years.

Peking is incomparably the grandest and most interesting capital in
Asia. The center of a civilization with a continuous history of nearly
3,000 years, its inner Imperial City has some of the spacious beauty of
Paris and its ancient temples and palaces with their rose-colored walls
convey a sense of classic antiquity. Standing on top of the great Tartar
Wall you could see vistas open through wide acacia-lined avenues
around the Winter Palace, across the gold and purple roofs and parks,
and the toy lakes mirroring constant azure skies, until the eye lifted
over the lacquered *p'ai-lou* and the heavy masonry of the gate towers
to the Western Hills, tawny in the distance.

Old Peking was also, like all Chinese cities, an overgrown village,
but a friendly and intimate one. Everybody seemed to know everyone
else, and cheerfully picked his way among the narrow hutungs within
the outer walled city, which were mostly unpaved lanes and in the
spring veritable canals. Flanking them lay the never-ending surprise
of pleasant pavilions and gardens hidden behind the walls which everywhere shut in the tile-roofed homes. Peking was a city of retired courtiers and soldiers of empire, of scholars and absentee landlords, of
monks and artisan merchants and of ricksha coolies speaking a cultured tongue; a city nobly conceived and nobly made, a treasury of
art, a place of gentle birth and of more knavery than downright wickedness; a city of warm vivid springs and shadowed autumns, and of winter
sunshine shimmering on snow-covered trees and frozen lakes; a city
of eternal compromise and easy laughter, of leisure and family love, of
poverty and tragedy and indifference to dirt; and yet a place of unexpected violence, where rebellious students coined the fighting
slogans of a nation, and blinding Mongolian dust storms swept down
from the Gobi Desert, leaving the graceful roofs strewn with the oldest
dust of life.

This languishing metropolis, which had seen so many *coups* and conquests in the past, was soon to be shaken as it had never been shaken before. Important events were already happening when we arrived.

Jehol, the last piece of "free" Chinese territory lying north of the Great Wall, was being forcibly annexed to Japan's new empire of "Manchukuo." Elsewhere, repercussions were beginning. In Rome an ex-Socialist editor named Mussolini was drawing cynical conclusions from the failure of the League of Nations to take action against Japan. He would soon seize Abyssinia. And in Berlin the Nazis had just strong-armed their Austrian-born paper-hanger to power over the Reich, which he would use to doom forty million people to death. But now millions of Germans reportedly swooned with ecstasy as they surrendered their honor and freedom to him.

From New York I received a delayed letter from my old schoolmate, Ben Robertson, on the *Herald Tribune*. He wrote:

"I was with Al Smith the night of the election when he heard that Roosevelt had won. I thought the Happy Warrior was going to cry. It was a bitter blow. Smith went down that minute with Calhoun and Clay and Webster and the other almost-weres. But he rallied and he said to us, 'What the hell, a Chinaman could have gotten in this year!' "

On the day Jehol fell Franklin Roosevelt was inaugurated and America's "Hundred Days" began. But peace and quiet soon descended on Peking and suddenly it was spring. America and its depression seemed remote and unreal to the foreign resident in China. To the Snows, the important thing one April morning was that we had found a house—no, a home—in Peking.

Unlike Shanghai, Peking and its environs were wholly Chinese-administered except for a Legation quarter a half dozen blocks long, enclosed by its own set of walls, where the foreign diplomats lived. Their small contingents of legation guards drilled on the *glacis* or held football, cricket and soccer matches or in seasonable weather played polo. Three or four Russian cabarets and a half dozen Occidental hotels clung to the fringe of the Quarter and provided the only "foreign-style" night life. Among these the Hotel de Pekin had large, sunny rooms and served French food of sorts, but its best feature was a roof garden which dramatically overlooked both the Forbidden City and the Legation Quarter. We stayed there a few weeks but were happy at last to be moving, as most foreign residents of Peking did, to live in a Chinese house.

The Peking dwelling was enclosed by plaster-over-mud-brick walls seven feet or higher, to keep out dust, wind, and prying eyes. Inside, the buildings surrounded a courtyard or series of courtyards separated by other walls pierced by moon gates or gates of more fanciful shapes. We had several Peking houses before we evacuated, but our first was small and new. Its outer gates were lacquered red and within the first courtyard was a moon gate. Behind it was an authentic dragon screen, to keep out evil spirits, which traveled in straight lines only. Beyond it lay a small pavilion filled with flowers and fruit trees, already a cloud of blossoms.

Peking measured its houses by *chien,* or lacquered beams exposed on the ceilings, usually about ten feet apart. "Here comes hundred-*chien* Wang," you could hear a ricksha coolie shout derisively. *"T'a ma-ti!"* And down the street would roll a silver-trimmed ricksha with its pompous-looking merchant in silk jacket. In my case it was "twenty-beam *Shih Lo"* and "Shih" meant "to bestow" and "Lo" meant "happiness." Such was the flowery meaning of my name, transliterated. "Snow" (*hsüeh*) itself could not be used; it was a name for women and a special favorite with prostitutes.

Our twenty *chien* added up to kitchen, dining room, master bedroom and bath, living room, guest room, and an office and library— all paper-windowed and tile-floored. There was also a wing with three servants' rooms and bath. Our rental was sixty Chinese *yuan* a month, then about fifteen American dollars. Did I mention earlier that one of the attractions of Peking was that a newspaper correspondent could become accustomed to living in the style of a bank president? Our cook, a houseboy and a private ricksha coolie cost us another fifteen dollars. And our servants were relatively "wealthy." My ricksha coolie owned two houses and maintained two wives, one in Peking and another in his native village. Foreigners paid their servants twice as much as Chinese did—and then there was the "squeeze" as well.

Peking's "Western-style" cooks were justly famous. When allowed to pick their own staff, and given a reasonable margin of squeeze in the purchases of provisions and all commercial transactions, they provided superior food and service at cafeteria prices. Most of us followed a system called "boarding with the cook," wherein the *maître de cuisine* contracted to feed us for so much a day, making deductions when the "master" dined out, and charging for guests. It averaged less than fifty cents a day per head. We hired one of Roy Chapman Andrews' former cooks and he did very handsomely by us, our food budget seldom exceeding sixty American dollars a month. Wines were extra, of course, but they were cheap, too, when bought from the local French and Italian monasteries.

At the frequent auctions a newlywed couple could buy enough blackwood or teak tables, chairs, cabinets, wardrobes, beds and chests to answer their modest needs for a few hundred dollars. Nym designed her own bamboo and wicker furniture and had it expertly made by an artisan who even managed to cut an easel-shaped plate glass top to fit an eccentric but entirely practical desk. With the addition of some Peking rugs, silk drapes, lanterns and lamps, as well as silver and chinaware also made to order, we set up housekeeping for little more than a thousand dollars.

At that, we were about broke when we were ready to enter Peking's unique Sino-foreign "society," which used to take itself quite seriously. The first requirement, after a home, was an adequate supply of engraved cards for the individual man and wife as well as for the joint Mr. and Mrs. Everybody had to conform to this hangover of Victorian days still religiously observed among Peking residents.

The newcomer had to call around personally to leave "cards" with anyone he wished to know socially, even though they might have already met. The master left a card for the master, the mistress left one for the mistress, and the joint card was left for the couple. One was not to forget, in the event that one found nobody home, to turn down the correct corners of all three cards. The young nonentity was advised by friendly old residents to make no mistakes in the order of the card-dropping and corner-turning. If a matron who considered herself Number Five in the social hierarchy discovered that newcomers had called on Number Seven before her she might punish them by not dropping return cards of her own, thus ostracizing them from her "set." By carrying out the ritual faithfully, one could expect early invitations to dine, dance or watch puppet shows or shadow plays or magicians at the homes of ambassadors, commandants, military and naval attachés, the embassy secretaries, and so on down the line.

Despite this queer preliminary, reminiscent of the courting dance of the goony birds, Peking society was far from stuffy. A genial community hospitably welcomed the new arrival, however poor or insignificant he might be—especially if the newcomer had a good-looking wife. Unlike those in Shanghai, most foreigners had a student's or scholar's interest in China, and few were there simply to make money. Even the business men had to study Chinese, for European languages were little known beyond the Legation Quarter. Although Chiang Kai-shek had proclaimed the dismal city of Nanking his capital, the foreign powers went on keeping their homes and embassies in Peking and diplomats satisfied protocol by making only periodic trips to the south. It was probably a political error for the Kuomintang to downgrade Peking, in a period when the Northern territories and China's relations with Russia and Japan were of foremost importance, and it was a psychological error among the populace. Most Chinese expressed their personal opinion by continuing to call the city *Pei-ching* (or Northern *capital*) rather than *Pei-p'ing* (or Northern peace) as the Kuomintang had decreed.

Nevertheless, life in the last days of Old Peking was no doubt more than a little pretentious and unreal. Peking "society" went on being preoccupied with card-dropping and such matters all the time a great war and revolution were gestating around it. For a while the Snows were no exceptions. Soon we bought a sleek Mongol racing pony and half of another, and joined a riding club. We took long rides through the autumn glory to visit the temples, and across the fields and meadows to the Summer Palace and the Black Dragon Pool near the Western Hills. For months it was a tranquil, uneventful and seemingly secure existence, in which there was plenty of time for everything, including my first serious attempt to learn the Chinese language.

Then the depression finally reached us. The Consolidated Press went bankrupt, and I was out of a job.

CHAPTER 2

By a Nose!

A FEW DAYS after I received that fateful cable from Horace Epes giving me the sad news that Consolidated Press was folding I sat beside the track at Paomachang, Peking's "gentlemen's racing club," and even my heart was sweating. It was a sunny week-end and the stands were crowded with foreign and Chinese gamblers and racing enthusiasts. After carefully studying the odds I had divided my money between the handicap and the sweepstakes. But more than money hinged on the outcome.

My problem was that I already had another job and didn't want it. My friend Jim Mills was in town on special assignment from the Associated Press; when I told him what had happened he came through with a solution. I could take over the Peking desk of his organization, he said, provided I would stick with it for two years. After that, he promised, I could become chief of the Shanghai bureau.

The question was, did I wish to be a spot-news chaser for the rest of my life? I had worked part-time for Morris Harris and the A.P. in Shanghai long enough to know the agency grind: covering everything, in dread of even a one-minute "beat" by the opposition; chained to a phone twenty-four hours a day. I was spoiled. I had had a very special kind of job with Consolidated. I had let conventional coverage go to the devil and read and studied when I pleased, and found news in what interested me. And what interested me was chiefly people, all kinds of people, and what they thought and said and how they lived, rather than officials, and what they said in their interviews and hand-outs about what "the people" thought and said. I had discovered that not many officials or bureaucrats really knew much about that. The A.P. discouraged roving, I knew, stylized everybody's copy to read alike, idealized anonymity, and wouldn't let a staff man publish a line elsewhere without home office approval. Why did anybody make a living writing except to be a person in his own special relationship to others? Yet the A.P. checks were regular if not sizeable.

So there it was: should we sell our years of freedom for those reliable checks and a pension? I had sold some fiction and thought I could live by that and writing articles and books. But I had no stake. A free-lancer without capital is only a slave adrift. I put Jim off for a few days, to think it over. Then I went to the bank and drew out our whole balance, a pitiful sum, for we were just then living beyond our means. Nym had said nothing to influence me, but I knew she wouldn't approve of bets at Paomachang; so I said nothing to her.

Shocked at what I had done, I sat next to her in the stand now and closed my eyes when the handicap was run, inwardly saying, "If I lose, that decides it. I sign on with A.P. If I win . . ."

After the race I opened my eyes and looked at the tally. My pony had come in second and I had trebled my money. I still said nothing and waited for the sweepstakes. This time I kept my eyes open. It was an impossible storybook kind of thing, and it happened to me only this once; but there was my number. I had drawn a horse, and now the beautiful little beast was winning.

"Darling," I said when it was all over and I had collected, "we're not working for A.P. after all!"

"It's going to be lovely starving with you."

"Thanks, but we aren't starving yet. I've just won the whole damned sweepstakes!"

Paomachang was a very small track and my winnings amounted to little more than a thousand dollars, but Nym's lap looked like the hoard of Ali Baba after I dumped the new bills into it. From then on she thought she had to watch me daily to keep me from the races. But I knew that I hadn't been bright, only lucky. The A.P. was in luck, too. They got a young Missourian, James D. White, for their Peking correspondent. He turned out to be one of the ablest men they ever hired.

Soon afterward an enraged Chinese groom, irked at a White Russian stablemaster for taking away most of his business, got even by feeding strychnine to more than a dozen ponies, among them our one and a half. We were about ready to drop riding, anyway, along with the racing set. We bought a pair of Japanese bicycles and found them superior in every respect except style as a conveyance in Peking. Then Sven Hedin gave us a beautiful white Sino-Russian hound, named Gobi. Second generation of a cross between a Kansu greyhound and a borzoi, he was the fastest thing on four legs in front of two wheels; he loved to fly along the level streets pulling my bike behind him.

Soon an American mail arrived with an envelope from the *Saturday Evening Post*. It had been a month on the way and inside was a slip which appeared to be a bill for seven dollars and a half.

"Did you subscribe to the *Post?*" I asked Nym, puzzled. "You'll send me back to Paomachang yet."

Nym frowned at the paper and plucked at her eyebrow. "I certainly did not," she said. "Do you think I've lost my mind?" Then suddenly she shrieked, "That's no bill, it's a check! And it's not seven dollars and fifty cents, it's seven hundred fifty dollars! For you!"

Still afraid it was a mistake we trotted off to the bank and presented the check at once. A little to our surprise it was cashed.

"We're rich!" I said to Nym. "We've got our stake. With the pay-off on my two gambles we can live here for a year." And that night we had Peking duck and champagne—with a tartar steak for Gobi.

The explanation came by the next mail. Months before I had sent an article to the *Post* entitled (after reading Spengler) "The Decline of Western Prestige." I had enclosed postage money and asked that the manuscript be forwarded to my agent when it was rejected. As I had had no word, I had forgotten about it. But here was a letter from George Horace Lorimer himself, congratulating me and buying the piece.

I got out a copy of my own letter to Lorimer and read it again. "What an impertinent ass I was!" I said. "But who would have expected Lorimer himself to read it?" I had said in effect that the *Post* was all wrong in its Far Eastern views and that its writers were out of touch. Japan was winning, not losing, and was getting richer and stronger, not going broke—the big myth of the time. Of course I was sure the *Post* wouldn't print me, I went on. I was an unknown. But I wished Lorimer to know the "facts of life" in the Far East before he sent my manuscript on its way.

Mr. Lorimer politely replied, in six pages, to correct my misinformation about their attitude toward new writers. He liked my story seven hundred and fifty dollars' worth, and hoped for more. It was the beginning of a beautiful friendship and of an alliance which would take me to every corner of the globe, for which pleasure the *Post* would pay me nearly a quarter of a million dollars over the next fifteen years.

My article was a condensed version of the last chapter of my first book, *Far Eastern Front,* which appeared soon afterward. The heart of it read:

> There can be no peace in Asia until the fruits of aggression are given up not simply in China but throughout the Orient. . . . With colonies everywhere in the East demanding freedom, will Europeans cling on, or will they have the courage to make definite efforts to liquidate their own conquests simultaneously with similar efforts [demanded] of Japan? . . . The step would by peaceful means, and with permanently civilizing effects, achieve a condition otherwise certain to be achieved by a series of bloody conflicts.

Alas, the people in London, Paris, Amsterdam and Washington who were the "kings of this earth" evidently did not read the *Post*. They would go on thinking it was much earlier than that, until Asia, in a tremendous upheaval at last, shattered their colonial timepieces forever.

CHAPTER 3

I Try a Headstand

"IF YOU WANT to understand China, Snow," said a bald, diminutive, hawk-nosed Sinologue named L. C. Arlington, pointing at the ground with a finger half of which was missing, "you've got to stand on your head and think *up!* First thing you do, master the language—that's a headstand in itself."

Arlington was then in his seventies and had been in China fifty years. The preface to his absorbing autobiography, *Through the Dragon's Eye,* was an epic all by itself, and only the beginning of his amazing adventures in China. He had been successively a shanghaied seaman, naval adviser to the Manchu Throne, officer in the Chinese navy (the knuckle he lost in the Sino-French war of the Eighties was the only casualty suffered in that farce, he used to say), official of the Chinese Customs Service, and expert on the Chinese theatre as well as the history of Peking. He had more "adopted" children—most of whom he put on the stage—than any man of his time.

Arlington adopted us in a way, too. He taught me a lot about China and Peking and I soon found he was right about the language. Without some knowledge of it no one can appreciate how greatly Chinese thought and behavior are influenced by the subtleties of their script. It has a life of its own that to this day dominates the present by its built-in reminders of past tradition and experience. Thanks to the good luck recorded in the previous chapter I was able to devote time to study it now and enter a world half way between journalism and academic life.

I have no natural gift for languages, and European languages are anyway of no help in learning Chinese. Between despair and patience, mostly on the part of my old Manchu teacher, Huang Li-shih, who knew no English, I did eventually learn enough *kuo-yü,* the national language of China, or what foreigners called Mandarin, to express myself and understand others in simple conversation. I never recognized more than 1,500 characters at best, but that was just enough to enable me to read some *pai-hua* ("plain speech"), the vulgate or written vernacular of the North. It saved me from remaining wholly a *hsia-tzu* or "blind man," as the Chinese call illiterates.

True mastery of Chinese is a lifetime job for a foreigner. There are 44,000 characters in the great *K'ang Hsi* dictionary compiled nearly three hundred years ago. Since then thousands of new words have been invented to cope with the inundation of modern Western thought and science. Scholars recognize from six to ten different and distinct forms of Chinese characters, tracing back more than 2,000 years before the Age of Pericles, down to the free-style abbreviations of today. Non-Chinese who can read and write sufficiently to consult the classics, as well as converse in correct tone and pronunciation, are very few. Of course one need know only the modern script to be literate, but "modern" might be held to include everything after the Emperor Ch'in (255-207 B.C.). The Chinese writing brush came into general use in that period and had a more profound effect than the invention of printing in China a thousand years later, or about five centuries before Gutenberg invented movable type.

To *speak* the language acceptably one should also know the four tones (nine in Cantonese) for at least a few hundred basic characters. There are dozens of homonyms in Chinese (even in identical tones) with different and often completely opposite meanings. Isolated characters (monosyllables) are in speech frequently unintelligible to Chinese themselves. Men often interrupt a conversation to write down a word for clarification. In my "blind-man" days when I would try to express myself in pidgin-English where no one understood a word of it someone invariably would lay a brush, inkstone and some rice paper before me, expecting me to write the characters for what I was saying. The assumption was that I was simply speaking some unknown dialect of Chinese. Writing, uniform and universal, would make it clear.

The old classical language is nowadays *spoken* scarcely more often than ancient Greek. For all practical purposes modern Chinese is polysyllabic even though the characters are written separately. It is the composition of these individual characters out of the original pictographs, ideographs, phonograms and other forms, and the creation of "new" words from character combinations, that makes Chinese as fascinating as the unraveling of a mystery story.

Since this is not a treatise on etymology one or two illustrations must suffice to suggest how the whole history and psychology of the people are wrapped up in their script in a way which has no exact counterpart in Western languages. In analyzing the pictograph for "surname" the student learns that it is a combination of the pictograph for woman with the pictograph meaning "to grow." But "woman," in turn, is simply man with breasts superimposed, a pictograph more plainly obvious in the older "seal character" in use 800-220 B.C. Going further, one would find that the character "grow" evolved from the pictograph for earth, plus something sprouting.

But why should "woman" be the radical or stem in "surname" instead of man? The answer must be that in the society which invented that character children took their family names from their mothers. And such turns out to be the historical fact. In very ancient times polyandry was the marriage system in China and children could be sure of their descent only on the mother's side. Hence they took matriarchal surnames, as is true even today in Tibet.

Finally, take the character *ai,* meaning "to love." It is made up of three "radical" characters, one superimposed on the other: the topmost character means "bird in flight" and "excited breathing," as from passion; the middle component is from the pictograph for "heart"; and the lower radical is for "man walking with dignity and grace." Integrated, they form the ideograph which not only means love and "to be subject to," "to covet" and "to admire," but in addition retains the imagery of each of its component parts.

These examples suggest how difficult it is to sever Chinese thinking from the cultural history of the land or to impose any unmodified ideology from outside so as to wipe out the past. Even if the Communists of today wished to do so they could not change the poetic calligraphy involved in the word "love." The characters for a boy, a girl and a tractor put together, for example, would not conceivably serve the same purpose.

I was enthralled by Chinese, although my study of it was too desultory owing to the necessity to continue to scrounge for a living. That first *Post* check and the Paomachang windfall did not last very long. When the Consolidated Press was dissolved the N. Y. *Sun* hired me to do a weekly column for a pittance which scarcely met the rent. I began to write for the old *Asia* magazine but it too had financial troubles and paid very little. For the next two years, while I was studying, writing a book and working as a part-time lecturer at Yenching University (which could pay me only a tiny honorarium), we lived chiefly on an occasional fat check from *The Saturday Evening Post*. All *too* occasional, then!

But it was in many ways the good life—ended too soon by war.

For one thing, we found a new home near Yenching and the Western Hills, which passed all expectation. I had met a Yenching-educated Christian Chinese banker named Jimmy Chuan.

"I have built a kind of retirement home in Hai-tien," he said. "That's the old village just south of the Yenching campus. I won't be ready to retire for several years and in the meantime we want to live in the city. Would you like to rent it while you're teaching at Yenching?"

I told him our circumstances and feared we couldn't afford it.

"Never mind the rent," he said. "Go and look at it. If you like it, pay me whatever you're paying now. Sixty a month?" He smiled. "Never mind, you take mine for forty!"

We cycled out and couldn't believe it. Inside the walls of Chuan's place was an acre of garden, fruit trees, and even a family-size swimming pool. The half-American, half-Chinese house was built U-shaped and perched so that through the living-room picture window you saw the Summer Palace and the Western Hills framed in breathtaking beauty. There were separate servants' quarters and a stable. The house itself was spanking new and each wing had a bath and a study.

We promptly moved to Hai-tien and found ourselves exurbanites as far as Peking proper was concerned. Our community now became the village itself, and the Chinese students and professors who mingled on terms of common intellectual and professional interest with a few Western students and teachers at Yenching, Tsing-hua and other nearby schools. Hai-tien itself was not part of the Yenching University campus, where most Chinese and foreign faculty members lived, but had been the home of Manchu bannermen who guarded the nearby palaces, the *Yuan-ming-yuan* (destroyed by European troops in 1860) and the "Mountain of the Ten Thousand Ancients" or Summer Palace. Residents of Hai-tien were of mixed classes but they spoke elegant Peking dialect and it was an excellent place to learn Chinese.

Yenching University had evolved from a missionary institution but was moving toward complete Chinese control, in accordance with the liberal ideals of its principal founder, Dr. J. Leighton Stuart, who was to be America's last resident ambassador at Nanking before the Communists took power. Stuart was largely responsible for raising the American funds to build Yenching and also for its distinguished architecture, a fine example of traditional Chinese, modified by Western materials and interior fittings and improvements. It was built in part on the site of the old *Yuan-ming-yuan* and retained some of the original landscaping, including a lovely lake in the center of the garden-like campus. On that lake on sunny winter days we used to watch aging Manchu retainers from Hai-tien give fascinating exhibitions of figure-skating on their sharp, curve-nosed, two-bladed native skates.

Here we lived in ideal circumstances for nearly two years, in touch with modern Chinese youth and thought on the university level, and within easy cycling range of one of the most historic and beautiful parts of China. There lay the old Bell Temple, the White Cloud Temple, the Jade Fountain and White Pagoda, and that whole cluster of holy places called *Pa-ta-ch'u,* amidst the groves and watered valleys of the pine-clad Western Hills—as well as the Summer Palace with its willow-shaded walks, its terraced buildings, its green lake and its marble boat. Such places, as well as the historical museums and most of the other buildings of the Winter Palace, the Temple of Heaven and the Altar of Agriculture, and scores of other wonders, had been open to the public since 1914.

And yet all this was but a pleasant mirage, on the surface of which the foreigner lived so agreeably on his favorable exchange rate, his extraterritoriality, and illusions that China would never change. Behind it an old society boiled and fermented toward an agonizing turnover of total revolution.   •

CHAPTER 4

Living China

WHEN I WAS living in Shanghai I began working with Yao Hsin-nung on a translation of Lu Hsun's "True Story of Ah Q," which remains the most influential single piece of fiction produced in the republican era, as Lu Hsun was its most important writer. After I arrived in Peking I invited Yao to come up and continue the collaboration. A graduate of Soochow University, Yao had never been abroad, but he had a facile command of English. Something rarer, among Christian-educated Chinese, he also knew China's classical and modern literature. Like all Chinese writers miserably paid for his original productions, he depended mainly on translations of foreign books into Chinese for a living—as was the case even with Lu Hsun.

Yao and I saw Lu Hsun in Shanghai several times and got his enthusiastic support for a projected book of English translations of contemporary short stories written in the spoken language, or *pai-hua*. It was Lu Hsun, Dr. Hu Shih, later Ambassador to the United States, and Chen Tu-hsiu, afterward secretary of the Communist party and subsequently expelled, who largely initiated the "literary renaissance" of 1919, which first firmly established *pai-hua* as the national language —a literary revolution scarcely less important than the political overthrow of the Manchu Dynasty.

Already revered as a scholar, teacher and great writer when I met him, Lu Hsun was a short, dark figure in his fifties, with bright warm eyes and a moist brow; he was incurably tubercular and had not long to live. Surprisingly, he had to stay in the French concession in hiding, and most of his books were banned by the Kuomintang Government. Although the Reds were later to make a national hero of him, Lu Hsun was not a Communist; only an ultra-conservative Confucian eye could discern anything very dangerous in his satire and humor.

"Ah Q" is the story of a typical illiterate coolie whose experiences, during the first revolution, show the utter failure of that event to reach the people. A near-equivalent in Western literature is the Czech classic, *The Good Soldier Schweik*. But Schweik at least had a place in the orderly military chaos of things, without knowing why. Ah Q had no place at all, without knowing why. Constantly baffled, seeing everything through a mirage of ignorance and superstition, knowing words and not their meaning, Ah Q goes from one humiliation to another, but each time philosophically rationalizes his defeats into victories and emerges as "the Superior Man." (See Confucius, see Nietzsche, see Walter Mitty.) Even when he is executed for a crime he did not commit, Ah Q goes to his death cheerfully singing, from a Chinese opera he did not understand, *"After twenty years I will be reborn again a hero."*

Communist intellectuals saw in Lu Hsun's story both an allegory of China's degradation in the world and the message that until they themselves carried the revolution to the illiterate peasantry, and brought them into the main current of modern life, China would never recover her lost greatness.

"Before the republic the people were slaves," as Lu Hsun himself put it. "Afterward, we became slaves of ex-slaves."

"Now that you have had the second or Nationalist revolution," I asked him, "do you feel there are still as many Ah Q's left as ever?"

Lu Hsun laughed. "Worse. Now they are running the country."

"Do you think Russia's form of government better suited to China?"

"I know nothing of Soviet Russia, but I have read much about prerevolutionary Russia and there are some similarities with China. No doubt we can learn from Russia. We can also learn from America. But for China there can be only one kind of revolution—a Chinese revolution. We too have our history to learn from."

It was through Lu Hsun (and Mme. Sun) that I met many of China's outstanding young writers and editors. Largely unknown to foreigners, they were, I discovered, the most popular and influential of the day with China's more serious-minded youths. Many of them, like Lu Hsun, lived in and out of hiding and exile, as their periodicals and books were in and out of legality or suppression. Few if any of those I knew were then Communists. They were Socialists in spirit, wanted freedom to agitate for reforms long since achieved in the West, and touched upon questions in their writing which the Kuomintang regarded as dangerous thought.

Yao and I made only a beginning of the translation of Lu Hsun's work before he had to return to Shanghai. After Yao left I continued, with the help of my tutor and some Chinese students, to explore fiction written in the vernacular. It was not often rewarding as literature but it was a thorough education in intellectual discontent. It opened many doorways into the thinking of people my own age in China and taught me something about the conditions under which writers worked —in constant fear, mixed despair and hope, and nearly always semi-starvation.

Pearl Buck and her husband Dick Walsh, who was editor of *Asia,* encouraged me by publishing many of these translated stories. John Day brought them out in book form, as *Living China.* This little volume may have had no significance as art but it was the first evidence of the growth of a modern spirit of protest and compassion in Chinese literature, and of a demand for social justice on the broadest scale, which for the first time in Chinese history recognized the importance of the "common man."

While Nym and I worked on this book we discovered that the giants of Russian literature had already made a far greater impression in China than most Western observers realized. They established a real cultural contact between the two countries hitherto unknown. The Russian tide came to China later than the European and American, reaching the intellectuals chiefly during the Nationalist period, when Pushkin, Tolstoy, Turgenev, Dostoevsky, Gogol and Chekhov were translated for the first time. By the mid-Thirties very few Soviet works had appeared in Chinese, and only the first volume of *Kapital* had been published. Even in the Red districts there was no complete Lenin.

After 1928 nearly all Russian works came under official ban. Many a student was arrested for possessing even *War and Peace* and *The Brothers Karamazov.* Later the Kuomintang "index" was extended to books by Dreiser, G. B. Shaw, Erskine Caldwell, Sinclair Lewis, John Steinbeck, and a long list of famous Western writers. Possession of the dangerous books could bring imprisonment or worse.

My own growing library of *sub rosa* books and periodicals was soon in constant use by Yenching students anxious to read the scarce or the forbidden. Not that any rigorous political censorship prevailed at Yenching; under Dr. Stuart we were relatively immune from surveillance imposed in other schools. Yenching was an upper-class institution whose students normally should have been political conservatives. But as the national crisis deepened, and class war merged with Japan's conquests in the North, a wave of radicalism began to spread there. By 1935 Yenching had unexpectedly become the birthplace of student protests which touched off a nationwide "rebellion of youth."

CHAPTER 5

"Between Fascism and Communism"

JAPAN HAD by now conquered nearly half a million square miles of China's territory in Manchuria and Inner Mongolia and was soon to reach deeper into the north. Simultaneously, Japanese diplomats urged Chiang Kai-shek to "stabilize Far Eastern peace" by signing an anti-Russian (anti-Comintern) alliance with them. That would have given Japan a legal position in China somewhat like America's post-war protectorate over Formosa. Tokyo contended that the Chinese were anti-Japanese merely because of Communist influence; if Chiang would only let Japan help him, Communism could be quickly crushed. But the Generalissimo had already suppressed all anti-Japanese organizations, and claimed he was nearing that final victory over the Reds which had eluded him for seven years. He feared that a Kuomintang-Japanese alliance would actually strengthen the Chinese Communists, politically, as it most certainly would have.

And yet, except for Japan's impatient and greedy seizures of Chinese territory, China and Japan might have found a common meeting ground. Ideologically, the two regimes seemed not far apart. The Kuomintang was much impressed by both Fascist Italy and Hitler's Germany. Chiang chose German officers to train his army, and Italians (before General Claire Chennault's day) to train his air force. Germans helped organize his political gendarmerie, the *Lan I Shc*, or "Blue Shirts," modeled after the Gestapo. Cadets in the Kuomintang military academies were taught the *fuehrer* principle of unquestioning loyalty to "Leader" Chiang, and that teaching soon reached public schools through the organization of Kuomintang youth corps.

The Kuomintang "tutelage period" was always a one-party dictatorship; no legal basis existed for an opposition. Although this dictatorship was inefficient and incomplete, opposition was possible only under shelter provided by militarists not yet wholly "assimilated," or in terms of open armed insurrection such as that led by the rival Communist party. There was no Bill of Rights, thousands were held in jail without trial, and executions went on daily, but as few records were published it was never possible to know just how many people were being killed.

Although the Reds had been driven to the West it was argued that the state power was still threatened from within and harsh measures were justified. Were the Communists really worse than either Nationalist dictatorship or Japanese conquest? I did not know, and I remained ambitious to find out, first hand. No correspondent had yet been inside the Red areas, but we did know that in rural China the toll of life had been far heavier than the outside world realized. On the advice of General von Seeckt a vast belt had been depopulated, burned and destroyed around the deeply "infected regions" in the south. Various official Kuomintang estimates of the dead before the early Soviet republics were finally destroyed in the Yangtze Valley ranged from two to six million people. Elsewhere, as the Kuomintang's own early slogans of land reform (originally for land redistribution) were repudiated and then became "subversive," the party frankly fell back on the old traditional alliance between the bureaucracy and the rural landlord-gentry class. Their hired *min-t'uan,* or local militia, were now armed by the Kuomintang and trained for war against the red bandits.

While all this was going on many foreigners lived in Shanghai and other treaty port oases blissfully unaware of the chaotic disintegration which was preparing rural China for violent revolution. This myopia was reflected in the testimony of Lt.-General Albert C. Wedemeyer a few years ago before a congressional committee. General Wedemeyer had never been in China before he replaced General Stilwell there during World War II, but he gave the senators a rather idyllic picture of that land in the Thirties. "So many observers with whom I talked in the Far East who had lived there many years," he said, "refer to this [as] the golden decade—mind you now, under Chiang Kai-shek's regime and approximately the same leaders whom we have today." *

Perhaps it glittered for a handful of foreign business men and their

* *Institute of Pacific Relations, Hearings:* Committee on the Judiciary, U.S. Senate, Washington, D.C., 1951. Part 3, p. 802.

native compradores. It was also a time when there was never a year in which millions did not perish in famines, floods, epidemics and other preventable disasters and when millions of farmers were losing their land. Chiang Kai-shek's Nanking government was always announcing plans to remedy these situations, and always postponing them, while the greater part of the national budget went into continuous campaigns of the Generalissimo to unify the warlord system under his single command. Consider one typical mid-decade report from my old "disaster" file of that period:

> Shanghai, March 26 (1935)—Twelve million people in the Yangtze Valley are in the grip of famine and face starvation. This news is brought today by John Earl Baker, special investigator [of the China International Famine Relief Commission], who has just returned from a long tour of the affected districts . . . Many deaths have occurred near the capital [Nanking] among starving people who have been using a sort of Fuller's earth for making soup to provide some kind of filling for empty stomachs." *

That is what I remember about the "golden decade"—that, and the growing fear and reaction among right-wing Kuomintang leaders who sought the answer to spreading rebellion in terms of ever-greater measures of repression.

In the cities the Blue Shirts soon extended the "White Terror" from the pursuit of Communists and Left Nationalists to include virtually all critics of the regime—non-party patriots, writers, teachers, editors, journalists and even business men. Debates and arguments raged in the middle schools and universities, where fascism and the "leader principle" had advocates among professors close to the Generalissimo. Yenching was anti-fascist, however, with a few exceptions.

Of course these terms had a limited meaning in China, and I don't wish to leave the impression that Chiang Kai-shek was an Eastern Mussolini or Hitler, whatever he may have aspired to be. Neither man was really a possibility in China; Europe's problems were vastly different. China was a backward agrarian state in which the choice of profound change or perish was no longer postponable. In the context of its history China *had to have revolutionary leadership,* just as China had to have it to survive in the time of Shih Huang-ti, two hundred years before Christ. And whatever else he was, Chiang Kai-shek was no revolutionary.

Under Chiang Kai-shek's government some attempt was made to

* *Peking Leader,* March 27, 1935.

establish rule by constitution and law, some roads were built, modern banks were established, some flood control work progressed, scientific study was somewhat encouraged, educational facilities improved, and women began to claim legal equality with men. Modernization along such lines was certainly more rapid than under previous regimes; had there been no Japanese invasion Chiang might have succeeded in unifying the country under right-wing dictatorship. But the whole pace of change was far too slow to cope with the deep crisis inside Chinese society. Increasingly Chiang resorted to despotism to hold back the tidal demand for revolutionary measures.

It was, however, unfair to call Chiang a despot and let it go at that. "He who wishes to establish absolute power, such as the ancients called tyranny," said Machiavelli, "must change everything." Chiang Kai-shek wanted absolute power, but he did not really want to change anything. It is not unfitting that his name, *Chieh-shih*, (Kai-shek) means "boundary stone," a fixed image indeed. In a time of utmost chaos he was often concerned with form, convention and propriety and inwardly concerned with prevention of change. He was not a great tyrant, only a petty one; he failed not because he was Caesar or killed too many people but because he killed too few of the right people; he never understood that his worst enemies were inside his own camp. Chiang was not resolute, only obstinate; not wise, only obsolete; not disciplined, only repressed; not original, only a scavenger among the relics of the past; and not ruthless, merely vain—as none knew better than the greedy parasites who surrounded and finally consumed him.

"Chiang?" laughed L. C. Arlington one day in Peking. "He won't last. He's not tough enough up here," he said, pointing to his bald pate. "He's no good at standing on his head, and even when he does he only knows how to think *down,* not *up!*"

Still, it seemed a real possibility that Chiang might lead China into the Axis, until Japan's invasion decided otherwise. Even Dr. Stuart, who had hopes for Chiang, considered it a peril, and encouraged discussion on the campus to help educate teachers and students concerning the real nature of fascism. He asked me to lead one faculty debate on the subject, in preparation for which I studied fascism systematically for the first time. And it was not the reports of fascism's enemies so much as the works of its apologists such as Pareto, and most of all Mussolini's own demagogy about the "Corporate State," and Hitler's ravings, which made a thorough anti-fascist of me. I now knew what

I was against, at least, and they represented most of it. I later discovered that my attitude was identical with Nehru's views of the time, as summed up in his *Autobiography:*

"As these pages show, I am very far from being a Communist. I dislike dogmatism and the treatment of Karl Marx's writing as revealed scripture which cannot be challenged, and the regimentation and heresy hunts which seem to be a feature of modern Communism. I dislike also much that has happened in Russia . . ."

At this time I also decided, as did Nehru, that whatever the ultimate truth about Russia might turn out to be, *"as between Nazi-Fascism and Communism* my sympathies were with Communism," not of love for its friends but of dislike of its enemies. One enemy at a time was enough for me; and it was Hitler, not Russia, who denied even the principle of human brotherhood and glorified barbarism and racial engorgement.

In these years I read some basic Marxist-Leninist texts and the history of Communism in Europe and Asia. Nym studied philosophy at Yenching, including a course in Hegel in which she excelled, although the lectures were entirely in Chinese! Both of us felt a growing conviction that the Communist-Nationalist war in China would in the long run prove more important than the Japanese war. But it was not Marx or Lenin or Stalin or Mao Tse-tung who reached me with the logic of Socialism.

At an auction in Peking I bought a complete set of George Bernard Shaw and read him thoroughly for the first time, all his prefaces and his plays. It was Shaw who convinced me that the advancement of mankind beyond the predatory stage of human development and the replacement of existing systems of economic cannibalism by planned co-operation for the common good, in accordance with the principle "from each according to his ability, to each according to his need," were attainable good ends and inevitable if men were to survive. While in my mind and heart I accepted the Fabian view of history from here on out, my conception of Socialism was to evolve with years and experience, until it merged with a general view of present history as man's last frantic improvisations on the road to that unification of the world where civilization may begin.

CHAPTER 6

We Spark a Rebellion

LATE IN 1935 students of Yenching University spontaneously staged a street demonstration in Peking which touched off nationwide protests that probably saved North China from falling to Japan by default. The idea and the planning of this outburst of patriotic indignation originated in our living room.

"Now I know," I said to Nym in the midst of it, "why people like W. H. Donald, Putnam Weale, Tom Millard and other newspaper men mixed up in China's internal affairs in the past. You can't just stand by and watch a lady you love being ravished and do nothing about it. And Peking is a nice old lady indeed."

Japanese demands of November were the climax of months of infiltration into "North China." We then used the term to mean Hopei and Chahar provinces, which lay just south of the Great Wall. After the conquest of Manchuria and Inner Mongolia, Japan had momentarily halted her armed advance when the Generalissimo directed his chief of staff, Ho Ying-chin, to sign a truce which in effect recognized the new status. The agreement set up an "autonomous" or buffer area covering the two large Northern provinces, of which Peking was the capital. But even within this area the Japanese used their troops to carve out a "demilitarized zone," between Peking and the Great Wall, and put a puppet in charge. From this zone they flooded North China with Korean and Japanese agents who bribed officials, took over what houses and property they needed, and opened scores of shops for the sale of cheap merchandise, heroin, morphine and opium brazenly smuggled in from Manchukuo.

General Sung Cheh-yuan, an old Nationalist soldier, held administrative responsibility over the Hopei-Chahar "autonomous" council. He was under such constant pressure that he had to shift officials and policies pretty much at Japanese demands. This had confusing results. For example, earlier policy had been to force opium smokers to take out licenses. Hundreds of violators of that law had been beheaded outside the walls of Peking, *pour encourager les autres*. This was somehow part of the Kuomintang "New Life Movement." But suddenly hundreds of other "Ah Q.'s," exactly like those beheaded, had to be treated tenderly when they patronized the Korean narcotics dens now elaborately protected by the Peking-Tientsin police.

At last the Japanese decided to end the farce and sever North China from Kuomintang authority completely. As they were not yet ready to go to war about it they called in their genius of intrigue, the mis-named "Lawrence of Manchuria," who had master-minded the Mukden "incident," General Kenji Doihara. Doihara reputedly put ten million newly printed Chinese dollars on the table and demanded that General Sung declare his independence from Chiang Kai-shek's Nanking government. And he produced documents, I was told by one of Sung's young secretaries, Ma Yung-han, purporting to show that the Generalissimo had already agreed in principle to replace Sung, if Japan insisted.

Such facts were more or less known to foreign correspondents; we had managed to cable something about it abroad. But the Kuomintang censors kept mention of Japan's demands out of the Chinese press. Doihara brought new troops into Tientsin and the legation quarter in Peking.* Then he hired some professional mourners, pimps, dope addicts and aging ex-officials of the old Manchu regime to parade the streets of the two cities, carrying placards demanding North China's "independence." Japanese newspapers reported "enormous popular support for a separatist movement led by General Sung," who in fact did nothing to foster the idea, but was afraid to suppress it.

One night my Chinese friend came from Sung's headquarters directly to see me. Ma was agitated to the point of tears. Old Sung, he reported, was ready to cave in to Doihara. He had repeatedly telegraphed Nanking for help against the Japanese if he resisted, but Chiang Kai-shek had given only ambiguous replies. Sung could not face an armed Japanese invasion alone, and he did not want to become another case for the impotent League of Nations. To keep Japan's armed forces out, he was going to set up a North China "separate" government.

"It's a pity," I said, "because Doihara is bluffing. I've just come back from two months in Manchuria and Japan, and I'm sure Japan isn't ready for war yet. In a showdown Doihara would back down."

"That's it," Ma replied, "but Sung can't gamble alone. It's all settled now. So we'll soon be another Manchukuo—lacking only Japanese troops."

* By the Boxer Protocol of 1900 the major powers were entitled to keep small guard troops in Peking and Tientsin.

The next day one of my journalist students, Chang Chao-lin, called in to ask about the rumor that Sung had gone over to Japan. Chang was then head of the student union at Yenching, which had secretly revived despite the continued ban on student organizations. He was a tall open-faced Manchurian who, like hundreds of other patriotic youths, was on the verge of turning against a government which denied legal outlets for their wrath.

I told Chang what I knew and he began to weep.

"Crying won't help," I heard myself saying. "We've got to act."

"What do you mean, *we?*" Chang asked, hopefully.

"Why, yes, what *do* I mean? I'm supposed to be neutral."

"But we're not!" broke in Nym. "Why pretend? Ed means we want to help—all we can. A lot of other American friends here are as mad as we are."

"Good," he said. "Then maybe you can help us get this published." He took a paper out of his pocket and we sat down and translated it. A rather pathetic petition to Chiang Kai-shek, it asked that he permit freedom of organization and speech, and "stop arresting patriots." It demanded a Bill of Rights, no less.

"It's too early to bring out this kind of thing—or too late," I said. "It won't save North China. In the first place most of the foreign press will just call it propaganda and the Chinese press won't dare mention it."

"But you could send it abroad."

"What good would that do? The Japanese would get it and some of you would be arrested for signing it. That's all."

"What else can we do?"

"I don't know," I said skeptically. "A few students . . ."

"A handful of students started the New Youth Movement that saved China in 1919," said Nym. "The whole country is just waiting for a sign that youth is still alive and they'll rise to back you."

I wasn't so sure. It was true that the New Youth Movement begun in Peking seventeen years earlier had brought on such an anti-Japanese boycott that Japan had had to back down in her demands for concessions and territory which would have made all China her vassal even then. But now?

Chang delayed issuing the "manifesto." He left us, determined to call another meeting of the union and lead an attempt to form an all-Peking students federation. Peking, with its dozen or more colleges and universities, and scores of middle schools and primary schools, was

still the student and intellectual center and conscience of the nation,
to which all others looked for leadership.

"What you ought to do," Nym said when he came back with Wang
Ju-mei, Ch'en Han-p'o and others to consult us, "is to stage a mock
funeral on the streets—make a corpse of North China being buried by
the Japanese and Chinese officials."

Her suggestion seemed futile to these earnest youths, who were
now passionately convinced that the fate of China rested with them
alone. The astounding fact was that momentarily it did, because in
China students had a very unusual role. For centuries scholars preparing for the imperial examinations and public office had held the
highest prestige, and this was still shared by modern students, to whom
the wisest gray-haired peasant was always ready to listen with respect.
Moreover, most students had influential relatives, and officials had to
handle them more circumspectly than coolies. At a time when no unarmed political party could exist, it was only in schools and universities that peaceful political protest could still be organized—as was to
prove true twenty years later in Poland and Hungary.

"Nym is right about the demonstration, if not the funeral," I said.
"A display by unarmed students opposed to the phony independence
movement might indeed make all the difference."

"If we expose ourselves we'll just be arrested and called red bandits," said Wang Ju-mei thoughtfully. "They'll never let us get onto
the streets."

"Not if *all* the students of Peking join in," I said, "and not if you
take the police—and the Japanese—by surprise."

"But how will anybody hear of it? The Chinese press wouldn't dare
report it."

"If *everybody* joins in—for you, not against you—they'll have to
report it," said Nym.

I promised that I would get other correspondents to the scene of
action and fully report it. What sympathy they won abroad would
depend on their own behavior and what sense their slogans made.

The names of the student leaders present then and in later conferences would still mean nothing to a Western reader, although they
were to become famous in China. Mostly Christians or Christian-
trained youths, they represented the highest calibre of the North China
student body of the time. There was not a Communist among them
and yet within a few years nearly all would have joined the Communists, in the patriotic war against Japan.

Back and forth the ball bounced, as the students formulated their own prescriptions about how to save China. For most of them it was the first concrete thinking they had done about what war with Japan would mean to them. What emerged was a series of demands on both General Sung and Chiang Kai-shek to reject Doihara's ultimatum, to end civil war, unite all factions for resistance to save China, begin "mass training and mobilization," and give people freedom to know the truth and prepare for what was coming. China must rely on herself alone, they proclaimed.

December ninth was chosen for the first city-wide student strike and demonstration. That was one day before General Sung was to announce the "separation" of North China from the South. Dr. Stuart knew that his Yenching students were "up to something," but he did not realize that they were contacting captains in all the other Peking schools, where underground student groups like Yenching's had come to life again with amazing swiftness. In a few days leaflets, posters and banners were prepared, first-aid teams were organized, couriers were chosen and instructed, and the general staff of a newly formed all-Peking students federation had mapped out a route of march.

On the eve of North China's greatest student demonstrations Nym and I stayed up most of the night copying out translations of the students' "demands" to release next day to the foreign press.

CHAPTER 7

Action

ON DECEMBER NINTH students gathered at a dozen different gates and memorial arches throughout the city. From these their columns converged toward the main streets and joined at the wide avenue leading into the Winter Palace, where a high Kuomintang official then had offices. There the students were to meet to present their petitions to the government.

It was the first time any of us had seen mass political courage displayed by educated Chinese youths, as apart from common soldiers, then still held in contempt. The sight was exhilarating to both participants and spectators. Thousands and thousands of blue-clad youngsters marched and sang their way to the Forbidden City in defiance of both their own police and conservative parents. Nothing like it had happened in Kuomintang China for eight years. Nym and I were ordinarily no parade-watchers, but we took our place beside the leaders of this one proudly. Other correspondents—notably, Frank Smothers of the Chicago *Daily News,* Jimmy White of the A.P., Mac Fisher of the U.P., and C. M. MacDonald, of the *Times*—shared our sentiments.

Caught unprepared and puzzled by the presence of sympathetic Westerners, the local police made only half-hearted and spasmodic attempts to interfere. Here and there when an arrest was attempted the blue-clad mass invariably surrounded the police, pressed leaflets on them, and shouted patriotic slogans. Usually the baffled police retired with grins of embarrassment. Weren't they also patriots? Then the whole fire department was called out and hoses were turned on the paraders. The youths swept on, drenched but triumphant.

Suddenly the political gendarmes, in black leather jackets, led by a nephew of Chiang Kai-shek, descended on the main column in motor-cycles and sidecars with mounted machine-guns. Flourishing tommy-guns, they pushed into the throng and indiscriminately clubbed boys and girls alike. Several dozen were arrested at random. But the job was too big for them; the crowd rolled on. For a tense moment the "leather-jackets" leveled weapons at the demonstrators in ready-to-fire position. A few rifles were fired in the air; the parade wavered but held. Correspondents and camera men closed in, hoping foreign witnesses would be enough to prevent a tragedy. We were. An officer threw up his hands and ordered his men to lower their guns.

"The Cossacks," Nym cried, "have joined the students."

Chinese shopkeepers, housewives, artisans, monks, teachers and silk-gowned merchants applauded from the streets, or ran out to get leaflets. Even ricksha coolies shouted the forbidden slogans: "Down with the bogus independence movement! Arrest the traitors! Down with Japanese imperialism! Save China!" The final meeting at the Heavenly Gate filled the immense plaza, where at last some of the police openly joined in the slogan shouting.

The first Peking demonstration made headlines all over the world and vernacular papers in defiance of the censors printed reports of it throughout the country. China was coming to life. Within a few days youth organizations sprang up in response in Tientsin, Shanghai, Hankow, Canton and all major cities, including at last even Nanking. Demonstrations began all over the country. Soon the students were joined by many teachers. On December 17th a second massive demonstration swept Peking and Tientsin and tens of thousands of students now joined the ranks in a more serious affair. Although many were injured and nearly 200 were arrested, a third demonstration was held a week later which for the first time called for an end to civil war in China and a "united front" to resist Japan.

Nanking vainly issued instructions to school principals to impose discipline and control, and in the South doubled and trebled guards around the schools. Sympathy and patriotic emotion had by then so permeated the police, officials and soldiers, however, that orders were only loosely enforced and few students were harmed. Under the shelter of an aroused public opinion the long-suppressed National Salvation Association was revived among adults and enlisted the aid even of conservatives in the organization of another boycott of Japanese goods.

The Japanese time-table, as we had guessed, was not prepared for any of this. The day after the first demonstration General Sung informed Doihara that he could not be responsible for proclaiming "independence" against the public will. Alarmed at the results of Doihara's abortive maneuvers, Tokyo now recalled him. Both the Japanese foreign ministry and the war office issued conciliatory statements denying any intention of using force to annex North China.

From now on Sung met all Japanese demands by dilatory tactics or by going off to "sweep the tombs of his ancestors," an old Confucian custom. It was an unusually protracted sweeping trip which was finally to convince the Japanese that nothing less than a major invasion would get them what they wanted in China. But by then internal pressures and external events would have left the Kuomintang no alternative but to commit the nation to all-out resistance.

The student rebellion of 1935-36 was the beginning of the end of China's non-resistance policy. Its greatest immediate impact fell on the Manchurian exiles in Peking. Manchurian (*Tungpei*) University students proved most active in extending the urban demonstration to the countryside. During the holidays many students poured into the villages to relate the facts about Japanese conquest of their homeland, and exhort the people to prepare for war. Others went to Sianfu, where the exiled Manchurian leader, Marshal Chang Hsueh-liang, was deputy commander-in-chief of Chiang Kai-shek's "red bandit suppression" headquarters. Marshal Chang welcomed them and gave them jobs as agitation-propaganda workers among his forces. Soon the whole Manchurian University shifted to Sian, which was shortly to become the scene of a rebellion that finally forced Chiang Kai-shek irrevocably into the anti-Axis camp.

Although the Japanese insisted that the whole student affair was run by Communists, the truth was that its leaders were inspired by Western national-patriotic ideals rather than any Moscow propaganda, of which there was little around at the time. Mao Tse-tung has said that modern revolutionary Chinese history embraced a period of thirty years, beginning in 1919 and covering six main "stages." The fourth "stage" was the December Ninth (1935) Student Movement. Communists are not slow to claim credit at any time, but concerning the "outburst of the December Ninth Movement of Revolutionary Youth" Mao admits that his party did *not* lead. "The strangest thing of all," wrote Mao, "was that the Communist Party was in an utterly defenseless position in all the cultural institutions in the Kuomintang-controlled area." *

In Pao-an within a few months I was to speak to Mao Tse-tung about the "outburst of revolutionary youth" as I had seen it develop from the start. It was clear to me that he knew very little about it. But it was also clear that he could not believe that mere Christian-trained patriots had begun it, and (of all places!) in Yenching, a college run by American "imperialists." Experts on resolving "contradictions," the Communists have never to this day quite figured this one out.

The truth was that the students of that period were neither pro-Kuomintang nor pro-Communist—merely pro-China.

This experience taught me that, among all the causes of revolution, the total loss of confidence by educated youths in an existing regime is the one indispensable ingredient most often neglected by academic historians of that phenomenon. The profound failure of the Kuomintang to play any dynamic role of guidance or inspiration in this critical period made it a symbol of pessimism, stagnation and repression and in the years of decision that lay ahead drove hundreds of the ablest and most patriotic young men and women to the Red banners as China's last hope. Among them were scores of Dr. J. Leighton Stuart's best Yenching-Christian students.

* *On the New Democracy,* by Mao Tse-tung, London, 1954. Page 260.

CHAPTER 8

"Wu Wei Erh"

SEVERAL FRIENDS encouraged me to apply for a Guggenheim grant to conduct a two-year field study of the agrarian crisis in China, particularly as it related to "red banditry." As far as I know only the Guggenheims gave fellowships in China, limited to one a year. One of my most enthusiastic sponsors for the project was (Jimmy) Yen Yang Chu, head of the Ting Hsien rural experiment. Yen sought to demonstrate that basic agrarian social, economic and political reform techniques could be applied in China by peaceful means under Kuomintang rule. If the Kuomintang failed, he believed, the Communists would soon and certainly impose the same changes by revolution. He was right; but too few listened. My other sponsors made strange company: Dr. J. Leighton Stuart, Dr. Amadeus Grabau of the Chinese Geological Survey, Lin Yu-tang, Lu Hsun, and—J. P. Marquand, who was then in Peking doing his Mr. Moto stories.

Alas, the Guggenheim board remained unimpressed. That year's fellowship went to a psychology student for "a study in Chinese racial and psychological characteristics as revealed by Chinese facial expression." The psychologist eventually turned up in Peking and for weeks went about scrutinizing the inscrutable Chinese with great energy. He hired a Chinese acquaintance of mine to tell people stories to make them portray pain, hilarity, anger, pity, desire, etc., while he took snapshots.

About that time the *Daily Herald* of London appointed a new editor who decided that it was time to enlarge their China service. I had been acting as a string correspondent for the *Herald* for several years; now they offered me a more lucrative post as special correspondent. As a chastened Guggenheim reject I was glad to leave the academic world and return to the "dynamics of reality," or chasing headlines again. We left our Hai-tien paradise and moved back inside Peking, where once more we found much for little, in the wonderful old mansion that had been Dr. Stuart's residence before Yenching moved to the suburbs. It was a huge rambling place with wisteria-draped walls that enclosed almost a square block near the old Fox Tower and embraced

147

a lovely garden, tennis court and stables. The Chinese greenhouse made a cool summer studio and a potting house served the same purpose in winter.

The *Herald,* although the official Labour Party paper of England, was privately owned by Odhams Press, a multi-million-dollar publishing corporation. Among its products was the *Feathered World,* organ of Britain's most patriotic poultry growers. Soon after we returned to Peking I received from the *Feathered World*'s editor an assignment to photograph a Chinese hen laying an egg on a dung heap. China's dehydrated eggs (packed by Armour) were then menacing the security of the British hen, and Odhams was leading a crusade to have the alien albumen barred from the King's markets. My wife replied for me. It was, she wrote, impossible to procure such a photograph for two good reasons: no Chinese hen ever announced the arrival of an ovum without some small boy rushing to the scene to catch the prize as it dropped; and dung being very valuable in China it never stood around idle in hills but was immediately put to work as fertilizer.

From the *Daily Herald* itself I received no such bizarre requests, nor any directives to "slant" copy. I often sent the *Herald* exact duplicates of articles I wrote for the New York *Sun,* although their politics were poles apart. It made no difference. The *Sun* never changed a word of my copy, while the *Herald* edited or rewrote almost everything. The arrangement seemed to satisfy both.

But if we had Colonel McCormicks who thought all Chinese were laundrymen, or psychologists who fancied that starvation looked "different" on a Chinese face, we also had some fine American teachers and scholars who, backed by their universities, became outstanding authorities on Chinese art, language, history, geography and general culture. In Peking they could work with the best native scholars and freely explore the archives, the museums and the living society around them. And here, also, in little more than a decade, the American Foreign Service built up a remarkable group of able young language officers.

The China career service had been made possible by the Foreign Service Act of 1924. That far-seeing piece of legislation was intended to free the foreign service from partisan politics along lines of the British career service. It sought to abolish the "spoils system," a hangover from Civil War days whereby the best posts abroad had been reserved for political appointees in reward for financial contributions made to the party in power. While the Act was still enforced, candidates for the China career service were selected by tough competitive examinations, and on the basis of merit, aptitude and general competence alone. The idea was that political appointees were eventually to be replaced everywhere, even as heads of legations and embassies, by this new generation of men trained to know the countries to which they were accredited, and how to safeguard America's fundamental and long-range interests in foreign relations.

Both China and Japan presented difficult language and social-political problems which required deep and constant study by such experts if our policies were not to become hopelessly mired in illusions and fantasy. In China especially the new career service speedily began to justify itself, and the quality and *esprit de corps* of our representatives notably improved. After 1941 our China language officers were to prove beyond any doubt their superiority over political appointees who sometimes could not even pronounce the names of the high officials to whose government they were accredited.

Men like Edmund Clubb, Edwin Stanton, Robert Smythe, John Davies, John Stuart Service, Raymond Ludden, Edward Rice, Robert Spencer Ward, Philip Sprouse, Laurence Salisbury, Arthur Ringwalt and a few others were soon to become a most valuable corps of specialists. As the best of them had to become conspicuous for their judgment in matters affecting the war years and the revolution, in contradiction to views held by certain Congressmen at home who lived in dense ignorance about China, the corps was destined to ultimate dissolution. Within two decades they would be rewarded for their hard work by slanderous attacks from McCarthy and the China Lobby until not a Chinese-speaking officer from the senior career service was left in the chambers where vital United States policies and decisions on Asia were made. Only a nation of very great power and wealth can afford such "conspicuous waste" and even the United States could not afford it much longer.

In the days when it never occurred to an American that to seek the truth about China was dangerous, we had an ambassador in Peking who encouraged all who did so. Nelson Trusler Johnson was our first Chinese-speaking envoy in China for many years. As one of the few men in our service who had opposed an Allied intervention against the Nationalists in 1927, advocated by our former envoy, MacMurray, he continued to think of the Generalissimo as a great leader and potential savior of China. But he stood above all for neutrality. He disapproved even of Americans who took sides against Japan, and he looked askance at my activity with the students. Mr. Johnson did genuinely believe, however, in the value of any and all work which

helped broaden our knowledge of China, although he tended to prefer projects which concentrated on the era of the *yin* bones or other
prehistoric periods. Nevertheless, when I published *Living China,*
which contained stories by many anti-Kuomintang writers, a number
of whom had been killed by assassins working for Chiang Kai-shek,
he wrote me a letter of generous praise for the effort and urged me to
continue my work on current Chinese literature.

Among Mr. Johnson's furnishings was a fine piece of calligraphy
which he carried from office to office. It was a famous Taoist motto,
Wu Wei Erh, Wu Pu Wei, meaning "through not-doing, all things are
done." For an America stubbornly isolationist in a world about to
catch fire it was an appropriate motto of the times. I also fervently
hoped that we could avoid entanglement in China. But I disagreed
with Mr. Johnson that we could be both of the world and above it, or
that we could possibly hang onto our special privileges in China and
end by not fighting either Japan or China—or both—to defend the
whole system of Western dominance.

These convictions were increasingly to place me in conflict with
Mr. Johnson's views of what was proper behavior for an American
neutral. But as a believer in "through not-doing, all things are done"
Mr. Johnson did nothing to interfere with my activities—not even
when, as was soon to happen, I became Boswell to Mao Tse-tung.

CHAPTER 9

I Cross the Rubicon

IN THE MONTHS just before I went to Red China and met the Chinese
Communist leaders for the first time I did not understand why things
obvious to me were not so to everyone else. That we were going to
get into a war in Asia seemed as certain to me as the logical way to
avoid it.

My own study and observation of the Japanese in Manchuria and
China convinced me that they wanted China not for a war against
Russia but as the base for a general assault on the whole European
colonial system. The United States would "inevitably" become involved—and I was opposed to it. For even if we won that war, I knew

by now that we were simply not equipped to decide the future of China. Our one way to stay out of the conflict was to renounce our special privileges in China and negotiate a new and equal treaty with her, as Germany and Russia had done, including the withdrawal of our gunboats and troops from Eastern Asia. This would have obliged the European powers to arm their colonial subjects for self-defense on a mass scale—which could in turn be effective only if accompanied by guarantees of national freedom worth defending. And why not? Was this not consistent with our American belief in self-determination?

Curious as it seems today, those views were enthusiastically received at the *Saturday Evening Post*. It also published my prediction of a major Sino-Japanese war well ahead of time and a forecast of its ultimate results. In an article called "The Coming Conflict in the Orient" I wrote, in June, 1936:

> In her great effort to master the markets and the inland wealth of China, Japan is destined to break her imperial neck. This catastrophe will occur not because of automatic economic collapse in Japan. It will come because the conditions of suzerainty which Japan must impose on China will prove humanly intolerable and will shortly provoke an effort of resistance that will astound the world.

But the United States was not Switzerland, despite the isolationist Congress of the day. Although we might do nothing to help China, I did not think that we would, in the long run, let the colonial powers down in Asia. Neither did the Russians think so. I wrote then:

> They [the Russians] trust that the burden of chastising Japan may fall to the Americans and the British before it is unavoidably thrust on the socialist shoulders of the Soviet Union . . . The Bolsheviks are convinced that Eastern war [with the West] will bring the Chinese Communists into power. And their prophecies, even when due allowance is made for wish fancy, are heavily freighted with historical logic.

Such expectations seem reasonable enough today, but Western policy-makers of the time ridiculed both notions. China, they said, would never go Communist. "The Chinese," was their explanation, "are far too individualistic." Secondly, "The Chinese will never fight. They're basically pacifists. Nobody can make soldiers out of coolies." They expected Japan to win a quick, complete victory in any major quarrel with China—and then turn on Russia.

One of the few foreign military experts to question either of those pre-war platitudes was Joseph Stilwell, then a colonel and our military attaché in Peking. "There's nothing wrong with China's human material," he said repeatedly, "but plenty wrong with the corrupt leadership. Under officers of high moral and technical qualifications the Chinese could become fighting men the equal of any on earth."

Stilwell had been impressed by the performance of the Chinese Reds against Chiang Kai-shek, as an indication of what the nation might do on a vast scale against an alien invader. For years they received no outside aid and always lacked modern industrial bases. They relied solely on a peasant economy. In major campaigns their small rural areas had been surrounded by numerically superior forces with ten to twenty times their fire power.

"Those Reds may be bandits, as Chiang says they are," Joe burst out to me one day, "but bandits or not, they're masters of guerrilla warfare. I don't know what they're preaching but to me it looks like they've got the kind of leaders who win. I mean officers who *don't* say, 'Go on, boys!' but '*Come on,* boys!' If that's the case and they had enough of them, they could keep the Japs busy here till kingdom come."

But neither of us then knew what the so-called Reds were. We didn't even know for sure whether they were "real" Communists. After nine years of civil war "Red China" was more *terra incognita* than Arabia Felix. I had confidentially proposed to both the *Sun* and the *Herald* that I go in and try to crack the blockade around the Communist-held areas in Northwest China. Both endorsed my plan. The *Herald* offered me all expenses and a handsome bonus if I succeeded. Harrison Smith, then of Random House, also made me a small advance against a possible book. With that support I went to Shanghai, where I again saw Mme. Sun Yat-sen. I sought her help, so that at least I should be received by the Reds as a neutral, not a spy. And shortly after I returned to Peking, in the spring of 1936, it was Chingling who made the arrangements. Through her I was put in touch with a professor in Peking who gave me a letter to Mao Tse-tung, together with other advice on how to contact the Red underground in Sianfu.

In June, 1936, just as the Generalissimo announced preparations for a sixth "final annihilation drive" against the Reds in the north, I set forth on this singular journey which was to affect my own life profoundly. Intensely excited by the prospect that lay ahead, I was aware, as I took the express for Sianfu, that I was crossing a Rubicon.

For once I was absolutely right.

CHAPTER 10

And Break a Blockade

I WENT DIRECTLY to the Guest Hostel upon my arrival in Sian, took a room and awaited a caller who introduced himself simply as "Wang Mu-shih"—Wang the Pastor—to whom I gave my letters of introduction. This fat and jolly English-speaking Christian (or ex-Christian) had come to see me and secretly put me into contact with Chinese Communists in hiding there. As plans to smuggle me into the Red areas involved the direct knowledge and help of the Manchurian army and its commander, Marshal Chang Hsueh-liang, I was now perforce made privy to a situation which six months later would erupt in the arrest of Chiang Kai-shek by his own subordinates in Sian.

Chang Hsueh-liang, former ruler of Manchuria, had retreated with his well-equipped army in 1931 in obedience to Chiang Kai-shek's orders not to resist Japan's conquest but to rely on the League of Nations. The Generalissimo later put Chang's Tungpei (Manchurian) Army—150,000 troops—to fighting the Reds, but as exiles they felt that their real enemy was Japan. The Reds' battlefield slogans and propaganda, "Don't kill Chinese! Unite with us to win back your homeland!" quickly infected their fighting morale. When the Communists won important battles and in ambush captured several Tungpei generals they treated them as honored guests. Mao Tse-tung and Chou En-lai spent days to convince them that they genuinely desired peace and a united front against Japan. Then Chou En-lai escorted the generals and most of their captured troops back to their own lines.

These tactics had produced magical effects. The "converted" Manchurian officers reported all their experiences to Marshal Chang Hsueh-liang, who himself then invited Red emissaries to visit Sian and discuss their ideas with him personally. Of these early meetings no word reached Nanking—although Chang Hsueh-liang was actually Chiang Kai-shek's deputy commander-in-chief of all China's armed forces. Chang secretly made a truce with the Reds and considered persuading the Generalissimo to listen to the Communists' proposals which he was now also convinced were for the good of China.

Chang Hsueh-liang, later widely vilified and misrepresented, was one of the few high officials on the national scene of China who had consistently acted from "pure" motives. His character was not to be judged by the fact that he had in his youth been a dope addict but by his successful fight to overcome the habit and undergo a drastic personal reform. He had, by accident of birth and the assassination of his warlord father by Japanese agents, had supreme power over Manchuria thrust upon him when he was still in his twenties. From the first he had supported Chiang Kai-shek's Kuomintang government at Nanking, to whose authority he peacefully acceded the vast and rich Manchurian domains. When the Japanese invaded Manchuria he and the bulk of his troops had been south of the Great Wall, helping Chiang Kai-shek extend control over North China—a move which was one reason for the Japanese action. Subsequently he saved Chiang Kai-shek's regime in two other major crises. Now, in the Northwest, however, he gradually became convinced that the Generalissimo intended to compromise with Japan, and might even join the Axis. To end the civil war in China, Chang was to choose the most unexpected and dramatic means—and perhaps the only peaceful means—at the cost of his own career and the sacrifice of his personal freedom for the rest of his life.

By the time I arrived in Sian a few important Communists were living inside the Young Marshal's own home. It was shortly after the student uprising in Peking, led at the outset by Manchurians, some of whom had already come down from Peking to lecture Chang's troops on their aims. Among them were two of my own students, Chang Chao-lin and Ch'en Han-p'o, who edited an army paper.

The Communists set up a limited liaison between Sian and Pao-an, which was then the Reds' tiny "capital" in North Shensi. With their help one morning I took off in a Tungpei Army truck for the great unknown.

Our road northward was one to evoke memories in any Chinese of the rich and colorful pageant of his people. In an hour we were in the valley of the Wei River. Here the early settlers who were Confucius' ancestors first formed a nation, based on the already ancient traditions of a rice culture and a system of ethics that endured for milleniums. Toward noon we passed the legendary burial mountain of Ch'in Shih Huang-ti, the greatest revolutionary builder in ancient Chinese history. It struck me then as oddly appropriate that the Communists should here work out a destiny for China with aims no less radical than those which Ch'in Shih Huang-ti imposed 2,200 years ago—one more reminder that China's revolution of today is rooted in time-space realities quite different from our own.

All afternoon we rolled on through fields of opium poppies ready for harvest, until as darkness fell we reached Lochuan. There I was surrounded by soldiers and hustled by a side door into the filthy inn where I spent the night quartered in a room next to donkeys and pigs. Between the rats and bugs I slept little. I was happy to be on the road again before dawn, threading through the spectacular loess lands of the Northwest.

Organic matter blown down from the vast deserts of Central Asia, over periods of many centuries, loess is a rich topsoil tens of feet deep but naked and easily eroded by the sudden, drenching rains which here alternate with periods of prolonged drought. The scenic results were fantastic. Hills like great castles stood between rows of mammoth scones or heaped-up ranges serrated and fissured as if by angry hands—queer, incredible, frightening shapes in a world of strange surrealist beauty.

"But where do the people live?" I asked my Tungpei escorts. We seldom saw a house among the cultivated fields.

"Look!" he said, handing me his field glasses. "*Yao-fang*—cave houses." Tucked in the folds of loess I now descried whole villages with a network of paths connecting them in ginger-colored hills. In this treeless land of cave-dwellers—much like the ancient cave-cities built by Cro-Magnon man in the Loire valley of France—even the wealthy landlords dug their homes, for warmth in winter, coolness in summer, and relative safety in all seasons.

That night I spent in Yenan, a hill-cradled walled town later to become famous as the Reds' capital for ten years. It was still in Kuomintang hands now. Beyond it everything was Red territory—reaching a hundred miles or more northward to the Great Wall, and westward two hundred miles to the plains of Ninghsia. Up with the sun again I left the city gate accompanied by a single Tungpei officer who saw me past his last sentinel. We shook hands, he saluted and I was on my own. With me was an unarmed muleteer assigned to guide me to the first Red partisan outpost. On his bag-of-bones donkey were my scant belongings—bed-roll, a little food, two cameras, and twenty-four rolls of film. I did not know whether he himself was a Red-bandit or White-bandit. For four hours we kept to a small winding stream between high walls of rock, and saw no sign of any human life.

I suppose I should have felt something like Melville's deserting sailors entering the forbidden cannibal encampment on *Typee,* but I did not. I was uncommitted for or against the Reds. I had not yet personally witnessed evil in them, though I had seen it in other systems of power. Nor could you call Mao Tse-tung and his followers a "conspiracy." It was simply an open armed struggle between two contenders, neither of whom had any more legal claim to authority than the armed following he could gather to impose it—immemorially the terms of power in China. I was genuinely curious to know whether the Reds might be better or worse—a journalist after a story.

My muleteer faithfully delivered me to a tiny village, the first we encountered inside Red territory. Here the head of the local "Poor People's League" received me suspiciously at first. On learning my mission, however, he hospitably found me a clean place to bed down for the night. In the morning he woke me early.

"You had better leave now," he warned. "White-bandits are not far away and you ought to get to An Tsai quickly, where you will be safe with our Red Army."

After gulping down some tea and a bowl of rice, I set off at once with a new guide and muleteer provided by the "Poor People's League." Within an hour we reached a lovely pool of still water and there I finally saw my first uniformed Red soldier, with a white pony grazing beside the stream. He wore a turban with a red star on it and a mauser hung from his hip.

"Who's the foreigner?" he sternly addressed the muleteer.

"My name is Shih Lo and I'm going to see Mao Tse-tung," I answered. "He is expecting me."

Having satisfied himself that I was unarmed and not leading any ambush he smiled and said, "Come with me to district headquarters."

Two hours later we rounded a knoll and a sizeable village of houses came into view. At the same instant I heard a chorus of yells that seemed to come out of the porous yellow earth. Looking above us I saw a dozen peasants standing on a ledge and brandishing spears, pikes and a few ancient blunderbusses—all pointed at me.

CHAPTER 11

Chou En-lai

I MUST HAVE HAD dismay written over my face because the Red soldier with me broke into laughter and snorted, *"Pu P'a!"* He pointed to the menacing spearmen. "Don't be afraid. They're only peasant partisans, drilling! There's a partisan school here."

As we came into a short street of houses a half dozen men emerged in faded gray or blue cotton uniforms which bore no insignia of any kind except a small red bar on each wing of the tunic collar.

"Welcome," said one in Chinese. "Come inside and have some tea." They were all officers, I discovered, as each man identified himself. The "tea" was merely hot water—*pai ch'a,* or "white tea," the impoverished Reds called it. The real thing was a rare luxury in those parts. In a moment we were joined by a slender figure of soldierly bearing who brought his heels together, touched his faded red-starred cap in salute and examined me with large dark eyes under heavy eyebrows. Then his face, half-covered with a beard of rather heavy growth for a Chinese, parted to show even white teeth in a friendly smile.

"Hello," he said. "Are you looking for somebody? I am in command here." He had spoken in *English*. "My name," he added, "is Chou En-lai."

This was a man for whose head Chiang Kai-shek had offered a reward of $80,000. At this time commander of the East Front Red Army, Chou would thirteen years later become the first premier of the "People's Republic"—Communist China. Now when he invited me into his quarters I saw a small room, half-cave and half-house, furnished with a stool or two and some metal dispatch boxes. Chou had his papers spread over the clay *k'ang*—a mud brick, flue-lined rectangular-shaped platform which serves as both bed and heating plant in this part of Asia.

"We have a report that you are a reliable journalist, friendly to China, and that you can be trusted to tell the truth," he said in rusty English. "Just tell truly what you see; that's all we ask. You will be given every help to investigate."

I talked with Chou until late at night and he answered most of my

questions with candor. With him, part of the time, were one-eyed Li
K'o-nung, head of an army communications section, and Yeh Chien-
ying, Chou's chief of staff. Li would one day become vice-minister of
foreign affairs in the Peking government, and Yeh Chien-ying a top
army commander during the final defeat of the Kuomintang.

Chou drew me a rough map of the territory then held by the Communists and described their military and political plans for the immediate future. These aimed chiefly at bringing an end to the civil war
and forming a "united front" with other armies to resist Japan.

"Then you're giving up revolution?" I asked.

"Not at all. We are advancing revolution, not giving it up. The
revolution will probably come to power by way of anti-Japanese war."
As for Chiang Kai-shek? "The first day of the anti-Japanese war," he
prophesied, "will mean the beginning of the end for Chiang Kai-shek."

The Communists would win, Chou said, because they know how to
organize and arm the peasants in patriotic war. Chiang did not. "Important sections of the Kuomintang army will in the course of the war
desert Chiang and follow us." What if the Nanking government did
not fight Japan but made peace? The Communists would anyway
move north to get into direct contact with the Japanese armies, Chou
said. "We have fought guerrilla warfare against Chiang Kai-shek successfully in South China with only peasant support. We can fight guerrilla warfare with their help against the Japanese even more successfully."

Chou then went on to analyze Chiang Kai-shek's strengths and weaknesses as a soldier and politician. He knew Chiang well; he worked
under him for three years as political secretary of Whampoa Military
Academy, of which Chiang was president. That was before the split
in the first Communist-Kuomintang alliance at the climax of the Nationalist revolution in 1927.

I was to see Chou many times in the future, and write a brief biography* of him and his brilliant wife, Teng Ying-ch'ao, but curiously
Chou's first remarks about Chiang Kai-shek were cancelled out by
him before I could publish them in my book. Events had by then
taken such an unexpected turn that Chou sent me a message asking
me to withhold his frank and disparaging opinions because once more
he had to acknowledge and work with Chiang as a national leader.
Only recently that interview finally saw print.**

* In the *Saturday Evening Post,* March 27, 1954.
** *Random Notes on Red China,* Harvard University Press, Cambridge, 1957.

Few Chinese were to make a more favorable impression on Westerners than Chou En-lai during his later career in Chungking as chief of the Communist delegation there during World War II. The grandson of a distinguished official of the Manchu Dynasty, and a former honors student at the American-supported Nankai University in Tientsin, he had also studied in Europe and knew some French and German. Boyish in appearance when I met him, despite his thirty-eight years and the beard, he was a person of charm and intelligence, and I thought that in earlier times he would have been a fastidious mandarin. Beneath his outer urbanity he had a tough, supple mind, but he did not strike me then, nor later, as possessing quite the mental dexterity, vigor and self-confidence of Mao Tse-tung, nor his gift of the common touch.

Chou ended our first visit by tracing an itinerary for me on his hand-drawn map, noting the names of people and institutions for me to see in each place. It added up to a journey (by foot and horse) of ninety-two days—an underestimate, as things turned out. Then he saw me off, with a company of Red soldiers, on a three-day trek to Pao-an, where I was to meet Mao Tse-tung.

CHAPTER 12

Compote with Mao

WHEN OUR SMALL cavalcade reached the crest of a hill overlooking Pao-an bugles began to blow and I could see horses and men scurrying up and down the brief main street below. Years of war and famine had reduced both the population and cultivated areas in North Shensi. Pao-an ("Defended Peace") itself was the ruin of a once sizeable frontier city. Remains of its ancient fortifications demolished by Genghis Khan could be seen far outside the town gates through which we entered.

"Welcome to the American journalist to investigate Soviet China!" "Down with Japanese imperialism!" "Long live the Chinese revolution!" Banners in English and Chinese were held aloft by a curious crowd lined up before a few dozen ramshackle huts and shops. At the end of the street waited a group of Chinese who included most of the central committee of the party and almost the entire politburo then in Pao-an. They introduced themselves and welcomed me.

Mao Tse-tung did not arrive until time for supper. He was a rather gaunt pale figure then, above average Chinese height, somewhat stooped, with large, searching eyes, wide, thick lips, a high-bridged brow and a strong chin with a prominent mole. His black hair had grown thick and long, on a well-shaped head—for which the Generalissimo offered $250,000, dead or alive. He gave me a firm hand, said a few polite words in a quiet voice and asked me to come and see him after I had talked to the others and found my bearings around the town. Then he ambled down the street filled with peasants and soldiers out for an evening stroll.

In this dusty, poorly provisioned lair the Communists had set up the paraphernalia of a tiny state: ministries of foreign affairs, finance, agriculture, public health, defense, education, planning—the works. A Red Army Academy headed by Lin Piao (one day to be acclaimed "liberator of Manchuria") was quartered in a series of caves which bunked about 800 students. "Publishing caves" brought out textbooks, newspapers and magazines. Many of them were mimeographed on the backs of Kuomintang propaganda leaflets—much as the monks in Europe during the Middle Ages used to write their lives of the saints over pagan manuscripts. Food consisted mostly of millet, cabbage and squash grown along the river, with pork, lamb and chicken rare luxuries.

The "foreign office hostel" was a compound of four one-room mudbrick huts, one of which was my temporary billet. There I often shared meals with various politburo members and their wives, whom I taught to play poker. Not far down the road was "Chairman" Mao's one-room cave. It had a single window and a door that opened on a lane guarded by a lone sentry. And there I soon found myself ending every day, or beginning it. Mao invited me down regularly to have hot-pepper bread—or "compote" made by Mrs. Mao from local sour plums. Afterward we would talk for hours, sometimes nearly till dawn. My written interviews with him ran to more than 20,000 words; besides that he told me dozens of tales which I neglected to record. In the end he related the story of his life—his childhood and youth, why he became a radical, how the Red Army grew, and the whole epic of its recent 5,000-mile retreat from Kiangsi, which the Reds called the "Long March."

There was a kind of lull in war and politics at that moment and

Mao had some leisure. Perhaps my intense interest and questioning also won a response in him. Frequently he put aside piles of reports or telegrams, and cancelled meetings, to be with me. After all, I was a medium through whom he had his first chance to speak to the world —and, more important, to China. Legal access to the press of China was denied him, but his comments published in English were bound to filter back, he knew, and reach the ears of most literate Chinese, despite Kuomintang censorship.

Since Mao later became the head of the world's largest state, numerically speaking, and a man who has posed great challenges to American policy in Asia, it is interesting to see that most of what has subsequently happened was forecast by him in his talks with me twenty years ago. He demanded, and said that there soon would be, a cessation of class war in China and a united front of all "patriotic elements" to resist Japan. He outlined in lengthy and accurate detail just the kind of "protracted war" he would and did conduct against Japan, and the manner in which it would bring the revolution to power. He also forecast an early attack by Japan on the European colonies, and against the United States, and was sure that Russia too would finally be drawn into a general war to defeat Japan—and end colonialism in Asia.

No doubt wish fancy played a role in these prophecies as well as Marxist dialectics, to which Mao traced all his views. I must note, however, that he promised no easy victory. He told me to expect Japan to win all the great battles, seize the main cities and communications, and in the process destroy the Kuomintang's best forces early in the war. Then a prolonged struggle would ensue in which Red guerrillas would play the principal role, building up their forces as fast as Kuomintang strength was dissipated. At the end of a war which he thought might last ten years the "forces of the Chinese revolution" would be far more numerous, better armed, more experienced, more popular, and would emerge as the leading power in East Asia.

Mao did not disguise those aims nor did I fail to emphasize them in my reporting. He never pretended that his party aspired to anything less than ultimate complete power. War against Japan was merely a preliminary to "completing the bourgeois-democratic stage of the revolution." He had serene confidence that Japan would bring that "opportunity" to China—had indeed already opened it. Nor did Mao and other Red leaders ever describe themselves to me as "agrarian reformers" or "capitalist reformers"—a fantasy of the most curious nature later blamed on me, of which I shall soon trace the origins.

"The Communist party," Mao said repeatedly, "will never abandon its aims of socialism and communism."

Word for word I wrote down all that "the chairman" had to say to the world and to the Chinese people. Anyone who studied his program in *Red Star Over China* could not fail to perceive how the Communists intended to reach and mobilize the peasantry in the vast hinterland soon to be left a political vacuum after the Kuomintang and the Western powers were driven from the treaty ports and the cities by the Japanese.

Inwardly I often smiled at the extravagance of Mao's claims, which then seemed more naive than Gandhi's hopes of conquering the British by "love-power." There he sat, with two pairs of cotton pants to his name, his army a minuscule band of poorly armed youths, facing a precarious existence in the most impoverished corner of his land. Yet he spoke as if his party already held an irrevocable mandate over "the workers and peasants" of all China, acted as if he believed it, and told the foreign powers just how a free China of the future "could" and "could not" co-operate with them. "Every man is an impossibility until he is born," said Emerson. Mao was real enough and yet still a kind of impossibility. For "everything is impossible," to finish the epigram, "until we see a success"—and at that moment Mao looked a failure.

But if, at first, I found him grotesque, his utter self-belief impressed me. He had what Mark Twain called "that calm confidence of a Christian with four aces." In his case the aces were Asian Marxism, his knowledge of China and Chinese history, his boundless faith in the Chinese people, and his practical experience in "making generals out of mud." His step-by-step reasoning gradually took hold of me as "just possible" reality. As his personal story unfolded, thoughtfully told, well organized and dramatic, I began to see that it was a rich cross-section of a whole generation seen in the life of a man who had deeply analyzed and studied its meaning. This life therefore was an important guide to understanding future events. Here was a man, I wrote in 1936, in whom "you feel a certain force of destiny, a kind of solid elemental vitality." Unconscious, inarticulate China's needs might be in "the vast majority of the people," but if social revolution could provide "the dynamics which can regenerate China, then in this deeply historical sense Mao Tse-tung may become a very great man."

Although I thus became more interested in Mao as a personality than in the polemics of the moment, it was not easy to extract his personal history. For days we had a kind of game in which I sensed that he was trying to decide whether he could entrust me with the truth about himself or whether I would misuse his confidence to distort or misrepresent what he said. Communist practice was to avoid personal discussion not only because in theory the individual was considered irrelevant except as a force in history, but because the death sentence hung over all Communists. Anonymity was an essential safeguard.

"But if you expect to end civil war and work with other armies in a united front," I argued with Mao, "the country has to know what kind of people you are. Propaganda for years described you as debauched, ignorant and illiterate bandits, practicing only arson, murder, plunder and free love. You've got to make yourselves living persons—not just political slogans."

Again he put me off.

One night when all other questions had been satisfied, Mao turned to a list I headed "personal history." He smiled at a question, "How many times have you been married," which I discovered had been mistranslated as "How many wives do you have?"

"Abolition of polygamy is a basic reform in our laws of sex equality," he said. When I explained the error he was mollified but still doubted whether time should be wasted correcting "personal gossip."

"Didn't you say that the life of George Washington and Carlyle's lives of the French revolution had inspired you?"

He picked up my questions and read them over again.

"Suppose," he suggested at last, "that I just give you a general sketch of my life? I think it will be more understandable and in the end all your questions will be answered though not in just this order."

"That's exactly what I want," I said.

To the series of nightly interviews that followed Mao brought sheets of his own notes. He was not giving me just dead facts to which I had to bring life, but a nearly finished piece of self-analysis and explanation of a generation of revolutionists. It was to become a book read by millions in China, and translated in every colonial country.

Mao's impact on his American Boswell is here part of my own story.

CHAPTER 13

Prophet in a Cave

MAO TSE-TUNG was forty-three, only fourteen years older than I, but he had lived nine lives to my two. He had much to teach me. He was an able sociologist and psychologist. If China had not been eighty to ninety percent peasant, if the majority of the peasants had not been poor families who stood to gain by land redistribution, and if the urban and rural owning class had not been so very small and its interests so firmly vested in an economy of scarcity, China would not have had the kind of revolution she had. But the facts were otherwise and Mao Tse-tung was their prophet. He and his party succeeded because they learned how to by-pass the owning class to form a corporative union between China's revolutionary intellectuals and the great inert peasant masses still living in the iron age.

Mao knew the physical contours of the land and the people who lived in it better than any political rival of his time. He had walked ten thousand miles across rural China. As a traveler of sorts myself, I was impressed. Even as a student Mao had tramped from farm to farm in summer vacations, working his way and sometimes begging. Once he lived on nothing but uncooked beans and water for a week as an exercise in "disciplining his stomach."

Mao's taste for such unusual excursions and his early discovery of and liking for poor peasants oddly enough could be traced to his hatred of his own father, a rich peasant, and his efforts to escape from him. He told me that his father's severity was a main cause of his rebellious tendencies from childhood—just as he credited youthful ideals and feelings of compassion to the Buddhistic influence of a generous, loving mother. Some of his early experiences may help explain the curious alternation between "moral persuasion" and violence which later marked Chinese Communist practice.

The elder Mao regularly beat his sons to secure unquestioning compliance. When he was nine, Tse-tung ran away from home in "moral rebellion" against a teacher who also beat him. His mother intervened and he was moved to another school. As his father's beatings continued, however, Mao soon rebelled again. "This time I had the support of the opposition party in the family," said Mao with a smile, "my mother, my brother and the hired laborer." Retreating to the edge of a neighborhood pond, he threatened to commit suicide by drowning if his father did not promise to "reform." The "enemy" capitulated.

"Thus I learned," Mao reflected, "that when I defended my rights by open rebellion my father relented, but when I remained meek and submissive he only beat me all the more."

When Tse-tung was thirteen his father made a deal for profit to marry his son to a woman six years his elder. Once more Mao ran away, wandering for days and working for peasants for his food and lodging. He was found by his mother and brought home, where nothing further was done to enforce the marriage contract. From then on father and son lived in truce but not peace, until Tse-tung left home for good.

An Oedipus pattern runs through the lives of many Chinese revolutionists. Mao simply seemed franker about it than most. Infant rebellion no doubt also accounted for his costive condition—a matter of such general knowledge in Pao-an that Mao's once-a-week bowel movement was an event for congratulations. When I asked him whether he preferred the relatively sedentary life he was leading as head of the "state" at that moment, or the "roving life" of combat, he replied:

"I prefer the military life. My bowels never worked better than during the battle of Changsha."

Denis Diderot once observed that "to keep the bowels moving freely is the great aim of life in all social conditions," a ribaldry to which historians in their search for "objectivity" may have paid too little attention. Mao's quip is an interesting revelation of personality. Here was a plain-spoken man any peasant could understand—a man with a sense of humor or sense of proportion about himself in relation to humanity.

On another occasion, when Mao and I were talking to Lin Piao, the cave in which we sat grew very warm. *"Ma-ti, t'ai jeh-ti!"* (Rape it, it's hot!) said Mao, taking off his pants and sitting down again as naturally as Gandhi in his loin cloth. He had a lively sense of fun and liked to tell anecdotes and hear them. Once he asked me to describe to him all I could remember of Charlie Chaplin's picture *Modern Times* and laughed till the tears rolled down his olive cheeks.

Mao was by no means all peasant. He was a good calligrapher and liked to write poetry. There was a romantic side to his nature and the several love affairs in his life are a revealing part of his story—beginning with his first wife, Yang K'ai-hui, the daughter of his ethics professor whom he met as a student at Peking University, and who was captured and executed during the civil war in 1930. He had excelled at literature and sociology in college, but as a propagandist he was a master of homespun talk peppered with earthy idioms. When speaking to the people he seldom used straight Marxist texts but drew allusions from folklore or commonplace history familiar even to illiterates. A favorite with him was the *Shui Hu Ch'uan* ("The Water Margin"), that forbidden epic about bandits in rebellion against the decadent Sung Dynasty. Pearl Buck has condensed and translated it as *All Men Are Brothers*—a book which tells us as much about Chinese character as *The Brothers Karamazov* tells about the Russians. I suspect that Mao identified himself with these bandit chieftains. The *San Kuo,* an equally great semi-fictional historical epic and familiar part of Chinese folklore, was also constantly and cleverly used by Mao and other Communists to give Marxist historical analyses acceptability in terms of native experience.

Mao was, in other words, a good politician who did not talk above the heads of his audience. When it came to serious "dialectical" works he was as literate as the next Marxist, however; he constantly crammed party texts to hold his position as the leading theorist, in competition with returned students from Russia. His advantage over the latter stemmed from his intimate knowledge of Chinese conditions and an ability to "take a curve" with any Moscow "line" of the moment—to adapt it and give it a practical local application.

From study of Mao's technique in manipulating dogma I came to a general conclusion that all political power is conditioned by the problems of its control, and all theory is modified by the practice of power.

Marxism gave Mao a modern method of analyzing political phenomena much superior to the muddled warlord-Confucianist concepts of Chiang Kai-shek. His lack of broad knowledge of the complex outside world was a later handicap but did not affect his maneuvering inside the arena of Chinese politics. Marxism and dialectical method were the equivalents of a philosophy and religion for Mao but he never claimed access to the final truth.

"In the great river of man's knowledge all things are relative," he once said, "and no one can grasp absolute truth."

I tried to define for myself the source of Mao's power in the party—just as a personality, and apart from his "objective" role, as the Communists would explain it. He was a complex character, with seeming contradictions. Where subordination of the individual to the mass will amounted to a cult, Mao was distinctly an individualist. Smoking was among the Communists considered an indication of lack of personal discipline and was discouraged; Mao was an incessant cigarette smoker. Most of Pao-an was up at daybreak; Mao worked at night and could seldom be roused before noon. He was not the only politburo member with a wife—women were extremely scarce in that camp—but the only one I noticed whose wife seemed completely under her husband's spell and domination.

Most of Mao's followers had Prussian haircuts. Mao hated to have his hair cut and wore it very long. His face was almost beardless, except for the few hairs that sprouted from the mole on his chin, which, following Chinese custom, were never cut. In contrast to the neat, alert and military bearing of Chou En-lai and others, Mao slouched when he walked, his shoulders bent, a peasant in his gait. When I took some photographs of him and Lin Piao reviewing cadets Mao gave the feeblest imitation of a salute I ever saw. Chou En-lai looked you straight in the eye; whatever he was saying, he always seemed anxious that you believe him. Mao had a way of gazing sidelong at you, waiting for the effect of his words and their logic to be understood, and challenged. Seemingly relaxed to the point of carelessness, he masked an ever-alert and imaginative mind.

Mao had an extraordinarily good memory. He was able to recall dates, names, exact conversations and details of incidents over many years. His method of bossing the party was not overt but indirect and subtle. He spent hours conferring with various committee members, sounding out their views and reconciling them with his own. After he had talked to each of them individually, and was sure of a consensus, he then stated his own opinion as a synthesis. He certainly believed in his own star and destiny to rule. But he was relaxed, natural and unaffected in his personal relationships. He built confidence and trust by his loyalty to those who were loyal to him. He was also magnanimous to those who disagreed with him. Those who fought against him and his ideas would in time lose influence but they were not purged or physically destroyed on the scale of Stalin's personal rivals.

Mao was good company. He was never at a loss for words or a subject of conversation. He enjoyed talking so much that it was hard to believe he was also a man of action. A comparable case is Winston Churchill, and indeed Khrushchev. Mao probably had as good an education, in his own situation, as either of those gentleman had in theirs. He certainly had as well-developed an analytical ability. His knowledge of the world beyond China was limited to the books he had been able to read in a life which combined action and thought in the intensest degree. His weakness, from the Western viewpoint, was that his judgments of all capitalist countries were arbitrarily conditioned by his faith in the Soviet Russian interpretation of Marxism. But even that could not suppress in him a deep curiosity about the outside world. He often expressed a regret that he could not both fight a revolution in China and see and know all the countries about which he had read in his youth.

Mao confessed his ignorance on a wide variety of subjects. He had the liveliest curiosity about the United States. He had never been outside China and thus knew nothing at first hand about a constitutional democracy in action; but he knew the American system in theory and had studied both our Revolutionary and Civil Wars.

Mao never attempted to recruit me to the Communist Party. No one else ever did. But once Mao asked me whether I expected a revolution in America, and if I would take part in it. If, I said, my own country were as poor and backward as China, if oppression and exploitation were as shameful and wasteful of human life, if American children were being bought and sold as slaves, if my country had always been a despotism and were now governed by individual military satraps unchecked by any people's power, if Americans had no suffrage rights and could neither elect nor impeach, if labor had no freedom to organize or bargain collectively, if our rulers used state banks to finance their private business operations and made no accounting to the public, if the highest families in power were the richest profiteers, if foreigners held our ports and controlled large sectors of our economy, if we had just lost the whole Northeastern part of the United States without a struggle, if no legal way existed to organize political opposition—if all those things were true of the United States as they were true of China, and if there were no way to change or improve either state policies or the conditions of life itself except by armed revolt, I would then indeed be counted in the ranks of the revolution.

"America," Mao smiled and said at the end of all that, "will be the last country to go Communist."

"Is China also going to be the last country to go democratic?" I countered.

"No, we hope it will be the second to go democratic," Mao replied.

"Meaning—Russia was first?"

"True democracy is possible only when classes are abolished and the people, not private capitalists, own the means of production."

Mao was not a blind believer in everything Russian. He was to prove no less capable of using Stalin than Stalin was capable of using him. In private conversation Mao blamed Russian Comintern agents for the disasters suffered by the Communist party during the counter-revolution in 1927. Stalin at that time headed the Comintern and Mao was in opposition to the "line"—as he was found to be several other times before 1934. Only then did his leadership finally win grudging acknowledgment in Moscow.

In his interviews with me Mao called the Soviet Union his "loyal ally." Over compote he referred rather satirically to the "Russian aid which never arrived." Indeed, no significant Russian material help was to reach the Chinese Reds for another nine years—during which they enormously grew in numbers and power despite the billions spent by the United States exclusively in aid of Chiang Kai-shek. Mao drew important lessons from the history of the American Revolutionary War and from Washington's guerrilla tactics. Despite continuous retreats and defeats he and Chu Teh kept the hard core of their army intact in a war of endurance and attrition, while waiting for the "main chance" when conditions became favorable.

Two decades of armed struggle built up in the Chinese Reds an independent national revolutionary tradition, battle-tested in a crucible of comradeship in which each man constantly held the lives of the others in hostage, which forged a unity among their leaders unique in Communist parties of the world. In this tradition even their worst defeats became glorified as moral victories of Chinese patriotism. A striking illustration is the way in which their defeat in the South and forced migration to the Northwest became known in their folklore as the heroic "Long March." Mao Tse-tung had much to do with this. He himself copied down his poem about it for me, which I render into English in the free translation I made of it, on the spot, with the help of his interpreter:

The Red Army, never fearing the challenging Long March,
Looked lightly on the many peaks and rivers.
Wu Liang's range rose, lowered, rippled,
And green-tiered were the rounded steps of Wu Meng.
Warm-beating the Gold-Sand River's waves against the rocks,
And cold the iron-chain spans of Tatu's bridge.
A thousand joyous li of freshening snow on Min Shan,
And then, the last pass vanquished, Three Armies smiled.

CHAPTER 14

People in a Hurry

AFTER MAO TOLD me his personal story I had no trouble gathering similar data about dozens of other Red leaders. A careful study of these testimonials could hardly fail to suggest that the whole national experience of China made a Communist victory inevitable unless the Kuomintang itself underwent a miraculous transformation to bring about deep, drastic and speedy reforms.

The plain fact was that in China (as in some other semi-colonial and colonial countries) the *Communist Manifesto* had a fresh and literal authority which in Europe had been lost to Fabian gradualism, evolutionary Socialist movements, and Keynesian economic practice. It was lost even more decisively in an America empirically evolving from a frontier society of free men and free land economy toward the exclusively middle-class society emerging as the ideal of the corporation state of today.

When Marx's stirring call to arms first began to be read by young people in China after World War I they did not see in it an analysis of conditions in Europe of February, 1848, but a true description of their own immediate environment. "The modern laborer, instead of rising with the progress of industry, sinks deeper and deeper below the existence of his own class," said Marx. Even in America relatively civilized labor legislation is scarcely a generation old. In China, with its child slaves and female labor, its twelve-hour day, its starvation wages and the absence of any protection against sickness, injury, unemployment and old age, and no serious possibility of collective bargaining, why should people have questioned Marx's prophecies right down to 1945?

The old security under the clan-family and the guild systems had collapsed and now the have-not was literally worth no more than his price tag in the market "purely as a means of production." Back of the defenseless position of labor lay of course the break-up of the old agrarian economy under the impact of Western trade and the bankruptcy of handicraft production brought on by machine products. Capital levies in the form of ever-rising taxes (in instances collected sixty years in advance) and usurious interest rates, and the consistent plunder of public revenues by thieving bureaucrats and militarists, had by the Twenties and Thirties reduced the solvent land-owning tillers to a minority. Aided by famine and war they threw millions of "surplus" sons and daughters of degraded peasant families onto the swollen labor market of unemployables. This process was years ago prophetically analyzed by R. H. Tawney. The reminder here serves to emphasize that the biography of almost every Red soldier I met revealed him to be a direct product of this mass rural bankruptcy.

To mention but two dramatic examples: Chu Teh, who was the Reds' commander-in-chief and Mao's military alter ego; and P'eng Teh-huai, his deputy C-in-C. Chu Teh came from a tenant peasant family in which five children were drowned at birth because of poverty. Of the Chu children who survived he was the only one educated; instead of being drowned he was given away to a childless relative who managed to get him into a school for landlords' sons.

P'eng Teh-huai was almost killed (for a minor filial offense) by a decision of his family counsel, but an uncle's plea saved his life; he was then indentured as a coal miner at the age of nine.

It required no sharp intuition to comprehend why, in a country where child workers of ten or twelve were often locked up at night, to sleep on rags beneath the machines they operated by day—as I saw even in foreign-run Shanghai—the *Communist Manifesto* was read as gospel. Nor need one ponder why Chinese who met Western democracy only in its role of foreign policeman defending "rights and interests" seized by violence in China, could readily accept Marx's scornful denunciations of its hypocrisy at full face value.

The second thing we biographers learned was that nationalism, the passion to assert China's ancient role as a great power, played a major part in attracting literate Chinese to Marxism. In the West the Communist party had no comparable appeal. In sovereign America, as I remarked earlier, the Communist subservient to Stalin's infallibility had to learn to despise "national patriotism," substituting for it a religious "belief in a saviour abroad." He had to be essentially a mythomaniac—and often remained so even after he became an ex-Communist.

In China patriotism, class war and Russophilia were more reconcilable, however. At the outset the party founders' initial acceptance of Marxism coincided with direct Russian help to Dr. Sun Yat-sen for the liberation of China from foreign imperialism. Class war was rendered readily acceptable because the small native bourgeoisie was in truth largely a compradore or collaborator class under the dominance of foreign financiers. And it was simpler for the Chinese to believe in Moscow's leadership because Russia's foremost antagonists were just those Western colonial powers who were likewise the immediate enemies of independence movements all through Asia and Africa.

It followed that China's outstanding Communists were not less Westernized but more Westernized, and not less nationalistic but more so, than their Kuomintang rivals. They were not horny-handed proletarians but for the most part came from the less than five percent of China's millions who possessed some secondary or higher education. Biographies I collected, later augmented by my wife's work,* showed that among the fifty "top" brains of the party and the army only two or three were of true proletarian (as distinct from peasant and intellectual) origin. (By 1945 the proletariat was better represented.)

Authoritarianism was, of course, an ancient tradition in Chinese political history. It long pre-dated Confucius, who merely codified the ethics which were subsequently used to rationalize the world's most stable system of dynastic and bureaucratic power. Social conduct as the criterion of individual excellence, and the subordination of the individual to the interests of group good and survival, were indeed sanctions of despotism implanted in Russia by (among others) the Tartar khans whose political advisers and wisdom came from China. Although Marx's version of all history as a perpetual class war was an innovation, his dialectical method had deep and ancient roots in Chinese thought. The school of Chinese dialecticians who followed Hui Shih (Fourth Century B.C.) anticipated the doctrines of progress and change (the constantly re-formed synthesis of opposites in endless contradiction) which Marx had lifted from Hegel and Hegel himself had borrowed from the early Greeks via German philosophy. For this reason Marxist revolutionary dogma as applied to the modern world seemed to many Chinese intellectuals not strange or alien but merely new wine in old Chinese bottles.**

These men were all in a hurry. Their own experiences, combined with their study of European and American history, made them painfully aware of China's weakness, backwardness and imminent peril of total disintegration. In their search for a means of coping with complex problems of individual and national survival, young Chinese men

* See *Inside Red China*, by Nym Wales, N.Y., 1938.
** For interesting comparisons between present-day Chinese Communist philosophy and bureaucratic sanctions, and Confucian and neo-Confucian techniques of power consult *A History of Chinese Philosophy*, by Fung Yu-lan, translated by Derk Bodde, Princeton University Press, 1952; and *The United States and China*, by John King Fairbank, Harvard University Press, Cambridge, 1948.

and women of initiative and intelligence gravitated toward an authoritarian and revolutionary doctrine because every other means had been tried and failed, because time ruled out gradualism, and because Chinese history repeatedly had sanctioned revolution as a means of salvation.

The usual arguments against Communists as apostles of violence and destroyers of "individual freedom" had small relevance in China's *realpolitik*. Freedom in the Western sense did not exist and political change was still something attainable only by armed supremacy. Called upon to judge the Kuomintang seizure of power for one purpose, few Chinese could distinguish in it any ethical superiority over the Communists, who openly sought power in the name of the "have-nots" at the expense of a minority of landlords, militarists, treaty-port bankers and—during the Japanese period—foreign conquerors.

Contrary to opinion held in America the Kuomintang never posed a clear moral alternative to the Communists but competed with them purely on a basis of efficient use of force. For educated youths joining the Communists it was simply a matter of practical judgment whether their method was the only one which would provide a personal solution as well as quickly close the appalling gap between China's industrial-scientific backwardness and the advanced nations of the world. Those who became convinced of this in the early days made a discovery which confounded all previous Marxist theory. They discovered that they could bring the "proletarian revolution" to power without urban insurrections.

Mao's faith in the peasant as the main engine of social revolution developed from objective experience and right to the end was not shared by the Russians. Orthodox Marxists elsewhere also continued to believe that a Communist movement could not succeed without an advanced industrial proletariat as its main force. In the beginning the Chinese thought that also. After their initial disasters (1927-30) in urban insurrections, when the party was all but destroyed, they had no choice but to fall back on the rural areas where Mao Tse-tung and Chu Teh set up its first sanctuaries. Real events thenceforth were to make the peasants virtually their sole material and mass support. Out of them was to come the strength which finally carried the Communists to national power, with little or no help from the heavily-policed urban working class—or from Russia.

"Whoever wins the peasants will win China," Mao Tse-tung told me in Pao-an. "Whoever solves the land question will win the peasants."

In Aristotle's *Politics* it is said, "Always and everywhere the desire for equality is behind rebellion." The desire for equality takes many forms, of course. Infinitely complex human needs and aspirations enter into the passions and energies of any revolution. Yet in the East, where peril of starvation was ever-present, belly-hunger alone was enough to turn millions of have-nots against have-gots.

The Reds never believed in land redistribution as an end in itself. But they saw that only by preliminary "land reform" could they get the peasants to join in a fighting alliance and later win their support for their main program. Remaining the party of the proletariat in theory and doctrine, the Communist intellectuals became in practice the party of the poorer two-thirds of the peasantry whom the Kuomintang, wedded to its landlord supporters, could not claim to represent.

"I believe," says the young page in Mark Twain's *Recollections of Joan of Arc*, "that some day it will be found that peasants are people. Yes, beings in a great many respects like ourselves. And I believe that some day they will find this out, too—and then! Well, then I think they will rise up and demand to be regarded as part of the race, and that by that consequence there will be trouble."

The Communists became in effect a mobile, armed, ubiquitous propaganda crusade spreading their message across hundreds of thousands of square miles of Asia. To millions of peasants they brought their first contacts with the modern world. To youths and women—for the Reds courted them first and last—they opened up unheard-of vistas of new personal freedom and importance. To the poor farmers they promised land and relief from ruinous taxes, usury, starvation and family break-up. To all they offered equality of opportunity in a new state free of corruption, devoted to the welfare of the common people, and founded on a share-the-wealth and share-the-labor philosophy. *Kung-ch'an-tang,* Chinese for Communist party, may be translated "Share-production-party."

The reasons why the fire at first burned slowly in China were the very reasons why it could not be stamped out. Poor communications, lack of roads, railways and bridges, made it possible to create enclaves of armed struggle over wide gaps between the modern industrial centers dominated first by the Western powers and then by the Kuomintang. In the hinterland the Reds could offer leadership and objectives to almost universal rural discontent, agitate and awaken new ambitions and build an army to fight for their goals. When they actually distributed the land, eliminated some of the worst inequalities, turned the old gentry-ruled village hierarchy upside down, and took no personal profit for themselves, the peasants began to accept them and finally merged with them.

What was also novel and appealing to peasants who had never known the meaning of a political party was that they were actually sought as "members." Was it surprising that they began to think of the Communists as "our" party? It did not matter that the new peasant proprietors were later to bear the burdens not only of their liquidation as a class, but of both fighting the revolution and the building of Socialism. It did not matter that the land given to the fathers would later be incorporated into collective farms of their sons. What mattered was that it had been found that "peasants are people" and were wedded to the party—which replaced the vanished protection once offered by the old clan-family system shattered by the impact of industrial economy.

"The people are the water and the ruler is the boat," said the revered philosopher Hsun Tzu, 2,200 years ago. "The water can support the boat but it can also sink it."

"We are the fish," said the modern Communist sons of Hsun Tze, "and the people are the water of life to us. We do not ride over the people but swim with them." And of this they made slogans the peasants understood.

CHAPTER 15

The Road Out

I TRAVELED far into Kansu and Ninghsia and met the Red Army in training and battle. This was a time when the Southern forces under General Chu Teh came out of a winter in Eastern Tibet to join up with the vanguard in the Northwest led by Mao Tse-tung, Chou En-lai and P'eng Teh-huai. It was the end of the epic Long March, the great retreat from the south which the Reds turned into that moral victory of survival.

The Red Army was quite apart from any other military organization I had seen: the incorruptibility of its officers, the equality of pay and rations among men and officers, the great emphasis placed on political training, and the army's role in the organization of revolutionary committees among the poor in every village. In brief, the Reds sought to make every man, woman and child active in some organization.

One of the more attractive things about the Red Army was the hundreds of children who accompanied it—runaway slaves, orphans, apprentices, or the sons of soldiers, whom you would in other places see as little beggars. Here they served as messboys, waterboys, actors, agitators, buglers, scouts, spies and even nurses. They were very well treated; I never saw one struck. I had no difficulty understanding why they called the Army *fu-mu* (father and mother) and loved the life. Many officers and party functionaries had already emerged from the ranks of these child camp followers who were affectionately called "little devils."

Opium was banned and so was the sale of children and of women as wives or concubines. There was the beginning of equality of rights as between sexes. Women shared in the land division. Education—within the means available—was free and universal. Teachers were, like other state employees, paid the same wages as soldiers and officers (five Red dollars a month) and the "government" supplied food, clothing, shelter and special allowances. Here the "bureaucracy" was no place to get rich; service in it was explainable only in other terms. But I need not further describe what was to become a revolutionary pattern or prototype for all China and has been since fully analyzed, pro and con, by many others.

As I look back over this summary of my days with the Reds I see that I have said nothing about repressive measures, knocks at the door at midnight, and concentration camps—of which I was to learn so much later on in Russia. I traveled widely and questioned many peasants quite freely. I had interviews which lasted hours (sometimes days) with dozens of Communists, mostly in their twenties or thirties, a few in the forties, two or three in the fifties: Red Army commanders and their subordinates, party and government officials. I wrote down a whole outline history of the party, of the Red Army, of the Communist youth and women's organizations, of the state security troops, of propaganda method and publication. I interviewed party theorists on policy and practice, past, present and future. I observed and studied political and military training and indoctrination, methods of bolshevization of conquered territory, of treatment of captured soldiers and of battle practice. The results of all this have been published elsewhere.*

The truth is that I saw little that could be called a "terror" in the Northwest and I doubt if any then existed. I must emphasize once more

* See *Red Star Over China* and *Random Notes on Red China*, op. cit.

that this was a period of transition in Red policy from an all-out struggle for power and uncompromising class war to united front tactics which sought to embrace all but the most irreconcilable elements of the old owner-ruler class. Persuasion and gradualism were the practice in bringing poor peasants into participation in both land and political reformations. I have no doubt that in earlier days in the South the Reds had behaved in a more extreme and uncompromising fashion.

Party membership in the Northwest then numbered no more than 40,000. Before they were driven from the Yangtze Valley the Communists had counted 400,000 members. In the last year of the Kiangsi Soviet and during the subsequent retreat to the Northwest, party cadres were reduced by ninety percent, while Red Army losses in battle and other casualties during the Long March (1934-35) exceeded 180,000, or two-thirds of their maximum combined forces in all commands. Just before I reached the Northwest the Communists' fortunes had stood at the lowest point in five years.

Lo Fu, then party secretary, told me that in excess of 500,000 party members had been killed between 1927 and 1936. He estimated that three million people had lost their lives during the five anti-Red campaigns conducted by Chiang Kai-shek in the Yangtze Valley. As for those executed by the Communist government while it was in the South, he insisted that political prisoners tried, condemned and executed did not exceed 1,000 "counter-revolutionaries." This figure was apart from combat casualties and doubtless excluded landlords, usurers and other "class enemies killed by the peasants" with Communist "encouragement" during earlier phases of the savage peasant war.*

What I can say is that the four months I spent with the Red Army were a highly exhilarating experience. The people I met in it seemed the freest and happiest Chinese I had known. I was never afterward to feel so strongly the impact of youthful hope, enthusiasm and human invincibility in men dedicated to what they conceived to be a wholly righteous cause. Perhaps if I had just come over from my own country I might have felt less of this. I might instead have judged the Reds

* In reply to an inquiry I made concerning the total casualties on *both* sides during the two civil wars in China, Rewi Alley, the New Zealand sinologue (and sinophile), who remained in China throughout all the conflict, wrote to me from Peking on May 19, 1956: "I have myself estimated that the deaths through political executions, Kuomintang 'cleaning up' in Kiangsi, Fukien, etc., in man-made famines in Hunan, Honan, etc., in 'incidents' [armed clashes or "border warfare" before the outbreak of renewed major civil war in 1948], and following the KMT-CP breaking of armistice negotiations, then in the general [civil war] struggle subsequently, all add up to something like *fifty million* from the break [counter-revolution] in 1927 up until 1949.

as antagonists of American doctrine or have recognized, in their assault on the *status quo,* some future menace to America. But China was then a weak, about-to-be-conquered nation, separated from us by ten thousand miles of ocean—and what sometimes seemed ten thousand years. It never occurred to me that Mao Tse-tung could pose a serious threat to the security of the United States.

The setting here was not Missouri but the poverty, ignorance, filth, brutality, indifference, chaos and general hopelessness which I had seen and felt in Eastern Asia for seven years, and which now largely environed my own thought. By contrast with the corruption and demoralization of the "in-office" oligarchies and the small and greedy possessing groups I knew, both the white and the brown, the Reds were men of probity and selflessness. Compared to their countrymen who also despised both the Japanese and the Kuomintang, yet docilely accepted living under either, they were at least ready to die to affirm the worth of an ideal they cherished more than personal survival.

I also felt an affinity to them because of their enthusiastic espousal of science, the practice of equality and fraternity among men and women, their insistence upon racial equality, their positive attitude toward the future. In contrast to the inert fatalism of old China, all this seemed to me on the good side. The reforms they enforced or advocated were not the country-club ideals of political freedom by any means. But they did offer the essential satisfactions of food, shelter and some kind of democratic equalitarianism for all, which I now knew to be the first demands of Asia. Perhaps their strongest appeal to me as a Westerner was their decisive rejection of mysticism and the gods that had failed the poor, in favor of the rationalist's faith in man's ability to solve the problems of mankind.

Their "foreign policy" calling for unity in resisting Japan also seemed right to me. It did not matter whether that aim corresponded to the Moscow line for a "united front" to "resist fascism and aggression." It did not matter what long-range advantages they saw in it for themselves. Japan had only to stop her anabasis in China at any time in order to thwart such aims. The fact was simply that Chinese could not defend the nation by killing one another. Though the Communists and the Nationalists would remain separate political species, the united front was a necessary symbiosis if the nation was not to perish altogether.

Chinese Communist policy thus had a stronger logic than the arguments against it—and then and later it suffered relatively little from the kind of agonizing contradictions between Stalinist absolutism and the objective needs of other parties which were, after World War II, to paralyze the Communist movement in Western Europe.

It so happened that I was the person through whom the Communists finally reached the Chinese public with their proposals for internal peace and unity. Just before I left Pao-an, Mao called me in and gave me his "terms" for the "re-union" of the Kuomintang and the Communist parties. He said, in brief, that if "other parties" were given some representation in the machinery of the state and a legal right to exist while the nation mobilized for resistance to Japan, the Communist party would now cease all attempts to destroy the Kuomintang by force, abandon the name "Red Army," place its forces under the supreme command of the national government, and agree to Kuomintang supervisory control even in its own territory.

I might add that such was my feeling of confidence among my new acquaintances that within weeks after I penetrated the blockade there I sent word to my wife, in Peking, to try to come to the Northwest and join me. She had at my request earlier sent down a non-Communist Yenching student, Wang Ju-mei,* who reached Pao-an in time to accompany me as a translator-interpreter during the latter part of my travels. Nym did bravely make the attempt to follow but she was not lucky enough to get out of Sian. Secret police had arrived from the Generalissimo's headquarters to tighten up the blockade around the Red districts preparatory to a new campaign. They had succeeded in denying use of the Sian-Yenan highway to all vehicles except those they personally inspected and cleared. Nym's contact with the Red underground in Sian was abruptly broken off and, dejected, she went back to await me in Peking. She was to return for an extensive stay in Yenan the following year; but now when I heard the news of her failure to penetrate the blockade I decided to return home as quickly as possible.

We had to take a very roundabout road out. A few excerpts from my diary of that long-ago period may convey the flavor of life in this oldest part of China destined to be the birthplace of the newest and perhaps most controversial society in its history.

October 12, 1936.

I left Pao-an at nine this morning, bound for the highway to Sian. Mao Tse-tung was still asleep, but everyone else came out to say good-

* Wang remained and dozens of students from Yenching later followed him to Yenan. He is today secretary-general of the ministry of foreign affairs.

bye. They walked me through the city gate and as far as the Red Academy, where General Lin Piao was lecturing a class in the open air. He and the cadets rose and shouted: "Peaceful good road, *Shih Lo T'ung-chih!* Ten thousand years!" The *t'ung-chih* meant "comrade" and was courtesy-talk, but I felt depressed as it occurred to me that not many of these youths had a long life ahead.

My horse was lean with many days of travel and rations of corn-stalks and grass. Now he trotted along briskly ahead of our half a dozen bodyguards, led by a young "steward," Fu Ch'in-kuei. All day we followed the narrow bed of the Pao-an River and just at sunset reached a farmhouse below a huge sandstone hill on the top of which perched an ancient temple. The hill looked like a giant beehive with its hundreds of caves hollowed from the stone and standing one above another along the only road.

October 13.

Here, as wherever we stop, we are guests of the Poor People's League. There is a festive air around the village as now in October strings of red and green peppers are hung everywhere and the green cabbage and golden pumpkins ripen in the fields.

Until now we have had little but millet-noodles to eat but tonight we had a feast: fried cabbage, potatoes (hashed-browned, at my insistence!), fried chicken, steamed bread and turnips. How little it takes to gladden the heart of a Chinese soldier!

"Good! Delicious!" everybody cried out.

"K'u? (Bitter)," asked a young soldier, jokingly. "Do you eat better in *Ta-mei-kuo* (Beautiful Country—America)?"

"I've seldom tasted anything more delicious," I said and I meant it. But what, I asked him, did he consider "really bitter"?

"If there is no rice we eat bread," he answered. "No bread, we eat millet; no millet, we eat corn; no corn, we eat potatoes; no potatoes, we eat cabbage; no cabbage, we drink hot water, no hot water, we drink cold water. But no water at all? Well, *that* we reckon bitter!"

October 14.

We have stopped in a hut high on a mountainside overlooking a green valley and the first rice fields I've seen since leaving Yenan. Our tumbled-down place is owned by a man from Szechuan who migrated twenty years ago. When I asked the size of his farm he called it "twenty mou *high*" (one mou = ⅓ acre) because it slants precariously uphill. "You have to be a *native*"—meaning a Shensi man—he said, "to get level land. *Slanting* land is all they'll give a foreigner. How is it in your country?" He pointed down the valley toward a beautiful rice field. "There's a man with a hundred *mou* of real land, now," he said enviously. "But I'm just poor Chang of the Poor People's League."

"Poor Chang" nevertheless produced several chickens, some eggs, potatoes and cabbage. Again we feasted, especially after Chang brought out some soup made of black beans, millet, bean oil and peppers. He proferred it to me with pride and beamed when I asked for more.

Chang told me that three of his sons were soldiers: one was a regular in the cavalry; a second was in the Red Guard; the third was a groom with a headquarters company. He had two younger sons. His one daughter squatted on the *k'ang* beside his wife and his sister.

Fu-ts'un, October 15.

Today we made twenty miles through wild country where all day we did not pass a house. Here the hills were thickly wooded and the brown rust of autumn lay everywhere. We saw pheasant, a few deer, and some wild goats and wild pigs. Across a valley two tigers streaked from one thicket to another, far out of range. We all fired at them and missed. Then we scolded ourselves for wasting ammunition. It was a day of beauty and an immense comfort to the eyes after months of barren hills and scrawny valleys.

An-chia-pan, October 16-19.

Loafing here for four days, I have picked up some new words. I have learned more Chinese on this trip, mostly without an English-speaking person along, than in two years of desultory study.

The young partisan leader in command tells me that he has been fighting guerrilla war in this district for five years. He had nothing to show for it—no "possessions" at all except his wife and child, who are staying in the same hut with us. As he had no winter coat and admired my army-issue sheepskin-lined jacket, I offered it to him. He refused. One day we sat on the *k'ang* and talked for three hours. He told me that the "white" troops had been getting more and more friendly. A few days ago he took a group of men and women to the edge of a "white" encampment and sang Red songs to them, with one man playing a *shansi*—a native guitar made locally. By two's and three's, he said, the soldiers gradually drifted over to them, talked and fraternized. Then the commander arrived and they could hear him shouting from some distance, "Shoot them! Fire!" He laughed.

"Did they fire?"

"Yes," he said. "They fired in the air. Next day they were all re-placed."

Tungpei Front, October 19.

Escorted here this morning by Pien, the first officer I met when I came into the Red districts. He led me now across no-man's land to a group of Manchurian soldiers waiting on the plain. We were met by an immaculate young officer wearing a gold sword and white gloves, and carrying a vacuum flask. We exchanged greetings. I shook hands with Pien. As he turned and marched back across the plain I took my last look at Red China.

The "white" officer led me to his regimental commander, with whom I dined. In the morning I left hidden in a Kuomintang army truck, ac-companied by another white-gloved officer. He saw me to the center of the capital, past the Drum Tower and then to a house inside Sian—where I was quartered at the orders of Marshal Chang Hsueh-liang.

My trip was over, but a near catastrophe almost rendered it worth-less right at the end. When I got out of the truck it was discovered that my bag was missing—with all my interviews, diaries and notebooks, and the first photographs ever taken of Soviet China. The explanation was that our truck had been loaded with gun sacks full of broken army rifles being sent in for repair; to conceal my bag, in case of search, it had been stuffed into one of the sacks. Twenty miles behind us, in the dark, all the sacks had been thrown off the truck at an arms depot.

Prolonged argument persuaded the drivers and officer to return im-mediately and retrieve the precious articles. I then stayed awake all night worrying about what would happen if the bag were discovered and confiscated by some suspicious Kuomintang gendarme back at the depot. At dawn my friends stumbled in, with the bag intact. I was doubly lucky, because shortly after they returned the city gates were closed, all roads leading into Sian were lined with the Generalissimo's bodyguard troops, and all traffic was stopped. The Generalissimo was flying in for a surprise inspection visit. It would have been impos-sible for our truck to return over the road we had followed, which skirted the heavily guarded airport.

The precautions taken to protect the Generalissimo on that visit proved adequate. But they were not to be enough to prevent his cap-ture, on a return trip a few weeks later, by some of the very troops assigned to guard him.

By then I was back in Peking and my story had been widely published.

CHAPTER 16

From Sian to War

TWO DAYS after I secretly returned to Peking our telephone rang. Nym answered it. Jimmy White was calling to make discreet inquiries concerning me. During my prolonged absence Nym had given it out that I was making a caravan trip through Inner Mongolia. Jimmy asked when she had last heard from me.

"Oh, I heard from him today," she said truthfully. "He's fine."

"You're sure?"

"Absolutely. Why?"

"We have a report from Sian that he was executed by the Reds. In fact, it's already on the A.P. wire in America. Know anything about that?"

I had hoped to get the major part of my story written for serialization (sending it out by hand for transmission from Dairen, to avoid censorship) before publicly reappearing in Peking. Now I could no longer postpone an accounting. I took over the phone and talked to Jimmy. Soon afterward cabled inquiries about my mysterious death arrived from editors in Britain and America. A few hours later I went over to the American Embassy and at a press conference released the main facts of my trip. My colleagues' and my own stories were promptly cabled back to China after they appeared abroad, and were printed throughout the Far East. I also sent the complete text of Mao's long official interviews, together with a general description of conditions inside Soviet China, to the *China Weekly Review,* which was widely read by students and Kuomintang officials.

All this created a sensation—and consternation at Nanking, where my name had been none too popular ever since the student rebellion. Nym had not improved sentiments there during my absence. While in Sian she had, acting for me as correspondent of the London *Daily Herald* and the New York *Sun,* extracted a provocative interview from Marshal Chang Hsueh-liang. Nym showed me her story in triumph on my arrival. Its chief feature was Marshal Chang's expression of sympathy for a united front with the Communists—the first such statement to come from any high Kuomintang official. She reported "rumors" that Chang himself was "planning an alliance with the Red Army."

Tokyo had demanded an explanation and the Nanking foreign office had promptly repudiated Chang's interview. But Chang himself had made no comment.

"He said a great deal more than that, off the record," Nym explained. "He wants Chiang Kai-shek to release the imprisoned students and to legalize the National Salvation Association. He wants a national defense government set up to represent all armies. He's dead set against another anti-Red offensive and I heard in Sian that he's even asked the Generalissimo to relieve him of any part of it."

As for my own reports, now, Nanking at first branded them a hoax, claiming that I had never been near the Reds. When I released some photographs to prove it the press bureau threatened to cancel my press privileges. Instead, both the Kuomintang and the Japanese sent agents to see me to try to find out how I had eluded the blockade. Japanese questions suggested that they thought I had been sponsored by Nanking. The Kuomintang intelligence seemed to think I had been flown in on some Russian plane. I told them I had simply walked in, from Mongolia. Anybody could do it. Why didn't they try?

Thus the details of Mao's proposals became known throughout China and Japan. Their logic appealed to many Chinese. Even at Nanking some officials privately conceded that Marshal Chang was right when he said that ten years of civil war had failed to unite China and that only national resistance could do so now. In November sentiment turned against Chiang's continued appeasement policy when there was renewed Japanese attrition in Suiyuan, a province on the Mongolian frontier. The Generalissimo refused to grant Chang Hsueh-liang's plea that he be sent with his Manchurians to strengthen resistance in Suiyuan. More student demonstrations followed, supported by strikes in Japanese-owned textile factories and boycott activities led by the National Salvation Association in defiance of government bans. The Kuomintang was bewildered by the open popular political activity in cities where the Communist party had long ceased to exist. Chiang's answer was armed suppression of the Shanghai and Tsingtao strikes and the arrest of more off-base patriots.

Such was the national scene when, six weeks after I came back from the Northwest, the duel between Chiang Kai-shek and the Young

Marshal reached its dramatic climax at Sian. Within that city Chiang's trusted Kuomintang gendarmes had already taken over from the Manchurian troops, who were ordered to the outskirts. Some knowledge of Red infiltration in the Manchurian army had now reached Chiang. At his orders many Communist suspects—but none of the principal Communists—were seized in Sian.

On December 7 the Generalissimo himself arrived in Sian with his staff and personal bodyguards, to assume personal command over the Sixth Anti-Red offensive. Several of his first-line armies were on the march to Shensi to replace Chang Hsueh-liang's troops on the Red front. Many of Chang's younger officers were on a list of "left sympathizers" scheduled for court martial as soon as the shift was completed.

Four days after Chiang returned to Sian, Marshal Chang's troops re-entered the city, staged a coup at midnight, and seized the Generalissimo and his staff. Next day Marshal Chang explained to the nation that this was a "patriotic act" to peruade the Generalissimo to carry out the will of Dr. Sun Yat-sen—to call a national assembly to elect a provisional representative government, to end civil war and begin national resistance, to grant legality to all "patriotic parties," to release political prisoners and grant rights of assembly and free speech, and to carry through the long-delayed agrarian reforms.

Chang's program was substantially the same as the proposals made to me by Mao, and almost identical with a seven-point manifesto circulated on December 1, ten days before Chiang's detention, by the Communist party. That the Communists worked in close collusion with the Young Marshal was further indicated by the fact that on December 11 their troops, in co-ordination with the Manchurians' own withdrawal to the south, moved into Yenan, southward to the suburbs of Sian, and eastward to the Yellow River.

I am tempted here to give a new "inside" account of the Sian incident, which so drastically changed the fate of Chiang Kai-shek. Many books* have explained the motives which caused Marshal Chang to take this extreme step, and to form the Northwest Defense Government in alliance with the Red Army. But the reasons why he decided to dissolve the alliance, to release the Generalissimo two weeks after his detention, and to return with him to Nanking and submit himself for trial —and an imprisonment which has lasted to this day, in Formosa!— have never been fully disclosed. In my own case I wrote of the Sian

---

* See *Sian: A Coup d'Etat*, by Mme. and Generalissimo Chiang Kai-shek, N.Y., 1937. *First Act in China*, by James Bertram, N.Y., 1937. *Donald of China*, by Earle Selle, N.Y., 1949. *Red Star Over China*, op. cit., etc.

affair with better than average knowledge at the time, for I was in touch with the Red and Manchurian underground both before and during the Incident. Yet my information also was incomplete.

Only recently I was able to present new data about Sian* which somewhat alters the historians' interpretation of the affair; but for the general reader I need not here repeat those details.

The Generalissimo feared, as he revealed in his diary, that he was going to be given a "mass trial" by the Reds, and perhaps be executed —as he had executed so many. Instead, he was subjected to what the Chinese called *ping-chien,* or "military persuasion." As an involuntary guest he had to listen to what his Manchurian subordinates as well as the Reds thought of his policies—his crimes of commission and omission, and the changes they believed necessary to save the nation. Beyond Sian all China, and the world, waited for the outcome of the unique political experiment.

Whatever Chiang Kai-shek did or did not promise the "National Salvationists" at Sian before he was released, the practical result was to end civil war. On Christmas Day the Young Marshal escorted the Generalissimo unharmed back to Nanking. The Generalissimo quietly called off the anti-Red offensive and personally authorized negotiations with the Reds. Officially, the Kuomintang now announced that the first task before the country was "the recovery of the lost territories" whereas formerly Chiang had always insisted upon "internal pacification"—annihilation of the Reds—as "the first task." Soon afterward tacit agreement was reached which provided that the Communists could retain their party organization but would abandon the name "Red Army" and become the "Eighth Route Army" as part of the National Army; that the Communists would cease attempts at violent overthrow of the Nanking government and transform the "Soviets" into a "Special administration area," and that the Kuomintang would convene the long-delayed "People's Congress," in accordance with the will of Dr. Sun Yat-sen, granting representation to all groups.

But Chiang's negotiations with the Communists had by June, 1937, reached a stalemate. The Manchurian army had been peacefully moved out of Shensi by agreement with the Young Marshal's subordinates. Once more the Reds were surrounded and blockaded. Mao Tse-tung and Chu Teh were told that their forces, also, were to be "reorganized" and transferred as separate elements, to other armies—a process which would have simplified their obliteration. Late in June I received a con-

* See *Random Notes on Red China,* pp. 1-12, op. cit.

fidential letter from Mao Tse-tung which expressed "anxiety and dissatisfaction" with the ominous trend of events. Destruction or advance into the northern provinces once more seemed to be their alternatives.

Chang Hsueh-liang had "saved" the Communists once. Now a second stroke of luck opened up broad and fertile opportunities for them. In July they were extricated from their precarious position by Japan's "providential" major invasion of China, which gave Chiang Kai-shek no choice but to shelve any and all plans for another annihilation drive.

Furious at the Generalissimo for even temporarily halting his anti-Red offensive, and angered by his rejection of their own demands for an alliance, Japan's militarists now announced that the task of "bringing China to her senses," as the phrase went, could no longer be postponed. With their unerring instinct for misreading Chiang Kai-shek's true needs, and their own genius for political miscalculation, the Japanese launched a campaign to "liberate China from Communistic oppression" and to "build a New Order in East Asia." This time no one would be able to halt the Japanese juggernaut until it had changed the face of Asia and smashed itself to pieces in the process.

A few days before the battle of Nanyuan, where I witnessed the beginning of the eight-year-long Sino-Japanese war, outside the walls of Peking, I finished writing the last chapter of *Red Star Over China*. In the closing paragraphs I indulged in some prophecy which seems appropriate to quote:

"Thus, only a great [Japanese] imperialist war, which is almost certain to assume the character of a world war, will release the forces that can bring to the Asiatic masses the arms, the training, the political experience, the freedom of organization, and the mortal weakening of the internal police, necessary for a revolutionary ascent to power . . ."

The noises I heard offstage were indeed heralds of the coming crash of empires. If I correctly understood Japan's role as the destroyer of the European colonial system, I was yet far from understanding all the long-range implications of involvement for my own, my "neutral," my native land.

CHAPTER 17

Exit from Peking

AFTER THE OCCUPATION and the early phase of the Japanese advance, Peking became dead as a news center. The *Herald* ordered me to the Chinese side of the front. I was glad of that but I could not leave without my long-lost wife.

While I was writing my book Nym had gone to Sian for a second try to get into the Red areas, to gather material for a book of her own. She had had to risk being shot when she climbed over the compound wall of her closely watched hotel at midnight and I knew that she had escaped only with the aid of an adventurous American business man. Three months had passed and my last word from her was that she was returning. Then communications were cut off by war. Daily I hoped to see her or get a message from her.

There were other reasons why I could not leave at once. Right after the battle of Peking my house filled up with political refugees, mostly university professors and students on the enemy's blacklist. Among them was the president of *Tungpei,* or Manchurian University. They felt safe with me; the Japanese hadn't yet begun molesting foreigners. I got these people out of Peking by helping to disguise them as beggars or coolies or peddlers, while others in the darkness of night climbed over the city walls which rose right behind my house.

Several of my former Yenching students were among those who fled to join the guerrilla organizations which quickly sprang up in the surrounding countryside. Through them I agreed to let some Manchurians set up a short-wave radio station and send and receive messages in my home. As a result I briefly became a kind of underground headquarters.

I was certainly no longer a "neutral."

One day the wife of a professor who had fled town sent a message to invite me for dinner. When I got to her house she introduced me to a Chinese woman with long bobbed hair who wore dark glasses. She at first meant nothing to me. Suddenly she burst out laughing. *"Shih Lo T'ung-chih,"* she cried, *"ni pu jen-shih wo!* You don't recognize me!" As she took off her glasses I saw the last person I could have imagined there. She was Teng Ying-ch'ao—wife of Chou En-lai, head of the women's department of the Communist party and member of its central committee.

Ying-ch'ao had been invalided with tuberculosis when I had last seen her in Shensi. Now she told me that she had come up to Peking in disguise, months before. She had been living quietly in an isolated temple in the Western Hills, where the dry Northern spring, and plenty of food and rest, had almost cured her. Knowing nothing of the Japanese invasion until the troops reached her village, she had fled across the fields, barefoot and her hair bound like a peasant's, to hide in her friend's home until she could get in touch with me.

"You're not going to stay here? The Japanese—"

Yes, she realized her life was at stake. She had to get out of the city. Once more I could be useful.

Rail communications from Peking to the sea had just been restored; one train a day took twelve hours to cover less than a hundred miles. The Japanese were searching all passengers and, at the Tientsin end, arresting anybody whose face suggested the possibility of political thought. Thus far they hadn't molested foreigners, however, or foreigners' servants. I agreed to escort Teng Ying-ch'ao to Tientsin, as our family amah, and see her safely through the lines, with the help of Jim Bertram, a New Zealand newspaper man and a good friend.

A few days later we boarded a car crammed with glum-faced silent refugees, among whom Ying-ch'ao quickly disappeared. She looked the compleat amah, with her bobbed hair miraculously transformed. Inside the jammed cars nobody could move. At Tientsin, which we reached after dark, I had a tense hour as we waited to get out of the barbed-wire enclosure. On the station platform we saw a dozen young Chinese yanked out of line and hurried off to the waiting military trucks. Their soft white hands, in contrast to their peasant garb, had aroused Japanese suspicions. Ying-ch'ao hid her hands in her sleeves.

"American," I said to the Japanese inspector, "American correspondent." And, turning to Ying-ch'ao, "Amah-san." She dropped her jaw in an idiotic grin at the sullen Japanese. He curtly motioned me on without attempting an examination, but contemptuously emptied Ying-ch'ao's straw luggage on the floor. Then, without even looking at it, he pushed her ahead.

Half a million refugees flooded the streets of the small British concession, waiting for passage on the few ships plying to the "free" South. Tickets weren't to be had. But foreigners, as a privilege of cabin passage, were allowed to take along a servant or two in steerage. Through a friend I arranged for Ying-ch'ao to play amah again, to a gentleman she never saw, and I personally settled her on her tiny spot on the crowded deck.

"Shih Lo," she said, her eyes filling with tears as I left, "don't go back to Peking! You won't be safe there long."

"Don't worry, Ying-ch'ao, I'll be coming soon. Take care of my wife if you see her before I do."

Back in Peking I waited impatiently for word from Nym.

One wet morning the guerrillas' liaison agent, Wu Ting, came in, excited. He reported that they had just beaten the Japanese to one of the imperial tombs (Prince Kung's, I believe it was) in the suburbs and had rifled it of a large quantity of diamonds, rubies, pearls, gold, jade and objets d'art. Wu proposed that he bring me the loot and that I sell it for them. He had a way of getting himself in and out of the guarded gates disguised as a camel puller. Instead of putting their superannuated camels to pasture the Chinese then used them to haul coal from the nearby mines, and Wu proposed to smuggle his loot in to me in a coal bag.

"How much is it worth?" I asked.

"A goldsmith's son is with us. He says the jewels alone should bring more than a million dollars. They'll have to be sold in Tientsin or Shanghai to some foreign buyer. No Chinese would risk it."

"But I wouldn't know where to go, or how much to ask for the stuff. What if I had to sell it for a lot less—or what if I lost it?"

"We'll take whatever you get. You're the only foreign friend we can trust to do it." Then he added thoughtfully, "You can keep ten percent for yourself, of course."

I shook my head and Wu's homely, pock-marked face wore a disappointed look.

"Well—" he hesitated, "then—fifteen percent?"

Fifteen percent of a million was not hay, but I had never accepted bribes and couldn't start now by taking money from these volunteers who badly needed it in the cause of their country. The vaguely illegal aspects of the case didn't bother me; it was one set of tomb robbers against another, and the natives had prior claims over the Japanese.

While I was thinking it over Wu continued to misunderstand me. "All right," he finally whispered, "keep a *quarter* of anything you get. But that's as high as we'll go."

"I won't take a cent," I said. He looked dejected. "But I will make another proposition to you," I went on. "Release those Catholics and I'll find a buyer for your jewels."

I knew that Wu's guerrillas had recently seized several Italian friars from a monastery in the Western Hills, on the grounds that they were "fascist allies" of Japan. Hard up for cash and arms, they were demanding ransom money from the Catholics. I had already advised them that this was bad practice and would hurt China's cause.

"You like the Catholics that much?" demanded Wu, wonderingly.

"It's China I'm thinking of," I said. "Fight one enemy at a time."

"Hao!" Wu said, *"hên hao!"* and it was a bargain. The brothers were soon released and I found a person who eventually disposed of the jewels. I never heard just how much they brought, but when nowadays fortune frowns on me I can't help thinking what a pity it is that I didn't come from good old robber-baron stock. I never again had so easy a chance to highjack a million dollars.

I was soon to make the pleasing discovery that money is occasionally earned by writing about bandits, however, as well as by being one. The first reception to my reports on the Chinese Reds was discouraging. Neither the New York *Sun* nor the North American Newspaper Alliance, with whom I had a string arrangement, used any of the thirty articles of my series. After they had held the copy for weeks without comment I resigned both jobs in disgust. I was mistaken in assuming that they had suppressed the stories; on the contrary, both the *Sun* and the *Times* (NANA's New York paper) wanted exclusive rights, and neither would compromise. But by the time I learned that I had recovered all rights and offered the material to magazines.

The Saturday Evening Post was the first to use the story. Then Henry Luce brought out two long picture stories in early issues of a publication just making its debut under the name of *Life*. After that I was flooded with more offers than I could accept. The *Daily Herald* of London featured my series on its front page and promoted me to chief Far Eastern correspondent. Immediately afterward *Red Star Over China* appeared and was an instant hit in England, selling over a hundred thousand copies in a few weeks. The Random House edition in New York sold better than any non-fiction work hitherto published about the Far East. I was later to publish more profitable books, but this success astounded me, as I had not believed that *Red Star* had a remote chance of "popularity" abroad.

Most of that good news would not reach me until months after I left Peking. Meanwhile the drain of feeding a houseful of refugees, as I waited to hear from Nym, more than once made me wonder if I might have to sell a diamond or two from Wu's loot, to keep me going. Then at last we received a delayed and garbled message from Nym, in Yenan, on our own radio. "All right," read the only part of her long message that got through, "better you come here."

It was enough. I packed off my guests one by one and put the radio in wraps with Jimmy White who was staying on. A few days later I began a roundabout journey, via sea and land, which eventually united me with Nym in Sian again. Then we crept back by the bombed-over railway to the sea at Tsingtao, where a quiet magic held us momentarily. The famous long white carpet of sand, at this season usually crowded with thousands of vacationists, became our private beach when for three days we did not see another bather. Never had that old German-built port looked lovelier, with its days a shower of gold and its nights gloriously cooled by sea-washed breezes mingling with the pine scents drifting down from the low hills. But over the closed cottages and the stillness of the half-deserted city there hung that curious expectancy of an event waiting to happen. Daily we expected to see a Japanese landing party roll ashore behind each hedge of blue-green surf.

I did not wait for them; after a week an unwelcome ship arrived with deck space for Shanghai, and our brief holiday was over.

CHAPTER 18

The Essence of War

CHINA'S CAUSE was now my cause, and I linked this sentiment with a commitment against fascism, nazism and imperialism everywhere.

I made the shattering discovery that what any man writes or says, can under certain circumstances lead people, even complete strangers, to actions which might end in speedy death. I felt personally answerable to the Chinese whose lives I had wittingly or unwittingly helped to place in peril. As I heard of friends and students killed in the war I realized that my own writing had taken on the nature of political action.

It was not easy for an American to do much for China, in contrast to what our business men were doing for Japan. After I covered the middle and the end of the Shanghai war—that costly futile repetition of 1932—I followed the path of flame and rape and slaughter across China to Hankow, to Chungking, to Sian, and once more to Yenan and back. I wrote many stories about war but I learned that a non-combatant observer, free to take flight, is not a true prisoner of war like the soldier. Here I felt, as I was often to feel more strongly in Europe later on, that even when the war correspondent's guilty conscience drove him to foolish risks no sensible soldier would take, still it was only a Yahoo kind of posture—full of sound and fury, but at best only an outsider's view of war.

My own "adventures" in the China-Japan war are mostly in a book* I wrote about what befell China before Pearl Harbor. Here I wish only to get down the *political essence* of that war which metamorphosed into a great social revolution.

As early as a year after the Japanese invasion a most curious thing became manifest. The defeated Chinese were not behaving according to the rules. Nobody could be found to make the surrender here in the way that Pétain made it in France or Horthy made it in Hungary. By 1939 Japan held nearly all the modern cities and the main railways in the most economically developed parts of China. Even before the Kuomintang government's retreat to Chungking the Japanese had destroyed the combat effectiveness of Chiang Kai-shek's main and regular forces. Henceforth he would passively remain about where the Japanese chose to stabilize an inactive front. But the strange thing was that although Japan won all the great battles she could never win a political decision and was never able to conclude the war victoriously.

The situation resembled the exasperating predicament of Napoleon, who defeated all the Russian generals in 1812, but never conquered Russia. "After the victory of the French at Borodino," wrote Leo Tolstoy, "there was not an engagement of any importance; and yet the French army perished." ** The Tsar and Kutuzov and all his staff realized that anyone who acknowledged defeat would simply not be obeyed by the people and would be disowned. It was that way now in China. When Wang Ching-wei, No. 2 man in the Kuomintang hierarchy, betrayed China and became chief of the Japanese puppet government at Nanking, the people spat on him and his influence vanished. The same thing would have happened to Chiang Kai-shek if he had surrendered. This fact was perfectly understood by Chiang

* *Battle for Asia,* New York, 1941.
** *The Physiology of War,* by Leo Tolstoy. N.Y. 1882.

himself. General Stilwell also perfectly understood that. Few other Americans did.

The illusion that we had to bribe the Generalissimo on his own terms "to keep China in the war," was to cost us very dearly. It was never his will that kept China in the war. Quite simply, Chiang never had the power to take China out of the war.

"With the burning of Smolensk," wrote Tolstoy, "the campaign in Russia took a form until then unknown in the art of war. There were only burnings of towns and villages and battles followed by precipitous retreats. The retreat after the victory at Borodino, the burning of Moscow, the pursuit of the marauders, the sequestrated provisions, the guerrilla warfare—all these things were contrary to the rules of military tactics. But in vain the French complain that the Russians do not conform . . . The *mouzhik* has raised his club in all its terrible and majestic power and, caring nothing for good taste and the rules, with a stupid but efficacious simplicity, striking out instinctively, falls upon the enemy and beats him incessantly." *

From 1938 to the end of World War II the Japanese were never seriously harassed by the defeated generals and politicians in the far west and south of China. It was the peasant who "raised his club" behind their own lines, the tireless guerrilla, seemingly nothing and nowhere, who was the uneasy jest of the conquerors by day and their dread preoccupation by night, the endless drop of water on the back. His unorthodox and irregular attacks provided the front that was never quiet, the enemy never defeated, the peasant partisan who would indeed never win the military decision against Japan but who nevertheless would decide the political future of China. And because the Communists alone understood this, and provided the peasant with leadership, trained him to steal arms with clubs, and combined revolutionary changes with national war to give him something to die for—because, in the words of Chou En-lai, they knew how to organize the peasantry and the Kuomintang did not—they were to emerge in 1945 ten times as strong as ever, while the Kuomintang emerged ten times as weak.

In 1938 Evans Carlson, then a captain in the U.S. Marine Corps, was the only American officer I knew, besides Stilwell, who grasped the significance of this amazing growth behind the Japanese lines. We had seen much of the Shanghai battle together when one night we sat in my hotel room especially heavy-hearted. In the course of our talk, he came to a decision which changed his life.

* Op. cit.

CHAPTER 19

Carlson Glimpses the Future

CARLSON AND I had just seen a fellow journalist rather pointlessly lose his life. The Japanese were attacking one of the last areas of Chinese resistance around the Settlement, a section called Nantao. Evans and I had gone to a water tower just inside the French concession to watch the show with Pembroke Stephens of the *Daily Telegraph*. And show it was. In that grotesque Shanghai warfare one could stand just inside the sanctuary of foreign territory and see a complete battle in cross-section—the exposed flank of Chinese positions on one side and Japanese on the other.

Stray or intentionally aimed bullets and shells fell around us as we took cover behind a brick wall. Stephens wanted a better vantage point for his eye-witness story; he climbed up the water tower and perched there. Across the small stream which separated us from battle someone must have spotted him. Suddenly the tower was sprayed with steel. No one could blame a soldier of either side for not knowing where the invisible line was. Blood and water dripped down on us. When the battle had passed on I followed Carlson up the ladder and came down again with Stephens. He was dead.

Soong Ching-ling, who was about to evacuate her home in the French concession, had sent me a bottle of Napoleon brandy a week earlier. Her note said, "This is almost the last of my father's cellar. Don't leave any of it for the Japanese!" That night seemed a good time to carry out her wish. We uncorked Napoleon and I offered a toast to Stephens.

"A brave man."

"He was brave, all right," said Carlson, frowning, "but he must have been damned unhappy about something."

"You think so?"

"Whenever a man risks his life recklessly he is having some kind of fight with himself inside. I know; I've done it myself."

Courage is one thing; the will to self-destruction something else. But coming from a man who had already had a reputation as a hero, and was in a few years to become a legend of Marine heroism in the Pacific, it was a remark I always remembered.

"That's not only the end of Stephens," Evans mused. "It's the end of Shanghai—and maybe the end of the war."

"So Japan has won?"

"China has lost her industrial bases now and it's impossible to fight a modern army like Japan's without industry. But has Japan won? I know what you're thinking, and you may be right. You're going to tell me Mao Tse-tung has the answer. Guerrilla war."

"You don't believe it?"

"I chased Sandino all around Nicaragua for a couple of years and I don't underestimate guerrilla possibilities in a big country like China. But it all depends on leadership—leadership and morale. Now I personally never met any Chinese like the generals you talk about—Chu Teh and P'eng Teh-huai and Lin Piao. Maybe they're different. If they really have got the kind of morale and discipline it takes—if their leaders are as resourceful as you say—if—if— But I'll agree that the future *could* belong to them."

"Why don't you go and see for yourself?"

Carlson's blue eyes narrowed, he pulled on his long nose and grinned. "I was coming to that. What would they do if I showed up at Chu Teh's headquarters—give me the old imperialist spy treatment?"

"I don't think so," I said. "Let me try to find out."

"Admiral Yarnell is my boss, of course, and if he agrees he'd still have to ask Washington. But you start the ball rolling and I'll begin working on my side."

The Eighth Route Army had representatives in Shanghai who I knew had radio communications with Yenan. I got them to send a message to Mao Tse-tung. Back came the response; Carlson would be welcomed, if Chiang Kai-shek consented.

A few days later Evans was on his way to Nanking with a letter to Chou En-lai, who was then the Eighth Route Army's chief of liaison at the Generalissimo's headquarters. Yarnell took some convincing, and Chiang Kai-shek still more, but permission finally came through. On a day when everyone else was evacuating Nanking in flight up the river to Hankow, Chou helped smuggle the big Yankee across the Japanese lines by way of the Red underground, and into guerrilla territory. He was thus the first foreign military observer (by several years) to confirm the paradoxical fact that as fast as the Japanese advanced, the Reds were expanding the physical area of their influence by carrying on a war of attrition far inside the enemy's perimeter of occupation.

Captain Carlson met General Chu Teh and all his commanders

and walked and rode hundreds of miles with them. He accompanied them on many small battles and saw them organize the peasants and train and arm them with captured guns. After three months he was so full of what he had seen that he came out feeling that he had to wake up America with it. His superiors refused and Carlson, a man of strong convictions, temporarily resigned his commission in order to write and speak freely.

The Communists didn't weaken Carlson's faith in American principles but he was greatly impressed with their army's training and indoctrination methods, its spirit of self-sacrifice and the high standards of personal morality and competence of its officers. Other American military observers in China ridiculed Carlson for his enthusiasm. It particularly irritated them that he thought *we* had anything to learn from *any* Chinese. But he had one intensely interested listener on high. He was sending confidential personal reports to the White House, for the President's very interested eye, alone.* Three years later Roosevelt would back Carlson's plan to set up that unique organization known as the Marine Raiders. In it he incorporated a spartan physical training regimen and egalitarian code of brotherhood between officers and men based on his experiences with the Eighth Route Army.

CHAPTER 20

We Start Something

THROUGHOUT THE WAR Americans spoke of China as part of the "world democratic front" and of her "national unity." Such terms were largely myths agreed upon among allies. We have seen why and how the Kuomintang government was obliged to tolerate the Communists in the Northwest; elsewhere, however, the party was not legalized. Laws providing capital punishment for membership were never rescinded, but a few Communists were permitted to travel back and forth on recognized war missions, and the Eighth Route Army was allowed offices and a newspaper in the capital.

* For a comment on this correspondence see *The Secret Diary of Harold Ickes,* Vol. II, page 327, N.Y. 1954.

It was not one country that fought Japan, however, but two Chinas —the "border government" (at first very tiny) run by the Reds, and the rest of unoccupied China run by the Nationalists. Meanwhile, among non-party patriots of all descriptions a real faith persisted that a progressive government representative of varied opinion and worthy of the people's spirit of devotion and self-sacrifice would emerge during the war. Out of such a faith grew the most original and hopeful experiment of the "united front" period—the Chinese Industrial Co-operative organization. It provided work and an education for tens of thousands of Chinese and proved indeed to be the forerunner of what ultimately became the largest producers' co-operative movement in the world.

Indusco—as the Chinese Industrial Co-operative movement was known abroad—was primarily the invention of Rewi Alley, Nym Wales and myself. It could never have got off the ground without the initial sponsorship of a strange pair of enthusiasts—Soong Ching-ling, and the British Ambassador in China, Sir Archibald Clark-Kerr, later to be Lord Inverchapel. The idea would never have occurred to us as possible at all if so-called "Free China" had not, by 1938, been reduced to an almost wholly agrarian and pastoral state. Control of Manchuria, North China and the lower Yangtze Valley had given Japan eighty percent of China's machine shops, ninety percent of the chemical, rubber and cement industries, most of the mines and railways, as well as the "modern" cities. More than half of China's skilled workers were concentrated in Shanghai alone. Displaced by war, thousands of them wandered about as refugees, with nowhere to work and nobody to organize and use them.

The general attitude of officials as well as most observers was that little or nothing could be done. China lacked basic industry; without it she could not make machines, and without machines there could be no production. After many discussions Rewi and Nym and I became convinced that they were wrong. We had the answer. One of the first people we committed was a young secretary of the British Embassy named John Alexander, whom we knew to be a co-operative enthusiast. John quickly fired the interest of Sir Archibald Clark-Kerr.

"Well, young man," said the Ambassador when John took me into his office, "the last time I saw you you were a newspaper correspondent. Now what's this I hear about you becoming an industrialist?" I handed him a copy of the "prospectus" Rewi and I had drafted, covering a survey of the nation's production problems and a general all-China strategy of "front-area, middle-area, and rear-area industry"—

industrial co-operatives—to meet some of them. By now I knew that the Ambassador, who had been in China only a few months, was a maverick among British diplomats. He was certainly the first one who had ever looked *me* up on his arrival.

While Sir Archibald read through our draft I studied his face and asked myself, once more, whether he could actually be real. Already he had broken from the snobbish patterns set by his predecessors. He liked to travel; he liked people; he wanted to know everything first hand; he was a liberal. Although Neville Chamberlain was still prime minister, Sir Archibald was openly anti-Axis, anti-Franco and anti-Japanese. He so expressed himself, off the record, even to American correspondents, whom previous British ambassadors had usually kept at a cool, disdainful distance. "My friends," he stopped me one day when I was "sir-ing" him, "call me Archie." He didn't even look like a stuffed shirt. With his bent-bridged nose, high cheek bones, and a ruddy complexion, all he needed was a feather in his head to be an Indian chief. Given a black patch over one eye he could also have been mistaken for a pirate—which one of his great-grandfathers really was, he always insisted: the gentleman left him a 6,000-acre ancestral estate in Argyll. Trained by Lord Allenby in Egypt, Clark-Kerr had been jumped over twenty men senior to him, into his first ministerial post. Now a vigorous young man in his fifties, he had a brilliant career ahead of him.

The Ambassador put down our plans for industrial co-operatives, lighted his Dunhill, and examined me speculatively.

"Let's hear it in your own words," he said.

"The idea's simple enough," I answered. "There's a vacuum—and we propose to fill it with something good before the bad takes over."

"Don't talk like Dr. Johnson. Get on with your story."

"The vacuum is the Chinese market. We want to fill it with Chinese goods before Japan floods it with hers."

"Fine. Where do you get these Chinese goods?"

"Exactly. Factories gone, workers scattered, machines destroyed or captured. But unoccupied China *has* the raw materials—a country almost as large as the U.S.A. It can be self-sufficient in food. It has unlimited labor power—three hundred million people to draw from."

"Yes?"

"For the first time in a century China has a protected market—cut off from the treaty ports and foreign competition, except Japanese. There aren't many tools, but there are enough for a start—our way.

We want to organize the refugees in small groups on a co-operative basis: those with money and labor, those with labor only. We'll put them all to work with what they have. Our answer is a solution for the refugee problem, the consumer goods problem and the war production problem, among others. Our 'factories' may be pure handicraft at first, but we'll organize a smuggling detachment to bring in more and more tools. They can be had. All we need is money."

"But why *co-operatives?* I understand they've failed here every time they were tried."

"Co-operative—to give the people a stake in the war—and the future. Yes, marketing, credit, consumer co-operatives—they have all collapsed in the past. But not *industrial* co-operatives. They've never been tried. The others didn't fail because they aren't suited to China. They failed because of corrupt, incompetent leadership—and powerful sabotage by local landlords, merchants and militarists. There were two exceptions. The "mass education" Ting Hsien experiment under Jimmy Yen's leadership proved that co-ops will work. They worked very well indeed in his one, protected county—till the Japs put him out of business."

"And the other exception?"

"The Red districts. Their whole economy, such as it is, has been basically state capitalism combined with co-ops. Are you shocked?"

"Not at all. That was my own conclusion. But co-operatives aren't a Communist monopoly. If so, England would have been bolshie long ago. Scandinavia likewise."

"Correct. They aren't Communism; they're industrial democracy. But they can work under Socialism, too. That's why co-ops are the logical economic foundation for a united front . . ."

"So Alexander has been telling me. You want to make a co-operative commonwealth out of China and cheat the class war. Is that it?"

"Co-operative enterprise is in the long run the only way out for China, short of Communism. It's probably the Nationalists' last chance."

"Suppose we foreigners agree on that. Where does the Chinese support come in?"

"We already have it. Mme. Sun Yat-sen is one hundred percent behind it. So is her brother, T. V. Soong. I've talked the whole thing over with T.V. and he has promised all the help he can give as a private banker. But neither Mme. Sun nor T.V. wants to come out in the open for it just now. You know why—the old family feud and jealousy. It's got to be sold to the Generalissimo first—and that means to Mme. Chiang and to Mme. Kung. The idea has to come from them."

"I see light." Archie's blue eyes twinkled beside his high-bridged Scottish nose. "I'm your choice for the salesman's job?"

I nodded and grinned.

"Suppose I did agree. Have you got me a leader I can pull out of my hat? And has he got the Chinese staff we need?"

"I'm glad to hear that 'we,' Sir Archibald. Yes, I think we have a leader. His name is Rewi Alley."

"Where do we find him?"

"He's Municipal Factory Inspector here in the Settlement and he probably knows as much about labor and labor conditions in this country as any foreigner alive. What's more, he loves the country in spite of all he knows; he's adopted two famine orphans and is putting them through school here. Irish-English, from New Zealand, a World War hero; his wartime buddies got him his job here. You can tell something about his background by the fact that his father named him after Rewi Te Manipoto, a famous Maori chieftain who fought the British Redcoats by guerrilla methods. But the main thing about him is that he believes in China. It's a religion with him. Speaks the language and likes the common people. Flaming red hair, a big head, a hawklike nose. He's built like a bulldozer: legs like sturdy trees. He's broad, tough and intelligent."

"Hmm. How do we get him?"

"You can get him released from his contract with the Shanghai Municipal Council."

"Could he put a Chinese staff together?"

"He's already recruited one—a nucleus of the best Western-trained engineers and co-operative experts in China. They'd go into the interior with Alley tomorrow if the government would give the go-ahead. Alley is definitely key man."

"And what are *you* going to get out of it, if I may ask?"

"Work—and maybe a story. My wife and I are prepared to spend as much time as it takes to put this idea across not just in China but wherever there's any sympathy for China. Give us the money and the tools and we'll do the job. We will organize committees everywhere to carry it out. America can't send China scrap iron and guns, as we're sending them to Japan. But we can send relief—this way. Productive relief—to help China help herself. That's our angle."

Archie ran through the pages of our prospectus asking questions as he went along. Finally:

"You think the Communists will back it up, too? We don't want it attacked as a British imperialist scheme to take over China."

"Soong Ching-ling is our guarantee about that. They won't attack her. If necessary, I'll go up to Yenan to get Mao's blessings on it, myself."

"All right," Archie said, slapping his hand on the desk. "I'll do what I can to help. But not a word about my part to anyone. Bring Alley round to see me."

We had a drink together and sealed the bargain. Thus I entered into a conspiracy with the most unorthodox and far-seeing British diplomat I knew and began a rich lifelong friendship.

Within a week or so the Ambassador had got Alley out of his Council job, with his pension paid in a lump-sum advance. They were soon on their way to Hankow. There Archie kept his promise and "sold" Alley to the Generalissimo, to Mme. Chiang and to Dr. H. H. Kung, who was premier and finance minister. Alley was appointed chief technical adviser and quickly gathered together a field staff of able and honest young men. He set up an organization based on the constitution we had drawn up, on modified co-operative principles, that provided for low-interest loans and private credits to finance the first co-op units, with workers entitled to buy over their shares and take full control as soon as they became technically trained to do so.

The amazing thing was that all this actually worked! By 1940 we had raised fairly large sums abroad. A two-million-dollar loan T. V. Soong made privately to Alley and myself, and state help from Dr. Kung, enabled Indusco to set up several hundred small factories, workshops, power plants, transports and mines. We had our own training schools, war veterans and war orphans vocational centers, printing and publishing houses, lunch rooms, clinics, nursery schools and character-study schools for illiterate worker-members and their children. Indusco was becoming a reasonably sound prototype of a democratic, co-operative society, producing a wide variety of goods of war value. Some mobile co-operative units functioned far behind the Japanese lines in North China.

The speed of this growth was accomplished with little help, except financially, from the government. The administrative and technical personnel consisted almost entirely of non-party patriots. Among these volunteers were highly qualified men and women with Western training, many of them Christians, who worked for scarcely more than their food and lodging.

Virtually free of graft and nepotism, the organization was for a time relatively immune from bureaucratic control. That very circumstance, a historical accident, was soon to mark Indusco as a target for destruction by the most reactionary elements in the regime it might have helped to save.

CHAPTER 21

I Become a Missionary

THE NATIONALIST CABINET had given Alley his appointment and earmarked funds for administrative expenses and a loan fund. Before we got started we learned that the promise was one thing, cash quite another. After a small initial grant, Dr. Kung held up payment for weeks. Meanwhile, Alley and his staff not only paid their own expenses but used their personal savings to finance some of the first experimental co-ops.

Not long after he reached Hankow I got an urgent appeal from Alley to come there immediately, "or baby will perish." I was in Hongkong helping Soong Ching-ling with her China Defense League and trying to set up a separate Indusco committee. I talked over Alley's message with Ching-ling and we decided I ought to investigate. There were only two planes daily to Hankow, but with T. V. Soong's help I got a reservation for the next day. At the last moment I was bumped off for some V.I.P. That unfortunate plane was shot down near Canton by the Japanese and nearly everybody on board perished in the Pearl River, including the beloved Hsu Hsing-lo, a Shanghai bank president and a member of our original Shanghai promotion committee.

"What's the crisis?" I asked Rewi when I reached his apartment in the old Y.M.C.A. building in Hankow.

"We can't get the Sage to part with another copper," said Alley, alluding to Kung. "The cabinet's earmarked a million for us but he's stopped our funds. I'm broke and my boys are about to leave me in disgust."

"I've heard Kung claims to be a great admirer of Jefferson. Why don't you remind him of what Tom said about money being like manure—not much good unless it's distributed?"

"The Sage thinks it's to lay eggs on—like that *Feathered World* editor of yours," Rewi cracked wryly.

"I knew you'd been having troubles; I didn't think they were this bad. If only you could get Clark-Kerr back here . . ."

"This is a job you can do," said he.

"Me? I thought you wanted me kept out of it."

"Well, it's too late. Mei-ling has already heard you were mixed up in it and she doesn't like it. She could get the Sage moving; but she won't."

"What can I do? You want me to go over and *k'o-t'ou* to her?"

"What I thought was that you could be nice to her—say you want to write about her work—how interested America is in her industrial co-operative scheme for refugees—volunteer to help her—it might turn the trick. Donald tells me she's never forgiven you for what you said about the Generalissimo in *Red Star*."

William Henry Donald was then Mme. Chiang's confidant, trouble-shooter and adviser, and Rewi's best friend at court. This remarkable Australian newspaper man, who had arrived in China the year I was born, had a gift of friendship akin to Alley's. He was physically as rugged as Alley—blond, blue-eyed—and equally as honest, fearless, frank and devoted to China. But where Alley worked with and believed in the common people, and learned to speak fluent Chinese, Donald gave his friendship and help to the rulers, and always disdained to learn the language. His contacts were limited largely to English-speaking Chinese; among them he often exerted amazing influence. As a correspondent for James Gordon Bennett's New York *Herald,* Donald had not only covered the rebel siege of Nanking during the 1911 revolution; he trained the guns which blew open that city's gates. Dr. Sun Yat-sen had made him "foreign secretary" of his first and brief-lived Nanking government.

In Shanghai Donald early met "Charley" Soong, the true "founder" of the Soong "dynasty." Charley was then a humble printer just beginning to make a fortune out of Chinese translations of the Bible. Donald's friendship with Soong Mei-ling began when she was still in pigtails. But he had not joined her and the Generalissimo when the Nationalists came to power. He distrusted the new regime, for reasons of his own. For services rendered to the former government Donald had been rewarded with control over China's first Bureau of Statistics. Following the establishment of Chiang Kai-shek's Nanking government, in 1927, the new minister of finance demanded that Donald kick back $5,000 a month to him out of the appropriation allotted his bureau. Donald resigned—and went to Manchuria to work for its ruler, Marshal Chang Hsueh-liang, who was still in his twenties.

It was in Mukden, in 1929, that I had first met Donald. He introduced me to Chang Hsueh-liang, and gave me enough background material to enable me to write a story which (rashly) predicted that Japan would shortly find a pretext for an armed conquest of Manchuria. Before and after that happened, Donald remained attached to the Young Marshal Chang, lent him strength and guidance which helped him get rid of the dope habit, and later stood up for him, as a man of integrity and loyal devotion to China, even after he had arrested the Generalissimo. Meanwhile he had, however, been detached from Chang Hsueh-liang's service and brought into the Generalissimo's camp by the persuasive Mme. Chiang, who knew a good public relations man when she saw one. He worked selflessly and indefatigably for her and for China, with no personal axe to grind. And it was as a skillful propagandist that he saw at once, when Sir Archibald Clark-Kerr sought to enlist his support for Indusco and Alley, its immense potential value as a means of winning sympathy for China's cause— and for his boss.

And now, at Hankow, Alley was telling me that Donald insisted that I had to do something to "square" myself with Mme. Chang if we were to get her fully behind the co-operative movement.

"You know I bent over backward to be fair to Chiang and Mei-ling in *Red Star*," I said to Rewi. "I told how brave they both were at Sian."

"Mei-ling doesn't care what you wrote about Chiang politically. She's hopping mad about your crack that he lost his false teeth when he was captured and made the soldiers hunt around for them in the dark!"

"It seemed a good human touch at the time—I'm sorry." By then I would almost have sold my mother to save Indusco. I said I would see Madame and lay it on thick about her war work. (She was really doing a lot.) I'd write up her support for the co-ops for English and American readers.

Just as I was about to leave to see Mme. Chiang, Rewi rushed in very agitated.

"For God's sake," he said, "don't say a thing to her about the co-ops! I've just had a talk with Donald and he says Mei-ling wouldn't touch your help with the proverbial ten-foot pole. She just heard you've been down in Hongkong working with Mme. Sun and now she's got the queer idea you're up here for no good—to 'do a job' of some kind.

If you mention co-ops it may be our kiss of death, says Donald. Not a word, not a word!"

It was too late to cancel my date. Mme. Chiang was in a rage from the moment I arrived. She spent half an hour denouncing anonymous "destructive critics" of her husband, herself and the Kungs, who were sacrificing everything for China. How much "they" had "hurt China" —those "destructive, cynical critics!" Yet she denied, when I asked, that she meant me. If not me, then whom? Her sister, perhaps? I never found out. I dared not ask any leading questions—she was almost hysterical. All I could do was hold my tongue for the good of Indusco and listen. Told verbatim, her outburst would have made a lovely story. But she asked me not to report a line of it and I never did. In anger, she was still an attractive figure.

My old friend Hollington Tong (a Missouri University graduate) was with me, in his capacity of director of war publicity. All through the "interview" I saw his hands shaking, and for the first time realized that the old words "tremblingly obey," in the imperial edicts, still literally applied to acolytes of the current dynasty. Holly trembled still more when, next day, we went to call on the Generalissimo. But Chiang was very courteous throughout our interesting talk—this time for publication. As far as I could see he showed no sign whatever that I had written a somewhat controversial book about China since I had last interviewed him. I doubt that he ever read it.

This little episode typified Alley's difficulties in maintaining a "united front" among the Chiang-Soong-Kung family in support of his project to "help China help herself." That all three Soong sisters eventually became honorary chairmen of the movement, that Dr. Kung and Dr. Soong both sponsored it in their separate ways, one openly and the other covertly, and that the "Gissimo's" own father-image portrait adorned Indusco's shops, was considered a major miracle by outsiders. It was in fact due to Clark-Kerr's diplomacy and prodding more than to any divine intervention, that Kung released some of his inflated dollars.

But this time we had to resort to another stratagem. "There's only one thing to do," said I. "We've got to tap that two million T.V. earmarked for us in the Bank of China."

"We're not supposed to go near that until the movement really gets going," said Alley. "If the Sage hears about it now he'll blow up. You know how he hates Soong's guts."

"He doesn't have to know where it comes from. We'll call it a loan from the Shanghai-Hongkong Promotion Committee, collected from foreign sources. Maybe Kung will be so flattered, as head of Indusco, that he'll cough up some cash of his own."

Deciding he had nothing to lose, Alley agreed. It worked! He and I signed the papers and back in Hongkong I had the bank transfer Ch. $200,000 (then about U.S. $40,000) to our committee. When forwarded to Rewi it pulled him through the crisis. By the time Kung heard about it some co-op units were already financed by it and in production. And sure enough, impressed by this "outside help," Kung soon came through with some loans.

I was to learn more about the Soong-Kung vendetta, but at this point I realized that the good publicity given to Kung and Chiang for starting Indusco was the chief reason it had been allowed to persist at all, after the initial gesture giving it "paper status," to please Clark-Kerr. The most important help I could give was to back up Alley by increasing publicity abroad, and capitalize on it to raise independent funds for him. The movement had attracted influential supporters in Hongkong. Since that island colony was still safe for the present we decided to make it our promotional base.

With Ching-ling's advice and help, and T.V. in the background, we now organized, under British law, an International Committee for the promotion of Chinese Industrial Co-operatives. Authorized to receive loans and gifts of money, materials and technical assistance, the Committee began to administer a revolving fund, with the Soong loan as nucleus. Clark-Kerr won the support of the Governor of Hongkong, and we were able to persuade the Bishop of Hongkong, Ronald Hall, a saintly and exceptionally able man, to devote a large part of his extremely busy life to the job of chairmanship. An impressive array of Chinese and foreign bankers, business men and philanthropists joined the board or backed it, and money began to come in.

All this was a wholly new field of activity to my wife and me; we worked at it with true missionary zeal. Late in 1938 substantial contributions were already in the offing in Britain and America, where millions of dollars were later contributed. It was in the Philippines that the warmest and most generous response first came from abroad. Persistent invitations arrived from the large and wealthy Chinese community in the Islands for Mme. Sun or myself to go there to raise funds for Indusco, and, incidentally, help "awaken" the Filipinos to the Japanese danger.

One afternoon at sunset Nym and I sat on the beach at Repulse Bay until the lights of the fishing sampans began to wink, as they prepared to spread their nets for the night's catch. Nym looked tired. So, I realized, was I. Dog-tired. My work had suffered from preoccupation with our "promotional" efforts so seriously that I had turned over my *Herald* job to J. B. Powell. I too had been spending my own money on Indusco, and soon we would be running low on cash. I had to get back to writing, I thought; I had a book to do, and some articles promised to *The Saturday Evening Post*. The Philippines, from where we sat, suddenly looked like paradise to me—and an escape from committees.

"Isn't it strange," said Nym, "that after all these years studying European colonialism, you've never seen how our own boys run the Philippines? Why not accept that invitation and go see what it's like? China will still be here when we get back."

CHAPTER 22

Interlude in Luzon

THE PHILIPPINES lay only two or three hours' flight from China by the Clipper ships of those days. Its northern territory reached within fifty miles of Japanese-owned islands off South Formosa yet few Filipinos then believed that what was happening in China was a prelude to disaster for themselves. Only the Chinese community, of more than 100,000, required little convincing that the Philippines were next on the Japanese schedule.

The Philippine Chinese, surprisingly homogenous and generally more prosperous than the Filipinos, were led by as patriotic and community-minded a group of rich men as I have encountered anywhere. They were chiefly from Fukien province, which also populated Formosa, and had only within the century, or a little earlier, arrived in Manila penniless immigrants. Now their multi-millionaires—such as Dee C. Chuan, Alfonso and Albino Sy Cip, and Yu Khei-thai—had by hard work, frugality and business shrewdness risen to commanding positions in the native banking, industrial and mercantile world. From the moment we landed in Manila they took us under their wing. Through them we discovered the moving gratitude and kindliness of overseas Chinese toward any Americans who genuinely tried to help their country.

Dee C. Chuan was among the more impressive Philippine Chinese, and their recognized leader. Dee told me that he had been a barefoot orphan when a childless merchant adopted him and gave him a start. Now he was reputed to be the richest Chinese in the islands. His fairness to his employees was proverbial and labor troubles were then said to be unknown in his many enterprises. One day at dinner he questioned me about the Reds, and my visits with them.

"We Chinese here in the Philippines," he said, "are non-partisan toward politics on the mainland. We think Sun Yat-sen's program was good; we always believed in him and we revere his widow. We are sorry the Kuomintang regime has not carried out his wishes and we know its shortcomings. But we hope for a wartime awakening. As for the Communists, if they're for the poor and want to bring an equal chance to everybody, that is what Sun Yat-sen wanted to do. I don't agree with all Mao Tse-tung says, but we respect him and his followers as patriots. Since they too fight against Japan they deserve our help. We want to discourage civil war and encourage democratic peaceful solutions. We want China to be a nation the world will respect. That's why we like Industrial Co-operatives and will aid them. It is the right idea for China."

Dee kept his word. As one of Indusco's staunchest friends he made generous gifts and secured money for loans which helped start co-operatives in both the Kuomintang and Communist areas of China.

Soon after our arrival Dee and other leading Chinese business men sponsored a large reception for us attended by high American and Filipino officials. Questions asked by Americans as well as Filipinos surprised me both by the general lack of information revealed and by the sympathy and good will expressed for the Chinese people's brave efforts at resistance. There was no joint Sino-American-Philippine war relief organization as yet. Indusco seemed ideally suited for that purpose—and to focus sentiment against Japanese aggression.

Thus, as the unavoidable consequence of our own commitment to China's cause, Nym and I had to take on the task of organizing the Philippine Committee for Chinese Industrial Co-operatives. Its educative and fund-raising activities naturally were anti-Japanese in their effects and soon aroused the ire of the local consul-general. So considerable was Japanese influence in President Quezon's office—particularly on his secretary, José Vargas, who later became an outstanding collaborator—that the Japanese consul-general succeeded in having a police permit withdrawn for a large meeting I was to address at the Teatro Nacionale in Manila. Paul V. McNutt, then American

High Commissioner, very promptly intervened to have the permit restored. He later told me that he had called Quezon and informed him that "as long as the American flag flies over the Philippines the rights of freedom of the press, assembly and organization will be fully protected."

The Japanese were even more annoyed when, further reflecting the High Commissioner's contempt, Mrs. McNutt herself became honorary chairman of the Philippine Committee for Indusco—as did the wife of McNutt's successor, Mrs. Francis B. Sayre. With this open support many American and Filipino volunteers entered into the work. Prominent among them in Manila was our chairman, the Rev. Walter B. Foley, who was to be killed during the war in Manila; and an outspokenly anti-Franco American business man, William R. Babcock, and his wife. In the summer capital of Baguio a branch committee headed by Mr. and Mrs. E. E. Crouter was very effective in stimulating the interest of American engineers in the mining community. Seventy of these engineers joined hundreds of other Philippine Americans who eventually petitioned President Roosevelt to earmark future loans, in our aid-China program, for the development of Industrial Co-operatives. Many of these friends were to perish in the war, and the Crouters themselves were to spend three long years in a Japanese detention camp.

By 1940 Eleanor Roosevelt, Pearl Buck and her husband Richard Walsh had sponsored an American Committee for Indusco. The movement had received so much favorable publicity in the Philippines that it dwarfed the official Chinese propaganda effort.

I did not spend all my time in the Philippines being a promoter. In the cloud-dimmed mountains of Northern Luzon, Nym and I discovered and fell in love with highland Baguio. A town air-conditioned by nature, and surrounded by lordly pines—some of them festooned with gorgeous wild orchids—it was about as near to a tropical paradise, à la américaine, as existed. We decided to make it our home base, as I alternately worked on a book and did reportorial assignments in the Philippines, and back in China, for The Saturday Evening Post.

It is pleasant to recall a time when Americans were really liked, as we were then in the Philippines. Although the liberating Tydings-McDuffie Act was motivated more by business interests seeking to cut off duty-free Philippines' imports to the U.S. than by any popular American demand to emancipate our wards, its effects created immense good will for us all over Asia. With the inauguration of autonomous government under President Quezon's administration, and complete independence guaranteed by 1946, most Filipinos were ready to acknowledge all that was good—and overlook most of the bad—about the years of American rule.

The immense majority of the common people of the Philippines were to remain unequivocally loyal to America and its democratic ideals all through the coming war; thousands turned guerrilla and doggedly fought the Japanese for four years. Even while I was still there, however, it was already evident that a few opportunists in high places were preparing to betray the republic, in the event of an invasion, and work for a Japanese and Axis victory.

If there were serious omissions in America's preparation of the Filipinos for political independence, our failure to build anything like adequate economic foundations for sovereignty was far more profound. No territory in the East—and few in the world—was better suited to provide a rich life for its people, in terms of both domestic modern industry and agriculture, than those greatly underpopulated and enormously valuable islands. Yet our rule resulted in their virtually complete dependence on imports of American consumer goods which the Philippines could make for themselves or readily do without, while the establishment of basic industry, and the training of cadres of technicians essential for the development of a modern state had scarcely begun.

Nowhere could you better see the grotesque results of an unplanned colonial economy under rampant laissez-faire than on a Saturday afternoon in Baguio, when the barefoot Igorots came up from the mines for their weekly encounter with American civilization. Dressed in nothing but scant loin cloths they would pile into yellow taxis and debouch on the main street. There these naked children of the headhunters would load up on face-painting materials and Baby Ruth bars and Coca-Cola—imported duty-free in a land overflowing with sugar—and buy "gaws and gewgaws." Then they would queue up to see George Raft knocking drunks around or shooting it out with other gangsters on the screen, imported from that glamorous world of violence and sin that sent its emissaries to tutor the simple savage. The Igorots at least still wove their own beautiful loin cloths, but practically every processed article the lowland Filipino wore, ate or used was duty-free American goods.

Reports from Rewi Alley and from Chinese engineers and technicians in the field concerning sabotage and political undermining of Indusco were by 1939 already troubling my conscience, as its publicist and spokesman for foreign support. I had after all seen only the hopeful beginnings of the co-ops in the best days of the united-front period, before the fall of Hankow. Now I heard that reaction, repression and demoralization were widespread under the government that had been pushed back to Chungking. Ching-ling urged me to return and see for myself what was happening. I put aside my book and went back to China, where further travels through the hinterland were to keep me for many months. This time Nym stayed behind, in Baguio.

CHAPTER 23

Dynastic Housekeeping

"OUR FRIEND Rewi Alley," said Mme. Sun Yat-sen when I next saw her, "seems to be in trouble again." Ching-ling was staying on in Hongkong as long as possible, rather than live under constant surveillance in Chungking, but her own intelligence system kept her well informed on internal Chinese politics.

"What kind of trouble now?" I asked.

"You might call it political fleabitis. You know the rhyme:

> Great fleas have little fleas, upon their backs to bite 'em,
> And little fleas have lesser fleas, and so *ad infinitum*.

Rewi is now a great flea in the eyes of the Kuomintang bosses, the Chen brothers. They're calling him a red-haired, big-nosed foreign imperialist! Indusco is becoming a success. The reactionaries want to eat it up."

"I know about that. Meng Yung-cheng wrote me that Chen Li-fu insists on another reorganization at Indusco headquarters. Every reorganization means more jobs for Kuomintang loafers on the headquarters payroll."

"Well," she said satirically, "they'll say it's their money, and they don't want any foreign imperialists telling them what to do with it."

"We're raising more money for administrative purposes right now than the government contributes. But foreign aid will dry up if Indusco becomes another racket for party hacks. It was guaranteed at the outset that the movement could develop free of the party bureaucracy."

"Maybe the real trouble," said Ching-ling, "is that you've been giving Alley too much publicity. Why don't you write an article about Dr. Kung?" She gave me a sly, quizzical smile.

"Do you want me to ruin China altogether? You know, I did go to see Kung with the intention of building him up as our patron saint. 'Oh yes, industrial co-operatives, I'm all for them,' he said. 'It's my dream for a long time. Yes, indeed,' he went on, 'my wife and I never did like to see our pure village girls going to work in the big city factories. It spoils their virtue. Mahatma Gandhi has the right idea: these spinning societies are just the thing to keep young girls working at home and out of mischief. We can't let our moral standards down because of the war.'"

"Did you know that Mme. Kung tried to get Rewi to leave Indusco and go back to manage one of her textile factories in Japanese-occupied Shanghai?" asked Ching-ling brightly.

"No! Well, perhaps I should write an article about that? Or about how absolutely astonished Kung was when he found out that the co-ops were not only making tools, machines and even hand grenades, but also making profits? All that, and saving the girls' virginity too!"

"Imagine our prime minister in a loin cloth!" Ching-ling choked over her tea at the thought of her brother-in-law as the Great Soul.

"Believe me, that's all Kung had to say; that's all he saw in the whole thing," I said. "Should I write about that? Or about his wife's speculations in foreign exchange? Or what I am told by Cyril Rogers, the Bank of England representative? He says British business men are all complaining to him about the excessive personal commissions Kung's office collects on the war orders he places with them."

"No, you should not write that—not now," she answered soberly. "In spite of all that, Dr. Kung and Mme. Chiang—and your foreign support—are the only chance we have of keeping Indusco alive and independent."

She was right about that, too, I discovered during the next few months after I had been in Chungking and then traveled hundreds of miles in the hinterland, up and down the "Indusco Line," part of the time with Alley.

By early October, 1940, more than 2,300 of our vest-pocket factories were spread across sixteen provinces and under the technical direction of seventy branch headquarters. They extended all the way from guerrilla territory, behind enemy positions, into the deep west of China, and from the Mongolian plateau to the highlands of Yunnan. Handicraft, textile, printing and transport co-ops had been the first to appear, but now there were small iron mines and foundries, coal and gold mines, primitive machine shops, flour mills, paper mills, sugar and oil refineries, and chemical, glass, publishing and electrical goods works as well as shops making medical goods, uniforms, hand grenades, wagons and tents. A quarter of a million people were already dependent on Industrial Co-operatives for a livelihood. In addition forty thousand affiliated home-industry spinners and weavers were engaged in filling an Indusco order to make blankets for the Chinese army.

All this activity was supervised by a field staff of only about one thousand educated non-party young people—trained engineers, economists, scientists, accountants, assorted technicians and organizers, among whom Rewi Alley was chief technical adviser. Their pay was minimal, and living conditions very rough, but they had pride and morale. They believed they were helping to build a progressive future for China.

But in this, under the Kuomintang government at least, they were doomed to early disillusionment.

It is necessary to remind ourselves again that Chiang Kai-shek and his cohorts were not elected to power but seized it. In 1938 party secretary Chen Li-fu claimed a Kuomintang membership of two million, but activists did not exceed two hundred thousand—scarcely two in five thousand. Eighty percent of the people could not read or write and owned little or nothing, and the Kuomintang held they were not "ready" for even local self-government. Probably not five percent of the people had attended secondary school. Not one in a thousand had been to college. Foreign visitors who met Mme. Chiang, and heard her beautiful Wellesley speech, or Dr. T. V. Soong, with his Harvard manner, often got the impression that they were typical of the Kuomintang ruling class. They could not have been more in error.

As far as the peasants were concerned, "government" simply meant the party-appointed local magistrate who ruled as of yore in collusion with the landlord-gentry folk and their local guards—five to ten percent of the populace. It was through them that the Kuomintang elite and its armed forces held what centralized power the Generalissimo administered as head of the state. Once the regime was driven from the coast by Japan, once it was cut off from its semi-industrialized bases in the metropolis, once much of its small modern urban middle class following was either lost to the enemy or debouched on the interior as bankrupt refugees, wholesale reform became imperative for the self-preservation of the Kuomintang. In the new setting about ninety percent of the population was peasant or living on the peasant economy. The great majority were have-littles or have-nothings. To run the costly, wasteful, corrupt and top-heavy bureaucracy and the army in the old way meant imposing impossible burdens on the peasantry.

"Wherever I am, there is the government," Chiang Kai-shek told me, and he literally believed that. But the corollary was "wherever I am not, there my government is not." Chiang's mandate did not prevail even in his own family, or over those most dependent on him. It was by virtue of disunity that he held power, not by unity. By keeping his subordinates weak and divided he himself appeared strong.

The Kuomintang government consisted principally of the national and local administrative apparatus or bureaucracy; the military hierarchy and armies more affiliated with it rather than commanded by it; and the "palace clique" or what the Chinese called the "Soong Dynasty."

The bureaucracy was controlled by the "C.C." clique, meaning Chen Kuo-fu and Chen Li-fu, nephews of the warlord and secret society chieftain who had first sponsored Chiang Kai-shek in the party. Ever after Chiang's split with the Reds, one or the other of the Chens always bossed the Kuomintang organization bureau and the secretariat. Through their chosen magistrates and the *tangpu,* or party branches (in close alliance with the urban and rural secret societies—actually, gangs), the Chens dispensed government patronage and collected tribute or "contributions" from the gentry and business men.

But the Chens did not own the army. That was dominated by their rival, the *Whampoa P'ai* and its sub-cliques, in the Generalissimo's headquarters. This was a group of generals trained at Whampoa Academy in Canton when Chiang Kai-shek served there as chief commandant under the Russian advisers. Few of them had ever won a battle, but as they were loyal to Chiang during the counter-revolution of 1927 they could henceforth do no wrong. The Whampoa clique and the "C.C." frequently clashed over divisions of spoils and patronage. Chiang mediated and prevented either from becoming too strong or independent.

Thirdly, the principals in the "palace clique" included Chiang and his wife, Soong Mei-ling; their brother-in-law, H. H. Kung; Sun Fo, the only son of Dr. Sun Yat-sen, who was older than his stepmother; T. V. Soong, the younger brother of Mme. Chiang; and Mme. Chiang's elder sister, Soong Ai-ling—Mme. Kung. Some people considered Mme. Kung more powerful than Mme. Chiang because of her controlling influence not only over her own husband but over her sister, Mei-ling, through whom she frequently swayed the Generalissimo. Her several grown children also shared the prerogatives of the "royal family" to some extent, as did the younger Soong brothers. Each member of the "Dynasty" had his or her own "sub-court" of near and distant cousins, aunts, uncles, friends and assorted acolytes and parasites. Among them contracts, favors and largesse were competed for in rivalry with both the "C.C." and the Whampoa clique. Here again the Generalissimo maintained a balance of weakness in the role of father-pacifier.

Chiang also used the state and semi-state banks of issue to keep the factions dependent on him. The Chen brothers operated only on the banking periphery while key banking positions were held exclusively by his brothers-in-law. Usually either Dr. Kung or Dr. Soong was finance minister. Chiang obviously preferred Dr. Kung, who had no party prestige and never openly opposed Chiang's demands; but Dr. Kung knew nothing about modern banking. "He has the mentality of a child of twelve," Cyril Rogers once told me in disgust. "If I were to record his conversations with me about banking and play it back abroad nobody would ever take Chiang's government seriously again." Periodically Chiang had to call in T. V. Soong to untangle the resulting chaos.

"T.V." certainly had the family's best-trained mind, and a good grasp of modern banking practice; he also had a vague attachment to liberal political sentiments which Chiang detested. In *Personal History* Jimmy Sheean gave a sympathetic picture of T.V. as a younger man, torn between Socialism as his ideal, and his inclinations toward moderation, compromise, comfort and respectability in practice. Although he finally sided with the counter-revolution, his political ambivalence continued. Emotionally he sympathized with his favorite sister, Mme. Sun Yat-sen, the only revolutionary in the family. His millions doubtless gave him a bad conscience which he sometimes appeased by helping Ching-ling and through her even surreptitiously aiding left causes. But as a "practical business man" from Harvard he had to stomach Chiang Kai-shek, whose methods he despised.

Western-oriented Chinese and foreigners sometimes envisaged T. V. Soong as the potential leader of a "liberal party" which might replace Chiang. This dream had no reality in the inner politics of the land. T.V. could have displaced Chiang only by violence, when he would of course have ceased being a liberal. He lacked the substance to be either a revolutionary or a dedicated reformer. Liberalism is a product of modern capitalism and China was still in a stage of semi-feudalism. Even Indusco was destined to wither in the dank air and deadly nightshade of Kuomintang politics.

I never met any foreigner who really understood the labyrinthine Kuomintang banking "system," but in practice Chiang, Kung and Soong ran the four government banks, including the Central Bank of China and the Bank of China, which held most of the hard money. Private and semi-private banks depended on currency loans and credits from these state banks but "connections" were necessary. Private bankers prudently rewarded the Dynasty and its allies with stock interests, so that those who made state fiscal policy directly profited both as principal stockholders of the major private banks and as participants in semi-state enterprises.

T.V. clearly understood the necessity to promote every kind of useful production and services. During the war his Bank of China financed many enterprises purely on that basis. For the most part he preferred to make money from some kind of actual production; his own code of ethics did not permit him to accept bribes. Dr. Kung had the shrewd rural-exchange merchant's eye out for quick profits in personal side deals, for which he and his wife became notorious.

While I was in Chungking the secretary-general of Indusco, an American-trained engineer named K. P. Liu, told me that Kung was again holding up operating funds earmarked by the Cabinet. Staff wages had not been paid for three months. One day Premier Kung's private secretary came right out and demanded a $50,000 bribe or cutback before he would advance any more money. Clark-Kerr once more intervened; but later on, when general demoralization set in, the cut-backs became standard practice. It didn't surprise me, as Rogers had told me that $5,000 had to be added on to the cost of every airplane China bought in England. After Kung began buying in the United States a personal "commission" of $16,000 was added on to the price of each of the Martin bombers purchased by China—or so I was told by Major (later General) Frank Roberts, our former military attaché.

In these years when the Nationalist government desperately appealed to the Western democracies to support the Chinese *yuan,* or dollar, Britain and the U.S. sank millions of pounds and dollars into what was called a "stabilization fund." This was supposed to maintain an exchange value for the Chinese dollar on the Shanghai, Hongkong and world markets. Only carefully selected Chinese and foreign banks were authorized to deal in limited amounts of foreign exchange. Of course the Japanese maneuvered to raid China's exchange reserves, but they had stiff competition from Mme. Kung and her agents. Mme. Kung not only regularly speculated in foreign exchange through her own bank, the Continental, in the Shanghai International Settlement, and through the American brokerage firm of Swan, Culbertson and Fritz; she was able to take advantage of inside information.

Rumors of Mme. Kung's more blatant exchange speculations were in several instances confirmed for me by our U.S. Treasury representative in China, Martin R. Nicholson. Nicholson had access to the books of the Shanghai Continental Bank and had seen the records of the transactions.

"It's Mme. Kung, not Japan," he said in disgust, "who is killing the Chinese dollar."

It wasn't just the dollar; that money would have fed and put to work thousands of war refugees. When I finally decided, in 1941, to report some of the facts about the Kungs' operations I showed my cable to Nicholson before I sent it to the *Herald Tribune*. "The facts are true enough," Nick pleaded, "but it may ruin China's chance of getting further American loans if you cable this. It will help nobody but the Japs. I'm keeping Henry Morgenthau informed and we're going to put a stop to this."

I never sent the story but the real reason was that I thought it might ruin Indusco.

Although the Kungs perhaps did more than any other single family to demoralize all Chinese officialdom, and their selfish behavior became more septic as the war dragged on, they were more conspicuous only because they were on top. They were personally nice people. Mme. Kung was especially charitable and philanthropic. They were after all only part of a general pattern, a prototype emulated on a smaller but more vicious scale in nearly every magistrate's yamen.

Admittedly, Chinese war profiteering was nothing to justify any smug sense of moral superiority in America. Some of our business men were sharing in the loot in China, while at home they also made war pay—as I was later reminded when I interrupted work on this book to write a story for the *Post** on the General Dynamics Corporation, one of our great producers of "weapons of deterrence." Parent stock in that company enriched its promoters by seventeen times from 1939 to 1956; today it is worth more than thirty to one on the original investment. That is even better than the nineteen firms which operated government-owned shipyards during the war, to make $356,000,000 on a

* *Saturday Evening Post,* Sept. 9, 1956.

capital investment of $22,000,000. At least American profiteers did produce the tools of war. Another difference as compared to China was that the American people could have done something about being robbed, if they had cared enough.

I have shown only one corner of the Chinese Augean stables. It is enough to expose the absurdity of the myth so sedulously fostered in late years by the Formosa Lobby, to the effect that decay and corruption of the Chiang Kai-shek regime did not begin until its very end. These are peccadilloes, of course, compared to the golden harvest Chinese officials were to reap from massive American lend-lease gifts after Pearl Harbor, but the moral rot was already far advanced before then. This miasma was not only to overwhelm Indusco but also to bring down General Stilwell a few years later.

Stilwell's orders were "to increase the combat effectiveness of the Chinese army." To do that he had to establish minimum controls over American aid in order to build a reliable, patriotic, well-fed and well-trained *national* army for China out of the coterie of feudal chieftains manipulated in a balance of weakness system by the Generalissimo. That made Stilwell a "reformer" and that, fundamentally, was why he could not be tolerated by the Dynasty, the generals-in-business, and greedy parasites from top to bottom. But the Stilwell story has been well told elsewhere, by Theodore H. White and Annalee Jacoby, by Jack Belden, by Brooks Atkinson and Tillman Durdin and others, as well as by Stilwell himself, and the U.S. Army.

Here I must return to the story of my own "adventures in the skin trade," if I may lift a phrase from Dylan Thomas.

CHAPTER 24

Further Disenchantments

IT WAS a day of triumph when Mme. Sun Yat-sen and Mme. H. H. Kung visited Chungking and together with Mme. Chiang inspected some nearby Indusco workshops, posed for still and moving-picture cameramen, and pronounced joint benediction over their "productive relief" efforts. This also helped put a momentary quietus on Japanese-circulated rumors—well enough founded in fact—that the united front was breaking up.

"A nice show," said Rewi, "but it won't stop the Chen brothers from continuing to sabotage. From their standpoint we're a menace. They thought we were a joke at first. Now all at once they realize that we're actually the largest working-class organization in the country—since free labor unions don't exist. So they call us Reds. We've got Reds at central headquarters, they say, so they get Kung to shove their so-called bookkeepers and accountants onto us. Now they are trying to get their stooges installed in branch headquarters. We'll soon be carrying two staffs everywhere—one to do the work, the other to guzzle wine and invent political slanders to report to Chen Li-fu and Tai Li."

"There's one safeguard," I said. "They can't get hold of the International Committee's funds. It's a set policy with us that only you decide where our money goes."

"That's what burns them up. That's why they keep calling me an imperialist and a Red. Can I be both?"

"You're worse; you're a missionary."

"Yes, yes, I knew that when you got me into this. Found it out long ago when I worked for the famine relief commission. Well, let them say what they like about us, as long as they don't stop us. I get my thanks from the looks on kids' faces when they get down to work. Lost, hopeless derelicts, mere beggars, discards; then we give them a job, teach them something, and life begins. They belong—a place to learn, a home instead of the jungle, a decent concept of living and working together! Makes animals into men! Oh, not everybody takes to it; we've got miles to go yet, but they're wrong when they say Chinese can't co-operate. They're born for it! Trouble is, nobody's ever tried."

"I still hear people say it can't work. Chinese are too individualistic, they say. Nelson Trusler Johnson, our ambassador, tells me that when I go to ask him to throw in a word for us with the Gissimo. 'Snow,' said he, 'stick to your last. *Wu wei erh, wu pu wei;* through doing nothing, all things are done. This isn't our war. The best thing for you and me to do,' he said, 'is to go on eating our bacon and let them do it their own way. *Industrial* co-operatives? They won't be ready for it in a hundred years.' "

"Horse feathers!" snorted Rewi. "The truth is that if we were failing we wouldn't be in trouble. We're a roaring success, damn it, and that they can't stand. Ching-ling is right: it's just what old man Sun was groping for—his livelihood principle brought down to earth. That's their only hope of democracy here."

If Rewi wasn't loved among party moguls he now had thousands of friends spread across the workshops of the countryside, where he had carried his message and money and tools from north to south. His blue eyes glistened when he remembered a scene from his travels— "the biggest thrill since we started to work."

"One winter morning we're leaving a little village on the edge of Mongolia when we hear tinkling bells, and a long caravan of camels comes out of the mist. Their breath turns to frost in the bitter air. As they go by we see the lead camel carrying a huge silk banner—our banner—and our triangle and *kung-ho* (work together!) slogan emblazoned on the big boxes of freight.

"It was a camel-pullers' transport co-op hauling products to the guerrillas, by God! I didn't even know it existed. The men with me who had come up from the warm south suddenly realized they were part of something that covered the whole country."

That was the kind of thrill (Alley went on) that kept Frank Lem, K. P. Liu, C. F. Wu and Lu Kuang-mien, our best engineers and organizers, sticking to their jobs despite every discouragement.

"It's beginning to take up more and more time," Rewi went on, "just springing our best technicians out of jail." He grimaced. "The funny thing is that we couldn't get an honest-to-God Communist to join our work in the Kuomintang areas if we tried! They need all their technicians in their own districts. Their eyes are on North China, behind the Japanese lines, not back here."

"That may get worse," I said, "but Chen Li-fu and his boys can't openly wreck Indusco as long as Mme. Chiang and the Kungs are taking credit and praise for it abroad."

"No," Rewi answered, "but they can slowly suffocate it. That's one reason they're setting up this so-called Co-operative Control Bureau."

The Co-operative Control Bureau would have been a great blessing if it had actually promoted co-ops, but it was another case of *yu-ming wu-shih* (name without reality) characteristic of the Kuomintang bureaucracy. It was all "control" and all "bureau" and no co-operatives.

Chen Li-fu made paper claims for some "farmers co-operatives" and wished to break Indusco to the same pattern. These farmers co-operatives theoretically were to unite tillers in credit and marketing associations.

"The way it works out," Rewi explained, "is that the Chen clique gives loans or credits to the local *tangpu* [headquarters] for a co-operative fund. The party henchmen and the magistrate get together with the landowners and form themselves into a co-op, which is actually a money-lending set-up. At best they simply re-lend the money to the poor peasants at a little less than the customary usury rates— say thirty to forty instead of forty to fifty percent. They just use the money themselves to corner local markets in grain, cloth, smuggled Japanese goods, and exchange speculations. Helps old man inflation hurry right along."

T. V. Soong was in America when the struggle with the Co-operative Control Bureau reached a crisis. I air-mailed the details to him asking him to intercede on the grounds that American opinion and support would be alienated if Indusco were turned over to the Chen brothers. Fortunately, he cared enough to cable the Generalissimo and Mme. Chiang some words to that effect. As a result Indusco successfully resisted "consolidation" under the Co-operative Control Bureau for some time. A more severe handicap arose later. It was the organized large-scale purchase of Japanese goods under the National Resources Commission, in exchange for China's raw materials. This operation was carried on by a government supposedly in mortal combat with an invader.

By 1940 much of the Western and Southern "front" in China had become inactive. The Japanese had gone as far as they wished and were trying to consolidate political control under the puppet regime at Nanking, headed by Wang Ching-wei, Chiang Kai-shek's former deputy-leader-in-chief. After Wang defected at Hankow many Kuomintang bureaucrats followed him as well as some Kuomintang commanders with their troops. As Wang's puppets now accompanied the Japanese they re-established business contacts with some former comrades in many "front areas," which became so peaceful that farmers ploughed up the earthworks and began to till their fields again. So-called no-man's-land often gave way to thriving markets in enemy goods.

Instead of suppressing this contraband to encourage production, the Chungking government took charge, and used its monopoly in certain raw materials to foster trade. In this way Japan was able to dump large quantities of cheap consumer goods into the "Free China" market and obtain tung oil, tungsten, wolfram, tin and other scarce metals in exchange.

The effects of this kind of competition on Indusco as well as other infant industry were crippling but not entirely disastrous. Coupled with the gradual freezing of state credits and operating capital, however, with increasing political interference which shut down many units for days at a time, and with rampant inflation, it soon made further Indusco growth impossible and mere survival dependent on emergency foreign aid. Runaway inflation was not at all inevitable in Kuomintang China. It was fostered by the government's lack of interest in production, nearly total lack of rationing, the vast unchecked preoccupation of party members, officials and army officers with bribery, hoarding and profiteering, and speedy emulation of the practices among all classes.

One of the main factors in the rural breakdown was the Chen brothers' control of the Farmers Bank of China, with which Chiang Kai-shek placated them when they complained bitterly about the Kung-Soong banking monopoly. After they took over the Farmers Bank the Chens spread corruption very wide in the rural economy. At the start, in 1940, they dumped Ch. $400,000,000 (then still money of sorts) into the gentry's hands in their "farmers co-operatives"—which had simply vanished in a year or two. Keeping the printing presses busy turning out paper money (with no collateral) they packed the pockets of followers who produced nothing but cornered what little others produced and much that later came in from America. Through this bank and others the Chens would, at the end of the war, advance "loans" which enabled them to grab state-confiscated enemy and "traitor" properties on the east coast of enormous value. Together with acquisitions made in similar ways by the Chiang-Kung-Soong group—in the name of "private enterprise" and "rugged individualism"—it probably constituted a large part of China's industrial assets.

The hope of the reformer was not yet dead in me when, in 1940, it became obvious that America would soon be at war with Japan.* We would then help China, I believed, take the path toward "progress during the war." Saul Bellow wrote somewhere that "as soon as people become free they feel responsible for everything; they think it's up to them to be in charge." Perhaps I wished to be "in charge" of the way our aid in money, materials and arms would be used in China. In this vice I was only a little ahead of drowsing America as a whole, which was yet to become aware that economic aid meant political intervention. Economic intervention *always* meant either bolstering the status quo or changing it. The important thing was to know that and make conscious plans to direct it.

In *Asia* magazine in July, 1941, for example, I argued that "the United States has the duty at least to secure minimum guarantees

* In "Showdown in the Pacific" (*Saturday Evening Post,* July, 1941) I predicted that 1941 would be the year of Japan's attack on the Western powers.

necessary for effective implementation of its aid." If America gave substantial *unconditional* help to the existing regime, I warned, the result would only increase its arrogance and corruption, and make it feel still less dependent on popular internal support, still less interested in production and self-help, and obsessed with personal enrichment through graft and profiteering foreseeable in coming "deals" with Americans.

The dilemma was real enough. It was to prove the central paradox of all America's war-time and post-war aid to China.

What I did not realize was how remote it was from the conscious desire of the American people and the Congress to assume any responsibility for the political future of China and Asia generally.

How earnestly this Candide-turned-reformer pleaded for comprehension in an America which was, he supposed, about to "take charge"! In 1941 I wrote:

"It would not seem desirable for the Communist Party to replace the Kuomintang . . . The Communists would have to enlist many of the present bureaucrats to form a government. If they were not merely to impose a new name on an old bureaucracy they would be compelled to break the latter's counter-revolutionary alliance with the gentry *with a ruthlessness and terror which would be widely misunderstood abroad.* The capitalist powers might take active steps to close China entirely as a capital market. The regime would have to rely solely on Soviet Russian aid . . .

"Nevertheless, the transition to a 'thoroughgoing democracy' must be made, and speedily made, or the Kuomintang may lose its mandate under circumstances painful for the entire world . . . The program of a co-operative state, based on a true rural co-operative movement closely integrated with true co-operative industrialization, co-ordinated in state planning, seems to me now to offer the only chance of laying the economic foundation for a victorious democracy in China without renewed civil war. *This is also, I suggest, the only kind of China in which the foreign powers would find any possibility of developing a market in the future."* *

I was simply dreaming, as many people in China were dreaming, of a "savior from abroad"—in my case, America. Only a person long cut off from the actualities of American life, as I was, could have assumed that America possessed any such coherent philosophy of intervention. America had no world ideological aims and no perfected methods of reform or revolution for export. Only a sentimentalist could have

* *The Battle for Asia,* N.Y., 1941, p. 367-8. Italics added.

imagined that our people, our Congress and our Government were ready to sponsor a co-operative economy in China, run by and for the people, as the only alternative to the triumph of Russian-oriented Communism there.

Ironically, it was to be the Communists themselves who would see the usefulness of the co-operative method of organizing the people, for their own ends, in a great transitional stage of the consolidation of their revolutionary power.

CHAPTER 25

That "Agrarian Reformer" Myth

"BAD NEWS about China is good news for Japan" was the thought that kept the more conscientious correspondents from spilling the most damaging facts about the Kuomintang regime throughout the war. Censorship was there; but censorship could be circumvented.

From what I had seen behind the Chinese front I knew that twenty soldiers were dying of malnutrition, preventable disease, neglected minor wounds for every one killed in combat. No wonder they looted and ran. Half the Kuomintang army was already barefoot, without overcoats, without medicines—all the necessities China could have made for herself. The generals had everything, and business, too. Few of us wrote about that.

Sons of officials and wealthy families bought their exemptions and sat around tea and wine shops loafing or trading; peasants were beaten into the army, ropes around their necks. On the streets of Szechuan towns you could see rich men throw scraps through the doors or windows of the more expensive restaurants to mangy children, and laugh to see them scramble like dogs. If you wrote very much about that you would be "helping Japan."

Among subjects foreign correspondents were expected to avoid, and for a long time did avoid, was the steady regression in relations between Nationalists and Communists. By 1939 the two parties and their armies were no longer true allies but merely two hostile Chinas committed to war against an invader.

By the terms of the Kuomintang-Communist "reconciliation" of

September, 1937, the Reds had agreed to change their soviets into "special administrative districts." They did abolish the soviets, change the name Red Army to the Eighth Route Army, as designated by Chiang Kai-shek, and stop confiscating and redistributing land. Thus they adhered to the letter of their agreement, but not to the spirit of it as Chiang Kai-shek saw it. For in the "special districts" they introduced what was called "the new democracy," a united-front system which spread wherever they went behind Japanese lines. This was equally hateful to the Generalissimo, but it did have this legal basis: years earlier the Kuomintang regime had promulgated a law which provided for establishment of local self-government where and when any provincial governor decided that the people were "ready" to exercise the voting franchise and end one-party "tutelage." No governor had ever found the people "ready," however. Now, of all times, the Reds did just that. Acting as *de facto* provincial authorities, they simply "transferred power," on the basis of the Kuomintang law, to "popularly elected" local regimes.

Few who did not witness it would believe that Communists in China could set up such a framework. But they did. I saw it working in 1939. My own reports* were corroborated by the testimony of many reputable American and European observers. Among them were missionaries, priests, journalists and teachers.

According to a rule Communists imposed on themselves their party members in the village, county and provincial councils were not to exceed one-third of the total representation. Generally they adhered to this. Kuomintang members were also allowed to participate but as the Communists were the best organized political group they easily dominated. That they did so by persuasion, exhortation and by personal example of disciplined and patriotic behavior rather than by simple coercion and force is, however, a matter of easily verifiable record.**

Wartime reforms realized under these "new democratic" regimes won widespread approval even in Kuomintang China, where many liberal intellectuals had long advocated the same program. Rents were reduced (maximum, 25 percent of the crop), gentry domination was curtailed or ended, usury was abolished, idle land and the land of absentee owners was put under group production, youth and women were brought into politics, unemployed persons were organized in industrial and agricultural co-ops, landlord militia gave way to self-de-

---

* See *The Battle for Asia*, p. 251-9, et seq.
** See The State Department's *White Paper on China*, Wash., 1949.

fense corps made up of peasant volunteers, and mass education and war propaganda produced new leaders among the non-landlord classes. The army and the populace became one. Corruption was kept to a minimum by collective control and stern punishment, ostracism, and disgrace.

In 1944-47 our own civil and military attachés lived and traveled widely in Red territory.

They confirmed the fact that there was no Communism or Socialism, but a system which equalized the war burden and inspired an organized populace with post-war hope.* This period of experimentation in gradualism was to last nearly a decade. It was to facilitate the relatively swift and smooth transition by which the Communists would later lead the country, stage by stage, from "coalition government" to the state socialism of today.

In Russia the Communists "seized" power at the center and then imposed it, under iron-clad boots, on the hinterland. The Chinese took long slow curves toward their goal. They created a multiple encirclement of the cities from the countryside until they could "slip into power," with the peasants obligingly holding the horn to ease them into the felt-soled shoes of the land.

Not at all understanding what was going on, and impressed by the Communists' wartime "experiment in democracy," some wishful-thinking foreign observers for a time persuaded themselves that the Chinese Reds had "abandoned Communism." They had "permanently renounced Marx and Lenin," it was said. An outstanding proponent of this view, an ex-Communist named Freda Utley, wrote and lectured widely in the United States to the effect that the Chinese Communists were not "real" Communists at all. They had become "an agrarian reform movement." They were "no longer a revolutionary Communist party but a party of social reformers and patriots." **

English-born but now a naturalized American, Miss Utley had been a minor Comintern agent in Japan. As an apostate, she was very hard on the Russians, but she gave her anti-Communist blessings to the Chinese Communist party. She convinced herself that it had turned its back on revolution. "The Chinese Communist Party," she insisted, "long ago abandoned its dream of establishing its own dictatorship. Its aim has genuinely become social and political reform *along capitalist lines.*" ***

* Ibid.
** See *China at War,* by Freda Utley, London, 1939, pp. 73-4, 253-4, etc.
*** Italics added.

Miss Utley was later to reverse her opinion so completely that she became a principal consultant and adviser on China to Senator Joseph McCarthy. That was during the period when McCarthyist demagoguery temporarily convinced large numbers of gullible people that "Red traitors in the State Department had sold China to the Russians." Miss Utley had meanwhile become an employee of the Kuomintang embassy in Washington, and had wholly abandoned her belief in the Chinese Communists as "capitalist reformers." Instead, she now ardently supported the efforts of the China Lobby, a group of Americans, including some congressmen, who worked closely with Chiang Kai-shek and H. H. Kung and their acolytes, to secure American armed intervention against the Chinese revolution.

Ironically, it was the defender of the "agrarian reformer" myth who served as an "expert on Chinese Communism" for the Senate committee on internal security, also. That deluded body spent many months holding hearings designed to prove that "American traitors"— including the State Department and the Institute of Pacific Relations —had "conspired" to deceive government and country into believing that the Chinese Communists "were not real Communists." The costly inquiries, held under the auspices of Senator McCarthy and Senator Pat McCarran, filled fifteen volumes, ruined the livelihood of many honest people, and profoundly misled the nation concerning the true nature of the Chinese revolution but they failed to turn up a single traitor or "country seller."

What must have infuriated McCarthy was that General Marshall, "armed so strong in honesty," had also felt obliged to give the lie to the Formosa Lobby on another major myth: that it was the Russians who intervened and brought the Chinese Communists to power.

"I had officers pretty much over all North China, along the Yangtze and in Manchuria, and I always felt that the reports I got were far better than those the Generalissimo received," said General Marshall. "He was being fooled time and again [with reports that Kuomintang battles were being lost to Russian tanks and Russian soldiers] . . . Always I was trying to find out anything you could put your finger on that was authentic as to Soviet influence or Soviet help in all this; I never got anything except the influence of what I would call the spiritual, or something akin to that . . . When it came to Soviet assistance at all, I never could get my hands on it . . . In the opinion of all my advisers and intelligence, *they* [the Russians] *were not supporting them*." *

* Institute of Pacific Relations Hearings, etc., pp. 1653-4, Washington, D.C., 1951. Italics added.

But a full decade before all this tempest was to arise in America, Mao Tse-tung had ridiculed to me, in what was to prove his last interview with the foreign press for many years, any suggestion at all that he and other Communists had abandoned Marxism or revolution:

"We are always revolutionaries," said Mao, *"and we are never reformists. There are two main objectives in the Chinese revolution. The first consists in realizing the tasks of a national democratic revolution* [i.e., anti-imperialist and anti-feudal]. *The other is social revolution. The latter must be achieved and completely achieved . . . The national revolution after a certain stage will be transformed into social revolution."* *

After this widely quoted statement few China correspondents personally subscribed to the "agrarian reform" myth. Paradoxically it remained the official propaganda line of the Nationalist government. Kuomintang officials continually tried to convince diplomats and correspondents that the Communists "no longer existed as a party" and had given up Marxism. Sir Archibald Clark-Kerr told me that Chiang Kai-shek claimed that they had "surrendered" and that it was wrong to call the Eighth Route Army leaders "Communists."

In a letter written to me on May 6, 1939, Earl Leaf, then adviser to Chiang Kai-shek on propaganda in America, said: "Please stop mentioning 'Communists' in your reporting." He contended that to do so was "playing Japan's game." He desired that "writers and correspondents [would] stop referring to the Eighth Route as a Communist army and stop calling Chu Teh, Mao Tse-tung and others as [sic] Communists."

A little later, when I was in Chungking, Chiang Kai-shek's news agency reprinted an interview Chiang had given a German correspondent in which he said flatly, *"There are no Communists left in China."* Accordingly, Kuomintang censors methodically deleted the word "Communist" from many dispatches. Meanwhile, a few over-zealous missionaries in America, seeking to "win sympathy for China," publicly helped to spread this impression to calm the fears of conservative Christian supporters. As for whether that "line" was also used in slick word-of-mouth propaganda by American Communists of the time, as some of their turncoats have asserted, I cannot say. It is obvious that they could not have made such claims without being aware of their fraudulence.

* For full text see *The China Weekly Review,* Jan. 13, 1940; and *The Battle for Asia,* pp. 289-91, N.Y., 1941. I repeatedly warned against myths to the contrary in my *Saturday Evening Post* correspondence, also. Italics mine.

CHAPTER 26

War within War

WHATEVER the Generalissimo said for foreign consumption, he had no illusions about the "existence" of the Communists. From afar he watched them flowing back into areas lost by his "regular" armies to the Japanese.

Theoretically, there was no reason why the Kuomintang could not have excelled the Communists in organizing and leading behind-the-lines resistance. Chiang Kai-shek made many attempts to do so but he never succeeded in keeping an effective guerrilla army in being. The basic reason was that Chiang would not or could not offer the common people any service or inducement to win and hold their loyalty and sacrifice—fundamental in organized partisan warfare.

"Chiang simply does not think *people* count," I remember T. V. Soong remarking to me privately. "His worst weakness is, he relies on military force alone." In a time of defeat and corruption, no weapon is better than the man who bears it. Chiang counted his rifles—and later his American planes and tanks—when he should have been counting men.

Chiang would not compete with the Reds in reform programs but in 1939 he reverted to blockading them. He withdrew his own First Army from the Japanese front and deployed it south and west of the "special districts"—leaving the Reds "free" egress only into the "conquered" areas. More than 300,000 of the Kuomintang's best-equipped troops were to remain immobilized in this way for the next six years, in so far as the war against Japan was concerned.

I first realized the severity of Chiang's blockade when I reached Sian, en route to Yenan, late in 1939. I need mention only a detail or two which convinced me that time had run out for regeneration in China by any means short of social revolution.

While in Sian I confirmed the rumor that Kuomintang concentration camps had again been reopened. They were filling up with hundreds of young people accused of "subversion" or "dangerous thoughts" or "planning to enter the special districts." Among those incarcerated were several members of Industrial Co-operative units in Sian and

Paochi actually engaged in filling orders for Nationalist troops. One of the boys was Rewi Alley's own adopted son, "Mike," whom Rewi had brought from St. Johns College in Shanghai to work as a technician for the co-ops. It took the intervention of Dr. Kung himself to get Mike released.

Only one or two carefully inspected trucks a week were allowed to put out of Sian for Yenan. I would not have been able to get through had I not carried letters from T. V. Soong to the commander of the Generalissimo's Northwest headquarters, General Chiang Ting-wen, and to General Hu Tsung-nan, commander of the First Army. I traveled not only as a correspondent but also as a delegate of the International Committee for Indusco, with a mission to inspect the Yenan depot originally authorized by Premier Kung himself.

My trip was to prove the last one permitted any foreign correspondent *for five years.*

On that trip, as before, I learned that the Communists in China wore no tails or horns that I could discern; neither were they guiltless or without blemish. In a land of narrow choices they were the lesser evil for the poor, who happened to be the vast majority. Times change, people change. For all I know they may today be relatively worse. No one can rule guiltlessly and least of all those whom history compels to hurry. But as long as Mr. Dulles forbids American correspondents to work in China it is hard for us really to know very much about it. But what I wrote about the Chinese Communists, while I knew and lived among them, was true, in so far as one man can know the truth at any time. No one has refuted it and it needs no apology or penitence today.

In *The Battle for Asia* I told, for people interested in history, how and why co-operative production—the nearest thing to democratic economic organization I ever saw in China—flourished and prospered in Communist-led areas more rapidly than in Kuomintang China, where material conditions were so much more favorable.

Now I need only add a footnote of personal experience which may serve to demonstrate how "open" the Chinese Communists then were to Allied assistance against Japan and where opportunity was ignored by the United States during seven years when the Yenan government desperately needed foreign help and received no aid from Russia at all.

Although the Chen clique attacked Indusco as "Communist inspired," the ironic fact was that Communists in the beginning were suspicious of and even hostile to it. Madame Sun Yat-sen was severely criticized by Communists for sponsoring Indusco. They told her it was a "diversionist bourgeois" organization. They resented the fact that funds from her China Defense League were diverted to a movement which had "nothing to do with winning the war."

In 1938 I wrote to Mao Tse-tung and gave him a complete account of Indusco, how it had started, its aims and methods, and how it could help in guerrilla warfare. I sent him a copy of the Indusco constitution. I argued that in view of the united front and the Communist acceptance of a "mixed economy" they should wholeheartedly support Indusco. At this time the Communists were still backing "producers co-operatives," which were actually a form of state-owned industry. I urged that they formally revise their co-operative policy to conform with Indusco principles.

This suggestion came up for consideration at a conference of "producers co-operatives" delegates in 1939. There it was voted to abandon the special features of the producers co-op. The conference adopted the constitution of the Chinese Industrial Co-operatives in its entirety. It was hoped that this change would "stimulate industrial co-operatives throughout the country and serve to demonstrate the Communists' sincere welcome for any united-front organization." *

When I returned to Yenan late in 1939, Indusco was facing a crisis there. Under Kuomintang pressure funds for the administration of Indusco had been cut off by Chungking. At the same time the producers co-operatives were being reorganized to conform to Indusco principles. In the absence of further aid from central headquarters in Chungking, the Yenan organization was threatened with bankruptcy. This emergency was met by help from the Border Government. It raised capital loans to keep Indusco alive. Financial help began to arrive from overseas Chinese. Despite all obstacles, there was a five-fold growth of Indusco within a year.

In connection with the promotion of this important international help for "front-line co-ops," I sought a clear policy statement from Mao Tse-tung. Since Indusco was later on to become one of the main economic weapons of the Eighth Route Army in its war against Japan and ultimately against the Kuomintang army, it is worth quoting Mao's declaration:

"Even if Chinese Industrial Co-operatives can do nothing for front-line areas and the guerrilla districts behind enemy lines, the work they are doing is very important in helping to restore industry in our rear. But it is in the war areas in the enemy's rear that Industrial Co-opera-

* *The Battle for Asia*, pp. 331-2.

tives are most needed and will find the warmest welcome from our troops, from the people, and from the government. By this means we can help achieve manifold objectives: 1) stop the penetration of enemy goods from the occupied areas to the rural bases of guerrilla warfare; 2) utilize China's raw materials and resources for our own industries and prevent Japan from exploiting them; 3) create economically self-sufficient bases of guerrilla warfare to support protracted struggle; 4) train our unemployed and unskilled labor so that Japan cannot utilize it against us; 5) maintain village prosperity by giving the farmer needed manufactures in exchange for food." *

Well over a million Chinese dollars were raised by Chinese in the Philippines and the South Seas before Pearl Harbor to support an "International Indusco Center" in the Border Regions. In 1940 virtually the entire work of Indusco in the guerrilla territories defended by the Eighth Route Army in the north and the New Fourth Army in the south was financed by special gifts and loans raised privately among overseas Chinese and American business men. Funds and sympathy were later enlisted for the movement through efforts of Indusco committees in America headed by Admiral Harry E. Yarnell and such distinguished citizens as Henry R. Luce and Arthur Upham Pope, and by other committees organized in England by Sir Stafford and Lady Cripps.

Even with the small capital then available, industrial co-operatives in the Shensi-Kansu-Ninghsia Border Region had, by October, 1940, already expanded to include iron and coal mines and iron works, small machine shops, drug factories, transport units and two small oil wells. By 1942 the Yenan depot came to be much the largest regional headquarters in the country, with as many workers as all the others in China combined.

At that time and in subsequent years only a few million American dollars invested in machine shops and small industries (secure in the cave-cities of the Northwest) could have vastly increased Japan's difficulties in North China. With a little capital the raw materials and techniques locally available could have been co-operatively organized to produce basic necessities, fortify civilian morale and make guerrilla troops virtually self-sufficient in secondary war supplies—grenades, rifles, machine guns and explosives. Later Japan might have thus been compelled to extend herself far more to hold down China while fighting in the Pacific. Private aid did something along such lines, but the Kuomintang blockade largely cut off imports from "Free China"

* For details see *Random Notes on China*, Harvard University Press, pp. 71-2.

while Indusco in the guerrilla areas had to capture (or buy and smuggle in) scrapped tools and machines from the occupied areas at great cost in human life.

During my visit Mao Tse-tung extended a welcome to American technicians and invited the International Committee to recruit organizers and send in inspectors to the Border Regions. He repeated his request for American technical and financial aid when we formally joined China as an ally in its war against Japan. The Generalissimo's blockade was not to be challenged by America until 1944 when, at Roosevelt's insistence, a few American political and military observers were finally permitted to travel in the guerrilla areas. But we were never to give the Border Governments a grenade or a rifle or a simple sewing machine during our long joint war against Japan. All our billions would go exclusively to the Generalissimo. It was thus not surprising that Mao Tse-tung saw in American wartime aid to China something which Americans themselves could never see: a repetition of foreign intervention against the Chinese revolution.

But it was not true that America consciously played such a role from the beginning. Although our policy consistently excluded help to the Communist-led war effort against Japan, American sentiment earlier did something to prevent renewal of civil war. The danger of that was implicit in the restoration of a blockade in 1939. It became acute when the Generalissimo in that same year set up a War Areas Commission in Sian, intended to liquidate the Border Governments, which were declared "illegal." Attempts to move Kuomintang troops in behind the Reds were resisted and sporadic fighting broke out along the borders of the guerrilla territory, both inside and outside the Japanese-occupied areas.

Chinese censorship policy demanded silence on this internecine strife and I did not attempt to elude it. Nor did other correspondents, anxious not to "hurt China's cause," report it as yet. It was not until the "New Fourth Army Incident" in 1941 that the gravity of this war within war behind and around the Japanese lines was finally exposed to the outside world.

CHAPTER 27

Massacre

THE NUCLEUS of the New Fourth Army consisted of Communist survivors left behind in Kiangsi "pockets" when the main forces of the old Red Army retreated to the Northwest in 1934. When Japanese troops overran the lower Yangtze Valley, Chiang Kai-shek ordered the remnants to reorganize as part of the National army under united front command. They were led by a Communist veteran, General Han Ying, and a non-Communist Whampoa veteran, General Yeh Ting. Most of their combat troops were north of the river, behind enemy lines. They had a base headquarters on the south bank, in unoccupied territory which supported some schools, a hospital, and a few workshops, all flanked by Kuomintang forces.

In mid-January of 1941 this New Fourth Army was suddenly ordered by the regional Kuomintang chief of the War Areas Commission to evacuate its one secure base and move north of the river, into Japanese-occupied Anhui province. After vain protests, some of the armed forces were ferried across the river under cover of darkness. About 2,500 remained. The Kuomintang commander insisted that they be moved also and sent an ultimatum. Accordingly, this rear guard set out for the river. As it included many school teachers, students, nurses, hospital orderlies and hundreds of wounded, as well as many artisans, it was largely unarmed.

Slowly the cavalcade wound toward the Yangtze, until late in the afternoon it had to pass through a narrow valley. In the middle of it a Kuomintang force concealed in the nearby hills opened an attack by hidden machine-guns, in a well-prepared ambush. Not many escaped alive. General Han Ying himself was killed and General Yeh Ting was severely wounded.

I learned details of this massacre from Liao Cheng-chih, the New Fourth Army's rear liaison officer, before any other correspondent. What affected me especially was that I had helped to raise foreign funds to set up an International Indusco Center for the New Fourth Army, which was training apprentices and operating a few small work-

235

shops to make supplies for the guerrillas. Now many lives and precious equipment were lost.

Once convinced that the story was true, I decided I had to report it regardless of how much it might "hurt China." It could well mean a general renewal of Kuomintang-Communist hostilities and the break-up of Chinese resistance altogether.

The New Fourth Army incident indeed proved to be a blow from which China's national unity never recovered.

My story would never have passed censorship in Chungking, where officials blandly denied any basis for it, but I was able to file several dispatches through Hongkong. For the first time I also reported the true extent of the blockade and the situation I had seen developing in the Northwest, which already assumed the proportions of a small-scale civil war. As a result all my fellow correspondents in Chungking got queries and London and Washington asked for immediate reports from their envoys. The Chungking government again flatly denied that anything had happened and once more cancelled my press privileges. In Washington Dr. Hu Shih, then Chinese Ambassador, insisted that the *Herald Tribune* prominently publish a statement in which he branded my reports as completely false. He took the line that there were "no Communist" armies in China anyway. He demanded, but did not get, an apology from my editors.

Several days later British diplomats were able to confirm the truth about the New Fourth Incident. They also reported to London that a large-scale Kuomintang offensive against Yenan was imminent. A partial admission now came from the Generalissimo, but he claimed that it was the New Fourth Army which had attacked him. Finally, in the face of Chungking correspondents' protests against attempts to suppress the facts which they, too, had tried to send out, censorship was temporarily relaxed. Soon the whole story of the near-collapse of the united front, so long kept under wraps, was being brought out for a good airing.

Later I was to learn that these dispatches had so interested Washington that negotiations for a new Chinese loan were suspended. Mr. Morgenthau had gone so far as to intimate that Chungking could expect no further financial aid from the United States in the event of any renewal of civil war.

There was thus an unmistakable indication that American wartime support for Chiang Kai-shek would be conditioned on his ability to maintain some kind of unity in joint resistance against Japan.

Yet it may not be correct to assume that it was only the unfavorable

Anglo-American reaction to the New Fourth Army Incident which restrained the Generalissimo from attempting an all-out offensive against the Reds. He certainly realized the implications better than his more hot-headed subordinates. Since nearly all the Communist forces were *behind* the Japanese lines, Chiang could not have fought them effectively without an alliance with the Japanese. This would soon have thrown the Chungking government into the Axis camp with Wang Ching-wei, and after Pearl Harbor would have left only the Communists fighting Japan on the side of the "democracies." It is not conceivable that America could have battled Japan in the Pacific while helping Chiang and Japan fight the Reds in China. The Chinese Communists would then doubtless have received American aid like any other anti-Axis force in World War II. How that might have influenced our subsequent relations with the Chinese revolution is a bootless speculation, but the result could scarcely have been worse, and might have been much better, than history as it happened.

What the United States Government did not realize, and apparently has never since realized, was that the political initiative in Chinese resistance had shifted even before Pearl Harbor. Graham Peck seems to have been one of the few people to perceive this. After four years of working with the O.W.I. in the U.S. Government attempt to aid China, he wrote in 1950:

"I believe the basic fact about recent Chinese history is that the years from 1937 to 1941—from the beginning of the Japanese invasion until Pearl Harbor—were the crucial ones. During that time the Communists showed they could exploit the emergencies of invasion in order to expand, while the Kuomintang began to lose strength because it could not or would not adjust to wartime problems. By the time China became our ally the trend toward a reversal of powers was so marked that we could have influenced it only through the use of more strength and knowledge than we had in China then. . . . By the time of Japanese surrender the Kuomintang had become so weak and the Communists so strong that nothing but full-scale American intervention, literally turning China into an American colony, could have defeated the Communists." *

Indusco was eventually to be entirely smothered in Kuomintang China. In Communist-led areas it not only survived and steadily grew but became a decisive factor in their final triumph. By 1953 Teng Chieh, a leading figure in the industrial planning group in the Peking

* *Two Kinds of Time,* by Graham Peck, Houghton Mifflin Co., 1950, p. 700.

government, would acknowledge this when he wrote in *People's China:*

"The Chinese Industrial Co-operatives, which began work in 1938 and won the sympathetic support of democratic-minded people at home and abroad, developed successfully only in the Liberated [i.e., Communist] areas. Much experience was thus acquired in organizing handicraft work on a large scale. *It was largely owing to such organization that the forces which were destined to liberate all China and lead her to [modern] industrialization were able to maintain themselves.*" (My italics.)

Moral: The co-operative methods in production which helped the Communists to "liberate all China" could have saved China for the Kuomintang. Perhaps capitalism will not everywhere dig its own grave, as Marx prophesied, but Keynes was surely right when he concluded that it is historically true that no order of society ever perishes save by its own hand. *Wheresoever the carcase is, there shall the eagles be gathered together.*

CHAPTER 28

Time to Go Home

> *To everything there is a season* . . .
> *A time to be born and a time to die*
> *A time to plant and a time to pluck up that which is planted* . . .

Chungking's belated admission of the facts on the New Fourth Army vindicated my integrity as an observer but it was an empty satisfaction. What it did was to cure me of my intensely personal sense of obligation toward China. At about the same time a still more incurable "missionary," W. H. Donald, finally threw in the sponge. Donald, in a last effort to awaken Madame Chiang Kai-shek to the demoralizing consequences of the graft and notorious profiteering activities of her close relatives, had appealed to her to curb them. Madame Chiang turned on him in a fury and said, "Donald, you may criticize the government or anything else in China, but there are some persons even you cannot criticize!" In a rage exceeding her own, Donald walked out, took the next plane for Hongkong, and thereby ended his distinguished career in China.*

Now I understood that there was no common ground left where youthful passions and ideals could compromise with corrupt and cynical old age, no room left for the have-gots and have-nots, the dictatorship of the right and the dictatorship of the left, to meet each other without murder in their hearts. The Japanese invasion had not stilled the fratricidal fires but had merely fed and spread them. They would burn for years yet and far outlast the war itself. That was the essence of what could be said about China, then, and it would be said many ways in many different time-space actualities; but no matter how often we said it we were not going to make Americans comprehend nor fail to be astonished and offended when the volcano finally erupted. What was more, some of them would never forgive us for having prematurely spoken the harsh truth.

I would still be for the cause of China; in the main the cause of the Chinese was on the side of truth, of right and of justice. I would be for any measure which might help the Chinese people to help themselves, for in that way only could they find themselves. I would be opposed to all uncontrolled charity to the rich-men's government which continued to feast as poor men starved and died; that could only increase the insolence of power and prolong the agony of an inevitable reckoning. But I would never again imagine that I personally was anything more to China than an alien corn adrift on vast tides of history with a logic of its own and beyond my power to alter or my birthright to judge.

Yet China had claimed a part of me even if I could make no claim on her. In place of my youthful ignorance of meanings of words and statistics there were real scenes and personalities—until famine now meant a naked young girl with breasts a million years old, and horror meant an army of rats I saw feasting on the suppurating flesh of still-living soldiers left helpless and untended on a charred battlefield; until rebellion meant the fury I felt when I saw a child turned into a pack animal and forced to walk on all fours, and "Communism" was a youthful peasant I knew fighting to avenge the execution of fifty-six members of his clan-family, held jointly responsible when three of its sons joined the Red Army; until war was the slit belly of a girl ravished and thrown naked before me on the streets of Chapei, and murder was the yellow corpse of an unwanted baby tossed onto a garbage heap

* *Donald of China* by Earl Selle. New York, 1950, p. 348-9.

in an alley near the Ministry of Health; until Japan's "anti-Communist leadership in Asia" was the feet and arms of orphan girls buried in the debris of a building bombed before my eyes, and inhumanity the laughter of idle men in silk watching one beggar choke another to death in a street fight in Szechuan over a handful of leftover rice; until I had seen dark frozen fear and cowardice in myself and courage and resolution in lowly men and women I had once childishly supposed my inferiors.

Yes, I would be part of that. And part of me would always remain with China's tawny hills, her terraced emerald fields, her island temples seen in the early morning mist, a few of her sons and daughters who had trusted or loved me, her bankrupt cheerful civilized peasants who had sheltered and fed me, her brown, ragged, shining-eyed children, the equals and the lovers I had known, and above all the lousy, unpaid, hungry, despised, peasant foot-soldier who in the mysterious sacrifice of his own life alone now gave value to all life and put the stamp of nobility upon the struggle of a great people to survive and to go forward.

Yes, I was proud to have known them, to have straggled across a continent with them in defeat, to have wept with them and still to share a faith with them. But I was not and could never be one of them. A man who gives himself to be the possession of an alien land, said Lawrence in his *Seven Pillars,* lives a Yahoo life; and I was tired of being a Yahoo. I was an American, I told myself, and now at last I saw myself as I was, an Ishmael in a foreign land, and drew back to avoid being engulfed in the deep.

The *Herald Tribune* had offered me a roving assignment through Siam, Burma, and India, and I resolved to take it up and go home by way of Europe. Early in February, 1941, I made a reservation on the Dutch line for Singapore. Under Joe Barnes the *Herald Tribune* had built up perhaps the best American foreign service of the period and I was proud to be part of it. With the most profound regret I broke this relationship, however, and abruptly cancelled a trip which might have changed my future. An urgent sense of neglect and failure in my domestic life suddenly came over me. My wife had already left the Philippine Islands, where she had lived for two years, and had returned to America. Perhaps if I went back at once the roots of love and trust could again be nourished to life on our native soil. Abruptly I cabled Joe Barnes that I was—after those "six weeks" that had lasted thirteen years—coming home on the next Clipper.

"You will come back," Ching-ling had said at our last meeting, after trying to persuade me to stay on. *"Wo-men suan ni shih ti-ti.* You're a younger brother to us. You won't be happy in America. You belong to China."

As we flew out of Hongkong and I watched the sampans and junks dwindle to brown leaves on the blue-blue water below us, I remembered her face, still youthful and beautiful, as she had said that, and I was moved again by her sincerity. I wondered if she was right, and half feared and half hoped she might be. Asia did seem my real home and America the great unknown. My body seemed torn from my spirit left behind.

Poverty is relative to time and place, and in the dying world of Western power in the Orient no white man was ever really poor; but as I drew closer to America, where success was the shadow of the figures behind your own dollar value, I regretted my improvidence. I had frittered away my savings on "war work," on a book that would earn nothing and on keeping two households going. I was "worth" less than when I had first touched Shanghai, in 1928, and the values I had lived by in China now seemed hardly convertible to gold. What, after all, was I taking home? I had no honor to show for my years but the physical ravages of malaria, dysentery and nephritis—not even an honest wound as souvenir. I was, I thought, a failure.

When you are lucky enough to reach the age of reflection you know that long life is not measured in years but in the number of lives you live. It is only in retrospect that you discern where one life slipped away and another began. As I slouched in the *China Clipper,* a depressed bundle of displaced tropisms, I did not at all sense that a new and exciting existence lay ahead of me. I was immersed in sadness and loneliness and a weariness of life new to me.

I did not know it but my flagging morale and mental fatigue were also traceable to a kind of slow starvation; avitaminosis had gradually seized me over a period of months. It was mostly fresh, nourishing food I needed. My weight had fallen from a norm of 165 down to 125. After I reached California I gained thirty pounds in a month. Then I went to a ranch in Arizona and forgot all about China and war and did nothing but eat and ride and sleep. One morning I woke up a whole man again.

About that time my "third life" really began.

PART THREE

THE OTHER SIDE
OF THE RIVER

A strange justice that is bounded by a river! Can anything be more ridiculous than that a man should have the right to kill me because he lives on the other side . . .

PASCAL

CHAPTER 1

Candide's Return

I RETURNED to America just in time to read a 1941 Valentine's Day message to the people from Mr. Republican himself. "It is simply fantastic," said Robert A. Taft, "to suppose that there is any danger of attack on the United States by Japan." It was also fantastic to Herbert Hoover. "The dangers to America today are less," he pronounced the same year, "than at any time since the war began." * Mr. John Foster Dulles thought then: "Only hysteria entertains the idea that Germany, Japan or Italy contemplates war on us." **

Not that Republicans were alone in their delusions. They were cheerfully echoed in the Communist line. "Something evil is happening in this country," as Mr. Roosevelt protested, "when a full-page ad placed by Republican supporters, appears, of all places, in the *Daily Worker*." *** Not only were Taft, Dulles, Hoover and the America Firsters and the American Communists used, along with congressmen led by eminent senators like Wheeler and Vandenberg, to frustrate Roosevelt's attempts to alert the country to imminent peril. They also found themselves in the company of such outright Nazi apologists as Merwin K. Hart, Father Coughlin, Fritz Kuhn and John T. Flynn. An "ominous combination," Mr. Roosevelt called it, "between the extremely reactionary and extremely radical elements."

In China I had been only vaguely aware of the divisive effects of the Nazi-Soviet pact which explained so much about our faltering policies in Asia as well as Europe. It was not till I encountered Theodore Dreiser in a Hollywood broadcasting studio that I saw all this puzzlement personified. I had gone there to be interviewed on a radio program. Dreiser appeared just before me.

"Some people say that though the British Empire is not perfect, still British democracy is far better than German nazism," the radio interrogator mildly suggested.

"My God! My Jesus God!" screamed Dreiser. "That's humbug for

* Sept. 17, 1941, in a speech at Chicago.
** March, 1939.
*** *Roosevelt and Hopkins,* by Robert Sherwood, N.Y., 1948, p. 193.

you! Read my new book, *America Is Worth Saving,* and you'll learn the truth! Is it Germany or Britain that holds half a billion Asiatics and Africans in slavery? Germany isn't fighting us, she's fighting British imperialism. Why don't Fuehrer Roosevelt and his friends ask England's *slaves* which is the greater menace?"

With some consternation I listened as the author of *Sister Carrie* and *An American Tragedy* denounced Britain as a "monster" and had nothing to say against Herr Hitler. How, I wondered, could an author full of such deep pity and indignation so underestimate the evil of Hitler?

He must be senile (he *was* seventy!), I told myself, as I watched him jump up and down in exasperation at the "lunatic fringe" of Americans who wanted to aid England. "No!" he wound up, "this time the Yanks aren't coming! To hell with that . . ." The emcee moved in quickly to call "time," after whispering to me, "Another second and we'd lose our franchise."

Dreiser took me home with him. If we had not spent several nights arguing, I would have wholly misunderstood him and never have read *America Is Worth Saving.* (It made more sense than his broadcast.) He had voted for Roosevelt and the New Deal; now he was bitterly against him, against the draft, against lifting a finger to help England or hinder Hitler.

"The British, the French, the Dutch, the Belgians, all these imperialists asked for it and by God I say let them take it!" Dreiser argued. "When did they do anything to give their natives any democracy? What did they do to save Spain, Abyssinia, China? And who's been arming Japan? British-American capitalism! Who backed Hitler at the start? Chamberlain! Daladier! And why? They miscalculated. They thought Hitler meant war against Russia, not themselves! Now they come crying to us for help, want us to fight their war, save their colonies. Say Stalin 'betrayed them'—making a deal with Hitler. Why shouldn't he? Didn't he just beat Chamberlain at his own game?"

"Most of that's true enough," I agreed. "But now it's 1941. Hitler has won Europe. The British Empire can fall, for all I care, but not to Hitler! Right now it's Britain alone, fighting for her life. And if Britain goes, who next? Russia. And after Russia?"

These dead polemics of that day need no further exhumation. I felt that I won all the arguments and was aghast that I did. How could I prevail against this great bulwark of an intellect whose genius and sincerity were beyond any questioning by me? The louder he shouted the less I believed the conviction behind the words was his own.

"All you say is logical only if you believe in the infallibility of Moscow!" I finally accused.

"Of course it is!" said he. "There's only one country worth helping to save in this mess. Russia! Snow, why aren't you a Communist?"

"Are you?"

"No; but not because I haven't tried, by God!" he replied. "They won't have me. I'm not good enough for them."

Good enough! Here he was, the nearest thing to an American proletarian writer the country had produced, telling me he wasn't worthy. "The Communists are particular, very," he went on. "I've done everything they've told me to do for years now but they still say I'm too individualist, too emotional, too undisciplined. I still have hopes though. What's wrong with you?"

"I was a Catholic once, like you. When I left I gave up believing in all popes. Stalin's no superman and I can't change my music every time he calls the tune. I was against nazism before the pact. If the Communists now want to call it an 'imperialist war' that doesn't change nazism for me."

The more we argued the more I convinced him of nothing. My position had its own contradictions, of course. I wanted us to help China *and* Britain yet I didn't want America to go to war. But I thought I knew one thing that Dreiser did not. Japan was going to drag us into the war whether we helped anybody or not.

My years in the East may have taught me that but they had not taught me anything about America or a man like Dreiser. He remained for me the key enigmatic figure among all the left-wing intellectuals who followed the Communist line of this period when they fought against Roosevelt's attempts to organize a defense and aid Britain but defended the pact and the partitioning of Poland by Russia and Germany.

Not so with Dreiser, who was finally to be found "good enough" to enter the party, in 1945, not long before his death. I was still puzzled when recently I came across an essay by Lester Cohen, who explained this act as a desperate final signature to Dreiser's lifelong search for a whole faith. Having found no hope for men in the real world he knew so well, he had to believe that absolute good did exist somewhere. Faith in Russia became for him, as for many much lesser intellects, belief in a saviour abroad.

In this respect Dreiser was like another North American artist of magnitude whom I came to know and like years later in Mexico— Diego Rivera. These were lions of men, stormy battlers with the raw materials of art and life, whose work will far outlast their politics because it was full of heart and the heartbeat was sound and true.

In 1941 Dreiser was thinking with his heart about China, at least, for no Kremlin interdict confused him there. Chinese resistance still had the blessings of Moscow, although Japan was Hitler's ally. Dreiser became so interested in the guerrilla co-ops in China that he helped form a Hollywood committee of actors and writers to raise money for them. He also introduced me to the League of American Writers, in which he was an important front man. As a result I was asked to be a principal speaker at a writers' congress in New York in June, 1941.

"Our life seems trivial and we shun to record it," said Emerson, and the incident I recall now seems trivial. Yet it was important to the "persona" we have been studying in these pages in relation to multitudes of other individual lives that make up society and sanction governments and in turn affect or are affected by them.

This congress was to be the last gathering of American writers summoned to act politically for many years. I was impressed by the famous names but troubled to find them supporting a platform which branded Roosevelt a "fascist," and upheld every act of Stalinist opportunism. They made no more sense than Taft or Dulles. When I refused to sign a manifesto couched in such terms I was told that it was "not meant to be a strait-jacket." They still insisted that I speak on the Far East. As American attention was then focused almost exclusively on Europe I was glad to take any opportunity to arouse people to the danger from the East.

I was, after all, not allowed to speak. The day before the meeting I was asked for an advance copy of my remarks. My script linked China's resistance with Britain's fight for its life, and asked for aid to both countries in the belief that the two wars were merging into one world struggle against nazi-fascist imperialism, and that Russia also would soon be drawn in. The only honest position to take at this time was "aid to any people fighting for its freedom against the Axis."

When the executive secretary of the Congress, Franklin Folsom, read what I intended to say he sent a committee to visit me three times to try to persuade me to delete these remarks from my talk. They were, Folsom said in a formal letter, "in contradiction to the fundamental convictions of the Congress." How, I asked, could a Congress called to "debate and discuss problems before intellectuals in the national crisis" have its "fundamental convictions" determined for it in advance?

I had not quite believed that the Communists were in absolute charge, as press attacks had asserted; I knew too many of the writers involved who were not Communists. Now I realized how their natural isolationist anti-war sentiment was being exploited simply to make headlines the Communists thought would please Moscow. I refused to alter my talk and the invitation to speak was withdrawn. I did attend enough of the "debate and discussion," however, to see how the few attempts to express independent or opposition views on foreign policy were simply smothered by a well-organized party claque which dominated all sessions. Resolutions proposed by the Communists were declared "unanimously" adopted. The Congress ended in a great fanfare at Madison Square Garden which denounced Britain for making "imperialist war," ridiculed Roosevelt as a "warmonger" and praised "peace-loving" Russia.

That was June 9, 1941. Twelve days later, "contradicting the fundamental convictions of the Writers Congress," Hitler's heretical tanks crashed into the Ukraine, taking Stalin's minions by surprise. The American Communist party, after several days of intense soul-searching, emerged from the fog to announce that the war had become a struggle of all "freedom-loving peoples" against the deadliest tyranny in history. Britain's "imperialist war" had ended and so had the League of American Writers. Both simply vanished.

I do not know how many writers who shared this humiliating experience in intellectual servility concluded from it that American Communists' total subservience to the Kremlin disqualified them from leading organized political, social and economic progress in the United States. I suspect that most of them did so, after recovering from the shock. The brief encounter was enough for me to see that the Communists here would eventually break up over their inability to think for themselves and work out a clear autonomous line of policy.

The truth is that a revolutionary party in a country nowhere near a revolutionary situation is basically a political anachronism. No country resorts to violent social revolution until the old order has exhausted all its means. The expedients still open to American capitalism were legion. One merely has to review all the conditions which in China made revolution inevitable to see that practically none of them existed in America to make that means of change the only alternative open to history. Marxist-Stalinist dogma built on the assumptions of Russian experience might be pertinent in many backward nineteenth-century economies. They lacked relevance when rigidly applied to the advanced industrial democracy of the United States. A party based on belief in a revolutionary saviour abroad was therefore like an army always preparing for a war already fought in a foreign land rather than the real struggle ahead.

But in 1941 it did not follow in my own mind that Communists in *all* countries would be permanently handicapped in the same way as the Americans. Nor was I any the less sympathetic with the Russian people's fight or the preservation of their independence and right to decide their own destiny in accordance with the laws of their own history.

I was soon to witness that struggle, perhaps the decisive political battle of the century, at first hand.

CHAPTER 2

I Meet the Army

OUR BEST BRAINS and worthiest patriots among the "interventionists" were impatient with anyone who wanted to "divert" attention to the Far East. In its demands for all-out war against Hitler at once the Fight for Freedom Committee and its powerful allies persistently ignored or underestimated Japan. Very few recognized Japan as a continental power now fully capable of conducting prolonged war against *all* the Western nations. Virtually everyone habitually wrote off Japan as "bogged down in China," or spoke about the "weakening effects" of her conquests, or dismissed her contemptuously as an Eastern Italy. Evans Carlson was almost alone among American military authorities who publicly warned us of the danger of a surprise Japanese attack on the United States. I have not read General MacArthur's intelligence reports for 1941, but I do know that when I saw him just before my return from Manila he was convinced that Japan would not touch the Philippines "as long as the American flag flies there."

"Churchill, like virtually everyone else in authority at the time," said Robert Sherwood, "assumed that it was the powerful Hitler who would decide when the time had come to attack the United States. The possibility that this act of incredible folly would be committed by the Japanese, the saving of whose 'face' had been the object of so much solicitude in Washington, was hardly worth considering." * That was

* Op. cit., p. 369.

true among both officials in the capital and army officers whom I met in great numbers during the summer and autumn of 1941.

Soon after my return I began to work exclusively for the *Saturday Evening Post*. For months I visited training camps and traveled with the new Army of the United States. The ragged morale among our draftees reflected the deep skepticism of a country wholly unconvinced that we faced any real peril. We had good physical material, our non-coms were paid better than Japanese generals, and there were no better-housed and better-fed soldiers anywhere. They lacked the unity of a cause and looked upon themselves as the victims of a warmongering President and a sorry hoax. If this was an "unlimited national emergency" why did they have to "play soldier," using broomsticks for rifles, stovepipes for artillery, jeeps for tanks and firecrackers for gunfire?

The army was so afraid of the vigilantes among isolationist congressmen that the facts of the war were not even discussed with the "selectees." Few could tell you what the Four Freedoms were. Officers were disgusted with a lend-lease arrangement which "took away the tools of their trade." They blamed *that* on Roosevelt. But they hated even more the isolationist Congressmen, in the overwhelming majority Republicans, who made it almost impossible to hold together any army at all. I remember getting an earful of that from General George S. Patton when I rode in his tank of the Second Armored Division for a couple of days during Louisiana maneuvers. As I left he said, prophetically:

"I've been frank with you, Snow. I have talked too God-damned much and you can ruin me. I can go a long way in this army if I don't put my foot in my big mouth. There's nothing that will kill a man in this man's army faster than getting in trouble with Congress. So don't quote me, whatever you do."

General L. J. MacNair, then in command of all field training, told me in September that we had only two divisions ready for combat.

Then there is this item in my diary dated August 14:

Went to call on Brig-General Omar Bradley, commander of the Infantry School, at 8:45. While I was with him an officer came in to report that news of the Roosevelt-Churchill meeting was on the radio. We went in and listened to Ed Murrow from London, who said the British weren't much excited. They had hoped for a declaration of war.

"No, it's not a declaration," I said. "It just makes it inevitable."

"Yesterday's vote on the draft extension—205 to 204—says a lot more to me," replied Bradley drily. "That's what worries us—this divided leadership. The morale problems in our camps would disappear overnight if the country and the Congress could unite, or at least agree that we need an army."

By December nothing had happened to change that deadlock in American opinion. The interventionists had won some support of labor after the Nazi assault on Russia, but their weight was more than counterbalanced by senators like Harry S. Truman, who now hoped for a policy to encourage the two evil genii to destroy each other, without committing us to the war. The *third* evil genie was still "hardly worth considering," although Mr. Hull was now negotiating with Admiral Nomura, the Japanese envoy. The America Firsters had more impressive congressional backing than ever. Col. Lindbergh's appeasement speeches were resoundingly echoed by kings of the press, such as Colonel McCormick, whose hatred of Roosevelt far exceeded their sense of national danger.

In spite of that noisy claque, however, the record shows that the President was by December soberly alert to the likelihood of enlarged Japanese aggression. Roosevelt's profound dilemma, as he stated it more than once, was how to get the bifurcated Congress to recognize the danger in time to avoid a national catastrophe. There is no evidence that his advisers ever dared to suggest that the Japanese themselves would solve it for him in the manner they did.

With a half dozen ways of achieving their objectives by a strategy of continued attrition, why *did* the Japanese choose the one and only way so certain to guarantee their eventual defeat? When all allowance is made for poor military intelligence and miscalculations of Japan's supreme leaders—the expectation of an early Russian break-up; the belief that Britain was knocked out of the war; the conviction that the U.S. would soon be isolated by an impregnable Axis-dominated Eurasian world—still the assault on Pearl Harbor remains a monumental "irrational act," to use Churchill's phrase. It could have been undertaken only by men whose passions completely blinded them to two decisive facts: the enormous war potential of the United States and the utter certainty that an act of unmitigated and unprovoked murder of Americans on American territory would bring our people to their feet in a unity and determination nothing else could have achieved.

If Pearl Harbor was "ignorance in action" on a national scale, the ignorance was not all on one side. If the Japanese could not understand our national character, neither did we understand theirs. Pearl Harbor was the climax of years of our own political blunders. It was also the product of the underlying ignorance of Anglo-American policies which had armed Japanese imperialism to ravage its weak neighbors, of Anglo-French-Dutch hypocrisy which had schooled Japan in the cynicism of colonialism while " irrationally" failing to lead their Asiatic subjects toward strength, freedom and equality, of two centuries of practical demonstration to Asia that the white man relies upon and understands nothing but force, and of decades of underestimation by the West of the fierce growing revolutionary resentment agonizing a continent, the redemption of which became the inner passion driving Japan toward imperial suicide.

I was now to hear similar views expressed by President Roosevelt.

CHAPTER 3

The Commander-in-Chief

NOT LONG AFTER that fateful December Sunday I was called to Washington to take a job with Army Air Force intelligence. At about the same time the *Saturday Evening Post* offered me an enviable assignment as its first war correspondent: a quick trip to India and China, and then to Russia, or "what's left."

On the last day left for me to decide, my dilemma was mercifully resolved by personal "orders" from the Commander-in-Chief. I had checked in for the weekly White House press conference and was talking to Wayne Coy, a special assistant to the President. The phone rang. It was Steve Early, to say that F.D.R. wanted to see me.

Our talk was all off the record but some of his comments covered matters I never saw discussed by him in print in quite the same way elsewhere. The President greeted me with a broad smile and a hearty handshake. He motioned me to sit down, took a cigarette for himself and leaned over to give me a light. He "knew me," he said, through *Red Star Over China,* and he wanted to "interview" me.

"How are things in China? Do they think well of us over there?"

The Chinese understood that he personally had always tried to help China, I replied. I held up my thumb. *"Lo Ssu-fu, ting-hao!* That means Roosevelt, very good. It's the salute I got from people deep in China whenever they heard I was an American—even when we were still selling war materials to Japan."

He grinned appreciatively. "Now tell me, what do you think of the statement Chiang Kai-shek made about India?" The Generalissimo had just been to Delhi and had issued an appeal to the British to grant India full self-government so as to bring the Indian people into the war as allies and equals.

I thought it was a fine idea, but would it do any good? "Wasn't it Churchill who called India the 'brightest jewel in our crown of empi-yah'?"

Roosevelt said he thought India might be "our problem" one of these days. "I don't really know what Winston thinks about the whole thing now. When I spoke to him during the Atlantic Charter meeting I got the idea that he *wanted* to do something for India but didn't know how."

I said I didn't see how we could fight a war for the Four Freedoms in Europe only and expect colonial peoples in Asia to get excited. We needed a Pacific Charter too. If the Allied powers would pledge independence for specific dates after victory to the colonies overrun by Japan, we might get some real military help from the millions of Asians. I had just written about this for the *Post*. He insisted that I give him a résumé of the unpublished article, and to my amazement this world's busiest man listened patiently while I did so.

"There are some ideas in that we can use," he said. "Let me have a copy of your manuscript and I'll get it into Bill Donovan's hands right away." I would be lying if I said I was not flattered.

"Snow, what would you do," he asked slowly, as if he had been mulling it over for some time, "about constituting a new government in India under present conditions? There is this Moslem-Hindu problem and there are the Untouchables and the princes and the minorities. The British say they have to protect all these people from each other; they can't transfer power because someone is sure to suffer. That's Churchill's argument. Now tell me, would you try to set up a government with guarantees for the rights and privileges of all the various religious groups, castes, princes, and so on? Or would you just give everybody equality under a constitution in a democratic framework something like our own in the early days of the confederation— would it work?"

What a question—for *me!* I gave him one man's opinion: India in stagnation for years because the British had been the great dam blocking up the flow and course of India's natural and national political evolution. India's problem now: how to get rid of outgrown feudal institutions, *not* how to perpetuate them in elaborate consitutional guarantees.

"Any new Indian government ought to be organized on the basis of a democratic constitution," I wound up oracularly. "There will be enormous problems but they're for the Indians to solve. Assuming, of course, that the Japanese won't invade, the longer the British hold onto power the more likelihood that the Indians won't be able to resolve their class and religious differences without a catastrophe."

"That's my own idea exactly! I'll tell you something else," said the President. "I think that not only have we got to get rid of religious bigotry and its backward social influence in India, we also have to get rid of the most reactionary religious power in our own country. Before long we are going to have to eliminate all church control of education. That belongs to the past. *All schools should be under secular control.*"

I reminded him that one of his predecessors had reversed the process in the Philippines, after the Filipinos themselves had broken with the Vatican and set up an independent Christian Church—the Aglipayans. It was President W. H. Taft who had paid his visit to Rome and settled the Philippines dispute with the Pontiff by returning church property seized by the Nacionalistas.

"Well, the Filipinos can change it again when they get their independence," said the President, "and we're keeping our promise about that—after we throw out the Japs. Now all Asiatics look to the Philippines and expect the other powers to follow. And we are going to have to tell our friends the Allies that they must have faith in the Orientals and their ability to govern themselves. It is true not only of India and Burma and Indo-China but also of Java and Malaya, and even New Guinea."

I sat up a foot or two.

"Now, the Dutch tell us they have already got self-government and democracy in Java, that they are going to give the people real power," he went on. "But what the Dutch and the British and the French mean is that they want a kind of self-government which will see Europeans still in the saddle a hundred years from now."

"They're dreaming! Whatever happens, the war means the break-up of the colonial system in Asia."

"Snow, it almost seems that the Japs were a necessary evil in order to break down the old colonial system, to force the reforms that had to be made. Of course, it's a shame that it had to be the Japs—" he grinned "—because the Europeans couldn't see the handwriting on the wall. I guess I'm a little prejudiced against the Japs. I come by it through my grandfather Delano, who sailed clipper ships to China. He came to know the Chinese well and loved them but he always had an intense dislike for the Japanese. I'm glad to know you think the Chinese like us. Do they get along better with us than with the British?"

I thought they probably distrusted us less than the British, I said. (In those days they did!) We hadn't had any wars or taken their territory. Still, we had never given up extraterritoriality; we had gone on sharing the benefits of imperialism without the onus.

He made a brushing-aside motion with his arms and said: "We should have got rid of all that long ago. Back in 1933 I did write a note to Secretary Hull and said I thought it was about time for us to give up extraterritoriality in China. Hull favored it but not his advisers in the State Department. He added with a sardonic grin, "Of course I didn't know enough about it to oppose the whole State *Depahtment!*"

Then he ran through a number of miscellaneous questions one after another. Did I think the Chinese would eventually "absorb" the Japanese as a race? Did they really intermarry? When a Chinese married a "Jap" was the child more Chinese than Japanese? He talked along for several minutes about the melting pot at work in Hawaii, where in his younger days he had got the impression that the Chinese produced the best-looking Eurasians and the best citizens. He supposed that the Koreans must be something like the answer you got when you married a Chinese to a Japanese. How did I explain the fact that the Japs hadn't been able to absorb the Koreans? Or had they? And would the Koreans support the Japanese in the present war?

"Not if we make an unqualified guarantee of Korean independence right now," I said. "Korea's one colony we can free and we ought to do so before any of our Allies get itchy fingers about it."

He: "Yes, we ought to do that. Japan is going to have to give up her colonies, that's the least she can expect. They'll have to find some other way of taking care of their overpopulation. That helped drive Japan to war, and it will probably still be there after the war and then *we'll* have to face it—what to do with that overflow."

He speculated leisurely about solutions, including birth control; and I took a sidelong glance at my watch. I had been there more than a half hour, while great and weighty decisions, I assumed, hung in the balance. F.D.R. had shooed away Admiral Leahy, his medical aide and Missy LeHand. I knew others were waiting in the offing. I had stood up to leave two or three times and he had motioned me back into my seat. Now he asked me about the Communist-led guerrillas and how they operated. I told him briefly what I knew and he seemed satisfied. It was about the same picture that he had got from his friend Evans Carlson, he said; they sounded to him like the kind of people who win wars. He wanted to know how we could best help China.

I could not resist the opportunity to put in one last missionary plug for Chinese Industrial Co-operatives. F.D.R. listened while I ran over the story, which he already knew in part, of Indusco's triumphs and travails. Then I made my point by suggesting that he ask Chiang Kai-shek to earmark some of our credits for loans and operating capital for Indusco. He thought he couldn't do it that directly. There was always that fear in him of giving Chiang orders like a "barbarian chieftain." But he said he would "let Chiang know that this is the kind of thing we would like to see develop there. I'll ask Chiang to keep me personally informed of progress. In that way won't he see the point of supporting it?"

I suppose I should have told him that Chiang wasn't the man to take a hint; he had to be pushed. But I felt I had gone as far as I could. I thanked him. As I stood up once more the President asked me what I was doing now and I told him my problem.

"You want to go overseas, don't you?"

"I've never been to Russia. I have an idea I might write something useful for the *Post,* whose readers probably know less about it than I do. But I won't turn down the Air Force if that's more important."

His eyes twinkled. "Oh, they'll manage without you, somehow," he said. "Take the *Post* assignment, do a good job and come back. The war's going to last a long time."

"May I take that as an order, sir?"

"That's an order!" he said emphatically.

"Thank you. Is there anything I can do for you while I'm gone?"

"Well, let's see, you're going to India first, aren't you? When you get there and see Nehru, say hello for me. I wish you would ask Nehru to write me a letter and tell me exactly what he wants me to do for India. You can send it," he added with a grin, "through our diplomatic pouch!"

He held out his hand at last. "Write me now and then if you hear anything interesting," he said, and the envious look of a man who loved travel crept into his wide blue eyes as he wagged his great head. "You can send it to Missy LeHand through the pouch and I'll get it. When you get back, give me a personal report."

That talk certainly made a better correspondent of me. The quickness and energy of his mind and its eagerness for information and special knowledge from the humblest sources was exceptional. You had a feeling that F.D.R. was abreast of the facts of the hurrying world; perhaps his physical handicap had something to do with his determination not to lag behind. He was open, he was accessible, his mind was not resistant to new ideas. His was that rare exception in the Neanderthal world of politics—a thoroughly modern mind.

I left F.D.R. deeply infected by his radiant intelligence and confidence, and with the conviction that he would, given the co-operation of Congress and the people, lead us to victory and a wise peace.

CHAPTER 4

End and Beginning

THE NEXT DECADE in my own life, and such work as I did which made some minute tangential connection with the larger pattern of history, might have been vastly different if I had been comfortably settled in my marital affections. I would not, for one thing, have been so anxious to go overseas again so soon. I would not have stayed so long abroad and thus "lost America" for a second time.

They say that one "falls" in love and "falls" out of it. The idiom correctly describes the sensations of the beginning and end of my marriage to Nym Wales. By the time I had rejoined Nym in America the image of love had fallen out of our eyes. Mutual transgressions rather than mutual trust were the focus; we were no longer met in unity but only in polarity, and efforts at reconciliation were wholly fruitless.

If the beginning of a marriage is sometimes *une sottise faite à deux,* its ending often makes more sense. Because we were foolish in the beginning we were wiser now. One thing I had learned and was too long in learning was that no institution is more important than life itself. No alliance could or should be preserved once it is clear that its creative possibilities are exhausted and the end is mutual destruction. By the time I was ready to leave for Africa that was clear to both of us. I was to make one last mistake: an agreement to a formal separation to "live apart as if sole and unmarried"—and a postponed divorce which delayed the tasks of reconstruction for years dreadful now to recall.

In Philadelphia, late in March, I picked up my credentials from the *Post*'s new editor-in-chief, Ben Hibbs. He gave me a letter introducing me simply as his "world correspondent"—because none of us knew by what route, so rapidly was the enemy advancing on all fronts, I might find my way back home.

Ben had taken over the *Post* in a crisis near a panic. Cancellations were pouring in by the thousands and advertising was flowing out. Under Wesley Stout's editorship the *Post* had remained last-ditch neutralist and anti-interventionist. Stout was a brilliant editor, daring and independent, but in his determination not to be taken in by Allied war propaganda and its domestic tools he made one blunder which ended his career. He published a series of three articles about Jews which attempted to examine the factual basis of anti-Semitism and German monomania on the subject. Although the pieces were written by a Jew, and in the main were objective, most of the nation was in no mood to listen to anybody whose views lent the least support to Nazi racism. The reaction was one of the swiftest and most disastrous in magazine history. Stout was out in a few days and Ben Hibbs was brought in to replace him.

Tall, lanky, Kansas-born, a Phi Beta Kappa, quietly and immensely competent, Hibbs managed within a couple of years to rebuild the paper and bring it to the top of the field again. But for years he never published anything touching on the "Jewish question."

Wesley Stout had originally invited me to join the *Post*. With Stout's resignation I considered the commitment cancelled. I asked Ben whether he was sure he wished to renew the offer, along with other headaches inherited from Stout. He promptly wrote a contract which raised my guarantee.

Some people thought it odd that the author of *Red Star Over China* should be found among the *Post*'s editors for years. My ties with Benjamin Franklin's lineal descendant were made long before that book was written, however; what people forgot was that the *Post* had published a digest of it. From the time of George Horace Lorimer's editorship, my association with the *Post* was always based solely on a reputation for consistently accurate reporting. Of that I was zealously proud. My reports sometimes contradicted the messages of the *Post*'s editorial pages, but it rarely insisted that the facts of life conform to its cherished convictions. Ben Hibbs and Martin Sommers, for years my immediate boss as foreign editor, were wonderfully considerate friends as well as great editors.

In 1942, as I got ready to go abroad, I did not know whether I would ever see the Kremlin. Max Litvinov, who was Soviet Ambassador in

Washington, had done what he could to get me a visa. Finally he told me that it was hopeless; my past writing had made me an "undesirable" in Russia. He suggested, as a last resort, an appeal to the White House to intervene with Molotov. While I waited to learn the result of this I took off for India, Burma and China.

Harry Hopkins' word did finally get me into Russia, but I was not to be given a visa until I had been overseas for months. From the taxpayers' standpoint Hopkins' intervention may have been a poor return in terms of reverse lend-lease. For my own part it had the advantage of enabling me to enter Russia without any feeling of obligation for a personal welcome or gratitude for the hospitality so conspicuously lacking.

CHAPTER 5

Lost over Africa

BEN ROBERTSON was waiting to go over to Cairo for *PM*. When I told him of my "orders" from F.D.R. to take the *Post* assignment in preference to the army job, he didn't seem properly impressed.

"I never had any doubt about that, Ed," he said. "One good war correspondent is worth two generals any day."

Ben didn't like it when I called him General Robertson, after that. I never saw anybody with such undimmed respect for the press. His sense of mission and obligation were just as intact as when I had first met him on the Missouri campus, where old Dean Walter Williams preached his journalist's decalogue to us. Ben went right on believing it, too, and trying to make his editors and publishers live up to it— with indifferent success—until he crashed in a clipper outside Lisbon a year later. Fortunately he had finally completed *Red Hills and Cotton,* the story of his boyhood, just before that last flight.

I almost beat Ben to the finish when, having in fact wangled a general's priority, I took off for India via Africa. The Air Transport Command then existed mainly on paper; we had only nine commercial clippers flying both oceans and there were a hundred people waiting for every seat. Even in Africa most of our planes and personnel were being ferried by Pan-American or other civilian pilots. Trans-Atlantic flying was still an adventure; the planes carried no ditching equipment and no parachutes. We got a pioneering thrill out of that early flight over the Caribbean and down across the incredibly broad mouths of the Amazon to Brazil, where we leaped the brine to Liberia in one long, dramatic hop.

I would cross Africa four times before I saw home again, but the repeats were routine pleasure trips compared to this initiation. Our crews had nothing but a narrow radio beam to guide them in and out. Some had only ordinary tourists' maps of Africa to use for bearings; if they got off the radio beam after dark it was blind flying in wholly unfamiliar country. Planes carried heavy overloads and there were frequent crashes. A bomber took off from Lagos just ahead of our Lockheed and disintegrated under a hot brassy sky on the 13th day of April, 1942.

We had flown over from Fisherman's Lake the day before, skirting the *Côte d'ivoire* (then under Vichy France) down to Dahomey and into British Nigeria. Next morning we left for Kano, following that bomber with its plane-load of doomed passengers. Half way up we had prop trouble and made an emergency landing outside a swarm of straw huts called Minna, where the pilot found a telephone and was able to call in help. The relief plane—a Douglas C-47—did not reach us till late afternoon and it was dusk when we skipped off again. We had a tail wind and made good time. When the co-pilot came out for a stretch he said we would be in Kano in a few minutes. But something went wrong and we slipped out of the radio beam and in an hour everybody on board knew we were rather hopelessly lost over Africa.

Kano was right up near Vichy's African frontier, where the Luftwaffe held power and took pot shots at Allied planes. We might easily drift over the Sahara, we knew, in ever-widening and aimless circles of flight. Another hour passed. Down below us the African landscape that by day had seemed devoid of life was now a bewildering pattern of thousands and thousands of tribal campfires. Some clustered so closely they looked like city lights and we were often deceived. The sky itself was dim but beneath it the earth was studded with those yellow campfires like a myriad of stars slung in an inverted canopy. And yet it was all crags and brush whenever we dropped low enough to examine the terrain, with the help of landing lights, for a not impossible place to nestle down for the night.

I sweated out enough flights on army planes after that to make me want to tip my hat to all pilots, but I never went through such a prolonged build-up to disaster as this one. We didn't have a parachute on board. If we couldn't get back on that beam, and it seemed about as likely as a blindman being able to put his finger on Sleepy Eye, Minnesota, on a desk-size globe, we had no alternative but to crash land. The pilot had not taken on a full fuel load for so short a flight and he was soon on the emergency tank and ready to drop the plane whenever we found a spot which offered an even "break."

After three hours it would have been almost a relief to put down anywhere. Our bucket seats held fifteen increasingly scared men. Not many were seasoned travelers. The crew themselves were youngsters on their second flight over a strange continent; anxiety ringed their faces. We had some engineers aboard, on their way to Iran to set up a supply line for Russia; various technical experts; a number of G.I.'s on detached special duty; an inspector of the U. S. Foreign Service, George Waring; and a naval captain, Milton E. "Merry" Miles, who was on his way to China to organize guerrilla intelligence and sabotage work. Later he became a famous admiral.

"What's better than presence of mind in an airplane accident?" joked someone. I think it was Waring.

"Absence," he said when nobody answered, "of body."

But after a couple of hours the jokes ran out and the suspense became intolerable. Several young soldiers got out pictures of their wives or sweethearts and stared at them in silence. A handsome corporal with soft, thin, blond hair wrote an interminable letter to his girl friend, his tears blotting every page. He had never been in a plane before and now was convinced he would never fly in another. One of the engineers continuously swallowed his saliva; he had a large Adam's apple which bobbed up and down with unbelievable rapidity. Another civilian engineer, a married man and a father, kept saying periodically, "Keep calm. Keep calm." Then he unbuckled his belt and went up and down the plane trying to sell his expensive gold watch for five dollars.

"I won't need it now," he said. "I won't need it now." When nobody would buy it he tried to give it to me.

The air was full of pockets and we hit them all; several of the men became quite sick, and a kindly middle-aged colonel fouled his trousers.

"Umph! We're still going around in the same circle," said "Merry" Miles as the plane sank and then sharply rose.

"How do you know that?" I asked, seriously.

"That's the third time we hit that same bump," he answered. "All this reminds me of being in a submarine when depth charges go off around you. You don't know whether you're hit until you try to come up."

A practical joker with a grin and an impish humor that had earned him his nickname, "Merry," he went on to tell me about the time he commanded a destroyer down in the South China Sea, where he "loused up" the whole Japanese fleet for several days. The Japanese were attacking Hainan when Miles came up and was given the "danger" flag and ordered to stay out of port. Instead he went right in, at the same time hoisting his personal "What the Hell!" pennant, an invention consisting of three stars, three question marks and three exclamation points. The Japanese admirals couldn't find it in their code book and queried Tokyo. Tokyo queried Washington and Washington queried Miles. By the time Miles' answer to Washington got back to the Japanese in Hainan, "Merry" had already collected all the intelligence he wanted and had left for other waters.

In between listening to "Merry's" anecdotes I was absorbed with my own reactions to the situation. I was not as nonchalant as he appeared to be but was just able to "hold face," as the Chinese say. As hours wore on and I recognized the odds against survival, it was interesting to discover that I could accept the idea of death in this way, if death it was to be. Before and since I might have frantically fought the idea of dying but at that moment I found I didn't greatly mind; I felt completely alone and I knew my exit would pain no one dependent on me. I was still young but I had lived more fully and in wider freedom than most men. I had seen some high windy places of the world and made a friend or two, and now I was glad that I had usually done what interested me.

All the same, none of my rationalization prevented me from carefully maneuvering myself into the seat which I calculated to be "safest" for the coming crash.

"I'm on it! I'm back on it!" we all heard our frenzied red-headed radioman scream through the open door to the cockpit. "I'm back on the goddam beam!" It was a minute-to-midnight salvation, literally so. When we neared Kano we had no trouble picking out the airfield. The boys had a ring of fire burning around it to guide us in, although we had been given up for lost.

After we landed, our pilot stepped out and measured the gas left in our last tank. "Four gallons," he said, and he must have been a Yankee because I remember he added, grinning, "more or less!"

CHAPTER 6

Desert Flight to Delhi

ANYONE UNABLE to understand what the Greater Aswan Dam project meant to Egypt, and why it was more wicked than clever for any statesmen to make a carrot out of loans to build it, should treat himself to an edifying trip down the Nile Valley from the Sudan. He will then see, as during this flight to India I saw for the first time, the shocking narrowness of Egypt's hold on mere viability. That long green slender ribbon of irrigated fertility, which runs from Khartoum for a thousand miles to the sea, alone makes human life possible in these arid plains. In most places the lifeline is only a few miles wide; from the air it looks more like a parkway set in limitless desert. As far as the veinous irrigation ditches reach out from the Nile the crowded valley floor is rich and fruitful, but a stone's throw beyond the last moisture how abruptly begins the still white glistening deathlike waste that is nearly everywhere else the face of Egypt!

Unless one realizes that the cultivable area of Egypt is hardly two percent of the whole country all outline maps of it give a vastly misleading picture.

In Cairo, at the head of the rich delta region, you would not think of Egypt as a desert land. Nor, during the war, could you take it seriously as a nation, at all, though it was then nominally an independent state. Just before I arrived the British gave old King Fuad an ultimatum, and ran a tank up his palace steps, to order him to install Nahas Pasha as the premier. Two other things I remember suggest the pulse of Cairo at the time. One was the fact that in Shepheard's Hotel they still had three service buttons in each room marked "maid, waiter and 'native'." The other item was something I heard at a party given for the Duke of Gloucester by Sir Miles Lampson, the British ambassador who had handed Fuad the ultimatum.

The grounds of the embassy covered vast expanses of beautiful, closely clipped lawn which I admired and commented on to a pretty English lady. I have forgotten whether the Egyptians broke the tops of the grass off *by hand,* as Indian gardeners did; they may have used shears but certainly no more advanced a machine.

"It must keep a hundred men busy just manicuring this lawn," I said, "what with watering and clipping—"

"What of it?" the English lady answered. "They're only Egyptians." It was so much according to the book of the pukka sahib of a period I thought vanished that I looked at her sharply; but it wasn't intended as irony.

Yet I did meet an English diplomat in Cairo, young Adam Watson, who made me realize that thoughtful Englishmen were fully aware of the consequences of the war for empire. At the British Embassy in Moscow Adam was later to become one of Lord Inverchapel's ablest assistants. What he told me during our first luncheon together in Cairo vividly impressed me, coming from a conservative. I made a note of it:

Watson was "positively relieved," he said, at the thought of losing India after the war. "Perhaps we can hold onto the Near East if you will help us," he said. "But of course we don't know what America will do. We do want Africa.

"It seems that the main power in the Near East will be the Soviet and yourselves. We'll never be able to compete in numbers with Russia. She will take Persia unless you stop her. We shan't be able to. Maybe we can save the oil at Basra, Abadan and Bahrein, but there, too, it depends on you."

An American who thoroughly agreed with Watson was Karl Twitchell, whom I met at Shepheard's at this time. A mining engineer and an old friend of Ibn Saud, he was going back to Arabia now on a government mission. Arabia had fascinated me for years and listening to Karl revived all my ambitions to see it. I couldn't have found anyone better suited to present my case at court; it was he who, while ostensibly looking for gold for Ibn Saud, had found him something far richer: the fabulous Arabian oil deposits. Two months after I left Karl I received, at his instigation, a personal invitation from King Ibn Saud to visit him in the holy city of Ryadh. I couldn't accept it then but the King's letter was later to make a press attaché out of me.

One day back in Cairo Twitchell showed us some fine Kodachromes of the Arabs, on a projector he was taking in to Ibn Saud as a gift. He ended up with some snaps of New Hampshire on a glorious October day.

"You won't be able to keep your king down on the desert after he sees that autumn," I remarked.

"Good Lord," said Karl, "I wouldn't dream of showing those pictures to the King."

"Why not?"

"Up till now I've never told him anything but the truth. If I showed him those golden trees and told him the leaves were real, not painted, he would never believe me again."

A week later I had dinner with Ben Robertson and Karl. Then I flew by the British flying boat *Cleopatra* to the Dead Sea and across the Holy Land and over Jordan's black tents, and barren Iraq, until we followed the Shat El Arab down to blistering Basra, where the Tigris and Euphrates meet not far from Sinbad the Sailor's home. After a day's flight above the shimmering Persian Gulf, skirting parched Iran, we came into Karachi at last. By then I understood what Twitchell had meant about that New Hampshire magic and the untraveled Ibn Saud.

Not only was Arabia a monochrome of barren sand, but from the time I left Brazil, and its nice, wet, green coast, until I hit India, it seemed there was little but gray and brown wasteland below us. It's all one world all right, as a coconut is all one coconut; but a lot of both of them is husk. The niggardliness of nature when it came to dealing out the juicy places to some of the dark-skinned peoples surely explains something about the so-called "backward" men and women in their lands that look so promising on our pretty, colored maps.

I reached Delhi in May in that withering time when all nature seems dead or dying, your body weighs a ton and even mad dogs and Englishmen stay out of the midday sun. I interviewed Lord Linlithgow, as aloof as his vast, sprawling red sandstone home they called the Viceregal Lodge. ("It will make a magnificent ruin!" Clemenceau exclaimed when he saw it.) Then I went by train to Allahabad to see Jawaharlal Nehru, for whom I had an urgent message from his publisher and a word from Mr. Roosevelt. The Indian National Congress met while I was there. It passed a resolution haughtily rejecting and condemning the proposals which Churchill had sent to Delhi by Sir Stafford Cripps, offering a semi-independent government in exchange for Congress' support of the war effort.

The Congress repeated its demands for absolute, immediate freedom and called upon the Indian people to oppose Japan by "non-violent non-co-operation," only.

In Bengal I found more heat, chaos and defeatism. I concluded that if the Japanese had the minimum force to support an invasion of Eastern India nothing was likely to stop them. Not the British, not the Indians, and certainly not America; we had nothing there yet but generals—and talk. It was a relief to leave that depressing scene for a few weeks when Major Richardson, General Stilwell's pilot, offered me a lift up the Brahmaputra Valley, to the eaves of the world in lovely, cool Assam, splashed with white tea roses and good whiskey. From there I flew across the "Hump" and over the hills of Northern Burma on one of the dozen transports then opening up our only supply line to China.

In Chungking I found a new post-Pearl Harbor attitude of "let George do it," George being Uncle Sam. Inflation, hoarding, speculation, corruption and bribery were racing merrily along unchecked. Among Kuomintang officials, army officers and bureaucrats the war, and local production to win the war, were now secondary matters compared to money-making opportunities involving hoarding and speculation in terms of increasingly plentiful American currency, lend-lease supplies and U.S. Army orders and largesse. The speed of deterioration within little more than a year since my last visit was ominous.

Correspondents in Chungking could get out few of these facts because of Chinese censorship. I waited till I reached Delhi and cabled the story to the *Post* quite straight. The British censors, having a devotion to the truth about China which did not carry over to India, let it pass uncut. As a result Mme. Chiang had me banned from her precincts, an inconvenience which had to be corrected finally by a few words to her from General George Marshall on behalf of freedom of the press.

But the story of how "we lost" China comes up farther on and I need not enter into further discussion of it at this stage.

I flew back to India with Colonel Robert Scott and we picked up a Japanese Zero near Mytkina, Burma, shook him off with the help of Himalayan clouds, got lost near Everest and finally came in at dusk with ceiling zero but a perfect landing on that tiny field at Dinjan hidden in the ample folds of mighty Katchenchunga's skirts. I fully appreciated those air-conditioned tea gardens only when I reached Delhi again in June. As we let down we were enveloped by dust which all but hid the capital. We stood for a moment under the wing of the plane and I found myself cooling off my hands by keeping them in my pockets. The mercury stood at 125 in the shade.

It is worse in Southern Persia around the wells at Abadan, where the heat climbs to 150 or more. And this, too, is one of the things to remember when trying to understand people who have to live here in the furnace lands of the world. That summer in Delhi before the rains came the earth seemed on fire. Even indoors chairs held the heat of stoves. Marble inside the old palace never cooled off even at night. There seemed no growing thing. Cows on the streets dropped in any possible shade to avoid moving and the sight of their great jaws hanging open was enough to make you instantly famished with thirst. I drank two gallons of water a day without producing a drop of sweat. And I learned to soak my mattress and sheet and climb into bed wet from a shower and pull another wet sheet on top of me, to lie under a punka or overhead fan. I'd wake up before long dry and burning hot and thirsty again. By repeating the operation several times I found I could get a fair night's sleep.

There was one blessing: no flies and no mosquitoes in that time of the great heat; and you remember that, when finally the rains take over. The rains are a big event in the furnace lands; salutes should be fired. Everybody wakes up even if it is in the small hours, and joyously walks into the sweet benediction of that first rain. The streets fill with people in all conditions of dress or undress who just stand and take a shower, silent and smiling. At the Marina Hotel the night the rains came a dignified Englishman with handlebar moustachios came out on the balcony next to mine and stood stark naked with his mouth open to the sky, howling with delight.

Ten days after that event I went to Wardha, in early July, 1942, for a last visit with Nehru and Gandhi before I took off for Russia.

CHAPTER 7

Debate with Nehru

How a natural personal attachment to the cause of one's own country can distort our understanding of the larger needs of justice! Not just America, and our European and Russian allies, but nearby beloved China seemed threatened by Mahatma Gandhi's ill-timed "open rebellion." At Wardha I found myself challenging Nehru's decision to support it.

I hadn't forgotten the contradiction between our British ally's position in India and our joint claim to be fighting for the Four Freedoms "everywhere in the world." Gandhi had often enough recalled his disillusionment with the British when, after using him to recruit Indians in World War I, they had let him down on their promises affecting Indian freedom. In 1939, after Britain arbitrarily placed India at war with Germany, without consulting any representative Indians, Gandhi led the Indian National Congress party to demand that Britain make good her claim to a moral cause by declaring Indian independence a fixed *"war aim."* Churchill did nothing of the sort until the Japanese attacked. Then, again, it was Gandhi who brought about the defeat of the Cripps mission.

"The Cripps offer," said Gandhi, "is a post-dated check on a failing bank." Indeed, British power could not have survived the war anywhere in Asia without American help, and the Mahatma did not yet know how to estimate that. He only knew intuitively that the time had arrived for positive action and he demanded that the British "quit India," at the moment Japan stood at its Eastern gates.

I could not question any Indian's right to act in what he conceived to be the nation's best interest but I argued with Nehru that the move would not bring India freedom and would only help the Axis powers. I contended that by assuming the partial power which Cripps had offered they could still organize the people, get men into the army and train them, and prepare to strike for full freedom "at the right moment."

What I did not realize as fully as Nehru and other Indians was how stubbornly Churchill would try to hang onto the empire in spite of what looked to everyone else like its early inevitable dissolution, whoever won victory in this war. And I did not realize how repugnant (if not positively immoral) it was to intelligent Indians to consider bartering their allegiance to the Crown at this late hour for the eventual "gift" to them of sovereign rights which the overlords had taken from them by force.

Once Japan's attacks struck into the European colonial pastures of Asia it became for all subject peoples a struggle which had their emotional, if not their intellectual, sympathy. Even Nehru was no exception. Why should Indians help the British vanquish Japan on the mere assumption that brown imperialism was worse than white? What kind of dignity could Gandhi achieve for India by warring on the side of her historic "oppressors" against the white man's enemy?

Nehru never put it so crudely to me, but in the days I spent with him and Gandhi at Wardha he made me see how they felt, and why, paradoxically, they honestly believed that the only way to save India *from the Japanese* was to revolt against the British. In my journal of the time I kept close notes of our off-the-record conversations.

"As I see the picture," I said to Nehru one day, "the fate of the whole world is being decided in the Nazi-Soviet struggle. If Russia collapses, India will be next. After all, you are an anti-fascist, a socialist, an internationalist, as well as an Indian patriot. With Hitler attacking from the West and Japan from the East, how would you feel if you found yourself their ally in fighting the British?"

"That's an odd question!" exclaimed Nehru.

"Maybe," I said, "but it's a question history may ask."

Nehru looked at me for what seemed a long minute. We sat on the mat-covered floor in a small house in Wardha used for headquarters of the Congress party Working Committee as they met here to be near Gandhi, whose ashram was in the neighboring village of Sevagram. There were big pillows to lean against. Outside it rained. There was none of the bustle, stir and confusion characteristic of political conferences. There were no cigarettes, no whiskey sodas, no typewriters in evidence, and no automobiles outside. We had had lunch, from small tin trays covered with dabs of diced vegetables and mounds of yellowish sweet rice. And now it was hard to believe that the men here, and one woman, Sarojini Naidu, in this small, bare house held the power to commit a great nation to revolt against the Viceroy whom I had left sitting in that regal air-conditioned splendor in New Delhi.

Nehru spoke patiently:

"I shall tell you why. For three years we did not think of independence as really urgent, but now it is just that very imminence of disaster which makes complete freedom imperative. We have to be free to defend ourselves, don't you see? We can't possibly win with English leadership at a time like this. Unless we assert ourselves decisively, India will go the way of Burma and Malaya. There is a growing feeling definitely favorable to Japan among our people. If Japan attacks we expect the British to lose—they haven't anything like an adequate force here—and after one or two battles our people would just passively submit."

"And yet I've heard it not only from the Viceroy, but from some Indians, that Gandhi could change the attitude of the country overnight just by issuing a call to support the war," I said.

"Don't you believe it," Nehru answered. "Gandhi's whole strength lies in his psychic appreciation of the feeling of the masses. He knows the people would support the war now only if national freedom were granted us first."

"But it isn't as if you had no freedom at all to defend," I went on, treading dangerous ground. "You have an amazing amount of per-

sonal freedom of speech, press, organization, due process, equality
before the law, and all that. At least Indian nationalism has more to
gain through an Allied victory than an Axis one. Is absolute independence at this moment a realistic demand? How can you act in a
vacuum without regard to events in the rest of the world right now?
Aren't you being too insular?"

Nehru bristled and at once caught me up. "Insular! Indian nationalism is no more insular than any other! Our social program, our social
consciousness, are ahead of many. We are ahead of China. I myself
believe absolute independence outmoded; we are all growingly inter-
dependent. But people have the right to self-determination. They have
the right to determine their own national interests. That's all we are
demanding."

What American could deny that? I had to backtrack. My remaining
argument was a practical one: although the British might not be able
to defeat the Japanese they could still crush any Indian civil disobedience campaign. To my surprise Nehru readily agreed.

"But that does not matter. What matters is how a nation goes down
or stands up. If we go down fighting we shall not be permanently suppressed. The only way to build up a spirit of resistance here is to organize against the British and then these organizations can be turned
against the Japanese."

"Inside" Congress information was that Gandhi now believed Japan
and the Axis were going to win. He felt that the presence of Anglo-
American troops in India invited attack which might otherwise be
avoided. Nehru never admitted that to me and he apparently never
believed in Axis victory. At Allahabad he had stoutly resisted
Gandhi's post-Pearl Harbor policy as inconsistent with "the attitude
of sympathy we have taken up toward the Allies" which would make
India a "passive partner of the Axis." But at Wardha he finally changed
his mind.

Right to the end, however, Nehru kept hoping for pressure from
Roosevelt to force Churchill to reopen negotiations for a liberally
broadened version of the Cripps offer. He made that perfectly clear to
Colonel Louis Johnson, the President's special representative in
Delhi. Even when he joined in the "quit India" resolution, on July 14,
he still managed to give it the character of a last-minute appeal for
American intervention. While demanding immediate freedom and the
right to form a provisional government, the Congress resolution promised Free India's co-operation with Allied troops, aid to China and
resistance to the Axis.

Nehru bitterly resented the fact that nobody in London or Washington believed his assurances or raised a voice on behalf of Indian independence as a war aim. No statesman of the "free world" came to his aid in this hour when he was almost alone in his belief that India could be swung round to active support of the Allies, if she were treated as an equal and sovereign power. And doubtless experience must have confirmed, in Nehru's mind, the wisdom of a foreign policy of "non-alignment" or "neutralism" which in the post-war years was so profoundly to perplex and disappoint Western statesmen who expected India to accept their bi-polar conceptions of a world dedicated to the prosecution of cold war.

It struck me as curious that there was not a sign of a spokesman for the Viceroy at Wardha, not even an unofficial observer, to follow the deliberations of the Indians at this fateful moment. No one tried to renew the search for a compromise. Later I realized that the Viceroy wasn't displeased by the course of events. The sooner he could lock up the Indian leaders the sooner the British would be free to save India without interference from the Indians.

"I am sorry to say it," Viceroy Linlithgow told me when I got back to New Delhi, "but the Indians have no political sense. When we go, the country will break up. India won't be ready for democracy for a hundred years yet. The only thing holding the country together today is the British Raj and the Army."

Pro-consuls and soldiers, even very sensitive ones, seldom are good judges of the revolutionary leaders who mature under their eyes. (Consider Pontius Pilate.) George Orwell, a far from obtuse observer, held an opinion similar to Linlithgow's. "If India were simply 'liberated,' i.e., deprived of British military protection," he wrote in 1941 in *The Lion and the Unicorn* on the basis of his service in India, "the first result would be a fresh foreign conquest and the second a series of enormous famines which would kill millions of people within a few years." And yet it was the waning days of Linlithgow's rule which saw one of India's most unnecessary famines. More than a million people died in it without the help of any new foreign conquest at all.

On the day the Congress high command reached its fateful decision at Wardha I went off to Sevagram for a farewell talk with Gandhi, who had asked for, and was now to lead, what he himself called an "open rebellion."

CHAPTER 8

"*Firecrackers, Begin Cracking!*"

WHETHER YOU SAW Gandhi against a background of wealth as a guest at Birla House in New Delhi or at the Desai mansion in Bombay or at the home of some other oppressed Indian millionaire subject of His Majesty, he always led the same ascetic life amidst his goats and spinning wheels. The complex simplicity of this routine often was achieved only by very careful staff work, however. "Gandhiji has no idea," as his wittiest disciple, Sarojini Naidu, once remarked to me, "how much it costs us to keep him up in poverty." But down at Wardha, deep in the Central Provinces, he had a kind of permanent set of his own, where Sevagram, his ashram headquarters, was typical of the discomfort of life in the tens of thousands of dusty villages which were the roots of the Mahatma's strength and the strength of Indian nationalism.

Wardha itself, a town of 30,000 people, held few charms visible to the casual eye. We stayed in the broken-down Circuit House, where the water was polluted and had to be purpled with permanganate before it could be drunk. Prohibition also prevailed in the town. Cholera was epidemic and malaria widespread. The soil was sandy, the landscape flat and uninteresting. The only difference between a hair shirt and Wardha was that the former was removable. All this doubtless helped explain why Gandhi chose it as the locale for his "model village." But perhaps I am prejudiced against Wardha; it was there that I caught dengue fever.

My Indian friends were hospitable and the Mahatma, with his kindness, gentleness and humor, was truly a "great soul" I was just beginning to know. He was in especially good form that day when with Arch Steele, then the New York *Times* correspondent and an old friend from Peking days, I bumped out to see him. We were conveyed, as customary, by that Indian instrument of two-wheeled torture known as the *tonga*. Gandhi had a very special one, its sides painted with the faces of Congress leaders. Gandhi's own face was right behind the horse's tail.

Sevagram, a cross between a third-rate dude ranch and a refugee camp, was a colony of mud huts with thatched roofs set in a cactus-sprinkled countryside. A dirt path led through the cluster to a hut that looked like the rest except that it was surrounded with a fence of sticks, and a *charka,* or spinning wheel, adorned the mud wall in crude bas-relief. A cow wandered by morosely and scrawny chickens strutted the yard. Inside, squatting barefoot on the matted floor, sat the toothless old messiah from whom all India awaited word. He was then seventy-four.

Amidst this collection of simple buildings, chickens and cows, in a place infested by scorpions and poisonous snakes, and kindly spinners and toilers carrying out his creed, between sessions at prayers, spinning, administering purgatives to relieve aches and pains of patients in his hospital where only faith-healing and home-grown remedies were used, Gandhi was about ready to deliver his ultimatum to Churchill. He distrusted science and surgery as much as he did Churchill, and he welcomed anyone who came to try his own personal mud-pack cure for high blood pressure. Here also he edited *Harijan* magazine and offered sensible advice both to young maidens on how to avoid being raped by enemy soldiers and to the Allies and the Axis alike on how to end the war.

And now, as he spoke softly out of this background, his words were so incongruous we found it hard to take in their meaning. He sat leaning against a big white pillow, his brown body naked except for a few yards of cheesecloth round his middle (and how I envied him in that stinging, prickly heat!) and over his large gold-rimmed glasses he peered down now kindly, now a bit petulant. He was going to lead a mass civil disobedience movement, he explained, on the broadest basis. It would be "the biggest in his life," but it would be non-violent in so far as he could make it so.

"And do you really expect the British to withdraw?" I asked.

"Of course if the British withdraw," he said, absently scratching his nose, "it would be a feather in their caps. But I wish to stress this point. There is no room left in the proposal for negotiations." He wagged his bald pate determinedly. "Either they recognize the independence of India or they do not. After that, many things could happen. Once independence is recognized the British would have altered the whole landscape."

Gandhi wanted an actual physical withdrawal, he said. "Next it would be a question of who would take over, God or anarchy."

Gandhi's semantics were often elusive.

"Yet you would want an independent India to withdraw from the war, would you not?" I asked.

"Free India will make common cause with the Allies. I can't say what would happen. If I can possibly turn India toward non-violence it would be a great gain. If I could influence 400 million people to fight with non-violence . . ."

"But would you oppose the use of military force to fight against Japan by a Free Indian government?" I insisted on pinning him down.

"No, it would not be right to do so."

"Then perhaps there is still a chance to reach some understanding?"

"Oh, no," Gandhi said firmly. "This time it isn't a question of [giving the British] one more chance."

"But this is a very serious action in wartime. It's treason!"

Absently pulling on his big toe and looking down at us in his child-like way, the gentle old warrior now touched off his heavy artillery.

"Oh, yes," he said, using for the first time the expression which was soon to blanket the country and the world, "it's open rebellion!"

Then he was silent. He leaned his naked brown body against the pillow. He looked very tired. His cheeks sank over toothless gums and his glasses slipped down over his nose. Behind him were two book-cases filled with religious books in faded wrappers, in the midst of which stood a single volume in a bright jacket labeled *Modern Armaments*. Beside him lay my own book, *The Battle for Asia*. A young Indian girl slipped in and whispered to him. He was needed in the hospital. He picked up my book and as he left the room he turned and said:

"You reporters are the firecrackers. Commence cracking!"

Nehru had told me Gandhi had been reading my book. "Your last chapter is just the way he sees it," he said. "Gandhiji wants to talk to you about it." When the others filed out I stayed behind, staring at a brown cow and a goat. I wondered what I could say to this brave old gentleman with whom I could not help feeling disappointed at that moment. I felt that he was letting down a cause greater than his own.

Suddenly I made up my mind. I turned quickly into the dusty road and left without telling Gandhi good-bye.

The rebellion was launched on August 2, when Gandhi, Nehru and all the top leaders were promptly arrested. Protest meetings and demonstrations took place everywhere and were met by arms. Thousands lost their lives. As soon as Gandhi was put away, in prison, the movement took on violent forms. By the following December 60,000 Indians had been jailed, Indian crowds had been fired on 470 times, and troops had been used sixty-eight times. Only when Gandhi undertook a prolonged fast did his countrymen desist and settle down sullenly to wait for his next command.

I still felt that it was futile. Only much later I saw why it was all a necessary part of a process Nehru had described to me. "India," he said, "has had its back straightened by Gandhi. He has taught us the value of unity in political action and during this period probably no other method than his could have succeeded."

One day I remembered what Nehru had told me about Gandhi "agreeing completely" with that chapter in *The Battle for Asia.* I read it over again. I saw that I had advocated more than a year before Pearl Harbor that America demand Indian independence as the price of our armed support for Britain. I concluded:

"It will be suggested that the emancipation of India would mean the end of British 'unity.' It may be the only way in fact to restore it. The strongest allies democratic England has today are Canada, Australia and New Zealand, and without the help of a certain former colony south of Canada she might not survive at all. A Free India could become as valuable an asset to England as a free America."

Touché, oh Mohandas Karamchand Gandhi! In my too narrow patriotism I kneweth not mine own child on the burning plains of India!

When I flew out of India into Russia I could not foretell that I would be at Gandhi's side and receive his blessing six years later, a few hours before his cruel death by an assassin's hand.

CHAPTER 9

Into Russia

A FEW DAYS after I reached Moscow I met an attractive young woman named Ilena, with whom I was to spend many stirring hours. But it was months before I ventured to ask her to let me take a close look at what caused the marvelous effect in her gray-blue eyes. They were cat-like, with elliptical lenses or pupils. I discovered that the phenomenon that put stars in her eyes also made her somewhat near-sighted. She could have had this corrected by a minor operation but she would not bother. When Ilena wished to see something at a distance she pulled down the corners of her eyes with her fingers and this trick brought them into sharp focus.

I suppose a believer in Freud's theories of eye-dreams may have a field day with the suggestion, but for me Ilena's eyes were symbolic of the way we and the Russians looked at each other. History had shaped or warped or deformed us so that we saw as through a glass darkly. Neither people seemed interested in making slight adjustments to clear up the view. In Ilena's case the defect was a rare personal adornment, but there was no such compensation for the stubborn myopia which persisted between the nations . . .

When I first arrived in Russia the fate of the world hung on the outcome of the battle for Stalingrad. Had the Nazis broken through there we would have been powerless to keep them from seizing the Mesopotamian oil basin and the whole Near East. The German tide incredibly was stopped on the Volga, where I saw the beginning of the end of Hitler written in the eyes of Marshal Paulus and two dozen German generals who surrendered with him admist the rubble and the myriad frozen corpses and fragments of corpses. In this victory of such enormous cost to Russia there was doubtless little or no altruism; the Russians died for Russia. It was fortunate for us that they had a Russia to die for. However much I came to dislike or distrust many features of the Soviet system, I never forgot Stalingrad. During that bitter winter alone Russia's losses dwarfed her Allies' combined casualties for the entire war.

Perhaps I entered Russia with standards somewhat different from those of my colleagues who had worked only in Europe and America. Anglo-American newspaper correspondents who then possessed any first-hand knowledge of Asia were few indeed. Fewer still knew anything about Asian Communism. My own years in the Orient had certainly altered my view of some aspects of life which shocked visitors fresh from modern plumbing or the bistro belt. To say that Russia is Eurasia rather than Europe is to state a truism, yet not many of us understood that. Russia struck me as the most technologically advanced of Asian nations, endowed with all the requirements for rapid future progress; many others noted only scarcity of bathtubs and the heavy privations imposed by war and ruthless dictatorship. They insisted on judging it purely as a backward *Western* land.

The Soviet Union is multi-national, of course, a continent in itself composed of sixteen republics in area more than three times as large as the United States, and with fifty million more people. By far the greater part of it lies in what the conventional cartographer calls Asia. There are somewhat more non-Russians in the U.S.S.R. than Russians. All its people share a heritage of centuries of life under Tartar and

Tsarist despotism which profoundly shadowed Russian behavior under Stalin, as under the Romanovs.

Accepting all that, I did not expect Russians to think and act exactly like Americans, Englishmen or Frenchmen. If I found some grays in the picture where others saw only black, it was also because I looked at Russia with half-Asian eyes, myself, eyes accustomed to poverty, hunger, disease, exploitation of women and children as private property, brutality and injustice by decree and the general practice of man's inhumanity to man commonplace in pre-war Asia.

The purges of the Thirties and the inquisitions carried out by Stalin and willing accomplices (including most of the present party Presidium) relieved me of illusions that I was entering Utopia. Once inside the Soviet Union I soon realized something else: that Socialism there was in no overt respect answerable to the wishes of individuals. This was a monopolistic society under a sovereign party wielding enormous near-absolute power, a condition which made possible its unique and mighty feature, a wholly planned economy at once of such dreadful and marvelous potentials that it might prove decisive in the shaping of the future of all mankind.

It was this unprecedented power to plan a nation's life, and the extremely complex problems of learning how to use that power in civilized ways, which provided the key to nearly everything good and bad about the Soviet Union, and which would constitute its basic challenge to the old planless economies and societies in the Western world. In it lay the explanation of all the unexpected successes Russia would score in the post-war world, right down to Sputnik.

To make a rough comparison to help anyone who has never visited the Soviet Union visualize it quickly, it might be described as a system something like we could get in America if all economic, political, social, legislative, administrative and judicial power were to be placed under a single corporative management. "If you look upon the U.S.S.R. as a monopoly in which the state owns every branch of production and controls every market," I once wrote, "the Politburo corresponds to the board of directors of one gigantic holding company. It holds the proxies of [millions of] party members who may be considered stockholders of the subsidiary organizations. They [party members] are in turn the managerial or steward class, who see that the company unions, made up of all the workers and peasants, keep in line . . . True, the [Soviet] constitution in no way makes that clear; it does not even mention the Politburo—or the NKVD, for that matter. It provides for a system of soviets, or representative councils, leading up to the Supreme Soviet and its Presidium, vested with power to appoint a cabinet. In practice, however, the Communist party selects all officials, from top to bottom . . ." *

Some years after I wrote that, Milovan Djilas, formerly an important Yugoslav Communist, would conclude that the Communist "corporation" and its membership constituted *A New Class*. Whether the word "class" was more appropriate than "elite" to describe the ruling party and bureaucracy (synonymous, to Djilas), membership in both was replenished from the two true producing classes, the peasants and workers. And this membership seemed somewhat more accessible to young people of such class origins than access to the *upper* bourgeoisie was to similar classes in most capitalist countries. Djilas' analysis would also be misleading without carefully noting other important discrepancies in the analogy.

While the Communist party monopolized all ownership and control, it did so as a collective body; no individual "shareholder" had personal resources of power outside it. Under private capitalism the owner of corporate stock can trade it or waste it, or use it to buy up means of production and labor to make private profits without regard for its social effects. "Stock" in the "new class" in Russia was distributed to ever-growing millions, shifting from older to younger people; but it was not marketable, not transferable and not inheritable. Also, it might at any time be "recalled," leaving the individual without material resources of prestige. Conformance of the individual to the collective or social will was therefore far more complete than it would be in the United States if a single corporation were to own *all* the means of production. In Russia even the greatest "stockholder" in the Communist party could not accumulate investment capital. Hence the personal-ownership-prestige motive played no role in his behavior compared to the party-prestige motive.

* Cf. *Saturday Evening Post*, October, 1952.

CHAPTER 10

A Point of View

ROOSEVELT once called Stalin a despot heading "a dictatorship as absolute as any in the world." Stalin himself admitted that all directives and laws derived from the party and its leaders, neglecting only to add that there was but one Leader. While I generally understood all this before I went to Russia, what I did not know, and what nobody could know without living among Russians for several years, was how the Soviet garment fitted the people, how they accepted it or were made to accept it, whether they would or could change it, and how, and what kind of policies these people could and would make possible or impossible for their government to pursue.

In the end I concluded that perhaps the most dangerous of all our delusions about Russia and her peoples was the belief that government and party were strictly one thing and Russian humanity another. There as everywhere else environment and history made the man, man made the society, and society made the kind of rule under which the individual was fated to live or die. No man is an island; neither was the government of Russia. It came to be and it persisted because it had firm foundations in the collective mind, the conscious and unconscious needs not of every individual but of the people as a whole. Every government mirrors its people's strengths and weaknessnes, their ignorance and their glory or wisdom, but above all it mirrors their will to survive and *perpetuate themselves in their own image.* "It is the frame of mind of the common man that makes the foundation of society in the modern world," said Veblen; and this was true of the U.S.S.R. as it was of the U.S.A.

In Russia all the ancient fear, suspicion and insecurity of life on the immense steppe with its open frontiers inviting invasion from east and west, and again and again subjected to and submerged by it, often had made unity of the mass at the expense of the individual the only alternative to national extinction. Any disposition on the part of the rulers to permit the organization of power at the bottom invariably had been interpreted as weakness, quickly exploited by assassins inside and outside the country, and followed by setback.

280

Russian history, brief in the evolution of nations, was chiefly an accumulation of three centuries of the Kiev tradition of identity of Church and State and of Byzantine law and art; of two and a half centuries of Mongol rule which taught the advantages of despotism in the molding and holding together of a rapidly forming empire; and of three centuries of tsardom under the Romanovs which further drummed home the lessons of submission of the one for the supposed interests of the many. It was not to be expected then that an infant modern working class and a few thousand nineteenth-century liberals and intellectuals, children of a Russian bourgeoisie very late to emerge, compared to that of Western Europe, could in a few years of revolution change the basic means of the state which were a thousand years in the shaping, nor change the national character of the peasant masses behind them.

Socialism is no exception to the rule that all great politico-religious movements possess two main human elements or sources of strength. One is realistic, rationalistic, the other idealistic or mystical. Once organized in terms of power, the realists who get control in the movement tend to exploit the idealists in order not just to perpetuate themselves but to institutionalize the orthodox, which becomes their vested interest.

Yet it is important to remember that it was not the perpetuation of despotism and inequality but its total extirpation, and the implantation of Western ideals of democracy, which were the aim and hope of the early Russian Socialists, from Bakunin to Lenin. Nor were the early Bolsheviks hypocrites when they had to revert to the means which they began their fight to destroy. They were true believers in liberté, égalité, fraternité, in the direct line of succession to leaders of European and American modern social thought: to Owen, St. Simon, Sorel, Fourier and Proudhon; to Jefferson, Paine, Bellamy, Henry George, Lester Ward and Veblen; to their own Kropotkin and Bakunin and many others in the liberal-revolutionary tradition. That they had to fall back on despotism as the only way to impose changes intended to end despotism was no more surprising than the resignation of the Jacobins to dictatorship, scarcely a century earlier, as the only hope for unity necessary to realize the aims of the First Republic.

The view expressed here that the political behavior of any nation can be adequately judged only by the yardstick of its own past is not original with me. Nations do not escape their history any more than individuals escape their chromosomes and genes. By and large all countries tend to cling to their traditional habits of thought and politi-

cal method regardless of parties in power or discrete objectives. Even
in revolutionary periods, when deep changes do occur which might
be likened to biological mutations or leaps forward or backward on a
grand scale, still the change itself is modified by impulses and inhibi-
tions carried over from former experience.

No doubt Stalin was a bloody tyrant guilty of most of the crimes
for which he was officially blamed only posthumously. But the people
accepted him in a way not understood by most of his enemies abroad.
That it was his closest disciples who made the accusations against
him which during Stalin's lifetime they always denounced as filthy
bourgeois slanders simply reflects their own joint responsibility for his
methods. All Joe's murderous despotism was seeded by the same Russian history that produced generations of boyars to whip their brothers
into service in the cause of unity and strength to resist the Mongol
Khans, and after them spawned the terrible Ivans, the pharaoh-like
Peter, the profligate Katherine, the part-despot, part-liberal, part-
Asian, part-European Alexanders.

"However weak you are, you must *pull* if you die for it," exclaims
one of Nikolai Nekrasov's characters. "So the Tartars taught us and
they left the knout as a remembrance." The Slav in the Russian might
yearn for individual liberty with responsibility. The Tartar in him
rejected it. The search for a middle ground, the essence of West European democracy, was in the end always alien to both ruler and opposition; in practice both equally despised it. To the Russian Communist, ex-Communist, or anti-Communist, Stalinist or anti-Stalinist,
government by free consent was government by compromise, rule
based on probability rather than certainty, heterodoxy rather than
orthodoxy, and weakness in exchange for strength. "Rotten liberalism"
became an epithet for it which even the sensitive Lenin, whose life
was changed by the execution of his idolized "liberal" older brother
by the Tsar, hurled at all evolutionists.

For the Bolsheviks, as for Ivan and Peter, government quite simply
had to be violent to survive. "The history of Russia," declared Stalin
in 1931, "is the history of defeats due to backwardness. She was
beaten by the Turkish beys. She was beaten by the Mongol khans.
She was beaten by the Swedish feudal barons. She was beaten by the
Polish-Lithuanian landowners. She was beaten by the Japanese barons.
All beat her because of her backwardness. She was beaten because to
beat her was profitable and *could be done with impunity.*"

Harsh, tyrannical, blood-stained and merciless as it has been to its
foes and imagined foes, the Soviet regime was the logical product of

Russia's somber past seen as a whole, of centuries of enslavement interrupted by violent surges forward toward human liberation, of many peoples on different levels of growth held together by an absolute power and orthodox faith made to prevail across 6,000 miles of vulnerable space reaching from the fringes of Europe to the Pacific Ocean.

Under the rule of the Russian Communists, using the knout wherever persuasion failed, the promise of "Socialist plenty" became a war against time and the future. A whole generation was sacrificed to the law of jam yesterday and jam tomorrow but never jam today. Led by the conceited, arrogant, cynical but definitely dedicated and infinitely shrewd and tough little man who called himself Comrade Steel, the party literally beat the backward, stubborn peasants onward and out of a morass of economic and social primitivism onto the high level of the great industrial powers in the brief span of thirty years. Many of the institutions it developed in the process were original, and both in language and outer form were curiously quite like those which the idealistic Bellamy foresaw and thought would finally lift man from barbarism. Stalinism was Socialism by knout instead of by common consent. Perhaps in America or Western Europe it would have been gentler. But the mere fact that in Russia Socialism did not at once liberate the human spirit no more proved Socialism a failure than the regression of fascist Italy, Japan, Germany and Spain necessarily proved that the freedoms of dissent must inevitably disappear under capitalism.

What World War II did prove was that Russia could no longer be "beaten with impunity." Not even by Stalin himself! By 1946, although momentarily crippled, hobbled, convalescent from wounds beyond conception abroad, the Soviet Union still was revealed as indisputably the mightiest land from the Pacific westward to the Atlantic. As one of the two great powers of the earth Russia was swiftly to pull abreast of Europe as she attained the means, at last, of completing her escape from the tyranny of a Tartar past, to enter upon broad new roads of development pointing in the same general directions as the West, and capable of moving along them much more rapidly, now, than many nations which had long held her in scorn and contempt.

Although that was foreseeable even during the war, an understanding of it had to be achieved by surmounting the most formidable obstacles placed in the observer's way by the Soviet government, as the following pages may demonstrate.

CHAPTER 11

Stalin's Guests

IN THE DAYS when Stalin was still the adored genius of geniuses to all loyal Communists as well as after the Twentieth Party Congress, when Khrushchev first depicted him as a homicidal paranoiac, a fear-crazed, suspicion-ridden despot and megalomaniac, any unauthorized or informal relationship with a foreigner (Communist or non-Communist alike) was certain to put the Soviet citizen under severe scrutiny and eventual interrogation of the dreaded political police.

Nevertheless, during World War II and immediately afterward there was a period of relative freedom when some Russians did risk friendships with the foreign devil. A number of Americans and Europeans got close enough to Russian women to marry them and acquire children and in-laws. I also came to know a few Russians on terms of some candor and even trust; but this was only after I had been in and out of Russia and been readmitted without betraying the confidence of those known to me or bringing harm to them.

Of course I met and talked to hundreds of Russians in the cities and villages under official scrutiny: bureaucrats, workers, teachers, students, artists, farmers, soldiers, Communists and non-Communists. These occasions usually followed a prescribed schedule and seldom led anywhere. You met composers like Prokofiev and Shostakovich, writers like Sholokhov, prominent actors, actresses, doctors, scientists and other professional people who were not, strictly speaking, party functionaries; but you could rarely see them privately. And of course Russians of position or official rank would not then risk expressing a private political opinion to a foreigner. The one exception was Max Litvinov, whose conversation I shall, now that he is dead, report in due course.

In general the policy of the Soviet press department was to promise everything and do nothing. Its ideal correspondent was one who would cable the reports and observations of *Pravda* and *Izvestia* abroad, adding only a few well-chosen words of approval. The game was understood by all; the correspondent's aim was to get a fresh, original and honest story and the press department's purpose was to frustrate him. Since everything was government-owned and controlled the odds against any important news break-through were enormous. It was quite impossible just to step off the street anywhere and drop in for a chat or an interview at random. In practice you could not visit a school, factory, hospital, government office, trade union, or any place at all where you might observe and question men and women at work, without advance official arrangements. Some of this may have been justified as strict security measures in war-time; but it had been true before the war and it would become much worse after the cold war began.

Gradually I became convinced that the policy of "no-show" was largely due to Russian inferiority and vulnerability and the Communist desire to hide it. German pillaging had destroyed the basis of even the meager pre-war standards of life. The primitive improvisations the country was forced to adopt could easily be made objects for superficial cheap ridicule by quick-trip foreign journalists, and often were. Until it woke up with a start about 1955 to the realities of the miracle of Soviet recovery, the American press continued to publish comparisons between the Soviet poverty and American prosperity as if Russia had never been through the most ruinous war and invasion suffered by any great nation in modern history.

In the first few years of the after-war, at any rate, Russia's excessive secrecy expressed not so much the need of hiding evidence of her strength as fear of the discovery of her grave physical weaknesses. If, a decade later, Khrushchev began to "open up" and to give the world a closer look, it was not only because Russia felt more secure (with the attainment of atomic stalemate) but because she had recovered from the major wounds of the war and could invite comparison.

Of course now, as before, the Russian language itself remained a formidable barrier between the Russians and other people. Yet the foreigner who speaks a little Russian, or even speaks it fluently, with the accent and appearance which stamp him as an *inostranets,* is about as conspicuous as a white man in China.

I toiled many hours over Russian phonetics, syntax, grammar and the complicated conjugations and case endings. I never got much beyond the ability to carry on a limited practical conversation and ponder my way through the dreary columns of the party—that is to say the only—newspapers. A few correspondents of Russian birth or long residence in Russia were better off. Alexander Werth, Henry Shapiro, Robert Magidoff and Edmund Stevens spoke excellent Russian. Yet they all complained that it merely meant they were more closely watched.

The truth is that correspondents in Russia have always been highly dependent on expert personal secretaries. There are women who have been doing this work since the revolution. During the war a few "new girls" broke into the ranks of the profession; several married foreigners and went abroad. It was generally assumed that all secretaries were regularly reporting to the NKVD, as the state security or political police were then called. The same assumption applied to all Soviet citizens who worked for or openly fraternized with foreigners. A few secretaries were obvious agents; the rest were women trying to make a living. Although they were all subject to interrogation or intimidation by the NKVD they showed little inclination to pry, provoke or propagandize. They all had to have party approval in order to work for foreigners and yet they included in their midst several of the bitterest anti-Stalinists I ever met.

Correspondents lived in the Metropole Hotel, which may have been a good second-rate hostelry in Tsarist days. When I was there it looked and smelled somewhat like a vast but failing whorehouse. Indeed, some Russian call girls circulated around it and the National, the other main hotel for transients. In Moscow the girls did the calling, however. Soon after the lonely stranger arrived a dulcet voice would come over the phone one evening, speaking in Russian: "Do you like Russian girls? Shall I call on you? Would you like to take me to the theatre?" or the equivalents. The stranger might not understand Russian but he would always have learned how to say *da* or *nyet,* and that was enough.

Commercialized amour was officially forbidden in Russia, and there were no brothels, licensed or otherwise. But there were available women, as elsewhere during the war. They were not interested in money but in gifts of food or hosiery or bits of lingerie. It was assumed that they must all be tabbed as spies by the NKVD. More likely the police just tolerated the situation because the girls really were hungry and had no other talent which could bring them a living in wartime, as was the case with women in Piccadilly, in London. Some of them were quite pretty. Some were ex-students of the ballet school or the foreign-language school who had been dropped for various reasons. Having developed a taste for foreign things, they could not go back to work in a factory or their former drab lives.

Before the war ended all the Russian call girls stopped calling.

The Metropole's guests ranged from minor foreign diplomats, stray or overflow personnel from the embassies, flyers, American fur buyers and correspondents to Moslem leaders from Central Asia, Mongolian tribesmen, Japanese newspaper men (our enemies but not Russia's), important out-of-town party functionaries (in for the usual report to the Kremlin followed by a discreet bacchanal), and a few European Reds awaiting orders from the Central Committee to set up satellite regimes in the soon-to-be-liberated states. Jack Margolis, a Cockney turned Bolshevik and married to a Russian, was sub-manager of the hotel. He kept an eye on us for the leather-coated huskies who hung around the lobby. Occasionally, but only occasionally as far as I observed, these NKVD stalwarts followed us on our appointed rounds.

These were the early war years when Walter Kerr, Bill Downs, John Hersey, Bob Magidoff, Maurice Hindus, Eddie Gilmore, Ed Stevens, Lee Stowe, Henry Shapiro, Godfrey Blunden, Henry Cassidy, Dick Lauterbach, Harrison Salisbury, David Nichol, and others lived in the Metropole. We worked sitting in fur coats and felt boots and let the hot water run in the bathroom to take the frost off the interior chill. We ate in a private dining room, beyond Russian eyes, such luxuries as cabbage soup, meat and potatoes. In addition we were allowed a monthly ration of bread, fresh meat, cheese, sugar or chocolate, vodka and wine from the Soviet "diplomatic store." Except for the absence of any kind of fresh food it would have sufficed, if we had been feeding only ourselves. Most of us were supplying employees, as well, which meant a Russian family or two.

My own "staff," a secretary and a courier, were well paid in roubles which I bought with American money at the diplomatic exchange rate that had no relation to actual purchasing power for anything but their starvation rations, mainly black bread. My "staff" were more interested in the bread I saved from the table and the sugar, fat, bread, wine and cheese allowed me than the roubles. These rations were worth thousands of roubles a month at prevailing black-market rates in war-time Moscow. We also used food and cigarettes for tips to waiters, hotel maids and others. A single piece of French pastry was considered a royal emolument.

During my first winter in Moscow the *only* fresh vegetables I had were two cabbages given me during a visit to a collective farm. I developed a mild case of scurvy and all my teeth wobbled in spongy gums; as a result I lost two sound molars. If this happened to a correspondent, whose diet was incomparably better than the Russians', the state of the native population may be imagined.

That winter we correspondents put on a touching drama of our plight before the relatively well-fed officers of the U.S. military mission and the embassy staff whom we invited to see it. They had never imagined such horror! After collapsing *en masse* from starvation due to the cruelty or sadism or indifference of our diplomats on the spot who had access to official or army rations then coming in at Murmansk and Leningrad, we evoked such pity from the Ambassador, Admiral Standley, that he cut us in as part of the official American delegation in Russia. Although the U.S. was then giving away on the order of billions a year in materials to Mr. Stalin's regime it was not until the American Embassy finally put correspondents on its own commissary list that we had enough to eat.

This discussion of items alimentary may seem disgusting unless you have lived under extreme austerity. In wartime Moscow people were always hungry. Outside their 10-to-12-hour work day, their minds were devoted to scrounging for something to fill the aching void. While Germany held Russia's Ukrainian breadbasket most Russians never had enough to eat. That did not apply to the banquet tables of the Kremlin. None of the Politburo's fat men lost any weight during the war. In fact Zhdanov and Shcherbakov visibly increased, and obesity hastened their early deaths. Except for the elite, the top-level bureaucratic and managerial class, however, rationing was geared to priority given the armed forces.

Communists took no chances on a repetition of the revolt of the starved and barefoot Tsarist army which preceded the October Revolution. The military came first in everything. But it must be said for the rationing system generally that it did prevent serious or mass famine. People somehow got the bare minimum needed to stay alive and produce. Malnutrition was widespread but I never saw any actual starvation, except in the battle areas. There were, of course, frequent unconfirmable rumors of bestial treatment of prisoners in the concentration or work camps.

Minor government employees themselves were always hungry. These included censors, interpreters, clerks and other workers in the press department. Most ravenous of all was our press chief, Nicolai Palgunov, who later became head of Tass News Agency. A nervous, extremely near-sighted individual, his vague vulture-like appearance fitted the nickname we gave him: "The Goon." It was an impressive spectacle to see him, at the occasional official receptions with a low enough threshold to admit correspondents, as he stood deployed before a buffet table heaped high with vodka, champagne, burgundy from the Caucasus, caviar, sturgeon from the Caspian and the state farms' bounty of roast fowl, ham, pork, venison and (The Goon's favorite) *chocolate*. As soon as Molotov and the other commissars vanished with visiting V.I.P.'s or ambassadors into adjoining rooms to dine and wine in exalted seclusion, the Goon would go into action.

He was the only man I knew who could, single-handed, not only cover both flanks as well as the front and rear of a twenty-foot banquet table, but also storm, occupy and thoroughly despoil and pillage it without any outside assistance whatever.

Knowing the Goon's fondness for sweets, some correspondents regularly contributed their monthly chocolate ration to him. It was hoped that the gesture would result in favored treatment. I discovered this belatedly and then for a time followed the custom. Pleased as a small boy by such consideration, he would always renew his promises of "improvements." Some people will promise to fulfill a reasonable request once, but the Goon was a man of infinitely more patience. He thought nothing of promising it ten or twenty times. His word was as worthless as a wartime rouble.

I must admit that the Goon stood a lot of nonsense from correspondents before the success of Russia's counter-offensives abruptly changed matters. Crimes committed by individual members of the foreign press included such acts as: throwing a typewriter from one side of the press room to another at a censor, an unfortunate near-miss; knifing to pieces one of those super-Mercator projection maps which show Russia the size of a whale, with all Europe reduced to a ventral fin; collectively presenting the Goon with a large box of laxative tablets temptingly camouflaged as chocolate drops; drawing handlebar moustaches on Molotov's portrait; and phoning the Goon at five A.M. to deliver an urgent (false) summons to the Kremlin.

In retrospect these antics, including acts of vandalism and sabotage of state property literally punishable by penalties up to death, do not seem amusing. But over the course of four years of frustration in Moscow they gained a certain flavor which brings some satisfaction in the re-telling. In a group of over-protected journalists, barred from most normal contacts, pretty much confined to the ghetto life of the Metropole, and compelled to deal with an inflexible and remorseless band of censors from whose often block-headed decisions there was no appeal, such childish mischief was understandable.

It came to an end in 1944.

By that time the Soviet Foreign Office was putting officials into new pearl-gray uniforms with braid and epaulettes, as in Tsarist days. It reflected recovery of confidence and a stiffening in Russian attitudes toward her Allies. From Molotov on down, bureaucrats acquired military rank befitting their new dignity in the service of a Russia now well on the road to victory. With the advent of fancy uniforms in the press department there came a new discipline. The first person to violate it was Ed Fleming, who then represented C.B.S. In a fit of exasperation he tore up his manuscript of a broadcast and threw it, so the Goon alleged, into the face of the censor who had just mutilated it.

"Hitler is *kaput,*" Fleming wrote, quoting a Red soldier he had interviewed.

"It is too early," the censor commented fatuously as he red-pencilled the statement, "to say that."

Throwing a censor's work into his face would probably have been enough to get a correspondent barred in any Allied theatre of war, and it was doubtless unreasonable of foreign correspondents in Moscow to take the view that the censor was a strictly Bolshevik invention. It is edifying to recall Leo Tolstoy's exasperation with the same institution under the Tsars. "You would not believe how from the very beginning of my activity," he exclaimed, "that horrible censor question has tormented me!" There is no record, however, that he actually assaulted the censor. Neither, Fleming contended, had he. He insisted that he had merely thrown the scraps of his dispatch into the air. But Molotov took the Goon's word for it and Fleming's press credentials were withdrawn.

Thereafter correspondents in Russia were models of deportment— inside the press bureau.

CHAPTER 12

Cecilia

RUSSIANS I KNEW well enough to visit in their homes or invite to my room, or join in an evening at the theatre or a week-end in the country, were as different from each other as characters out of Tolstoy or Dostoevsky. There was a uniform poverty, of course, a propertyless state common to all. (But don't imagine Russians are not as "materialistically-minded" as anybody else.) Dictatorship can exact obedience and superficial emulation; it cannot really de-personalize people. Behind the facade of nominal conformity one found in Russia, as anywhere else, true-believers and skeptics, honest patriots and cynical careerists, the warm-hearted and the cold-hearted, youthful idealism and embittered old age.

There were naturally more able-bodied women than men in wartime Moscow. After three years I could call many women by their patronymics, but I knew few Russian males well enough to use the intimate form of address. Probably my experience was not unusual. Russia is one of those countries where the male ear is impatient with the stranger struggling to express himself; whereas the female is sympathetic, intuitively understands, and is more likely to be amused by an atrocious accent and grammar which merely disgusts the male. I gratefully remember all the kind and helpful Russian women I knew, beginning with Cecilia. She was my first secretary in Moscow.

Cecilia Nelson was not really Russian but Finnish and she was more American than either one. Her parents had fled to America from Tsarist oppression. Carried away by enthusiasm for the October revolution, they brought Cecilia back to Russia with them as a child. With thousands of other repatriated Finns they helped set up the autonomous Finnish state of Karelia. Eventually their farm was collectivized and Cecilia, herself no farmer, chose to marry a Finnish boy who played the trombone. "Toik" was his name. He was good enough on his brass to make Svassman's jazz band, which was Moscow's best.

Thus Cecilia came to live in Moscow.

Blonde, blue-eyed, freckle-faced, she remained as Middle Western as corn flakes. She tried her best to conform to Soviet ways, rules and regulations, but her heart was not in it. Since it obviously embarrassed her, I seldom tried to engage her in political discussion. I spent some pleasant days with her and "Toik" in and around Moscow. They had a tiny summer datcha or cottage which they shared with the family of a Russian newspaper man, Sam Gurievitch. Sam's wife was the only psychiatrist I ever met in Russia, or even heard of. During the battle of Stalingrad Mrs. Gurievitch worked in a base hospital there. She was supposed to handle battle fatigue or shock. I saw her back in Moscow again while the Stalingrad fighting was still going on.

"Don't tell me you cured all the shell-shock cases already!" I said.

She smiled faintly. "They gave me only two patients all the time I was at the front. Russians soldiers do not suffer from battle shock like the British and Americans," she explained. "It is bourgeois!" She arched her eyebrows. "As there was nothing for a psychiatrist to do at the front I asked for transfer to the rear."

I did not know her well enough then to appreciate the irony in her voice. Indeed, I did not realize how thoroughly convinced Communist dogmatists were that psycho-analysis was a fraud. As far as Russia was concerned, the war was won without any help from Dr. Freud.

Thanks to Cecilia, I met some Russians tolerant enough to listen to me torture their language. Cecilia's own Russian was easy for me to understand. She spoke it with an American accent and was more at home in English. But she was an excellent secretary and good companion. As Toik worked till early morning with Svassman's band, broadcasting or entertaining, Cecilia often went with me to the ballet or dinner, where her husband would join us later.

Restaurant parties in Moscow were extremely expensive. That meant that it was virtually mandatory, when you were host, to get everybody drunk. After I had accumulated a number of obligations I managed to reserve a table at Aragvi, a Caucasian restaurant, and one of the few places open during war-time. By borrowing food and liquor tickets I got enough credits together to feed two dozen people on shaslick and trimmings irrigated by ample vodka and wine.

Among the guests was Zoya Feodorovna, the movie star, whose brother and husband were both in the Red air force. They were soon to be killed; but that evening Zoya was gay because she heard direct good news of them from some fliers dining at the Aragvi. One after one they came to embrace Zoya and drink with her; she seemed to know every pilot in Russia. I don't recall how many I met that night but there was one I won't forget. He was the most persistent drinker and talker; as the evening waned he became the most affectionate. He not only repeatedly kissed Zoya good night but in the old Russian manner he unexpectedly gave *me* a bear hug, and a kiss.

I awoke about noon, when Cecilia arrived several hours late, looking pale around the gills. The first mystery was a pair of women's pumps in my briefcase. I had positively no recollection of returning to the hotel or of climbing the stairs or getting into bed, much less about any strange pumps.

"Don't worry," said Cecilia. "They must be Zoya's; nobody else could afford them." Late that afternoon Zoya did phone, in some desperation, to ask about the missing treasures. She was enormously relieved to recover them.

Those pumps were made to order for her, a prerogative she enjoyed as a "people's artist." On the black market they would have been worth five or six hundred dollars. Zoya evidently had, in her hazy leave-taking, mistaken my briefcase (an improvised vodka-bag) for her own and stuffed her shoes into it when she was changing back to valenki. Heavy snow and ice lay on the streets and valenki, the knee-high felt boots of Russia, were the only proof against that bitter 20-below frost.

"Who," I asked Cecilia when she returned from Zoya's, "was that heavy-set pilot who kept embracing everybody? He tried to kiss me good night! He looked familiar, somehow."

"No wonder," she said. "That was Stalin's son, Vassily."

Cecilia was as much in the dark about many aspects of Soviet life as I was and her interest and curiosity matched my own. She was wholly unaffected by Communist suspicion and distrust of the foreigner. A naturally modest girl, she had all the spunk, the stubborn independence and courage of her people. I'll never forget the dressing-down she gave the Goon, with the excuse of speaking for me.

It was at the end of my first stay in Russia. I didn't expect to return, so I had nothing to lose but my temper. On my farewell visit, the press chief started off with the usual amenities, but I cut him short. I told him he had not only wasted my time but had deprived the great American public of learning something useful about the U.S.S.R. Giving him no chance to break in with excuses, I itemized each of my complaints and called him a "liar, hypocrite, defeatist, obstructionist and outstanding saboteur of Soviet-American friendship."

The Goon knew a little English, but to make sure he understood every word I asked Cecilia to translate right along with me. We even rehearsed the choicer bits in advance. She was wonderful as her voice mimicked me, rising and falling in indignation and mock pity. She, too, had been waiting a long time to hear it said. I left a written list with the Goon of all the people, institutions and events he had promised to arrange for me to see. I concluded by saying he was doing Russia more harm than Goebbels. I had, I said, protested to Stalin.

Cecilia was as red as a radish when she wound up; the Goon stared at her speechless.

I half expected to find my luggage out on the street when I got back to the Metropole. In fact I hadn't written Stalin yet, but I had sent a letter to Alexander Shcherbakov. He was then Stalin's Politburo member in charge of the whole Soviet information apparatus. That evening his secretary phoned to ask me to come to his office. When I saw him he gave me a flash-bulb smile and—*reductio ad absurdum!*—asked whether I was satisfied with my visit.

I repeated all my complaints, and those of other correspondents. I made the Goon sound more anti-one-worldist than germ warfare, which he was. So, of course, was Shcherbakov, as I knew. All the Goon's decisions were in accordance with Politburo directives but I pretended I was telling him something new.

He listened impassively. Only his small, red, porcine eyes bored into me, intense and sardonic. The late Mr. Shcherbakov had a reputation for ruthless cynicism. Attached to Shcherbakov's great trunk were short thick arms and soft pudgy hands with perfectly manicured pink—*pink!*—nails. He was a George Orwell creation to a T. Virtually all Politburo members appear to be compulsive eaters, a well-known manifestation of insecurity feelings, but Shcherbakov led all the rest.

At the end of my harangue he conceded that perhaps there had been one or two oversights. Things would now be arranged. As he was aware, however, I was about ready to leave. If you missed a plane reservation in those days you might have to sit it out for another month before you got another. I had only two days left. Very well; he would do the best he could. He did prove at least that a word from the Politburo was all that was needed to open every closed door and window in Russia. It turned out to be six days, not two, for the plane was delayed: six days in which I met more helpful people, and accomplished more, professionally, than in any previous six weeks.

By the time I left Russia I was wondering if I hadn't misjudged things somewhat. When eventually I returned to Moscow I at once tried to get Cecilia back to work for me. Unfortunately she had taken a job with Robert Magidoff. Several years later, after I had left Russia for good, a painful thing happened to them.

Bob was himself a native of Russia, having been brought to America as a child. He did not go back as part of a returning family of exiles, like Cecilia. He re-entered simply to report what had happened to the country of pogroms remembered by his parents. He had always been among the "friendly correspondents," hoping for better Soviet-American understanding. He fell in love with and married a talented and beautiful Russian girl named Nila. A fiery personality, Nila had once been a revolutionary; she was imprisoned in the Lubyanka for a few months as a Trotsky sympathizer. By the time she met Bob she had become sufficiently "disinterested" to become a secretary for an American.

Nila Magidoff was in America during the war. She made scores of speeches for Russian War Relief to help raise the many millions of dollars given generously to aid her former countrymen. Gifts and honors were showered on her by Americans, for whom she personified Russia at war. When she went back to Moscow to join Bob she was an American citizen but she expected to be at least warmly received, if not officially commended. She was instead regarded suspiciously.

Once the cold-war weather began, the Foreign Office had no use for people like Bob and Nila. They knew too much about Russia and it took too many police to keep track of them. Our good friend Cecilia involuntarily became the finger girl for their ruin. According to the official version, Cecilia began to suspect Bob when she found letters in his file concerning technical information of a "secret" nature. On poring through his papers she found evidence so grave that she felt bound to denounce him to the state. Bob and Nila, who had done so much for Russia, were summarily condemned without a hearing and expelled as "imperialist spies." The irony of it was that, on his return to the U.S., Magidoff was also dropped by both N.B.C. and McGraw-Hill.

When I read of Cecilia's part in this event I could not believe it. Afterward Bob explained. She had been picked up by the state security police and held *incommunicado* at the Lubyanka until she agreed to "reveal" his espionage activities. Officials reported that "incriminating correspondence" had been seized in which McGraw-Hill had ordered Magidoff to commit specific acts of espionage. In fact all the letters, as later published, were merely a routine exchange, sent through the open mail, concerning subjects of ordinary and legitimate journalistic interest.

Poor Cecilia! I was glad she had at least had the pleasure of calling the Goon, face to face and with heartfelt sincerity, "Russia's outstanding saboteur" before this humiliation shattered her brave, cheerful, honest soul.

CHAPTER 13

Some Russian People

SOMEONE HAS SAID that a nation is only an individual multiplied, but of course no two individuals are the same. That is why nations have not one character but a host of contradictions, and Russia has always ranked high among the unpredictables. Every correspondent's reporting on a country is influenced by the drama of his personal encounters with the people. One may despise a government, and an honest man may find it hard not to despise most governments, but no one can hate a whole nation if he has liked anything in it.

The Kremlin built a wall between Russia and the outside world but it could not altogether shut out the warmth, the elemental vitality, the wholeheartedness and the wonderfully attractive humanity you found, once you were inside the country, imparting a logic of their own to all Russia's puzzling paradoxes.

About the young children nobody could have two opinions. They were irresistible. One winter day, jammed in a streetcar, Cecilia and I found ourselves next to a red-cheeked boy of nine or ten. He reminded me of a White Russian child Nym and I practically adopted in Peking. He was like one of those strangers you sometimes glimpse for a moment on the street, or in a shop, who give you the feeling that if someone would just introduce you there is no doubt you would become fast friends. No one does; you pass on and wait for another incarnation to bring you together.

In this instance the boy looked at me with open, curious eyes; he was the quiet one in a group of chattering schoolchildren. I said hello to him. Detecting a foreign voice he asked politely whether I was an *inostranets* and what kind. I told him I was American and he smiled and said he had read *Tom Sawyer* and *Huckleberry Finn*. I was born on the Missouri River, Cecilia said, close to where Mark Twain lived. His eyes lighted up.

"My name is Dmitri," he volunteered. "What's yours?"

When I said *"Sneg"* he laughed. Snow is a funny name in Russian. It reminds people of Father Frost, the Russian Santa Claus. Dmitri took my hand, shook it impulsively and held on. His wide blue eyes were as fresh and open as the summer sky over the steppe. I remembered some éclairs I had been saving from the dining table for my courier. I thought Dmitri might appreciate them still more.

"How long since you've eaten pirozhki?"

"So long," he replied nostalgically, "I've forgotton the taste."

"Good," said I. "Come with me and we'll have tea and pirozhki and I'll tell you about boys in America."

"Delightful!" His eyes sparkled.

As we approached Red Square I began to force my way through the crowded vestibule. Dmitri held onto my hand tightly, but I became aware that he was anchored at the other end. I looked around and saw a large, sharp-faced woman.

"Where are you going, Dmitri? Stay here," she commanded. "I am Dmitri's teacher," she said turning to me. Alas, what had been a spontaneous gesture of communication began to seem awkward. Leaning over Dmitri I whispered my room number in the Metropole Hotel, and asked him to come later. He still clung tightly to my hand, however. Suddenly the teacher, if teacher she was, gave a powerful jerk and pulled him loose. They lurched back against the other children.

As I got off the street car I thought the gawking spectators of the little drama looked equally divided between those for and against my side of the tug-of-war. Probably they thought we were husband and wife quarreling over our child, a scene familiar enough in Moscow. "Come and see me, Dmitri, when you can! Any day!" I shouted as I jumped from the step.

"I shall come," shrieked Dmitri over the screwed-up faces. He never came, of course.

I got better acquainted with a Cossack boy of thirteen named Guy Pushnestikov, with whose family Alex Werth and I spent a few days while I was in Kotelnikovo, during the fighting along the Don River. German soldiers had been quartered in the Pushnestikov home for five months just before we arrived. During that time the three Pushnestikovs—Guy, his mother, and his grandmother; the father was somewhere with the Red Army—had existed on a few slices of bread a day and the leftovers (if any) on the plates of the five foreign soldiers crowded into their tiny three-roomed bungalow.

"They didn't behave like gentlemen, there's no doubt about that," Mrs. P. said. "At the same time this is war. How do we know they're not just as decent as our people, in peacetime?"

Guy was only slightly more bitter about it. "They didn't consider us cultured or their equals or even people, really," he said. "We were just slaves in their eyes. They only used us boys to look after their cows and made the girls keep house for them and clean up dirt. If a girl was pretty and would sleep with them she would get better food, but not many did. The rest of us had to do all the work but they gave us nothing. Still, as Motka says, that's war for you."

Otherwise, he never complained. Although he was as thin as a stick he never asked for anything. He was very proud. At meal time, Alex and I were guests at the Red Army's table, where we ate much better than in Moscow. From time to time we filched portions of bread, sugar, butter and potatoes to carry off to the Pushnestikovs. They refused to touch anything but the bread, insisting that we would need it ourselves.

"We're used to being hungry," Motka said, "but you aren't and you'd suffer."

Guy considered himself well on the way to "culture" and tended to patronize his peasant mother, who could scarcely read. He knew Pushkin, Gogol, Turgenev, Chekhov, Tolstoy—and Marx, Engels, Lenin and Stalin, of course. He was a Red Pioneer and would soon be a Young Communist; and for a Communist he believed anything was possible. His mind was already busy with the future. He hadn't the slightest doubt, now that the Germans were driven out, that he could be anything he chose to be. Most of his schoolmates were planning to become doctors, scientists, engineers or teachers. But he?

"I'm going to study navigation and command a ship," he said confidently. "I've never seen the sea but I've read a lot about it. I'm pretty good at geography."

He too had read Twain. *Life on the Mississippi* was his favorite book. One of his reasons for wanting to be a navigator was to see America after he had finished his studies in Moscow. And he was so sure, I asked, about getting to Moscow?

"I'm at the top of my class," he retorted. "I see no objective reason why I shouldn't."

"Objective" was his favorite word. I asked whom he regarded as the greatest man alive.

"That depends on your standard," answered the cool little Cossack cucumber. "Everybody is great for somebody, yet some consider nobody great. If you are a scientist or an engineer you would say one thing, if you're a politician you would say another. Some years from now people will have opinions about living men quite different from ours."

These pearls of wisdom dropped in his thin little voice with great cheerfulness and aplomb. Five months of German occupation hadn't shaken his self-confidence.

"And you take America, now, you think your richest man is greatest."

"Is that so? And who is richest?"

"Morgan first, then Ford. America worships capitalists, not politicians."

Whatever the system did to older Russians, for youths like Guy it was accepted as the best of all possible states. Thereafter I took it for granted that he would one day pilot his Russian ship into New York and drop in to see me. I am still waiting.

Then I remember an old man with a wooden leg who buttonholed me as I walked down the muddy street of a collective farm outside Moscow. He had lost his leg "to the Kaiser," he said, but he had been doing a full day's work as a toiling peasant in this same village ever since. He was now past sixty. He dragged me into his sparsely furnished but neat one-room cottage while he ordered his wife to pour me a drink of fresh warm milk. He harangued me about the war situation as it looked to an old soldier. He gave me a dozen reasons why it was imperative for the Western Allies to land in Europe that year—it was 1943—or all would be lost. At last he wound up by begging me to transmit his entire statement, in code, of course, to President Roosevelt. He was quite serious.

It took me a long time to make the old gentleman understand that I was not a high official, nor any official at all, and could not possibly influence decisions about the conduct of the war.

All at once he laughed, said *"Nichevo!"* and got out some vodka to offer me a stiff one for the road. The reason I never forgot his face was that at that moment it radiated the warm good will among unsophisticated people who work the earth and grow things, all over the world; that, and the toast he offered. The first toast in those days almost by law belonged to Little Father Stalin. But the walnut-faced old farmer flouted the convention.

"To the triumph," he said passionately, stomping his wooden leg on the floor and repeating it, *"of all that is good in humanity."* I think it was probably the best toast I heard all the time I was in Russia.

But I did drink a stronger drink: of blood, or so I was told. Russian blood.

The deep love of the Russian people for their land will always be epitomized for me by that little incident that occurred in a cave dug into the high bluffs on the edge of the Volga River below Stalingrad. The Nazis had just surrendered the frozen ground of the totally destroyed city, and half-dead Germans crawled around the smouldering rubble, as we sat down to talk to General Vassily Ivanovich Chuikov. Nothing he said about that great battle stays in my mind now, but I clearly remember Clara Yeramenchenko, a young Ukrainian with the women's service troops. They were volunteers, like our WACS and WAVES, but they carried arms and worked right with their men in the battle zones. A former school teacher, Clara had been in Stalingrad all through the fighting.

Outside, it was twenty below zero, but in Chuikov's cave the heat was unbearable. When Russians heat a place at all they do it, as they do most things, beyond the limit. Burning inside with vodka, I got up to look for some water, a rare commodity at the front, where a drink meant either tea or vodka. Clara Yeramenchenko offered to find water for me and disappeared in the darkness. A few minutes later she returned lugging a bucket, from which she filled glasses for us. The water was ice cold and delicious.

Looking at me quizzically, she said, "It's better than wine, isn't it?" I nodded and she refilled the glass.

"Of course it's better," she exclaimed with sudden fierce pride. "It's holy water: the Volga mixed with our Russian blood!"

Clara was young and desirable and she must have left a lot behind her, in the Ukraine, worth living for. Thousands like her, though perhaps not so pretty, did not get through that winter alive. I don't know how much she loved Stalin or the party. By the brave tilt of her head, and the fire that flashed in her dark eyes when she said "holy water—the Volga mixed with Russian blood," I knew how she felt about Russia.

CHAPTER 14

Ukrainian Symphony

IN THE WINTER of 1944, after repeated appeals to Molotov, I finally got permission to make an "individual" trip to the reoccupied areas of the Ukraine. Part of that republic was still held by the Germans when my new secretary, Anna Yermolayeva, and I reached Kiev, half-demolished and half-depopulated but still beautiful and picturesque, sitting high above the Dnieper. The Ukraine had been the most advanced part of the U.S.S.R. and alone accounted for nearly half of all Soviet industrial production. It suffered heavier war damage than any other part of the Union or any single country of Europe.

Of the millions of Soviet military and civilian dead, probably a third were Ukrainian losses. New data on Soviet population available in 1956 made some American demographers conclude that earlier estimates of war losses in the U.S.S.R. were greatly understated by the government. It is possible that twenty-five to thirty million people perished in Russia during the war. One official in Kiev told me that about ten million people had "disappeared" from the Ukraine alone.

To a great extent the Ukraine was rebuilt by the labor of its women and children, and German prisoners.

In the midst of the ruins I met a Ukrainian woman violinist who introduced me to the Kiev Philharmonic Orchestra. She had come to see me at the hotel after learning that an "American official" was staying there. She asked if I could get word to her sister, who was in America, that she had survived the war but that all her relatives in Leningrad had starved to death. Her sister was an actress named Koryus, who had recently appeared in a Hollywood film called "The Great Waltz," widely shown in Russia. I agreed to carry her letter. Then she invited me to meet the director of the Kiev Philharmonic. We had a meal together.

"To Ukrainians," said the director, "music is bread."

The orchestra had been reconstituted on the first day after the Germans were driven from the city. It gave a concert when Kiev was still smoking and being de-mined; frequent explosions provided the effect of bass drum interpolations. On learning the date of the orchestra's next scheduled appearance I expressed regret that I would not be around to hear them. In the morning the director sent me an invitation to attend a rehearsal that afternoon. On arriving at the hall I was told that they had gathered there to give a full-length concert of whatever music we cared to hear. I had never encountered such cordiality toward an American in Russia and I assumed they were merely making a gesture which they did not expect to be taken seriously. But the orchestra leader said that they would be offended if I did not accept.

"Americans are liked in the Ukraine. You helped feed us after the famine in the First World War. American engineers helped build our industry. Now America is sending us food and clothing. You sent us weapons to fight Hitler. Your boys are dying with ours in a common cause. Now here you are, the *first* American we can see since the liberation. We want to thank America by giving you a concert!"

Who could refuse? Anna and I sat down, the only audience in that vast hall, and listened solemnly to a program we had selected on the spot. We chose all Russian and Ukrainian composers, with the single exception of Grieg. They were pleased, of course, and played superbly.

Afterward, members of the orchestra crowded around to ask many questions about American music, orchestras, theatres, the war and opinions of Russia. I deplored my ignorance of home. Nearly all those people had relatives and friends in the U.S.A.; they felt close to us. Many said they longed to visit America.

Finally I asked how I could reciprocate their kindness.

"There is one way," said the director thoughtfully, when I repeated the question. "We desperately need *strings*. Could you get some strings for us in your country?"

"Strings?"

"Violin strings, cello and viola strings, harp strings. And reeds. Reeds for the wind instruments. We stopped making them during the war. But in America, perhaps . . ."

It would be easy to buy them, I thought; the problem would be to bring them over. Then I remembered that Averell Harriman was in Washington but would be returning to Russia soon. I promised to wire him from Moscow. The director looked grateful enough to give us an encore then and there. And he did!

In the Ukraine even officials seemed cordial and reasonable in contrast to the bureaucrats of Moscow. I left convinced there was much good-will for us in the Ukraine. Of course I assumed that the orchestral performance was arranged by the party propaganda department, but who cared? The people were genuine in their friendliness; that was what mattered. I was therefore hugely surprised when on my return to Moscow the chief censor, Mr. Petrov, refused to pass my radio message to Harriman. He sent it back to me by my courier. I went up to see him at once.

"Why do you suppress a simple request like this?" I demanded.

"Strings and reeds are not needed here," he said coldly. "Soviet production is ample. We don't wish to bother Ambassador Harriman with unnecessary trifles."

"But good Lord, *you* aren't bothering him; that's my personal request. I know he'd be delighted to help. All he has to do is pick up a phone and somebody's sure to contribute the things. If not, I'll pay for them. They won't take up any space in his plane."

"Nyet," he repeated. "Even if it were true about the shortage, this would be valuable news to the enemy. I can't let it go out."

"That's idiotic."

He looked at me suspiciously. "Where did you get that information?"

"I beg your pardon?"

"I mean who misinformed you about the strings?"

I quickly decided to let the matter drop, for the present.

"Oh, just something I picked up on a train," I said.

"You mustn't believe everything a stranger tells you," Petrov smirked.

This experience strengthened my growing impression that the great moral and creative force of the Russian revolution was dwindling in proportion to its canalization in the old rigid channels of the bureaucracy.

CHAPTER 15

Youth

OLGA MISHAKOVA was deputy secretary-general of the Komsomol, or Communist youth organization. She assured me at a diplomatic reception one night, on top of several vodkas, that it was perfectly possible, "for a serious purpose," to meet all the young people I wished to meet, without going through the press department. The next morning I walked into her office.

If it is youth that makes revolution, it also makes counter-revolution. Unless the idealism of youth is invoked and mobilized, no revolution can occur and no counter-revolution can be successful.

I told Olga Mishakova I wanted to know Soviet youth, teen-agers and below, because they were possibly the most important people in the world for Americans to understand. She gave me a new and calculating appraisal. A handsome woman in a Juno-esque way, Olga had hair the color of taffy and wide blue eyes which, if you looked closely, seemed cold, severe and shrewd. The story about her was that she took her former chief's place in the Komsomol after appearing as a witness against him when he was liquidated by Vyshinsky in '38. Anyway, she was a favorite of Stalin's; and she did keep her promise.

Under her sponsorship I met youth leaders in schools, factories and colleges, and I acquired an interesting guide for these travels in the person of Vera Andreiyevna Smirnova.

Vera was a faithful Communist who managed also to be an appealing human being. She had a pleasing low voice and soft, wavy hair, a strong brow and strong, capable hands. She was quiet and grave; she had none of the Russian tempestuousness. She never used make-up and she was one of those rare women who look better without it; she had glowing milk-white skin. She wore simply cut garments of rough materials: padded coat, cotton dresses, cotton stockings and plain, sturdy shoes. She was not really beautiful but she had some quality which made young men stare wherever she went, and she seemed wholly unconscious of that.

Vera was twenty-one when I met her and had already had a hard apprenticeship as a machinist. That was during her student days in a *tekhnicum*. While she studied engineering she worked part-time at subway construction. Proudly she showed me the tile mosaic of the station she "built." By the time the Germans reached Moscow she was able to take charge of the gangs throwing up earthworks in the suburbs. Now on Mishakova's staff to organize the "youth labor reserve corps" while on leave from Moscow University, where she yet had to get her engineering master's degree, she was temporarily assigned to show me around.

Vera was my first real encounter with a second-generation Russian Communist pure in faith and pure of heart. She was probably a little too much the model child of Lenin's teaching to be typical, but she was certainly not unique. The quality you found among people like Vera, and a large segment of Russian youth whether in the party or not, was a much more serious-minded dedication to study and hard work than was common among American college youths as I remember them. Education was still a novelty here and they cherished it. They looked upon it more as a privilege than a right.

Some American friends who saw me with Vera began to smirk and say, "Where'd you find Cinderella?" They could not see that she was in herself *news* to me. She taught me things you would never learn from a newspaper but not what *they* thought. Mishakova had told her I wanted to meet Komsomols. Very well! She brought me to them, the young and future elite of Russia, in every branch of activity.

I learned most from my visits to the *tekhnicums,* something I'd waited vainly for the Goon to arrange. These were like our high schools combined with vocational training schools or technical-scientific prep schools. But we lacked any exact equivalent in our system. At the *tekhnicums* I saw the working out, in practice, of a new educational system: planned, from the nursery up, to produce the required numbers of workers, technicians, teachers and scientists needed to fulfill state industrialization and cultural programs foreseen for as far as *thirty* years ahead.

Gradually I became impressed by the realism of Soviet education, less haphazard and aimless, if also less free, than our own. Again, it was the kind of thing described in Bellamy's *Looking Backward* more than half a century earlier; and here, at least, the results might have pleased him. Socialist planning might be bludgeoned into the Russian

people in other respects, but nobody complained about the vastly enlarged educational opportunities open to all nor the guarantee of jobs
awaiting graduates. In this field many other nations had something to
learn from the Soviet prototype.

Despite handicaps of the war, Soviet education was adhering to its
program with remarkable continuity. It was rapidly changing the whole
composition of the nation from a predominantly semi-literate peasantry
into masses of well-trained or scientifically educated men and women.
This human transformation had already begun to alter historic Russia
itself in just about every conceivable way, as Vera and her friends
made me realize. Watching and listening to them, I understood that it
would not take another hundred years but a mere decade or two
for the Soviet system to rebuild its war-shattered economy, and then
to surpass its own achievements by far, bringing to Russia "the possibility of a higher standard of living than any nation in Europe or
Asia" within ten years after the war.*

It would not be surprising to me, therefore, when under the stimulus
of the cold war Russia was able to graduate twice as many scientists
and engineers, in 1955, as the U.S.A., and attain a level of production
second only to the same competitor.

Vera was pleasant but business-like, at times almost brusque with
me. She had no use for frivolity. She often went to work for eight or
ten hours after she had spent half a day with me. She got less to eat
than I did; invariably, she declined my offers of dinner or food. Our
relations remained so formal that I began to think she must be completely ascetic. Then one afternoon she phoned unexpectedly and
said she had a free evening. Would I like to take her to dinner? She
dined, enjoyed a bottle of wine and relaxed. We then talked, and for
once she talked about herself, until Moscow's early-summer dawn.

Vera's own parents, she told me, were workers who could barely
read and write; they were the first generation off the land, and her
great-grandparents were serfs. Her father died when she was ten. In
the old days that would probably have meant, for one of her class, that
she or her older sister would have become objects of charity or perhaps prostitutes. But both Vera and her sister went through school
right up to and through college, supported by the State. They were
good students; both won scholarships. Vera still lived solely on her
stipend. She really thought the Soviet state was run in the interests of
the people, and *by* them. When you considered her own career it was
not hard to see why. The greatest treasure she had in life was her

* *The Pattern of Soviet Power,* N.Y., 1945, p. 212.

education. It lifted her miles above her own people's past, and for that she owed (she felt) everything to the State.

"Anybody who studies," she said, "can get the finest education our country can offer. Would that have been possible under Tsarism? My parents were poor people. A penniless child like me would never have got through more than a year or two of school. In my college class of more than 90 engineering students *not one* was the child of educated parents. Now girls may study anything men study. There were 27 girls in my class.

"The Soviet system seems to me the most democratic. I have not seen any other, that is true; but I would like to. I would like, so much, to see America and to know how people live there. I *can* do that. If I study I shall get there some day."

Study was in her mind the whole currency of freedom; and it was all open for her to take, she thought. None of *her* family had been affected by the purges.

Purges? Yes, there were still "bad" people in Russia. She could not say whether everyone arrested was guilty. Mistakes had been made. But she could not conceive why she should oppose the regime or that anyone would cut short her opportunity.

"Now tell me, please, can children from American families like mine become engineers? Does the State support them while they study? Is it true that Negroes have no such rights? Is it true that they do not find jobs when they graduate?" She listened as I tried to explain "freedom of choice."

"But if you do not have national economic planning, how can young people know what to study or where they are needed?" she asked. "Who tells them? The corporations? But cannot the owner of the corporation just decide for personal reasons who shall work and who shall not? Don't the few who own the means of production have everything? Those who work hardest may have nothing?" I deferred answering that to ask:

"You think you have complete equality of opportunity in the U.S.S.R.?"

"Oh, no. That is for Communism in the future, when the principle 'from each according to his ability, to each according to his need' will prevail. Right now we are still in a Socialist period. People are rewarded 'in accordance with the work performed.' Only those who don't work may find it hard to eat. In the old days here those who didn't work at all often ate and lived the best. Is it not so in your country now?"

The idle rich? We had some, yes. The average working-class family in America lived far better than the average Soviet family. They were better fed, better clothed, better housed, than all but the top bureaucrats of Russia. I showed Vera *Life* and the *Saturday Evening Post,* with their pictures advertising appliances and conveniences: the modern tubs and johns, vacuum cleaners, cars, a hundred commonplace things. A low-level approach, I admit; but I was curious to see her reaction. She examined the magazines page by page with bulging eyes.

"How many in America could enjoy all such things, such living?" she asked.

"Most of our upper and middle income group," I said. "Say sixty or seventy families in a hundred."

"*All* of our Soviet homes and kitchens would have been like these in a few years if there had been no war," she said confidently. "Now it will take a little longer, that's all." She was as sure of that as some people are of salvation.

I spoke of the party hierarchy as a privileged class in Russia. She smiled tolerantly. How could that be? Was she not a party member? Did they not all get the same food, same housing, as other workers? Important state officials were different, of course; they were rewarded in accordance with the value of work performed, however, not because of party membership. Party members were no "class." They did not depend on wealth or inherited power for their advantages. Had not her own career demonstrated that anyone could advance to a position of high trust and responsibility?

As for the lack of personal freedom? Vera simply didn't understand, or she understood only very incompletely. Was it freedom to live, to study, to work, to have a career, love, marry, bear children, help Russia? Didn't she have all that? Freedom of opinion? Ah. Everyone had the *duty* to discuss and understand state decisions in complete freedom.

Vera's answers were the straight party line, all right, and I had heard them before; but she interested me as the first adult Communist I knew who had wholly *inherited* her faith. She knew nothing first-hand about capitalism and privilege derived from ownership; there was no personal rancor or passion in her anti-capitalism. Her generation, the generation today doing the most important productive work, simply has no memory of another way of life. For everyone in Russia now thirty-five or younger what happened before the Bolshevik revolution, even what happened before the last great purge, is simply pre-history.

Vera belonged to what Arthur Koestler called "the generation born after the flood." How could you convince people like Vera that private ownership was more democratic or "idealistic" than social ownership? President Eisenhower confessed his own failure to do so in the case of his wartime friend, Marshal Georgi Zhukov. "[In America] a man can earn what he pleases, save what he pleases, buy what he pleases," the President explained to a press conference. "Now I believe this because I believe in the power for good of the, you might say, the integrated forces developed by 170,000,000 free people. But he [the Communist—Zhukov] says that 'We say to the man, "You can't have those things. You have to give them to the state,"' and this is idealistic because they ask these people to believe that their greatest satisfaction in life is in sacrificing for the state, giving to the state. . . . So when you run up against that kind of thing, look . . . I think you could run into people you would have a hard time convincing that the sun is hot and the earth is round." *

About one in every six or seven Soviet Russian citizens was a Communist or a Komsomol. It was as respectable to be a Communist in Russia as to be a deacon in Boston or a Rotarian in Sioux City. It was as enviable to be a member of the Central Committee as for a New Yorker to have a seat on the Stock Exchange or in the Union Club.

The Soviet state may be profoundly modified, but private ownership of the means of production will never be restored. State ownership and state planning are the granite facts on which the edifice of modern Russia has arisen. They could be destroyed only by physically erasing the U.S.S.R. itself.

Few among the many anti-Stalinists or anti-Communists would be ready to pay so awful a price to bring the edifice toppling in ruins.

CHAPTER 16

Dear Mr. President

RUSSIA WAS a police state, all right, but it was also among the most dynamic, and just then probably was the most exciting and important, if the most perplexing, of all the nations on earth. I was often enraged by Russia but never bored. The mere physical experience of living there more than compensated for all the petty annoyances: the feel

* N. Y. *Times,* July 17, 1957.

and taste and smell of the frosty air, the deep sparkling winters, the long, cold, zestful nights and brief bright days, the apple-cheeked children, the old women muffled in shawls and padded greatcoats, the ice-coated buildings, the streets like tunnels between the walls of snow piled high on the walks, the feeling of time brooding in the vast, empty, windy Red Square and around St. Basil's stick-candy colored domes, the dark Moscow River flowing silently under the Kremlin's walls and its many-windowed white palaces now in curtained darkness, and the awareness always of being on the edge of the fabulous Russian landscape reaching to the Pacific Ocean, stretching around us in the titanic ocean of steppe, its long waves broken only by the islets of white birch, and atolls of huts made of heavy logs, and in them and in the flat cities ever the wholehearted, vital Russian people, the sense of upheaval yet of direction and of destiny in them, the sense of a decisive duel going on here between elemental nature and man, the sense of turbulence being forced under control, and of a turning and twisting and shaping and re-fitting of everything into still elusive new forms.

How Mr. Roosevelt would have liked to have had my chance to see the Russian people and their tremendous puzzling world! His travel itch frustrated by his invalidism, he roamed the earth in his mind's eye and in the books others wrote about it, and the letters they wrote to him.

Write to me, he had said as I left him. And write I did.

Moscow, August 14, 1944.

"Dear Mr. President:

"I have been back here for nearly two months, and that is about the time-limit for fresh impressions—the 'feel' of the place now as compared to my last visit.

"When I left Russia it was winter and a cold, half-twilit country masked everywhere in white. In Moscow you seldom saw the sun. Now it is summer and so is the expression people wear in their faces. The camouflage has been scrubbed from buildings and the grim, tense scowl everyone wore in winter also seems largely scrubbed away. Part of this is just summer with its warmth and light; Russian character changes with the seasons. But it is also the consciousness of victory, and knowing that the worst is over, and confidence that there will be a future . . .

"Now that the offensive has reached Poland and our own forces are hammering toward Paris the Russians are thinking more about postwar problems, though publicly there is little discussion. The anonymous citizen thinks even more intently about a pair of shoes, a suit, repairs for a leaking roof, a shorter working day and some leisure, and above all enough to eat. How they long for peace! Now that it seems near, privations get harder to bear. Everyone is tired, tired; and the difference is that now people talk about it. People in their thirties and forties, working three years without a rest, have aged ten or fifteen years: teeth falling out, arthritis, eyes failing, a lot of the diseases of old age afflicting them, hastened on by semi-starvation and overwork.

"Moscow now has more people than before the war, when crowding was already serious, with over four million inhabitants. It is harder to get a room than it is to get into the Kremlin—almost. I know divorced couples who have had to go on living as man and wife for years solely because neither could find a bed elsewhere. Hospitals are also filled beyond capacity. Yesterday I went to Gorki Park, out on the Moscow River, where I saw dozens of veterans (overflow from the hospitals) sleeping on cots in the open. Many were trying out new crutches and artificial limbs. It seemed there were more armless and legless men than people still whole.

"It is hard to find a Russian who hasn't lost somebody close to him. My teacher lost her two sons; on my return I learn that her husband is dead; she is only 34 and her hair is all gray. My secretary has heard nothing from her husband, assumed dead for two years. The two maids who look after my room report themselves newly widowed. Each has also lost an only son. The other evening I visited Zoya Feodorovna, a movie actress, and her sister. Their father was killed in 1941; soon afterward their only brother followed him. While I was away each got the news that her husband was killed.

"Zoya and her sister enthusiastically study English in their spare time. English language study is now compulsory in the middle schools and it's the most popular language, I'm told, in colleges and in universities.

"I find ordinary Russians now ready to concede the importance of American help and even to exaggerate it. They see American goods on display in the stores, American cars and trucks in the streets, American clothing on refugees from the war areas, and extensive distribution of American war relief food. I have had Russians tell me they think 80 to 90 percent of all the Red Army's supplies have come from us—an impression I can't say I bother to correct!

"I predict that the Russians will turn to the tasks of peace with about the same energy they have applied to winning the war. More than one Russian has said to me, 'We have learned how to work during this war. We have mastered the machine. We will never go back to the old ways!'

"Pierre Cot, who was in the French Cabinet before the war, made a four months' trip around the recovered areas, studying rehabilitation methods. He was allowed to see more than anybody I know. He told me that he was convinced the Russians would recover their pre-war *industrial* output in *five* years. He said their planning of reconstruction generally had been fitted into a long-view scheme of things, so that actual reconstruction of all the ruined cities might take fifteen years.

" 'Russia,' he said, 'will be growing and developing at a faster rate fifteen years from now than it would have been able to do had there never been a war!'

"To sum up:

"1) The public wants peace. All are tired. The public is resigned to a Russo-Japanese war and many think it is part of the price Russia must pay for American aid. Russians are grateful for that aid.

"2) The process of the war itself, the advance of the Red Army and the flight of Hitler sympathizers, creates in Eastern Europe a kind of political vacuum in which a new type of government will emerge, not democratic in our sense, not Soviet Communism, *but* pre-Socialist.

"3) The Russians are laying down some fundamental plans looking toward long-term co-operation with America. But there is no indication that this country intends to abandon its own system. There is renewed emphasis on the study of Marxism. There is no sign of the party grasp of affairs, in all phases of Russian life, losing its strength.

"4) A disturbing change from the past is the spread of anti-Semitism. Even a year ago one rarely heard anti-Jewish remarks and I never heard Jews complain of discrimination. Now there is a lot of this. Some fear that something like the old quota system used in Tsarist days is being revived in the universities, in science and the professions. I have heard Russians say that the Jew always finds a way to keep out of the front-line, that the Jew stays home and speculates while the Russian fights, that the Jew is crafty, etc. The fact that they make such remarks to a foreigner shows how matter-of-fact they must be. People attribute it to the effectiveness of Hitler's propaganda among the villages of occupied Russia, and wartime nationalism, which has made Russians more race-conscious than at any time since the revolution."

Within three months I was to get a sharp correction to my optimistic view of the Russians' "fundamental plans looking toward long-term

co-operation with America," and a direct warning that officials were
thinking more about the possibilities of another great war. It came just
in time for me to carry back to Mr. Roosevelt personally. The source?
A friend of peace, surprisingly enough, in the ministry of foreign affairs!

CHAPTER 17

Warning from Litvinov

MAX LITVINOV was the one high official who ever conceded to me
that Soviet press policy was unnecessarily stupid. I had known Max
since his Washington days. In Moscow I could even ring him up directly once in a while for an appointment. Usually there was a secretary
to write everything down, as in any other official interview. One day,
October 6, 1944, he received me quite alone. Our talk was strictly off
the record and I never published it. Today it cannot harm anyone to
quote from "the Litvinov warning" which I delivered to the President.

Litvinov had for me personified the hope that a means might yet be
found, after the war, to reconcile the "absolute" truth, the infallible
Stalinist truth, in some workable compromise with the West. Had he
not been Foreign Minister for a decade? Had not his doctrine of "collective security" been a real influence in the world before the Nazi-
Soviet pact? Surely the fact that he was still a vice-commissar had some
significance. It must mean that somewhere in the Kremlin there remained common sense enough to guide our relations toward an honest
formula of co-operation in the gigantic tasks of post-war reconstruction.

Yet on reviewing my notes I honestly cannot find any reason to
suppose that Max personally expected anything of the kind. He had
done more than any individual to raise the prestige of the U.S.S.R. in
the society of nations and to win a measure of respectability for Bolshevism. In Moscow his achievement was not understood and he was
hated and regarded with contempt by his successor, Molotov, a man
in every way his inferior. Long a resident of England (his wife was
English) Max was the only surviving Old Bolshevik who had thoroughly assimilated Western European culture. Short, rotund, almost
benign-looking with his crown of white hair and his large near-sighted

eyes, he was by nature a warm, emotional man who really loved humanity and hated the waste of war, which he did not believe necessary to establish Socialism, or the "salvation" of mankind. He did not let these sentiments betray his intelligence. What he really saw ahead was heavy trouble for all of us.

The root of the post-war crisis, he predicted, would again be Germany. We would not be able to agree on what to do with the Germans, and they would end by dividing *us*. He thought the basic reason for this was the inability of the British to think about Europe in any terms except the traditional balance-of-power system; now they were going to get the *Americans* to try to restore it.

Events were clearly placing Russia in the position of the strongest power in Europe, he said; therefore all Anglo-American hopes of rebuilding Poland or Germany "as a springboard against Russia" were vain. The day had already passed when Russia could be "excluded from Europe." Incredibly, the Anglo-Americans were going to make that attempt once again, he thought.

I asked: "Do you think the war will end by eliminating fascism or will there still be a base for it? I can't see it in Eastern Europe or in Germany. The only other possibility is France, but France is not going to play that role."

"I have no faith in France," he said flatly. "De Gaulle and all the rest—they'll repeat the history of the past decade. And there's still Franco and there are plenty of fascists [sympathizers] left in Britain . . . The French under De Gaulle are making a show of getting rid of the fascists [collaborators] but the worst are left untouched. The old crowd will survive—and with them the corruption, intrigue, compromise. France needs a thorough purge and nothing less will save her. She won't get it—not under De Gaulle, anyway."

But surely Franco would have to go, I insisted. How could he stand after the war with nothing but the Vatican to lean on.

"Who will put him out? The Spanish people are powerless. The French won't move a finger . . . Do you see any sign of the British or Americans being dissatisfied with Franco? No, he'll stay."

"So the answer is that Western Europe *will* be reorganized as an anti-Russian bloc?"

"I'm afraid so, things being what they are on both sides. Look at the Polish issue. The British and particularly the Americans don't even want to throw out the old crowd there!"

Such candid pessimism was extraordinary to hear from any Russian at that moment, and particularly from one so well-informed and wise as Litvinov. So far, he said, the Allies had almost wholly avoided discussing basic European settlements. When we finally did get down to them, he predicted, it would be too late; our mutual fear, ignorance and suspicion would by then have raised insurmountable barriers.

"Many people think both you and Maisky are being wasted," I said. "As the two men in Russia who know most about America and England, it seems odd that you aren't playing more important roles. Or, excuse me if I am mistaken—maybe lots of things are going on behind the scenes . . ."

"No," he laughed, "what you say is true. We're on the shelf . . . This commissariat is run by only three men and none of them knows or understands America and Britain."

"Three? Molotov, Vyshinsky—?"

"And Dekinasov."

"Dekinasov?"

"He was Ambassador to Berlin during the time of the pact. He is the man who sat next to Ribbentrop for a year. That's *all* he knows about Europe."

I understood then that his own pre-war policy of seeking Anglo-American and French co-operation—the policy of collective security—was still basically repudiated. As long as Molotov headed the foreign office it would mean that the Kremlin saw little qualitative difference between Nazi imperialism and Anglo-American imperialism.

"On the outside," I said to make this deduction explicit, "it looks like this government believes everything that has happened shows that its policy was right in 1939, in making the pact with Hitler, while everything that led up to it was a failure. In other words, there is no recognition of the fact that it was your policy, before 1939, that largely made it possible for us to be allies—*in spite of that pact?*"

"That's correct. That is the way *they* look at it." By "they" Litvinov meant, first of all, Stalin.

However much he may have disagreed with Molotov's methods, however, Litvinov firmly believed in the necessity for Russia to "get rid of the old crowd" in both Poland and Germany. It was fantastic and dangerously unrealistic, he said, to revive Russia's fears by insisting on fulfilling what he called Churchill's "absurd promises" to return the "London Poles" to power in Warsaw. "The old Beck crowd," as he called it, was "through."

"Poland has got to be friendly toward Russia and must abandon the idea that she can be a springboard against us and in that way get back her sixteenth-century empire. Before the war the Becks and Sosnkowskys offered their services in that respect to Germany. Now they offer themselves to Britain and America. We won't have it."

Even if we could agree on Poland, I said, the real stumbling block of Germany would remain. Did he see any possibility of a united Germany after the war?

"Why are you so interested in a *united* Germany?" He smiled grimly.

"What I want to know is whether your government foresees in the predictable future anything like a Germany in one piece again, under a single administration?"

"If—*if*—the Allies could agree on how to re-educate the Germans, how to make them harmless and peaceful people—then maybe we could get a *small* but unified Germany."

"Your emphasis shows you think we won't be able to do that."

"No," he said slowly. "we will not be able to agree on a common program for Germany."

"So the alternative is the break-up of Germany into small states?"

"That's my opinion."

"Does it mean going back to all the pre-Bismarckian states?"

"Not all thirty-five of them! But probably the most important national divisions. Maybe in time each will become an autonomous republic."

"But without any center?"

"Without any center—at least not for a long time."

That prospect certainly was not disturbing to him. Litvinov had formerly hoped that the wartime Anglo-Russian alliance could be transformed into an all-European defense pact. That hope was fading fast.

"Britain has never been willing to see a strong power on the continent," he said. "The idea of *collaborating* with a strong power for peace is too alien to her thinking. She is at work in France and Italy and the Lowlands undermining our alliance already."

"But aren't you doing precisely the same thing in Eastern Europe?"

"Yes." He grinned. He was afraid they were. "We're drifting in the same direction. If only we had made our purposes clear, if we had made clear the limits of our needs, to each other, good diplomacy might have been able to avoid the conflict. Now it is too late. Suspicions are too rife."

Abruptly he startled me with a strange question:

"If it came to a choice in war, if the United States had to choose between supporting the British and supporting Russia, is it absolutely inevitable that you would support the British? Would you think the Republicans more likely than the Democrats to line up with the British?"

He was not smiling. I rarely learned so much from a single question.

Remember, this was October, 1944; the German collapse was still six months away. Yet in the Narkomindel (Foreign Office) they were already worrying about the next war! I said I imagined that in the long run U.S. foreign policy would turn out to be about the same, regardless of which party was in power. But I could see no logical reason for the U.S. to go to war against Russia. Thus far, at least, there was no basic conflict of vital interests. It was hard to foresee an early Russian challenge to America's dominant position in the world market. And certainly we had no direct boundary disputes. With the British, on the other hand, our economic rivalries had been intensifying; our interests were in conflict in the colonies, especially. But strong emotional and traditional ties bound us, and the British well knew how to exploit them.

"A war against Britain or the dominions today would seem unthinkable unless the British made crude, unthinkable blunders; and no one in the past forty years has shown greater skill at the gentle art of maneuvering American opinion than the British," I concluded.

"In other words," said Litvinov, "if British diplomats were as bad as ours, America might fight Britain instead of Russia!" He was laughing now. But what he said was not a laughing matter.

His feelings about Germany were those of most Russians: that in its division lay the only guarantee of the peace of Europe. From this time on I assumed that Russia would never let go of Eastern Germany. Not, at any rate, until Russia was sure, had an absolute guarantee and a reliable force to back it up, that the German people would never again support a hostile or warlike combination against her.

Some of Litvinov's remarks about Soviet attitudes toward Germany seemed so important that I wanted to carry them immediately to our then Ambassador, Averell Harriman, whose views I knew to be much more optimistic. I asked permission to do this. Now it may sound strange; any other Soviet official would have taken it for granted that whatever he said to any foreign correspondent would at once be reported verbatim to his ambassador. But not Litvinov; he was familiar enough with American reporters to believe they honored their word when asked to keep a confidence.

"No, I must ask you *not* to discuss our conversation with anyone at all in Russia.

"You're going to Washington in a few days. If by any chance you should see the President you might tell him what I've said. He's the only man—*the only one,*" he said slowly, "who can improve relations now."

So *that,* I concluded, was why he had risked his head by speaking so frankly to me.

A few days later I returned to America and faithfully delivered a twelve-page memo to the President containing a full record of this conversation. Just before he left for the Crimea Conference Mr. Roosevelt wrote to say that the notes were of "tremendous interest" to him.

I was never able to speak to Litvinov under conditions of similar freedom again. When I returned to Moscow I saw him once or twice at receptions, but he did not give me another appointment until after Japan had surrendered. On that occasion a "secretary" was present and took notes. By then we had the A-bomb to worry us.

"The bomb won't change conventional diplomacy or military thinking," he said. "Things will still stay in the same old ruts of power politics, spheres of influence and balance of power. It won't change your diplomats' way of thinking or be used in any new way and the bomb won't be an American monopoly very long. We'll soon have it, too, for our protection. So will other powers. When everybody has it then nobody can use it. It will be like poison gas and germ warfare."

He was the first man I heard express that opinion.

One other question I had discussed in my earlier interview with Litvinov was whether the Russian people wouldn't be "ready" for the use of some personal freedom after the war. Hadn't they proved their loyalty to the regime, and wouldn't the party feel secure enough to tolerate genuine freedom of speech even within its own ranks?

"*I* think so," said Max, shrugging his shoulders. "But what I think doesn't count. *They* don't think so. No, there won't be any great improvement in this respect until the other powers give up the hope of destroying us by force."

"You mean destroying Communism?"

"I mean destroying Communism."

We had completed the circle, we had boxed the compass, we were back at the old fear of encirclement. Even for Litvinov, I saw, "necessity," the oldest argument of tryanny, was not altogether without its justification for the harsh denials of freedom.

CHAPTER 18

Was It Treason?

THE IDEA of the loyal opposition has no tradition in Russia. As far as I could see, it would not be wanted or tolerated, even if an opposition party had won post-war power. We have seen how scornfully the Russians in ages past rejected "government by compromise" and why Russians had no experience in the kind of democracy whereby successful parliamentary systems seek to reconcile conflicting interests. It seemed to me illusory in the highest degree to expect Russians suddenly to adopt such a system.

"Galya Kaganova" taught me something about the possible consequences of an abrupt legalization of political opposition in the Soviet Union. Almost certainly some people would utilize their freedom to enthrone another despotism—which would then quickly suppress any opposition.

Galya was not her real name; I must somewhat camouflage her story. Despite the anti-Stalinist turn, and news I lately had that "Galya" was no longer around, still I think it wise to protect her against any possible exposure. The basic facts set forth are true; the one described faithfully mirrors the real person.

Let us say, then, that she was a teacher at the Foreign Language Institute. I met her at one of those infrequent "teas" arranged over a table of vodka by VOKS, the state agency for the promotion of friendly cultural relations with foreigners. To help out a publisher friend, in New York, I had asked VOKS to find someone to synopsize new Russian books for me, in the hope of turning up something suitable for American publication, and my own education. Galya, the VOKS secretary told me, would be just the person for it. We made an arrangement on the spot. Thereafter she began to meet me once or more a week.

Galya had a good command of English, German and French. She was in her mid-forties but looked older: lean, brittle, graying, with a parchment skin stretched across a bony face tied together by the knot of a new-potato Russian nose. She was probably pretty once. Now very near-sighted, she did not wear glasses, but in her ancient reticule she carried a lorgnette framed in mother-of-pearl, a last cherished relic from the pre-revolutionary past. Using it, she was a different person. New life came into her wintry cheeks; it awoke a gleam in her eyes and softened her voice, which normally would cut a board. I doubt if she showed that lorgnette often. After a meeting or two I sensed that she was crazy to talk. At first she evaded all personal questions and seemed both embarrassed and contemptuous. On the third occasion I saw her, she had made up her mind.

"My family belonged," she said, "to the aristocracy. The *Ukrainian* aristocracy." She looked at me as if she expected me to be shocked or to disbelieve her.

To tell the truth, I did not know exactly what the Ukrainian aristocracy was. She did come from a wealthy merchant family on her father's side; her mother was of Ukrainian rural gentry stock. She had as a child lived briefly in Germany and she had been studying in a fashionable Tsarist finishing school when the October revolution occurred. She had two strong reasons for hating the Reds: her family had been completely ruined by the revolution and the Ukraine, which she considered culturally far ahead of uncouth Russia, had been "put back a thousand years."

Soon after Lenin seized power Galya's father had wilted away like a figure from the *Cherry Orchard,* leaving his wife and children a mansion in Leningrad but little else. They lived for a time by selling their personal possessions, one by one. Presently their home was expropriated. Penniless outcasts, they went to Moscow to look for work. Galya's mother knew how to embroider and found a job as a seamstress. Galya began to teach. She put her younger brother through an engineering school, while they all lived in a single tiny room. Then she married a professor of engineering, "a Russian but a zhentulman through and through," who took a job under Kaganovich.

Things brightened up for a few years. In the late Thirties Galya's husband and brother were arrested during the purge known as the *Yezhovchina.* Accused of sabotage and conspiracy, they were both executed. According to Galya they were wholly innocent and Kaganovich knew it but refused to intervene. Vyshinsky had declared them guilty. Who dared dispute him and Stalin's wrath behind him? Not long after that tragedy Galya's mother drank veronal and died.

Somehow the police had lost interest in Galya. She was now an officer in her neighborhood buildings committee and had done so well that the party invited her to join and insisted that she become head of the district fuel committee.

"It's simply because I am honest," she told me. "There's no one else they could trust with the fuel!" She took the job and somehow avoided joining the party, so she said. I believed her.

Gradually she revealed her profound disgust with the Soviet state, with the war and with "Communism's allies," including Britain and the U.S.A. "I live to see them beaten," she said one day, frowning bitterly. Her pale eyes flamed. "Every Communist should be slaughtered, the way they slaughtered our best people. You foreigners who help them now will in due time suffer also from your mistake, mark my word!"

In Hitler's victory Galya saw the last great hope. For the old Russia she had loved and lost? The Russia of the throne, the aristocracy, the French-speaking, German-speaking bourgeoisie, the gulf between the very rich on top and the millions of ragged, illiterate, brutalized peasants on the bottom? No, she knew that that could not be brought back. But it could be avenged! So could her murdered husband and brother! Only Hitler could put the "Red swine" out of the way and restore Ukrainian and White Russian culture to its majesty and splendor. What if it did mean being ruled by Germans for a generation or two? Was it not the Swedes, the Germans, the French, who in their conquests had civilized Russia?

Galya ridiculed the notion that ideological differences were involved in the war. It was simply a question of dog eat dog. Democracy? Freedom? Self-determination? Bosh! Wait and see! These words meant nothing in the kind of Europe Stalin wanted. Only Americans were naive enough to believe this war had anything to do with freedom.

"Lies! Lies!" Galya would cry as she tore through the books or the papers and journals I received as a correspondent. "P-p-propaganda! R-r-r-rubbish!" Whenever it was a story of German defeats or embarrassment she refused to believe it. She had been given only one-sided news for so many years that even the most independently authenticated facts often failed to convince her.

She did not believe a word she read in the Russian press about Hitler's atrocities and the extermination camps. "Puh—rr-opaganda!" she would mutter, incensed. "Exaggerations! Maybe Hitler exterminates a few Communist rabble. What's that compared to the slave camps right here in Russia? Why don't you and your American colleagues write about them?"

"First of all, there is censorship. But aside from that, who knows the facts? For instance, how many camps are there? Where? How many people in them? For what?"

"Scores—scores of camps. Millions of good Russians in them. Millions!"

"Galya, get me the facts about just one camp, where it is, how it is run, how many are in it. I'll write that when I leave."

But when it came to furnishing details, Galya was not very helpful. Perhaps she did not know; perhaps she was afraid to go quite that far. The best she did for me was to tell me the true story of one family in her block, which I did write, immediately after the war, in a composite, non-traceable form.

"Tell me this, Galya," I said one day. "If Hitler did come in, would you expect him to abolish concentration camps here? Wouldn't it be far worse: genocide reaching nobody knows how far, plus ideological persecution?"

"Ah, you are so naive! Do you think we can destroy Bolshevism without killing anybody? Of course, the leaders, the worst criminals, will be executed."

"How many? A thousand? A million? Ten millions? And Komsomols, too?"

"As many," she said colorlessly, "as necessary."

"The Germans have been welcomed everywhere as liberators in the Ukraine!" she always insisted. When I got to the Ukraine soon after the Red Army began recovering it I found a different story. Many Ukrainians had been ready to embrace Hitler or anybody who might free them, but the Fuehrer never gave them a chance. He scorned nationalist sentiment and grabbed the great collectives and turned them over to greedy German burghers to operate as feudal estates, with the peasants returned to actual serfdom. Tens of thousands of non-combatants were arrested, murdered or put into concentration camps. A steady stream of women and young children was exported in box cars to do forced labor in camps, factories, farms or brothels in Germany.

Galya shrugged her shoulders when on my return I told her what I had personally seen and heard. "Hardship? Injustice? Destruction? Of course! How can you have war without them? But here we have had the same thing for years in *peacetime!*"

She herself was opposed to killing Jews; it was against her religion, she insisted. But didn't they ask for it? Wasn't it a fact that even in Russia the Jews always managed to avoid being sent to the front, and got safe jobs in the rear? That they always ran the black markets and made money while others stupidly died at the front for them? When you got right down to it, who else but the Jews were left in Moscow these days to sleep with the soldiers' wives?

Although the Soviet press published many stories giving prominence to feats of Jewish heroism, and battle statistics belied the other slanders, Galya was not the only Russian who repeated them and apparently believed them. Habits of the pogroms died hard and the poison of Hitlerism quickly revived them. Even the terrible revelations, the fully documented and illustrated horrors of Maidanek and Dachau, would not altogether put an end to anti-Semitism in Russia. The Little Father Stalin, himself, was soon to prove that . . .

Yet I never heard Galya make an indiscreet remark in public. She was, I knew, highly thought of at the Institute: a quiet, efficient worker. No one else at the Metropole, none of the secretaries I knew, dreamed that she held treasonable opinions. She both repelled and fascinated me. She was good for me in one sense; a useful penicillin against an endless spate of propaganda. She presented a problem, too. Weren't the Nazis she loved our deadly enemies, the same people who were murdering our own American boys? In England or America, in wartime, I would have had her locked up. In Russia it was somehow not quite the same; here there seemed less chance that she would get a fair hearing.

Anyway, I had no proof that Galya and her nameless "engineer friends" were really German agents. She said they nightly listened to the Nazi short-wave broadcasts and translated and disseminated them. She could have been shot for that alone. But I thought she lacked the necessary emotional stability for the spy role. I also dismissed the thought that she might be an *agent provocateur*. Why would the NKVD bother to ascertain my private opinions? Why would Galya be wasted on me instead of being thrust into a foreign embassy where she might be really useful?

And why would the Communists deliberately sabotage their own purposes by introducing a woman to persuade me that there wasn't a new Russian novel or non-fiction work worth translating? For we never did find a single suitable book. "Trash! Lies! Stupidity!" was her unvarying comment. And as nearly as I could make out her judgment in this matter was often sound.

Of course I knew other Russians working for foreigners in Moscow who were anti-Communist. But I never heard of another Galya, hostile to the whole "freedom-loving camp," as it was then called, and a Nazilover fervently hoping for Axis victory.

"Galya!" I would say incredulously after one of her outbursts. "How do you know I won't turn you in to the police?"

"Ha!" she would snort. "You are an American—you're too soft-hearted. This is not your quarrel. You won't become involved. You Americans! You know nothing about Russia. None of you!"

Sometimes I was amused by her, and always I felt I was learning something about a face of Russia hidden from most people. Only occasionally her arrogant contempt for America got under my skin.

"You will see," she told me. "If Hitler is defeated, your turn comes next. Do you think Stalin is not laughing up his sleeve at you for saving him? Your ambassadors, they are fools: boasting of their personal 'influence' on Stalin! What children you all are! Do you think Stalin will keep any of his promises? Of course not! I prophesy war between you: war, war, war!"

Curiously, Galya did not hate Stalin personally. She even bore him a grudging respect. "He is better than all the rest," she said. Hadn't he killed many, many Communists? In some odd, inverted or paradoxical way Stalin personified for Galya the great Russian tradition of leader-despots. Was he an interim image to substitute for the Tsar and her own apparently inadequate father, while she prayed for Hitler?

The German retreat became general and was overwhelmingly confirmed. Galya grew more and more depressed. As I watched the green, red and blue rockets sprayed across the Moscow sky to celebrate Red victories she would turn her back and refuse to look. When it was over, the veins stood embossed on her forehead and her face would be pale as death.

"Hitler has a secret weapon," she would incant. "It is almost r-r-ready. My engineer friends know what it is—ter-r-r-ible! When it comes everything will collapse here, turn to dust and ashes. *We* shall escape; we know the secret. *We* shall have our celebration then, our rockets will make flames in the sky. We'll dance on Bolshevik graves!"

It was like that right to the last time I saw Galya.

Not long ago I met a British correspondent in Washington whom I had known in Moscow. I asked him about mutual friends; then I remembered I had once introduced him to Galya. I inquired about her, by her real name. I was prepared to hear the worst.

"Galya Kaganova? Oh, of course, I saw the old *blad* every time I took a cable to the Nark. She's the toughest censor working there. Highly thought of by the press chief, too."

But very recently I had news that she had been "prohibited to live in Moscow." That could mean anything up to having her body short-ened by a head.

That's Russia for you.

CHAPTER 19

The "Peaceful Revolution"

BEFORE THE END of the war it was evident that the Red Army would not bring to Eastern Europe any return to things as they were before Hitler, but would foster "peaceful," police-managed revolutions throughout this whole area.

"In the irony of history," I cabled my editor from Moscow after I returned from newly occupied Rumania and part of Poland, "it has turned out that Nazism, which set out to overthrow Communism, has succeeded in destroying *laissez-faire* capitalism. Eastern Europe will never be the same again. Here capitalism as we know it will cease to exist." *

That was as far as I could go in a dispatch which had to pass Soviet censorship in 1944. Hitler had dug capitalism's grave all right, but the rest of the truth was that the Russians were enthusiastically inter-ring the corpse. The basic facts which dictated this process looked simple to the Russian people. Not just Communists but nearly all Rus-sians felt that their country had a moral right to "correct" the causes of evil not only in Germany but in neighboring allied states. It was the Germans who had attacked Russia, not the other way round, and Germans who had drawn Russia's armies into Europe, not the Russians who had invaded Germany.

Russia's dead outnumbered the losses of the other Allies, combined, by more than ten to one.

"No government ever formed among men," exclaimed Winston Churchill after seeing some of the devastation, "has been capable of surviving injury so grave and cruel as that inflicted by Hitler on Rus-sia!" More important to most Russians than injury to the "government," however, was the human toll, a mountain of skulls, and the wasteland made of the richest part of the nation. Of the 28 to 30 million Soviet

* See *The Saturday Evening Post*, Nov. 11, 1947.

people drafted into the armed services during the war, more than fifty percent were killed or wounded, in addition to five million men taken prisoner. Civilian and military dead combined exceeded 20 million. Behind them the Nazis left half the Soviet coal and iron industry in ruins, and destroyed half of all Russia's electric power, steel and machinery-making industry. Six million buildings were demolished: housing and office space equivalent to all pre-war housing and office space in Arkansas, Arizona, California, Connecticut, Florida, Maine, New Hampshire, New Mexico, Oregon, Vermont and Washington, combined.

Whatever resentment Russians harbored against Stalinism was momentarily forgotten in their disgust with the Nazis. They expected their armies to secure punishment of the guilty, retribution for some of the injury and the kind of transformation in all Eastern Europe which would prevent it from ever again serving as a springboard for maniacal invaders. Even though at the end of the war Russia truly was exhausted and licking her wounds she was still manifestly the strongest nation in Europe. The U.S.A. alone was now her military peer. This formidable fact made it fantasy to expect Russia to restore in Eastern Europe a private-ownership system which, from the Communist point of view, had mothered a monster that all but destroyed her.

The Red Army was bound to fill the political vacuum left by the Nazi collapse with *something*. It was argueable that it had no choice but to impose its own brand of ideological goods. The triumph of the Red Army was inseparable from the triumph of the political system which produced it. Neither the Army nor the Party knew or understood any other system.

What we would soon forget or ignore, also, was that never during the course of the war did the Anglo-American powers actually demand of the Russians that they prohibit the teaching, spread and organization of Communist thought in the countries they occupied. Assertions were made later that Russia had broken "promises" to that effect. In truth, Russia's acceptance of the phrases "self-determination" and "free elections" never required her to repudiate Communism in those countries nor deny help to those who advocated it. We were, as Galya said, simply enchanted by the spell of our own rhetoric, ignoring the hard reality of the various armistice agreements signed by the Allied representatives in Moscow. Those agreements *explicitly* authorized Russia to "eliminate" the influence of all elements "hostile to the Red Army." Obviously that could only mean, since the Red Army was empowered to interpret the words and was itself inseparable from the

Communist party, the elimination of influence "hostile to Communism" as well.

Nor could that retribution seem illogical to non-Russians who had actually witnessed the primitive regressions of German power under Hitler imposed wherever he carried the swastika, for the sole ideal of ennobling a myth—the paramountcy of a German super-race at the cost of exterminating or reducing to slavery all the other children of Greece and Rome, of Judea and Egypt, of Hindustan and Muskovy. "We must resort to all means," said Hitler in *Mein Kampf* "to bring about the conquest of the world by the Germans." In any other country since the stony ancient Persians such a man would have been laughed to extinction. In Germany it was characteristic of Hitler's supporters— by no means *all* Germans—that they were totally lacking in humor.

"If our hearts are set upon establishing the Great German Reich we must above all things force out and exterminate the Slavonic nations— the Russians, the Poles, Czechs, Slovaks, Bulgarians, Ukrainians, Byelorussians. There is no reason why this should not be done," said Hitler. All that was required was order and organization, step by step: first the immolation of the "sub-races," with top priority for the Jews; then would come the turn of the "sub-men" of Asia, and the cleansing of mongrel America. Thus it actually happened that over all Europe some 6,000,000 non-combatants were systematically slaughtered in the Nazis' efficient death plants, where "nothing was wasted."

It was at Maidanek, in Poland, that I fully realized why Russia would never again permit Prussian power to revive in Eastern Europe. There I first saw an enterprise operated solely for the purpose of reducing men and women and their children from the condition of upright, ambulatory beings to so many kilograms of fertilizer for Nazi vegetable gardens. Later I saw Dachau and Mautthausen in Western Germany, but neither surpassed Maidanek in necrological interest. This ghastly abattoir derived its efficiency from a curious combination of German peasant virtues of thrift, order and obedience and the racial arrogance and spiritual meanness of the Prussian in a manner which perfectly epitomized the very "soul" of Nazi philosophy.

CHAPTER 20

Tweedledum—and Tweedledee?

"THOSE WHO have not seen the Germans will not believe that there exists a nation especially to personify cruelty and brutality," warned Tiberius, who was well acquainted with the subject. Of course we know that evil is no inherent monopoly of any people. All the same it is odd that 2,000 years after Tiberius, Germany was still able to produce Hitler and Himmler, and millions to emulate and obey them.

A visit to Maidanek was bound to make a student of the long story ponder more than once over the old Russian proverb which says, "The German may be a good fellow but it is safer to hang him."

Maidanek turned out a total of well over a million corpses of men, women and children of German, Austrian, Polish, Hungarian, Russian, Ukrainian, Rumanian, French, British and others of Jewish or partly Jewish or only allegedly Jewish descent. Many political prisoners of non-Semitic origin were also immolated here. It was a self-sustaining factory on the whole. It had its own power plant, its various shops, its extensive gardens, and its miles of prisoner-built roads winding between high watch towers that connected walls and barbed wire. It had a fire department; no one was permitted to burn ahead of time. Its raw materials were human minorities and their labor and its products were loot, corpses, fertilizer and soap.

Everywhere at Maidanek it was neatness, cleanliness, order, efficiency, economy; the complete absorption of the German master of detail. All possible cash was extracted from the victim before he was killed. On his arrival at Maidanek the prisoner surrendered his luggage which often included everything he owned, for he had been falsely promised that he was to be "settled" in "new territory." The last touch, after he had been starved and worked to complete exhaustion, was the removal of any gold or platinum crowns and fillings from his teeth before he was confined to the ovens that burned day and night.

All the pathetic personal belongings were collected in a large storage depot, a former Catholic church in the town. It took us hours to go through this macabre used-clothing shop, which was like a huge Macy's stocked with all Third Avenue's hand-me-downs. Each item received was carefully entered in the ledgers and a record was kept of its sale or disposition to some deserving German family at home or German "pioneers" in conquered Ukraine. Inventories included nearly every conceivable article of clothing for both sexes and all ages. One room overflowed with children's garments. In one corner was an assortment of baby potties. Another held a large collection of children's toys and books smudged by small hands. I saw old buttons sorted out in piles, and half-used tubes of toothpaste. Even rags were fumigated and preserved and entered in the ledgers.

The most grisly place was the large out-building filled with the shoes of the dead. Tens of thousands of pairs, awaiting assortment, lay one on the other. They were somehow more tragically eloquent than close-packed bones, or the looted, naked corpses I had seen stacked like marbled cordwood on frozen battlefields. Here were little red slippers, gold evening pumps, tiny sandals, children's boots, the high-laced shoes of elderly women, worn clodhoppers of peasants, the frayed *valenki* of the Russians, and rubbers from Akron, Ohio. I read labels from Moscow, Warsaw, Paris, Berlin, Vienna, Munich, Antwerp, New York, Madrid, Rotterdam! The shoe of a crippled woman, with its built-up sole six inches high, lay near a truss and a knee-length brace.

Nothing was wasted.

I remember a colloquy I had with a little *Obersturmführer* named Theodore Scholen. He was one of several Nazi guards taken by surprise near the camp and brought back and identified by the surviving inmates who took us around and explained the works. Scholen now freely recalled some of the details of management. Among these was the date November 3, 1943, when a record was set up at Maidanek which not even Buchenwald surpassed. On that one day more than 18,000 persons were gassed or shot and burned.

Yes, looking back on it now, Scholen said, Maidanek must indeed have been an extermination camp; at the time he had simply assumed they were all "guilty." Guilty of what? How should he know? "Orders" did not say. It was not his affair; he insisted that he himself had never taken part in the actual killings.

"Then who was responsible?" I was later to put the question to dozens of Nazis, right up to General Goering, when I was with the Americans who captured him near Berchtesgaden: and always with the same result.

"Orders," Scholen said, "Berlin." ("Hitler," Goering said.) Not the camp commandant, not Scholen, and not any of the nineteen young Nazis who had worked under Scholen. Just "Orders."

"Hasn't it occurred to you that you will be tried as a war criminal?"
I asked.

He gave me a look of hurt surprise. *"Ich bin nur ein kleiner Mensch!
I obeyed orders!"*

General Orders was the only criminal. But the Russians were convinced that the criminal was Germany itself. Tens of millions of their next of kin had been murdered by Orders. They were determined this time to stay on German soil until the schizophrenia was resolved. For that reason even some anti-Communists sanctioned the "peaceful revolution" in Eastern Europe.

Here it may be asked whether the Communists did not suffer from exactly the same disease. Was there any real difference between the Stalinist concentration camp and the Nazi death plant? Between the ideological inquisition conducted by the NKVD and the inquisition conducted by the Gestapo? Between murder in the U.S.S.R. rationalized as "historical necessity," and Nazi mass genocide and sterilization of racial inferiors? If Communists and Nazis used the same means how could there be any basic difference in the results?

Weren't they, in fact, simply Tweedledum and Tweedledee?

The answer is no, they were not.

I say this knowing that it flies in the face of years of cold war propaganda that equates Russian Communists and German Nazis absolutely. That delusion has been particularly popular in America, and it is dangerous. No one can justify or minimize the heavy-handed crimes of the Russian dictatorship. But neither can anyone begin to understand why Communist values have survived and spread over a vast area of the world unless he comprehends that *despite* those crimes and a similarity of methods between Nazi and Communist there did remain quantitative and qualitative differences: differences of means and ends, and obvious differences in results.

"The means employed determine the nature of the ends produced" is an axiom in mathematics. But as soon as it is applied in political judgments involving the use of subjective standards of "good" and "bad" the formula can no longer be stated absolutely. Here the truth lies closer to LaSalle than to Gandhi: "Ends and means are so entangled that changing one you change the other too."

Good ends can never "justify" bad means, and it is doubtless true that good ends can never be attained by wholly bad means. But it does not follow that the ethical or moral value of the end or aim is irrelevant merely because the means appear "bad" to us. It matters a great deal.

What is "good" and "bad" about ends and means depends on where we sit, naturally. In a world where most leaders of men, wherever they sit, now accept science as the basis of civilized progress, it is axiomatic that "good" ends are those which contribute to the evolution and enlightenment of mankind as a whole: the general advancement of the races, recognized as biological equals, and capable of common social effort for the common good. "Bad" ends are ends which would deny the plausibility, desirability or even the possibility that "within the four seas all are brothers." And the nadir of all bad ends leading back to the night, it will scarcely be disputed, is surely the ambition to impose the supremacy of one nation or race over all others by means of enslaving or even exterminating whole peoples.

Therein lay the basic difference between Germany and Russia, or at least between the Nazi and the Communist. The Nazi's aim was perfection for himself at the expense of universal darkness for others. The Communist aim, often compromised though it was by bad means, retained its human connections, its lineal relationship to the evolution of mankind as a whole, and to ends of liberté, égalité and fraternité.

In many countries other than Russia and Germany tyranny and wickedness and racial arrogance have been empowered to commit atrocious crimes against their neighbors. But in no modern state except Germany, not even Japan, has it been possible to win popular adoration and blind obedience for leaders openly committed to the use of systematic plunder and extermination of their neighbors for the end-ideal of racial supremacy, and for racial engorgement in what amounted to systematic reversion to cannibalism. Edward Crankshaw defined this difference very succinctly when he wrote:*

> But in the last resort the German failure, which so far differentiates Germany from all the other nations of the West, including Russia, is a "rejection of that reality which includes one's neighbors." It is idealism gone rotten; and until they can learn to accept a reality which includes people, the Germans in their restless and insane striving for something better, will remain dangerous to those who content themselves with trying to make the best of the world as we know it to be.

Russian Communists often lost touch with "people," but during their worst moments they never dared repudiate the Socialist faith in the essential one-ness of mankind, or in evolution and the ends of international unity and brotherhood. This in itself tended to place limits on the extent to which the party could equate itself with evil in the methods of police rule. Communists could never overtly reject "the

* *Gestapo,* by Edward Crankshaw, N.Y., 1956.

reality which includes one's neighbors," and cast off all restraint as Hitlerites did. This explains the phenomenal fact that the Communist dictatorship could suppress individual freedom at home without altogether destroying Russia's power of attraction as a center of hope and liberation for racial minorities and men oppressed by imperialism or otherwise weak and lagging behind.

President Roosevelt was well aware of this paradox of ends and means in Russia. He knew of course the means by which the Communists ruled Russia. But because no Western Christian and democrat could seriously quarrel with the aspirations of the revolution or the liberation of mankind which Communism steadily proclaimed as its end Roosevelt never despaired of achieving limited co-operation with Red Russia in peacetime, of dispelling her fears of encirclement, and of giving her a sense of belonging to the family of men of good purpose.

Such was the enduring impression I was soon to receive from F.D.R. in person when during a swift visit home I saw and talked to him in the last hours of his life.

CHAPTER 21

An "A-Political" Relationship

THE PRESIDENT constantly checked information he received through official sources by keeping in personal touch with newspaper men as well as dozens of other informants. As far as I could learn this practice was seldom followed by senators. I was mistaken, however, in assuming that they were altogether indifferent to correspondents' activities. Some of them were to display a keen interest in our private lives in Moscow during the war. I discovered this only when I read the full record, by courtesy of Senator James O. Eastland, of the Senate investigation of the "loyalty" of John Paton Davies.

I first met John Davies many years ago in Peking, often saw him in various parts of China, and shared minor adventures with him. I came to value his intelligence as a foreign service officer. During the war our paths crossed in Cairo, India, Washington and, finally, in Russia, where he arrived early in 1945. His career was ruined, once Joe McCarthy had put the finger on him.

John had been well on his way to an ambassadorship when in 1950 Joe Alsop, the columnist, wrote a series of articles which flatteringly blamed him, John Stewart Service and General Stilwell for the success of the Chinese revolution. It seemed that they had acted contrary to the views and wishes of Alsop and General Chennault on China. Senator McCarthy picked up Alsop's charges and—General Stilwell being dead—added Davies to his list of those master-minds in the dreamy State Department who had "sold China to Russia." Alsop later changed his mind and manfully conceded that Davies and Service might have been right, after all; but it was too late to save them. Service was illegally fired and was later reinstated on orders of the U.S. Supreme Court; by then his usefulness was over. Davies underwent prolonged and repeated investigations held in the hope of turning up some more plausible reason for his dismissal than the appeasement of McCarthy. The efforts proved fruitless and imputations of disloyalty were finally dropped. He had, however, become a political embarrassment to John Foster Dulles, who fell back on his discretionary powers to find Davies vaguely guilty of incompetence. He was dismissed, without any pension, just before McCarthyism somewhat disintegrated under the glare of television lights.

Davies' hearings were originally held *in camera,* but his testimony was later published, all the same, by the Senate Sub-committee on Internal Security. Not long afterward another witness made some unkind remarks about me under the cloak of immunity extended to slanderers by Senator Eastland's committee. The witness was Harvey Matusow, who has since been convicted of perjury in another connection and sent to jail. Matusow had already retracted his lies about me and others when I wrote to Senator Eastland to demand a complete record of the Institute of Pacific Relations inquiry, in which I found Davies' testimony incorporated. On consulting the index of the fifteen-volume monument to the art of irrelevance, I discovered extensive references to myself.

It seemed that John Davies had once recommended to his chief, George Kennan, who was head of the State Department's policy planning, that I be put to work on a proposed operation known as "Tawny Pipit." Through the intervention of Undersecretary of State Walter Bedell Smith, Davies was saved from divulging to the senators exactly what I would have been expected to accomplish for Tawny Pipit. General Smith told the investigators that the nature of the project was so highly secret—or "sensitive"—that it would have disastrous effects on our security if Davies were obliged to explain.

As the matter is still under wraps I can only guess at what he had in mind. Knowing John's nature, however, which combines a sense of satire and imagination not encountered every day in the State Department, it seems reasonable to surmise that the outstanding characteristic of the tawny pipit, which is its "loud song delivered in flight," contains a key to the mystery. As a mobile correspondent of some special presumed knowledge of the cold-war enemy, it may have been hoped that I could be used to evoke counter-calls from the other side of the river which would help the Department analyze propaganda and intelligence objectives and techniques of the Cominform.

Tawny Pipit was abandoned without ever having become airborne, but it provided a reason for the Senate inquiry's long digression into my private attachments in Moscow and into matters which I had never remotely imagined could engage the attention of the august U.S. Senate. One must at least admire the devotion, above and beyond the call of duty, which brought the senators, in hot pursuit of our internal security, to haul themselves up to room 424 of the Senate Building during a hot August of 1951 to listen to John Davies' reminiscences. Consider a few fragments:

> Mr. Sourwine (Senate counsel). Do you recall whether you ever wrote any letter to Mr. Snow?
> Mr. Davies. Yes, I think I did.
> Mr. Sourwine. How extensive was that correspondence?
> Mr. Davies. Very limited. He had a girl friend in Moscow. I remember his inquiring about her, and my writing back and saying that the NKVD had not gotten her and she was all right.
> Mr. Morris (another counsel). Can you name this girl, Mr. Davies?
> Mr. Davies. I don't remember what her name was. She was a girl who had contacts with people in the British Embassy. She was—we all recognized her as somebody that the NKVD was trying to use on us. She was a cute dish.
> Mr. Sourwine. You say somebody in the NKVD was trying to use her?
> Mr. Davies. We assumed that.
> Mr. Sourwine. You say you all recognized her?
> Mr. Davies. "Recognized" is the wrong word. We assumed that . . .

> Farther on Mr. Sourwine asked: "Had you met her?"
> Mr. Davies. "I had just met her socially."

> Mr. Sourwine. And you say she was Mr. Snow's girl friend?
> Mr. Davies. I don't think—I think that—
> Mr. Sourwine. You did use that word, didn't you—his girl friend?
> Mr. Davies. I think it was an a-political relationship.

Mr. Sourwine. What does an a-political relationship mean?
Mr. Davies. A relationship without any political connotation.
(Discussion off the record.)

It is tantalizing to go off the record at this point, but after all it was a hot day in August. We are not privileged to know how accurately Davies' enlightenment of Mr. Sourwine corresponded to Dr. Kinsey's reports on the a-political activity of the American male. It must have been enticing, because when they returned to the record it was with the emphatic request that Davies supply "her" name as soon as possible. "Girl friend" now became "young lady":

Mr. Sourwine. Since you presumed the young lady to be an NKVD agent, why was it that you told Mr. Snow the NKVD did not have her yet?
Mr. Davies: A totalitarian state devours its own, you know.

That answer didn't resolve the contradiction, however, and as the Senators may still be worried about this threat to our internal security, allow me to introduce her. She was Ilena Sergeievna Yasnova, although fellow correspondents and friends around the embassies knew her by another name in the last year of the war when she was my frequent companion. Since all the facts are, along with unwarranted conclusions, now collecting dust in the files of the NKVD, there is no reason to withhold this scientific information from our own researchers.

Yes, she was attractive. But an NKVD agent? Hardly. Not unless you would call every Russian citizen who had any kind of overt friendship with foreigners an "agent." That would include quite a few "girl friends" who married Americans and later became good American citizens. Of course all Russians were subject to a sudden summons to the Lubyanka, to be warned of possible consequences and required to answer questions. Not wholly different, in fact, from the way an American associated with Soviet Russians at home may be invited to co-operate with the F.B.I. In Russia the alternative for an American visitor was to avoid all informal contacts with the natives, which was no task at all! Those who did so learned nothing and might better have stayed at home.

As far as I was concerned, I thought, no risk was involved. I was a legitimate correspondent-editor, and no spy. I had no secrets to hide from the YMCA, as Moscow Americans used to call the NKVD. The shoe was on the other foot. If my friendship with Ilena involved unforeseeable risks in a fantastic future American jungle world of guilt by association, it was a different matter for her. She was immediately vulnerable, as her mother later gave me to understand.

Ilena was determinedly a-political, to be sure. "Everybody knows I do not understand politics," she would say if anyone asked her a marginal question when she was with me. "I am too stupid. Perhaps it is because of my eyes, no? Let us talk art or music."

It was Tanya who introduced us, three years before Davies met her. Tanya was the tempestuous, tawny-headed wife and secretary to Ronald Matthews, correspondent of the *Daily Herald;* and Tanya was far from a-political. Tanya had taught foreign languages and had known Ilena as a student. That first time we met I remembered only that she was passing fair, bubbling over with enthusiasm, and had azure eyes of a singular shape.

I did not see Ilena again until, months later, I walked through the Kremlin park one spring day and there she sat on a bench reading a book. Having studied some Russian I threw discretion aside and tried a few words. She was very kind about my efforts. She spoke no English but I soon discovered that her French was better by far than my Russian—and my French.

Ilena was then twenty-one and a student at Moscow University, where she had earned a scholarship that paid her tuition and a stipend of several hundred roubles a month. Her specialty, about as far from politics, war and NKVD as you could get, was history, theory, principles and practice of *art*. She had to do another year at college and postgraduate work, when she hoped to win the status of *aspirantura,* accompanied by a good income. It would qualify her to work for one of the state museums of the Soviet Union. Ilena's dream was to be a director of the Tretyakov Gallery and then escape from its dreary Brullovs, Lebedevs, and Repines, to become a buyer in France and pick up all the latest Picassos. She was, I learned on better acquaintance, also interested in studying the works of such artists as Schiaparelli and Dior.

Ilena was the only child of an orthodox and devoted party worker who was a biochemist in a state laboratory. In her busy career she had not spent as much time with her daughter as she would have liked; to compensate for this she had (she feared) over-indulged Ilena in some respects; her mind was "not well disciplined in a political sense." Her stepfather, also a scientist, was busy with his affairs and remote to Ilena. She could not remember what her father (an army officer) had looked like. He had taken permanent leave when she was a small child, by writing his wife a post card informing her that they were divorced. Now, after many years, Ilena's stepfather was entrapped by a younger comrade, and also wanted a divorce, which Ilena's mother thus far had refused him. The time of the post-card divorce had long since passed and now it took solid reasons, and a long wait, to win a divorce before a Soviet court. Meanwhile, Ilena lived with her grandmother.

I didn't know anything about Ilena's family affairs during my first year in Russia. She was working hard at school and after hours was occupied with the Komsomol, visiting hospitals and collecting firewood from the surrounding forests, and other duties. Between trips to the war areas I did take her to dinner once, with my secretary, for the utilitarian purpose of questioning her about Soviet education during wartime—how students were separated between university and *tekhnicum* levels, hours, curricula, social relationships, and so on. Then I left for the Middle East and Western Europe.

When I returned I saw a lot of Ilena because she worked for me after school as a courier. The Moscow courier was a kind of assistant to one's secretary, to save her time running errands or standing in queues for rations or waiting for the censors to put a dispatch through the mangle. Even such rather lowly employment was then coveted (and sanctioned by the foreign office); times were extremely hard and the work for a foreigner meant needed good food. Ilena got the job, my secretary told her her duties, and sometimes I did not see her for days. I remember having the distinct impression of speaking increasingly fluent Russian to her. Then one day I suddenly realized that she had spoken English—with a strong accent, to be sure, but understandable enough, and in a pleasing, rather breathless voice. Her English somehow put her in focus as a person identifiable with my own world.

Startled, I asked how and where and when she had learned English, while I was still groaning over preliminary struggles with the subjunctive mood and despaired of ever learning to speak the lyrical, maddening Russian language. She had, she explained, merely changed her language *spetsialnost* from French to English. And now, less than a year later, she was almost fluent.

It was not long after that discovery that I drew her to the window one day to make a careful inspection of the phenomenon that literally put stars in her eyes. I saw that they were just the color of blue-green Kashmir sapphires and were perfectly elliptical—and elliptically perfect.

"Why, you're a Siamese cat!"

"You don't like my eyes?" she asked, quite gravely. "But they are good—I see *so* well. Are they ugly?" And all this tumbled out in an unexpectedly tremulous voice, as if a picture I admired had magically come to life.

"Ugly! They're the most unusual eyes I ever saw! *Ochin prikrasni!* They're beautiful, simply beautiful!"

And so they were. But there was nothing I could do about it. Nym and I were formally separated but she had not divorced me. I especially wished to avoid any serious entanglement in Moscow.

I drew back to neutral observer's territory and stayed there for weeks. Then gradually I began to take Ilena to the ballet, the theatre and the opera, where she was much at home, the best-informed "a-political" companion I could wish for, and as such much pursued by some young lonely hearts of the British Embassy.

CHAPTER 22

Du Temps Perdu

ONE OF the things I had missed in Asia was more than a decade of music, for which the falsetto singing and wailing Chinese violin were no adequate substitute for anyone but a native. (Music and dancing in Southeast Asia are a different matter.) In Russia music was a second language offering ready contact with the emotional and cultural life of the country. People in the U.S.S.R. sing a great deal, song has a vital place in army as well as civilian life and every Soviet nation contributes to the wide variety.

During the war the air was filled with music day and night. Quite wisely the Communists cut down on their long party harangues over the air, which are the equivalents of our commercials, and relied upon broadcasts of pure music to evoke patriotism. Whole symphonies and operas came over without any slogans or political soap interrupting.

Great amplifiers hung above the streets and it was eerie to hear them pour oceans of sound into the wide, ice-coated, curfew-cleared plazas, which they seemed to crowd with the images of Bach, Beethoven, Mozart and other immortals. I never hear Grieg's stirring first concerto without thinking of one frosty evening when I walked with Ilena around Moscow's Kitai Gorod, the Chinese City, our footsteps muffled by soft snow and our felt boots. Except for our muted voices not a sound could be heard. Suddenly a Niagara of music crashed into the vast spaces of Red Square. The piano seemed sky-high as its mighty thunder rolled along the Kremlin Wall and St. Basil's turnip domes danced in the moonlight.

One "diplomatic" privilege conceded to foreign correspondents then was access to good seats at the Bolshoi Theatre. In that vast structure resplendent even in wartime, its imperial plush in spotless glory, its jeweled candelabra ten thousand sparkling mirrors of iridescence, you could still see the world's finest classical ballet. The enchantment of the Bolshoi and the lavishness of its production contrasted with the eternal drabness and grayness of Moscow, especially wintry Moscow; so that to step from the street into all that glitter, the scarlet and gold on elegant ivory, was to enter Russia's only fairyland, where every *tovarishcha* became a Cinderella for the night.

"To come here," as Ilena put it, "is for us to live longer."

The night Stalin took Churchill to see the Moscow ballet the Bolshoi looked as though a couple of tons of gilt and polish had been newly poured on it. They sat in the old Imperial box under the flashing candelabra, flanked by Molotov and Eden. (Near them, on the edge of his chair, sat Nikita Khrushchev, his sycophant's smile no doubt masking homicidal thoughts for which Joe would have cut him down by a head had he read them.) Churchill got an ovation which pleased him from an audience that was Moscow's elite. His own applause for Galina Ulanova's superb *Giselle,* one of the more rigidly conventional ballets in both form and content, was equally enthusiastic. As we filed out of the theatre Stalin passed not five feet away from me in the momentarily almost empty lobby. I noticed for the first time how very short he was; shorter, even, than Churchill. He must have taken a wrong turn; he gave me a puzzled glance as if waiting to be directed. Then a guard caught up and marched beside him and he was gone.

Both Stalin and Churchill obviously enjoyed themselves and a certain grace between them subtly relaxed everybody. "Both gentlemen had a lovely time," as Tom Barman said afterward. He was Churchill's P.R.O. for the visit. "You might in fact say that in their agreement on *Giselle,*" he added, "there was a perfect meeting of Tory minds."

Ilena laughed till the tears came when I repeated the remark.

As the Germans retreated farther from the capital, more halls and theatres opened their doors and we heard frequent concerts: inevitably Tchaikovsky, Borodin, and Rimsky-Korsakov; and Khachaturian, Shostakovich, Prokofiev and other moderns. No Russian artist, incidentally, was subject to draft call, and most of them stayed in the capital throughout the war. Prokofiev conducted his own music when Ilena and I went to hear him.

I remember going to the Conservatory for the first concert of Rachmaninoff the Soviet government permitted after many years. Rachmaninoff had been a Tsarist sympathizer before the war; just before his death in the U.S. he came out in warm support of the Fatherland. The intimate ovation given his music on this occasion was as if an elder were returning to lead the massive chorus of the clan.

Ilena had gone to a famous Moscow school, No. 34 I think it was, attended by children of Kremlin officials. Among her classmates was Stalin's daughter Svetlana, with whom Ilena had played in the Kremlin. She had known other "advantages," as a daughter of "an old comrade," and yet in her lifetime she had never had a room of her own. Her mother and stepfather had a sparsely furnished flat with one pocket bedroom and a tiny kitchen, where I visited several times. Ilena's toothless grandmother of eighty-two had somehow managed to hang onto a relatively spacious first-floor room in an old mansion. If all went well Ilena would inherit it. It was perhaps her foremost ambition. The old *babushka* knew it and kept her in virtual servitude under threat of disinheritance.

Most of Ilena's friends and schoolmates lived no better. Many lived not as well as she did. Rents in Moscow were even lower than in Paris but you could not, as in Paris, get living room for key money or bribes, since all quarters were assigned solely by the bureaucracy. Living space was a prime arbiter of domestic life. Once we were invited to the wedding of a schoolteacher and a writer. Just before our arrival the fiancé learned that the two-room apartment (in which he had expected to be ensconced with his bride) had been taken away from the teacher and awarded to her former spouse. Disgusted with the collapse of his dream of liberation from his own closet-sized rathole, the bridegroom called the whole thing off. With no hard feelings, however, the jilted fiancée invited him to stay and share the wedding supper—mostly salami and vodka rations contributed by another correspondent and me.

As a friend of Ilena I was politely received where she took me. If I had suspected that her life was being complicated by our association I preferred not to think of it. She knew all about me and there were no avowals between us. But you don't prevent people from walking together just because the road is clearly marked dead end. I simply ignored the sign until Mme. Yasnova came to see me one day and drew it to my attention.

First, did I know how much Ilyenachka's studies were "suffering"? In a few months the term would be over. If her marks fell further she would lose her "stipend," and with it her chance for a career. Secondly, she said awkwardly, she was sorry, she liked me personally, she perfectly understood the situation, and so did Ilena. But politically I was bad for her. Did I know that Ilena had dropped out of the Komsomol? Just dropped out, because she "didn't have time" for meetings. Perhaps that had nothing to do with me. But would *they* know that? She denied that she had been officially warned; her motherly apprehensions could have been entirely a-political also.

It was true I had heard little about Komsomols lately. I had not known that she had resigned. That was a serious step, like leaving the Church in Italy. Had I any right to interrupt the pattern of her life or make it seem unworkable? True, I had never tried to undermine her faith in the regime. What would it have accomplished when I had no alternative to offer? But wasn't our mere association enough to do that?

For a girl like Ilena, her mother continued, separation from the party was a lifetime handicap. On top of that, friendship with a foreigner! Although now a grown woman Ilena was politically still a child, her mother insisted. She had perhaps had her own way too much; she was brilliant but headstrong; she let her emotions rule and ignored consequences. We were close allies now, but how would it be after the war? Who knew?

How much did I think of Ilena? Enough to agree not to see her any more?

Faced with the question suddenly, I realized there could be only one answer to it under the circumstances. I knew her mother was right. I could not let Ilena give up anything irrecoverable for which I could suggest no adequate alternative. School, work, career, all Ilena's future were in jeopardy.

But Ilena was there, too, in tears. And Ilena had a stubborn will of her own. Defiantly she refused to join the compact. Her mother was exaggerating everything, she said—except about her studies. If the Foreign Office did not want her to work for me they would say so. I could not tell Ilena what to do. Neither would I withdraw my promise to Mme. Y., who was also in tears. For an hour we argued in stalemate, mother and daughter in intense, tearful debate I could not follow. Suddenly Ilena, being Ilena, turned all summer and smiles. They embraced; they had made a compromise. Very well, she would catch up on her studies. She would again lead her class. She would stop seeing me, but only until she got her degree.

Thus I won and lost. Mme. Y. and I understood that this was the end. Both mother and daughter again broke into tears, for different reasons. Then they embraced, we all embraced, and they wept some more. Finally we drank a bit of Russian cognac to seal the bargain and they left, smiling!

Romance—in Moscow? The Montagues and the Capulets—ending not with a bang but a whimper. The whole scene seemed unreal to me and I was still reflecting on it when a pale dawn shouldered aside the raw Moscow night.

Ilena stayed away and I did not call her. Moscow again became the city of wintry pinched faces and gray frosty souls and streets dark with ice. I was glad when I had a chance to go to England and the fog and buzzbombs for a few weeks, and then home once more.

For all I knew I would never see Ilena again.

CHAPTER 23

Last Talk with F.D.R.

IN FEBRUARY, 1944, I was once more in Washington waiting for a plane to Europe, when the President returned from Yalta. The day after he made his report on the conference to a joint session of Congress I sent him a line of congratulations which I assumed he might eventually read when I was somewhere in Germany. The White House phoned to invite me over before my departure.

Jonathan Daniels led me into the Oval Room where the President was going over some papers with Admiral Leahy. He looked up and flashed a warm smile as he reached out his big hand.

"You've been doing a lot more traveling than I have," he sang out. "I enjoyed that book of yours, *People on Our Side*. You kept me awake half the night on board the *Quincy*."

I mention this not solely for egotistical reasons, but because the main thesis of that book proposed that the U.S.A. sponsor and help finance a series of post-war colonial liquidations in Asia and ultimately in Africa—the only sure alternatives to a whole series of bloody colonial wars and social revolutions. I had discussed this briefly with the President. I knew that he hoped to make it a cardinal aim of

American post-war policy to bring about the speedy attainment of freedom and equality for all colonial peoples.

Over in Africa he had, he said, listened to Lord Runciman describe the virtues of British colonial rule, apparently oblivious to the fact that visible evidence of native misery on all sides belied his claims. Finally Roosevelt burst out impatiently to say that after all the profits the British had made in Africa it seemed to him that they should have been able to do something better for the people. "Why don't you put back a little to develop the country? Tell me, Your Ludship, how much do you suppose you have sent back to England for every shilling you put in there?"

Runciman made a quick calculation, he said, and came back coolly, "I should say it's paid back a pound on the shilling so far."

" 'And the people,' I told him, 'certainly look it!' "

When he was through with Leahy that day Mr. Roosevelt called me over again and sat me down and started searching around for a paperweight I had sent him, a bust of Gandhi. "Where's Gandhi?" he called to an aide. "See if you can't find my Gandhi."

I had by this time, in 1945, become very pessimistic about the future of our relations with Russia. The President's optimism now renewed my own hope. A day or two after this talk his dispute with Stalin over interpretation of the Polish agreement became serious and it was still unresolved when he died. Some commentators suggested that this "disillusioned" Roosevelt and shattered his hopes of continued collaboration for peace. The speculations seemed premature to me. I believe Roosevelt would have left nothing untried, within the limits of his responsible power and imagination as a great politician, to avoid a post-war armaments race.

In my talk with him of May, 1944, he had made it clear that he wholeheartedly believed in the alternative of frankly accepting the Russian giant as a great and dreadful neighbor with whom we had to learn to live and share world power and authority and whom we had to try to understand if we could not learn to like. At that time I had just finished reading Forrest Davis' series of articles in the *Saturday Evening Post* called "The Great Design." Those articles still give us a remarkably good insight into Roosevelt's thinking about Russia at the time: his aim to remove Russia's historic fear of exclusion from Europe, to convince Russia that capitalist democracies were capable of accommodating necessary changes by peaceful means, to extend a helping hand to the Soviet Union as a "member of the family" in exchange for her co-operation in maintaining world peace, and to open up broad possibilities of useful competition between the two systems, both adhering to an international defense organization—as opposed to reversion to Marxist dogmas about "inevitable" violence and war followed by revolutionary change.

The President said that Davis had "done a good job" but when I asked about his phrase "the great gamble" used to describe Roosevelt's policy toward Russia he said "gamble" was not the word. Was it a "gamble" to co-operate for peace when our alternative was to begin right then to prepare for World War III?

"I am all for trying to make a lasting peace after this war and a world we can live in together," he declared and meant it.

It seemed clear to me that Roosevelt recognized, as a practical politician, the necessity of defining spheres of influence in making a workable peace. Even in 1944 on his return from Teheran he had spoken to me of Stalin's demand to "get the Ukrainian part of Poland back inside Russian borders" as reasonable. He also thought it "reasonable" to turn over East Prussia to Poland. "If what Stalin wants is to get these noblemen's estates [referring to the Polish Ukraine] and give the Poles East Prussia in exchange, there shouldn't be any objection to that, should there?" he asked.

Churchill was far from eager to go along with that arrangement, and doggedly resisted recognizing the paramountcy of the pro-Soviet Polish provisional government set up in Moscow.

Now, in March, 1945, Roosevelt more than ever seemed to think of himself as the peace-maker holding the Big Three together. He was the middle-of-the-roader, he thought, with Churchill representing the right, Stalin the left, and himself the cement of the united front.

"I got along absolutely splendidly with Stalin at Yalta," he told me, almost exultantly. "I feel I finally got to know the man!"

Recalling Litvinov's notes, so full of pessimism, I asked him about the doubts he had expressed, and whether Yalta had cleared up basic questions of long-term controversy, particularly the predicted breakdown of co-operation in Germany. They hadn't settled every detail, of course, but on the whole, he said, Yalta had put everything straight.

"What about Russia's Free Germans and captured officers?" I asked. "Don't you think the Russians intend to use those people for administration of the areas they occupy, and won't this lead to two kinds of governments there?"

"Of course they are going to make use of their Germans to help administer and police," he answered, undisturbed.

"Their Free Germans are Reds," I said. "Does that mean we won't be able to have a common policy [with Russia] in Germany?"

"Obviously the Russians are going to do things in their own way in areas they occupy. But they won't set up a separate administration [independent of the Allied Control Commission] to rival an arrangement made for all Germany."

Formal co-operation in the partitioning of Germany, rather than identity of political aims in the occupation, thus seemed all that he expected at that time. In reality little had been settled at Yalta about the "arrangement" for all Germany, but it was evident that Roosevelt believed all questions could thereafter be negotiated by mutual compromise.

"I got the impression that the Russians are now fully satisfied," he said, "and that we can work out everything together. *I am convinced we are going to get along*." (The emphasis was his.)

Now I think *"Obviously the Russians are going to do things their own way in the areas they occupy"* was probably the controlling phrase there, and perhaps in Roosevelt's concept of a Russian policy in that period. Was it also a key to any *entente* which might have survived the war as regards both Germany and Japan?

I previously said that we went far toward legalizing that principle when we signed the armistices laid down in the Balkans. "In some of these [Soviet-controlled] countries, notably Hungary, Rumania and Bulgaria," wrote General John R. Deane, who was chief of our wartime military mission when I was in Moscow, "the Soviet program has been carried out with the stamp of American approval." * Even in the case of Poland, despite face-saving concessions to the Polish émigrés in England made at Yalta, basic agreements left the Allies little reason to doubt that the Russians were going to be the major influence in the formation of post-war Polish government, for some time to come. We might have set specific limits to the degree of that influence and the way it could be exercised had we attempted it before 1944. But there was no basis for the later claim that we could have altogether superseded it or excluded it. Not, that is, except by World War III.

General acceptance of that reality—the emergence of new spheres of influence as a "natural" outcome of the war and hence the foundations on which peace had to be built—surely was the underlying reason for the "success" of Yalta. To me that alone could explain the buoyant optimism there apparently shared by highly sophisticated politicians

* *The Strange Alliance*, by John R. Deane, N.Y., p. 321.

on both sides who had for years distrusted each other and whose very political existence depended on avoiding self-deception.

"We were absolutely certain," Harry Hopkins told Robert Sherwood after the Crimean conference, "that we had won the first great victory of the peace, and by 'we' I mean *all* of us, the whole civilized human race. The Russians had proved that they could be reasonable and far-seeing and there wasn't any doubt in the minds of the President or any of us that we could live with them and get along peacefully for as far into the future as any of us could imagine. But I have to make one amendment to that—I think we all had in our minds the reservation that we could not foretell what the results [of Yalta] would be if anything should happen to Stalin." *

Stalin! How odd that Hopkins (of all people) should have foreseen possible failure growing out of an untimely death for Stalin rather than F.D.R.! Reared in a democracy, where no man is considered indispensable, it is difficult for us to believe that severance of anything so tenuous as the relations of one individual with a given time could decisively change our fate. And perhaps that was not true of Roosevelt; perhaps the cold war had to be followed inexorably to its foreseeable end—the present truce imposed solely by profound mutual fear, or what Churchill himself finally correctly named "peace by balance of terror."

And yet it is easily possible to list, among mutual provocations which swiftly destroyed Roosevelt's "great design," a half dozen errors committed on our side which he would almost certainly have avoided.

But—back a moment, back to Roosevelt on Russia—and China— and to Mrs. Moses Taylor's harem in Morocco.

CHAPTER 24

From Mrs. Moses Taylor to Yenan

IN MOROCCO I had spent a night in Mrs. Moses Taylor's celebrated Moorish castle outside Marrakech, where F.D.R. and Churchill had been guests a few months earlier. There I heard that the President had asked to be carried up to the love nest, which had deep cushions

* *Roosevelt and Hopkins*, by Robert Sherwood. N.Y., p. 870.

behind discreet marble lattices overlooking a turquoise pool set in harem quarters said to surpass the sultan's palace in splendor.

When I mentioned my visit to Mr. Roosevelt he said he had a story about it which he would give me to "save for my me-moirs." So here it is.

"Did you ever see anything like those bathrooms?" he demanded. "I never knew they made bathtubs like that. I nearly drowned in mine. The trouble with them is that they aren't quite big enough to swim in but if you lose a piece of soap you have to dive to find it!"

"Just who is," I asked, "Mrs. Moses Taylor?"

"I don't know except that she's an American widow with pots of money. She's been living in France and Morocco for years and she doesn't like That Awful Man!"

"Oh? I assumed that she must have given the army the place as a patriotic gesture."

"Not at all. What happened was that Mrs. Taylor knew one of our young vice-consuls. She apparently liked Pétain's France but when the Nazis moved in she got worried finally and went to see her friend, the vice-consul, and asked him to take custody of her castle in Marrakech and look after it for her. Well, when Churchill and I decided to make a trip down there they began looking for a place for us to stay and the vice-consul came up with Mrs. Moses Taylor's wonderful house with its wonderful bathrooms. We had a marvelous stay there and everybody was happy about it except the poor vice-consul."

"Don't tell me he was lost in the bathtubs?"

"No, it was worse. Mrs. Moses Taylor heard about our visit and when the vice-consul got back to Casablanca she was waiting for him in fury. She came into the consulate and berated him for betraying her trust. He wanted to know what he had done. 'Done!' she said. 'Done? Young man, I left my house in your care in good faith that you would protect it. And what have you *done* with it? Why, you made it into a hotel for common tourists and not only that, you put That Awful Man in my very *own* bedroom! How do you think I feel having *that* man sleeping in *my* bed! As if that wasn't enough, you put Churchill in my house, too! Everybody knows nobody in England hob-nobs with him but the Communists! I want my property back immediately!' The young man apologized profusely but he couldn't help her. At that point our army decided to requisition Mrs. Moses Taylor's castle and make a hostel out of it. She's been mad as a hatter ever since!"

For once I could add a detail. "When I was there," I said, "the bedrooms you and Mr. Churchill slept in had been *sealed up,* at Mrs.

Taylor's request so I was told. We all assumed it was done to *honor* your visit; but now I get the point!"

F.D.R. raised his eyebrows. "I didn't know about that but I'm not surprised. The old lady probably had the rooms fumigated first to prevent any possible contamination!"

Roosevelt liked to tell anecdotes and I liked to hear them, so that our conversation was very far from systematic; but if there was one recurrent subject on which it was less desultory it was China. He was baffled and yet acutely fascinated by the complexity of what was happening there, which nobody explained satisfactorily to him: myself included. He understood that our wartime aid was actually a form of political intervention in China and he genuinely desired, I concluded, that it be used in ways which would both keep China in the war and bring about social, economic and political progress. But how to do it?

By 1945 Roosevelt was more than ever puzzled by Chiang Kai-shek as a man and a politician. When I last saw him he had just heard about a breakdown in negotiations Pat Hurley was then conducting between Yenan and Chungking. It was "very disappointing news," coming after earlier reports that a formula had been worked out. The President said Chiang Kai-shek had "raised some perfectly absurd objections" to the Communists' requests for certain guarantees along lines of a bill of rights which appeared "perfectly reasonable" to F.D.R. These requests were implicitly promised in an agreement to legalize the Communist party, which General Hurley himself had signed as a witness at Yenan.*

Mr. Roosevelt asked me what I thought of Chiang, and whether I "liked" him. I replied briefly along lines I had already written in *The Battle for Asia,* not very flattering, I fear. As for whether I "liked" him, I had interviewed him several times but I really did not know him personally. He said "hm" and looked at me shrewdly and went on:

"I never was able to form any opinion of Chiang at Cairo. When I thought about it later I realized that all I knew was what Mme. Chiang had told me about her husband and what he thought. She was always there to phrase all the answers. I got to know her but this fellow Chiang! I never could break through to him at all. I'm hoping Pat Hurley will be able to tell me a little more when he gets back."

By now he recognized the growing strength of the Chinese Communists as the effective government of the guerrilla areas. He was considering giving them direct help against Japan, as a matter of military

* *U.S. Army in World War II. C.B.I. Theatre, Stilwell's Command Problems,* by Charles F. Romanus and Riley Sunderland, Washington, D.C., 1956.

expediency. He may also have thought it useful to beat the Russians there; he asked me now whether they were "real" Communists and whether the Russians were bossing them. Were they aiming at a proletarian dictatorship or only, as some people were saying, "agrarian reformers." I repeated what I had written many times: that their immediate program was agrarian reform, or agrarian egalitarianism, but that they were Marxists with Communism as their ultimate goal.

The President asked a few questions about what, concretely, the Eighth Route (Communist) Army could do with our aid in North China. He then said that we were going to land supplies and liaison officers on the North China coast, as we drew closer to Japan. All this was of course off the record. Heretofore, we had given no military help to the Communist forces. I assumed that in any such commando operation we would try to find Kuomintang people to work with also. I wondered how the Reds, who controlled most of the North China population beyond the roads, railways and cities garrisoned by a Japanese, would react to that.

"I suppose the position is that as long as we recognize Chiang as the sole government we must go on sending all supplies exclusively through him? We can't support two governments in China, can we?" I asked.

"Well, I've been working with two governments there." The President threw his head back decisively. "I intend to go on doing so until we can get them together."

This last conversation reflected a certain new coolness in attitude toward Chiang Kai-shek and a growing impatience with his obstinate resistance to basic reforms necessary for his own self-preservation. It was now five months since the Generalissimo had won his personal victory by forcing Roosevelt to withdraw General Stilwell rather than give him the authority to reorganize, retrain and otherwise impose the minimum improvements needed to save the non-Communist Chinese armies, and the government itself, from complete disintegration. The Generalissimo had had his way, but at the expense of bringing to the President's close attention the most noisome details of inner corruption, demoralization and incompetence in Chiang's military and political household. As the authors of *Stilwell's Command Problems* shrewdly observed:

"In retrospect the Generalissimo's triumph acquires an aspect it probably did not wear at the time. It was the last diplomatic victory he was to win for many years. In May, 1943, at the Washington Conference, Roosevelt had been solicitous in his concern not only for

China but for the personal position and prestige of the Generalissimo. Not three months after the Generalissimo had forced Stilwell's recall, Roosevelt met with the Prime Minister and Marshal Stalin on Russian soil at Yalta, February, 1945. The attitude the President there adopted toward the territory and interests of China suggests that the Generalissimo's triumph of October, 1944, was one of the steps that led to the Manchuria partition of February, 1945." *

What a difference it might have made in the Generalissimo's fate if he had kept Stilwell in command, and thus been able to hold him, and through him, the U.S.A., responsible for the integrity of Manchuria after the war! Most of the terms covering Russia's entry into the war against Japan might still have been accepted even if Stilwell had held that responsibility in China. The end results might have been vastly different.

Just what did Roosevelt, who then had these secret terms of Yalta concerning Manchuria and China fresh in mind, foresee as the possible future of our own relations with the Chinese Communists? What did he mean when he said that day, "I'm working with two governments [in China] and intend to go on doing so . . ." ? Did he regard the presence of our diplomatic and military observers in Yenan as a form of de facto "recognition," and an earnest of American material aid to come?

The answers still remain a mystery.

"Don't forget to write," he called as he sped me on my way with a warm handshake, "and tell me what you see."

A month later he was dead—"laid sweet in his grave," as Emerson said of Washington, and "the hope of humanity not yet subjugated in him."

Plans for military collaboration with Yenan were soon afterward abandoned. With that went our chance to find out what the Chinese Communists would do if given help by the Western allies, as happened in the case of Tito and Yugoslavia.

* Ibid., p. 469.

CHAPTER 25

First in Vienna

I RETURNED to Europe and entered Germany barely in time to collect on the *Post's* promise to let me cover the last phase of Hitler. As we moved swiftly from Stuttgart to Munich and into Austria I discovered what peaceful, obedient and ingratiating hypocrites defeated Nazis could be. Inwardly they regretted nothing, as Marshal Kesselring had the candor to state openly, but "the mechanical inferiority" that had lost them the war. There was no sense of shame or guilt in the Germans I saw, and nothing like the humility and deep moral shock that I was to sense, some months later, in the defeated Japanese.

Germans in the West began at once to offer their full support to the U.S. Army against Russia, while Germans in the East volunteered to help the Red Army demolish the Yanks. If the Allies were now to punish Germany by keeping her divided between them, it was equally clear that the Germans instinctively felt that their own recovery depended on their ability to keep the Allies divided over Germany. That was my conclusion after interviewing top Nazi war criminals from Goering to von Rundstedt, and talking to rank-and-file Germans by the dozen.

The day after V-E Day I was in Salzburg, hunting for a loose car. Now the Germans were surrendering all their transport and I wanted wheels of my own. General J.M. "Iron Mike" O'Daniel of the Third Division helped by giving me an official license number and an order entitling me to any motor I could grab. My needs were modest. No Daimlers, Mercedes or Dusenbergs for me; I had seen too many junked on the road for want of a minor part. I prowled the ordnance dumps looking for a German Ford. When at last I found one, "Kilroy was there," in the person of a tough sergeant asserting squatter's rights. While we argued, a young officer in charge of the car pool came up and I introduced myself.

Finally I met a soldier who had heard of a war correspondent— besides Ernie Pyle.

"Are you *China* Snow?" he said, believe it or not. "Guess I've read about everything you ever wrote. My name's Ledmann. What can I do for you?"

Recovering from the shock I told him to call me Ed and I brandished my order from O'Daniel. "Just a—just this one very small Ford," I begged.

"Okay, Ed, it's yours," he said with a flourish. "Call me Bob. Why, in a way *you're* why I joined the army. Wanted to see China! I studied Chinese at the University of California."

"So then the army sent you to Germany. That figures."

We shook hands as the sergeant shuffled off in disgust. I drove Frau Lizzie to Schloss-Kleisheim, the old Hapsburg palace which was temporary divisional headquarters. For the first time I began to believe we had won the war.

During the subsequent week I drove around the Austrian Alps, to Hitler's lodge at Berchtesgaden, to Innsbruck and the Yugoslav border, to Atter See and Trawn See, and to help liberate a cache of champagne and fine wines in one of Ribbentrop's guest houses. Then I crossed the Danube to visit Linz, where I joined forces with Jack Bell of the *Chicago Daily News*. We were the first American correspondents to reach Mautthausen concentration camp and we found an O.S.S. lieutenant there named Jack Taylor. He had been slated for execution but in the last-minute confusion had managed to survive by oversight.

It was Taylor who first gave me the idea of going on to Vienna, which was then forbidden territory. Nobody knew exactly what the Russians were doing there, whether they were setting up a puppet Red regime or were going to honor their agreement with their Allies to help Austria establish a freely elected government. U. S. troops then occupied Austria west of the Enns River; British troops held the Brenner pass and the Austrian Tyrol; and the Russians held Eastern Austria, including Vienna and the hundred miles west of it up to the east bank of the Enns.

Taylor introduced me to an Austrian inmate, Dr. Hans Becker, a former cabinet minister in the Dollfuss government whom Hitler had first imprisoned, at Dachau, as early as 1938. Though free at last Dr. Becker was, like many at Mautthausen, too weak to move. In any case he could not have crossed the Russian lines. But he knew about the new "all-party government" in Vienna; the underground had kept him well informed. He entreated me to try to get to the capital and bring out the story, as well as news of his wife whom he had not seen for seven years.

Encouraged by Becker's introductions to people in Vienna, I decided to try to crash the Russian lines. I went to Enns, where our troops faced the Russians across a narrow bridge. Colonel William E. Carraway, our G-2 under General Reinhardt at that outpost, flatly told me the projected trip was impossible; the Russians absolutely refused to let any American beyond the bridge into their part of Austria. I wouldn't succeed, he was sure, but he wouldn't prevent me from trying. I was comforted with the knowledge that he would report me missing if he heard nothing of me after two weeks.

Jack Bell wanted to join up and I said fine. We picked up K-rations and whiskey, not enough, but something. Then I drove Frau Lizzie up to the bridge and showed my pass, made out by General Reinhardt. The guard shook his head and wouldn't let the car through, but I yelled *"Tovarishch!* Boris!" and out came his superior, Captain Boris Melbiakov. He knew me, the Amerikanski who could speak a little Russian. I had walked over the day before and we had exchanged drinks and toasts and hailed eternal Russo-American friendship.

Now I brought out the promised whiskey and we went inside the toll house to sample it. Again the young Russian woman who had been with *Gospadin Kapitan* appeared; again we exchanged compliments; again we were allies. This time I asked why I couldn't "drive up the road a few miles, to visit the Hapsburg palace." Melbiakov clammed up, insisting that his orders forbade anyone to cross the bridge. I tried my trump. I still had my Moscow press credentials and a resident's permit. I flashed them before his eyes. I mentioned "my friends" the Russian generals I had interviewed—and some I had not.

"You mean to tell me, comrade," I said in a hurt voice, "that after all we have been to each other I can't have one small look at your old imperialist palace?"

"Orders!" he yelled, but he was weakening. We had another drink, we sang another song. Boris praised Americans, I praised Russians, we all praised the alliance, victory, world peace and brotherhood!

"Not even one little old look at your palace?" said I.

Vera said *pochemu nyet* to Boris.

"Pochemu nyet?" Boris suddenly asserted rather than asked. He picked up his field telephone. He spoke to his commanding officer. Enormous static ensued. Boris held the receiver to my ear. I heard some snorts, barks, splitting oaths, then loud music. A celebration going on in their street, too. My friend took the phone again, listened for several minutes, shrugged at me, yelled *da da* and *sposiba,* and hung up.

"Be quick," said he. "What is it! Go, I tell you! Well, be off—"

Leaving the whiskey behind, Jack and I fled for—we hoped —Vienna. Our main regret as we rolled away was that we had not brought along more gas. We had two jerry cans, ten gallons, hardly enough to reach Vienna and return.

Frau Lizzie performed like a darling. We were stopped five or six times at roadblocks "womaned" by the big blonde Amazons the Red Army brought to Europe for traffic M.P.'s. All we did was to show my Moscow credentials and our U. S. Army accreditations, smile and look idiotically dumb. Helped by Lizzie's new coat of regulation olive-drab paint and official numerals and insignia, we got by.

At dusk we were inside Vienna, following Becker's hand-drawn map, down empty streets, to the apartment of Mr. and Mrs. Hans Roggenberg, who were to hide us. They were Austrian-born Canadians who, caught in Vienna at the outbreak of war, had secretly joined the Austrian underground while posing as loyal to Hitler. Their apartment on top of a six-story building, opposite the old palace, had been bombed and had no light. A third of their roof was gone. Once they had read Becker's letter they made us comfortable in a sheltered corner and gave us ersatz coffee. Then they helped us, with Austrian connivance, hide our car in the abandoned U. S. Embassy.

We fed the starving Roggenbergs some K-rations and again regretted not having filled our Ford with them. After a month of Red Army occupation Vienna had no more horses, cats or dogs to be butchered. The bread ration was cut to one loaf per week. Somehow the Austrians had expected the Red Army to feed them better. They had forgotten that 600,000 of them had fought in the Wehrmacht. True, the Allied declarations had drawn sharp distinctions between Germany and Austria. The latter was to be "re-established in freedom and independence" under Four-Power supervision. But the Russians weeded out the pro-Nazis and did not share our sentimentalism about the Viennese.

The Red Army was having its turn now, here at the end of a long, cruel, blood-stained road, the 1500-mile march from Stalingrad, every mile of it bordered with Russian dead. They had come in hungry and thirsty, their eyes dazed with the smoke of war, and they took what they could find, not too bothered about apportioning guilt between the German and his cousin. Austrians looked and spoke like Germans. Had they not cheered Hitler and his moment of glory in Russia?

The Red Army's first act was to requisition food, cattle, transportation and labor, with its own needs taking priority. No wonder every Austrian I met asked one question: "When are the Americans com-

ing?" The good Americans, who arrived self-contained and self-suf-
ficent in conquered countries, who demanded nothing from the people,
who even fed the enemy's slaves in concentration camps.

Remembering the good Dr. Herbert Hoover, Viennese believed he
would be generous again. The Red Army's food demands were not
the real reason for the famine. The Germans had looted the city before leaving; the Reds merely finished the job. Now the occupational
army was reduced to only a few thousand, however, and the main cause
of the food crisis was the total breakdown of transport, the isolation
of the city market from the Austrian hinterland. The Russians were
in no hurry to correct that. They sent home every wheel or machine
they could trace to German ownership. Dr. Karl Renner, the aging
former President of the Republic that Hitler conquered and smashed,
was alarmed. He asked Marshal Tolbukhin, the Russian commandant,
if they weren't mistaking Austria for Germany.

"Don't worry," the Marshal replied, "when we are all through with
you Austrians you will still have enough to buy out what will be left of
Germany! Then the Americans will come and give you more than we
take away."

It was the Roggenbergs who told us of four American flyers who
were held at the Vienna University Klinik. They took us by back
alleys to visit them. The Americans had been shot down over Austria
just before the end of the war, and the Russians, coming upon them in
a wayside dressing station, had brought them in by truck as far as the
Klinik. Then they too had forgotten them. Promised special rations
never arrived. The flyers had, like the other patients, been living on
nothing but bread, a few ounces daily. One lad was still extremely
weak from a leg amputation. The other three, though badly hurt and
seriously undernourished, could be moved.

"Suppose we took them back with us?" I asked the director of the
Klinik.

"*Verboten!* I am responsible. They can't be moved without the
Russian commandant's personal authorization."

"What if we just came and took them away by *force majeur?*" said
we. "What could you do about it, eh?"

He shrugged his shoulders and smiled. He could, he thought, turn
his back. We left the last of our spare rations with the flyers after promising not to return to Enns without them.

During the five days we stayed in the Roggenbergs' flat we secretly
saw nearly every member of Dr. Karl Renner's Austrian "cabinet."
We even met and interviewed Franz Honner, the minister of the in-

terior. He was an Austrian Communist, but he did not betray our presence to the Russians.

Our gas reserve dropped to the point of no return, and gas couldn't be bought at any price. The Russians had made it a capital offense to hoard gas against official confiscation orders, and they held the only supplies. We thought of disclosing ourselves to them, to appeal for help, but now we had the flyers counting on us to get out. What if Tolbukhin threw us in jail for illegal entry or as spies?

At last the Roggenbergs persuaded the local representative of the Swiss Red Cross, a Mr. Fern, to part with some petrol he had been hoarding against the possible need for a quick get-away: first, from the Nazis, and now from the Reds. He filled one jerry can for us as if it were his life blood. It might have been better if it had been. The fuel he gave us, we were soon to discover, was heavily diluted with water.

We left loaded with messages: from the Roggenbergs to British intelligence; from Mr. Fern to his government; from Mrs. Becker to her husband; from Austrian underground leaders to the *Resistance* in Paris, and to Milovan Djilas, in Belgrade. Cardinal Innitzer, whom we had stealthily visited in war-torn St. Stephen's Cathedral, had given us an appeal to broadcast for food and medical supplies. His ruins were filled with refugees. Then we picked up Green, Lawson and Skinner, our flyers. It was exceedingly painful to all to have to leave their buddy behind. We swept down the Ringstrasse and out of Vienna the way we had arrived. Incredibly we were again not challenged until we were well out on the highway.

For the last forty miles we were convinced that Lizzie would choke on Fern's gas. I had to stop every five miles to take the carburetor apart and clean it. None of my invalids aboard could help. Jack Bell had lost an arm in World War I and couldn't clean a carburetor, but he was the best one-armed driver I ever knew. He was a lucky one, too, because just before dark we at last crept and coughed our way onto the Enns bridge. I was relieved that Boris was not at the gate. Another Russian officer, with orders to prohibit anyone from going *eastward,* had to admit that he had no specific orders to prevent us from proceeding *westward*. He let us through.

Next day we gave General Reinhardt and Colonel Carraway a detailed account of our trip, the first report on Austria under Red occupation to reach SCAEF.

I returned to Paris and filed my own stories to the *Post*. I took Frau Lizzie down the Loire and across the then deserted early-summer roads of Southern France. We spent ten days at the Carlton on the

Riviera, at army expense. Again as I lay browning in the sun at Cannes, I thought that victory was ours, but I was not to enjoy its fruits for long. Back in Paris I found orders from home to hurry on to the Far East, by way of Russia.

But how could I abandon Frau Lizzie? The problem was solved for me by Bob Capa, Morgan Beatty, Charles Collingwood, Jack O'Riley and Jack Belden, who relieved me of eight hundred dollars in a murderous poker game. I had to sell Liz to Henry Brandon of *The London Times* to buy my way out. That was nothing; Collingwood lost his Dusenberg *and* his Mercedes the same night. O'Riley probably bought his Bucks County farm with the winnings.

Days later, in Moscow, I heard by way of grapevine G-2 of the aftermath of the Snow-Bell breakthrough to Vienna. When our reports were published in America they had started a chain of inquiry which ended in an investigation by Tolbukhin to see how we had "taken" his command without his knowledge. Jack and I had never once been stopped or interrogated by any of the security police. Since neither of us explained in our dispatches who had helped us in and out, or mentioned names or places of friends in Vienna, Tolbukhin probably never found out.

Jack and I had a clean beat on the Vienna story that lasted for six weeks.

CHAPTER 26

Hiroshima in Moscow

WHEN I FIRST saw Moscow it was a city still under partial encirclement: late fall and already bitter cold, no moon, a total blackout at night, streets sheathed in ice, buildings camouflaged and the Muscovites covered up, too, only red noses and anxious eyes peering out under padded cotton or fur hats, their faces drawn with hunger and fear.

Three years later, when I went from Paris through Stockholm and Helsinki, and entered Russia by way of Leningrad, it was early summer. Perfect days and pale blue skies lent some of their serenity to a harried people. No longer formless padded bundles, they emerge in recognizable human shapes; their winter-shut faces open, they smile. Light cotton dresses reveal that the women have figures, and the young Russians very good ones. The long white nights give young men leisure to pursue romance; darkness lasts only three or four hours, in the north, and everybody lives outdoors.

Leningrad still conveyed a sense of beauty along the Nevsky Prospekt. Years of neglect, followed by the long German siege (which cost the city a quarter of a million lives) made it a bad jest now to call it "the Paris of Russia," as it once proudly boasted. Leningrad was still a "window on Europe," as Peter the Great said when he built it, but it would take a long time to restore its past greatness.

In Moscow again I was back in Asia. A hot new fear would soon begin to spread, after the bomb fell on Hiroshima. Even before then, distrust and suspicion were poisoning the atmosphere between the Allies. The chance of peace talks being held in any spirit of mutual accommodation dwindled daily.

Soon after my arrival in Moscow in June I met Max Litvinov at a diplomatic reception. Were things better or worse, I asked, than when I had last spoken to him, before Yalta?

"Worse," said he, promptly. "Why did you Americans wait till right now to begin opposing us in the Balkans and Eastern Europe? You should have done this three years ago. Now it's too late, and your complaints only arouse suspicion here."

Few Americans realized, then or later, that Russia had begun pressing us, as early as December, 1941, to reach agreements not only on the future of all Eastern Europe, but "on such far-flung subjects as the future of the Rhineland, Bavaria, and Eastern Prussia," as Harry Hopkins pointed out.* The American position was that everything had to wait for settlement by a peace conference; Congress would never ratify secret agreements. Secretary Cordell Hull's delay was fatal.

Ambassador Harriman was painfully aware of this when, confronted by the fait accompli of Red Army occupation of the Balkans, he approved of the terms of the armistices offered the peoples there. From then on the Russians expected us to accept the same pattern elsewhere. When I asked Harriman whether we had not erred in failing to reach advance understandings about all these areas he took the position that we had been "deceived" and that our troubles were entirely due to Russian "bad faith." I quote from my journal:

"Harriman said [in confidence] that he had first supported the general policy of extending lend-lease aid to Russia without any polit-

* See *Roosevelt and Hopkins,* page 401.

ical strings, i.e., without demanding [concrete] political commitments in exchange. He himself initiated the principle of it, at the first Harriman-Beaverbrook conference on the matter. But after our deliveries increased substantially and lend-lease became a vital factor, he changed his mind, Harriman said, and would then have been ready to insist on terms, in Eastern Europe, 'to impose our own pattern there.' Nevertheless, he kept that opinion to himself; he did not challenge Cordell Hull's policy of deferring serious political debate till the peace conference.

"Of course," said Averell, "if we could have foreseen events we might have acted differently. But who could anticipate Soviet behavior in Eastern Europe? Nobody!"

In fact plenty of people did foresee it, even before we signed the prototype armistices. And Harriman himself was not so naive as the foregoing sounds; not toward the end, anyway. How many a diplomat must have understood, at the end of an assignment in Moscow, the feelings which made Chekhov exclaim: "What if this life were only a rough draft? What if we could throw it all away and start on a clean sheet?"

Sir Archibald Clark-Kerr, then British Ambassador in Moscow, gave me this off-the-record picture of President Truman at Potsdam:

"On first contact Mr. Truman made a very good impression, with those blue eyes magnified under heavy lenses, his energy and vitality, his directness and candor, his forthright subaltern air of do or die. But as the conference wore on his vacillations became rather trying. He would take up a point one day and say, 'No! No, no!' beating the table with the sides of his hands. Then everything would come to a halt. But the next morning, after he had talked to his advisers, he would come back and pass over the same point with a mere nod of approval. Pretty soon people stopped taking his snap judgments seriously."

Roosevelt's tragic death, which deprived Churchill, at Potsdam, of his closest wartime collaborator, Churchill's own cruelly timed political defeat and retirement in the midst of the conference, and Truman's newness in office and hence his lack of intimate knowledge of past private conversations among the Big Three—all played into Stalin's hands.

In the absence of any specific Anglo-American accord to guide us for remodeling and reforming Europe, Russia did have the immeasurable advantage of knowing what she wanted, which was simply to *change* the pattern of life wherever Soviet influence could reach. As is known, Truman also innocently strengthened Stalin's hand by ordering Eisenhower to withdraw all U.S. forces from a great area of Central Europe which the Americans had overrun in the last days of the Wehrmacht. This vast belt of land, 400 miles long by as much as 120 miles wide, included a large slice of Germany and Czechoslovakia which a prior allied zoning agreement had allotted to the Red occupational forces. Churchill had pleaded with Truman to postpone withdrawal of our troops until after the Potsdam meeting. He wanted to use this means of bringing pressure on Stalin to live up to Churchill's expectations concerning Poland, and to slow down the bolshevization of the Balkans. Truman's advisers thought otherwise, and the order, which Churchill tells us in his memoirs "struck a knell in his breast," was carried out. Churchill felt that this costly and premature decision made it certain that Stalin would prevail, at Potsdam, on the most important questions left over from Yalta.

Relying on his advisers, Truman had made another mistake. This was the President's abrupt cancellation, immediately after V-E Day, of all lend-lease to Russia. The advantages of keeping lend-lease alive for purposes of negotiation, quite aside from humanitarianism, seemed obvious. To end it in such a tactless manner needlessly aroused suspicion and deep resentment just as Russia was about to fulfill her commitment to us to enter the war against Japan. As a result of these errors, the United States needlessly threw away its most powerful pieces in the chess game at Potsdam.

Russia's alternative was always implicit in the Red Army's new position in Eastern Europe won by victory over Germany. She could, if deprived of American aid in her post-war reconstruction needs, return to the old lines of class war and revive the Comintern, to cause the Western Allies a maximum amount of difficulty in their attempts to restore the pre-war status quo in Europe. Only the blind could fail to see that Russia could no longer, in Stalin's words again, be encircled "with impunity." *

It may be questioned by historians whether it was not still another decisive error completely to exclude the atomic bomb from Potsdam bargaining with Russia. At any rate it was a mistake soon afterward to *announce,* as Churchill and Truman did, that the secrets were to be held as an American monopoly, especially since scientists knew that they were already within Russia's early reach.

With the surprise atomic bombing of Hiroshima, two days before

* In *Stalin Must Have Peace,* N.Y., 1947, p. 182, I myself pointed out that the attempt was "quite certain to fail" and could only lead to a rearmament race of the most dreadful and futile nature.

Russia declared war on Japan, we were all inevitably committed to a new and different kind of war among ourselves. In Moscow you could feel it in the air. From then on intelligent Russians knew that a fearful and altogether unprecedented power was now to become the arbiter of their lives. Once more their hopes of any real relaxation of tension in the world were doomed.

The atom bomb was played down in the Soviet press but the army knew, and soon every soldier, that they must have it. Weary workers knew it, too. The generation chewed up by past Five Year plans all knew that yet more years of sacrifice would be demanded now to crack atoms for their gods. They knew that this was a trick "messieurs the capitalists" were not going to lend-lease to them. Scientists knew, teachers knew and even the children of Moscow knew that Russia must not lag behind us in the atom age. And yet every sentient person in Russia also soon knew, almost as soon as every conscious American knew, that great war, war among the giants, was simply no longer possible if man were to survive.

Everything that war had taught us up to this moment became obsolescent a few days after Hiroshima. The yet unwritten memoirs of the statesmen and generals were already out of date. Wartime lessons and agreements now meant far less, or far more, than the words said. Pre-atomic concepts of defense and offense, of buffer zones and balances of power, of social systems and political systems, were abruptly rendered archaic. Man's knowledge of Nature seemed suddenly doubled or trebled, and most of it was knowledge learned since all but the youngest of politicians and statesmen had left school. Despite this, we would follow the old worn ruts for years before men grew new habits of universal thought and action commensurate with the awful power unleashed by the atom.

Eisenhower himself seemed to foresee that at the time he came to Russia with Marshal Zhukov. Ike was the first foreigner Stalin ever invited to stand beside him on the marble podium, over Lenin, in Red Square. Just below them I also stood for five hours that day, watching the victory parade. Returning with Zhukov from a visit to a collective farm, Ike invited seventeen generals to the American Embassy for an informal snack. By the time they left, early in the morning, they were all making harmony with "I've Been Working on the Railroad"—led by an NKVD officer! But none of this deceived anyone about the big atomic mushroom now hanging over the future, as Ike admitted one afternoon in Moscow.

"Before the atom bomb was used," he answered a private question privately, "I would have said yes, I was sure we could keep the peace with Russia. Now, I don't know. I had hoped the bomb wouldn't figure in this war. Until now I would have said that we three, Britain with her mighty fleet, America with the strongest air force, and Russia with the strongest land force on the continent, we three could have guaranteed the peace of the world for a long, long time to come. But now, I don't know. People are frightened and disturbed all over. Everyone feels insecure again."

It is also interesting to remember now that neither Eisenhower nor other American officers then in Moscow were anything but pleased with the announced terms of the "alliance" Stalin had made with Chiang Kai-shek's National government in China. Major-General John R. Deane, chief of our mission in Moscow, thought that we had "definitely settled the Chinese internal question, and sealed the fate of the Chinese Reds." He told me in mid-August that "both the spirit and the letter of Stalin's agreement excluded any possibility of Soviet help for the Chinese Communists." He went on:

"General Wedemeyer [Stilwell's successor as commander in China] is completely confident that we can realize our policy of support for Chiang Kai-shek, and he ought to know. Stalin has what he wants in Manchuria—the Port Arthur base and his railway—and he isn't going to jeopardize that in a Chinese civil war. Even if he did, we have too big a headstart. Wedemeyer says we now have armed and trained thirty-six divisions for Chiang, by far the most powerful army ever seen in China. Stalin's treaty is the finishing touch for the Communists. With our backing Chiang will force them to surrender or break up into guerrilla bands and outlaws easily destroyed piecemeal."

I didn't agree. I said: "The Chinese Red Army has become too big, it controls too large a part of China, it holds the allegiance of too many people, to be liquidated even by Stalin."

John Davies, who was then second secretary of our Embassy in Moscow, and the only person there who knew China very well, thought as I did. We had both read something else between the lines of the dispatches from China—not published locally. Manifestoes issued from Yenan by Mao Tse-tung and Chu Teh were totally at variance with the terms of the Stalin-Chiang pact before it was published. Right after Russia entered the war against Japan, Mao and Chu had denounced Chiang Kai-shek as a "fascist." They called upon Japanese troops in China to surrender, *not* to the National government, but to their own Red commanders. Obviously Moscow had failed to inform Yenan of the terms of either the Yalta agreement or its negotiations with Chiang Kai-shek for the Sino-Soviet pact. In neither case did Russia make the slightest overt move to champion the special interests of the Communists of China.

"Here is more proof," I wrote in summing up a discussion on the subject with John Davies at the time, "that Kremlin policy is first and always aimed at advancing the national interests of Russia, and cannot place the interests of any other party on the same level. The effect in this case will not destroy the Chinese party but *will* strengthen its nationalism and independence."

When Mao Tse-tung did belatedly discover what sweeping official support Stalin pledged to Chiang he could not but reverse Yenan's policy and accept the offer of General Patrick Hurley, our maverick Ambassador in Chungking, to arrange for peaceful negotiations with the Nationalists. But in his heart Mao did not, as historians are now well aware, accept the advice which Stalin tendered to his Chinese comrades, at this time, to accept the best terms they could get from Chiang and resubmit their territory to his command.

Mao's first responsibility now was not to Stalin but to China's own large independent revolutionary forces. Not even the atomic bomb was to cheat them of an early triumph.

CHAPTER 27

Sweet and Bitter

A FEW DAYS after I returned to Moscow I had lunch with Sir Archibald Clark-Kerr. Suddenly he asked, "Why did you come back again —really?"

"Isn't that an odd question? I go where I'm sent."

"Don't try to fool me, young man. Your story is China now, and you know it."

"I do, and I'm on my way," I claimed, and I believed it. "As soon as Russia gets into the war with Japan I'm going out by way of Manchuria." Who could have foreseen that Japan would surrender two or three days after Russia declared war, or that Russia's Manchurian frontier would then be buttoned up as much as ever?

Just as I left him, Archie persisted. "You are not keeping anything from me," he growled. "She's been pointed out to me at the theatre, you know. She's very charming and I don't blame you."

So much for privacy in Moscow, I thought, as I walked across the Kremlin bridge above the dark, gray, swollen, early-summer river. But Archie was wrong. I had seen nothing of her since my arrival, and I didn't intend to, nor to linger around Moscow a day longer than necessary.

When I reached my room in the Metropole the door was unlocked, as I had left it. Even before I entered I sensed that she was there. In the old-fashioned alcove, with its worn velvet drapes that bravely tried to make a sitting room of the place by day, she sat quite still, her proud youthful figure chic in a Stockholm dress, her face as radiant as spring.

"Ilyachka!"

"*Lubimets!*"

When she finally spoke again, laughing and crying, she said, "School is over. I am free! I came through as the first in my class!"

"That's—wonderful!"

"*Khorosho?* So now—I take my job? I want to help you."

"No." I tried to make it sound firm. "No courier needed. I know my way around now."

"You can make me believe that?" She stretched the corners of her eyes wide with her fingers and laughed. "I can see through you. No courier? Good, then I increase myself to secretary."

"Ilena, you don't want to be a secretary. Why, you're, you're too good for that. You're a full-fledged curator or something by now!"

"Nonsense. I shall go to Mr. Molotov and ask him to write me down as secretary officially by the Narkomindel, yes?"

"It will ruin you all the same."

"Ruin?" She twirled and ended with her arms wide and pale hair flying. "Then *ruin,* let her commence! At once!"

She had her way and I was very lucky. She was not just a decorative companion but a good helper who knew how to partition work from personal life. We went on excursions and interviews and met a few celebrities, more available in the brief interregnum of peace, people such as Ilyushin, the aircraft designer, and Dmitri Shostakovich, the composer, Mikhail Sholokhov, the novelist, and Professor Tsitsin, head of the Soviet Academy of Sciences.

Tsitsin, a robust extrovert who makes me think now of Walter Slezak, boasted then about Soviet perfection of "perennial wheat," which turned out to be a premature claim. He also told us another Soviet "secret": the Elixir—no less—of Long Life, an odd thing to find in the land of sudden death. According to Tsitsin, Russian scientists had established the reason for longevity by research among centenarians in the U.S.S.R. All their men and women over 100, one as old as 140, had lived all their lives on honey as a main or staple item of diet. And not just honey, but the *dregs* of honey. They were mostly bee-keepers, these old ones, who could not afford to eat the refined honey they produced but consumed the "waste" at the bottom of the hive, where the heaviest concentrations of bee pollen and other excretions collected. The Academicians were now conducting extensive research into the nutritive properties of various kinds of pollen. To cynics it all sounded suspiciously like a pleasant project designed to keep Prof. Tsitsin well supplied with honey. He admitted it was part of his diet. For the general Moscow public honey was unobtainable.

"I should live," Ilena drily added later, "to see just some of the top of the honey and let Tsitsin eat the bottom and live twice as long!" But I was so impressed with Tsitsin's claims that I wrote a humorous story for the *Post* about him called "Don't Throw Away Those Old Bee-hives!" Ben Hibbs, sensibly, filed it in the basement.

One afternoon Ilena came in smiling and shivering at the same time. "Can you guess where I was last night?" she asked, pulling her eyes wide and looking straight at me. "The Lubyanka. By 'invitation' to tea! Try to refuse! They wanted to know about you!"

"And what did you tell them?"

"What was there to tell? What you think of Russia? What questions do you ask me? What politics we discuss."

"What did you say?"

"That we never discuss politics. Do we—much?"

"Of course not."

"They were interested in your former secretary, Cecilia. And Miss Hu Tsi-pang, the Chinese correspondent. They want to know what she says to you in Chinese!"

"Yes?"

"I do not know anything about Cecilia and I cannot understand Chinese!"

The attitude of Ilena's friends toward Communism reminded me of Catholics of my boyhood toward the catechismic teachings of the Church. Here Communism came with one's mother's milk, a condition of life. Ilena had been through years of classroom study of Marx, Lenin and Stalin but I rarely heard her quote one of them. She was fascinated, however, by stories I told her about Chinese Communists, real, fighting revolutionaries. They were as remote and exotic to her as the people in the *Arabian Nights*.

To be a Communist in Russia was not bad form but good form—or good conformism. Many youths were dissatisfied with aspects of the regime and hated Stalin enough to fight against him, if given the opportunity. But they did not think of reviving private capitalism. Youth wanted more of everything for itself but gave no more sign of wanting to be ruled by millionaires or their deputies than Americans exhibit any conscious yearning for commissars. The huge gap between the pretensions of Soviet politicians and the social realities was obvious enough, but the Soviet youth had no more difficulty reconciling it with his ambitions than the average opportunist in any established society had in conforming to its folklore in order to advance his own interests. It was only in the older generation that you met people troubled by the disappearance of that unselfish idealism which had for them been the spirit of the revolution.

One of Ilena's aunts, whom I shall call Katerina Mikhailovna, had some interesting things to say to me about the change in this respect.

Katcha was nearing fifty then, a short, dark, tired woman with fine black eyes. She made a living teaching, she spoke some English and she had once spent a whole year in the U.S.A. At that time an ardent revolutionary, she had gradually become disillusioned. Her father, mother and sister had all died in Odessa during the mass famine that followed the great no-planting strike against Stalin's collectivization. Her husband, an engineer who had also once been a party enthusiast, was now a kind of political parolee obliged to work in Kamchatka but permitted to visit Moscow once a year for two weeks.

Katcha cited her youngest brother as "typical" of cynical Russian youth compared to the idealists among her own generation of revolutionists.

"You can't blame him," she said. "He almost starved to death with my parents, and after he became an orphan a gang of thieves fed him. He joined them. They murdered some people and they were caught. Every one of them was executed except Piotr. He got off because of his youth; he was only thirteen. I had good party standing then and I was able to get him admitted to an engineering school. But after three years of it he became a chauffeur! Soon after that he was drafted. Now he's been all through the war without a scratch and what do you think he feels? Nothing! But he collected more loot in Europe than any man in his company. He told me proudly that his house in Moldavia—he married a girl there—is so crammed with loot from Bucharest to Berlin that it simply won't hold any more!"

"I suppose it gives him pleasure thinking about every German he's robbed," I said. "Revenge is sweet?"

"No, not revenge. You have to hate somebody to want revenge. And Piotr doesn't hate anybody nor love anybody except possibly his wife. He is not anti-anything, not anti-Nazi and not anti-Communist, not anti-capitalist but just pro-Piotr. He fought the war on a strictly material basis and was lucky. No hard feelings. He came home with his loot."

"There is one thing missing in Russia which I think may still exist in America," I said. "It is not at all what I would have thought before I lived here. You know what it is?"

"Love? Do a few people in America still know what it means?"

"That isn't quite the word, at least not in English; but it's fair enough. The word I'd have used is charity. A stale old bourgeois word, charity, and yet as St. Paul used it a word of the deepest sense of brotherhood. It means giving something in humble acknowledgment of the insignificance of any living man and his institutions but in salute to the giant fact of eternity living in every man. I don't think it's possible, Katcha, except in a society where the individual has *some* right to have and to hold some means of his own survival—and by that right has the power to give it, in charity, to another."

"Everybody isn't like Piotr," Ilena broke in heatedly. "I remember an officer in a hospital I visited with Komsomols. To talk, I asked him did he hate just the Nazis or did he hate the Germans, the people. Understand? *'Konechno!'* he said. 'Tomorrow we may be friends, right now the Germans are enemies. I hate them. In war there must be the enemy, otherwise how can one kill?' My question was not so silly because he answered so; he had been thinking. 'To hate—the hatred' he said—how is it?—*la moralité de la guerre? Oui?* He said, 'Hatred is the war's morality. War without hatred has no more meaning than sleeping with a woman without love.' He had that much love to give, do you see, and yet he had to hate somebody with it."

Katcha moodily stared at her and smoked a cigarette in silence.

"He had walked on the mine and it shot up," Ilena added thoughtfully. "He was—*châtrer un homme*—how does one say it? Yes, castrated."

CHAPTER 28

Pros and Cons

"WHEN I WAS a young Communist we didn't care what we wore or ate, we didn't think about fancy dresses and lipstick," said Katcha, looking sideways at Ilena, who always managed to be neatly groomed despite the dearth of cosmetics and couturiers.

"I am not a child any more, Katerina Mikhailovna," Ilena retorted coolly, throwing back her head and glancing in a mirror.

"Our cause," went on Katcha, grinding out her *papirosa* and ignoring Ilena, "our cause filled our bellies and that was enough. We were idealists, we were making revolution to build world Socialism. Our leaders loved the people, the lowliest of humanity. Now? Equality as an ideal is considered old-fashioned; differences in pay and everything are like anywhere. The aim is just to get on top and to hell with the bottom dog until he bites. Why, it's cannibalism; it's just like America."

I cited the case of Vera as one Communist idealist. Katcha conceded exceptions. But even the Veras, true believers, were seeking social acceptance in high circles, she said, dreaming of careers and material prizes.

It was an odd complaint of which few foreign observers then were aware. Most of us were busily looking for signs of incipient revolt against the economic and social system in Russia long after the main implications of Socialist ownership had become ingrained mass habits of thought. It was not fear of pro-capitalist plotters that prolonged the severity of the dictatorship so much as certain inner necessities evoked by power itself—and by Russian history.

With all its lost dreams of new freedoms and its other disappointments, however, Katcha's generation recognized the substantial legacy accumulated for heirs of the future. Russia stood, a nation industrialized, disciplined in the techniques of science, with education free and universal and opportunity constantly enlarged.

Inequalities persisted in the Soviet state, but not parasitism: there were no idle rich, no unearned ease, no pashas or sheiks living on the largesse of foreign oil companies; no maharajahs keeping their harems and villas in luxury while tenants went naked and their children were

367

full of rickets and worms; no retired politicians living on the loot of office, and no retired generals collecting stock options as "directors" for grateful corporate merchants of deterrence. There were political opportunists, but no lobbyists buying votes for millionaires bent on further plunder of the public oil, water-power and other natural wealth; party labor bosses but no labor crooks building private fortunes with union dues; and yet it was true that there were officials who lived as well as officials anywhere.

There were NKVD torture chambers. Secret trials and executions still occurred. There were still "correction" camps where labor was exploited for state profit. On the other hand there were no pimps, professional perverts, shills, whoremongers and gangster underworld combines run on big-business principles. There were peddlers of misleading propaganda galore, and cultural ignoramuses in control of the party line were roadblocks in the way of truth more formidable than many an advertising agency. There was no freedom of the press or assembly except under party sanction. But there *was* this kind of freedom: freedom from peddlers of phony cults and patent medicines, sex trash, comic books, pornography in general and latrine gossip purveyed as "confidential" freedom of the press. Not only the government but every organized sector of Soviet life devotes more time and effort to the promotion of mass cultural education by means of awakening interest in and appreciation for classics in literature, music, theatre, the dance, the visual arts, than in any country. All this, as with everything else in the U.S.S.R., has its political content, of course; who pays the piper calls the tune.

The Russian working class has long had its free clinics, hospitalization, medical care, creches, rest homes and old-age pensions. The enormous blunders of post-war Soviet political tactics and strategy, the Stalinist crimes and stupidity at home and among the satellites, would for a time obscure such facts; but history must record that Soviet initiative did lead the world in many reforms which were only later emulated in the free "West."

Nothing in all this incomplete inventory means that Americans should exchange their virtues or vices for Soviet ones. They not only should not and would not; they could not. They could not simply because no people can escape from its history and the peculiar genius of its own culture any more than a man can borrow a different body and throw aside the old. But the body itself is changing, in Russia as elsewhere; the new mintage of humanity is not an exact copy of the old. Each generation, though it has to learn everything all over again for itself, adds a link. In these times the linkage increases apace. The transformation of man, minute though it is, is both what he was at the beginning and what he is becoming by changing circumstance and change imposed on circumstance by himself. The nation that was Russia yesterday, an ignorant backward peasant mass, is not the Russia of today, with its millions of educated highly trained youths eagerly reaching out and demanding new satisfactions, new freedoms. Not any more than America is still the unplowed country of the free frontier.

The original slogans of the revolution, "land! bread! freedom!" meant something quite different to the peasants of Russia in 1917 from what they mean today, and something different also to American onlookers from afar in both generations. The fulfillment for Russian youth of today, in terms of security in their livelihood, of more to eat and wear than their parents had and of educational opportunity far beyond anything conceivable in the old Russia make Soviet society, on its own level, as dynamic as any in the world.

CHAPTER 29

Farewells Should Be Sudden

EVERY MAN obviously does possess a measure of "free will" and is responsible for what he does. Yet how narrow the limits are! Do they really include freedom to choose when to replenish life any more than when to deny it? Each act turns out to be as complex and yet as inevitable as the first step in a man's life is to the second and to the last.

That was another thing I learned from Ilena. She knew very well the limits of courage, self-reliance and freedom open to her. In a land of anxiety she faced life with zest and hope, rejoicing at the day's offerings in a small world of her own choice within a vaster world beyond control. Because of that, what could have been merely a wayside adventure took on a deeper meaning; the hazard involved for her shadowed it with vague and formless peril. It was something felt but not defined, not even when I had to leave abruptly for India and the Far East.

The northern lights had already dropped below the horizon again when I left. "I'll be back in half a year," I told Ilena as we parted. So

370 THE OTHER SIDE OF THE RIVER

brief was that summer sun that her skin was still only the palest gold.

Months passed during which I waited anxiously to hear from her. At last she managed to send me a long letter, through the embassy pouch, which reached me in Japan.

She was all right. She had a library translation job, until she could resume work on her *aspirantura* degree.

"We have had another election," she wrote. "What a nice day! We were all decorated, the streets so gay, bands playing, people laughing and smiling and so polite! Pardon me this, tovarish, and pardon me that, *tovarish*. Could it really be Moscow? Who do you think won through it all? 99% voted for our 'bloc of Communists and non-party members'! What a victory! *Ils ne font qu'un!* [As like as two gloves.] But we shall speak of it later."

At the end of her letter she quoted a line I had taught her from the lament of that becalmed English sailor of long ago: "O Western wind, when wilt thou blow . . ." That was all.

Ilena was strictly *a*-political.

Another winter and summer went past before I was reassigned to Russia. But the curtain had already begun to descend and meanwhile I had written a series of articles that attempted to show both faces of the basic problems of "co-existence," which I considered the only alternative to co-extermination. My editor had in good faith advertised them as "the Russian point of view." Soviet officials didn't agree. In New York, Andrei Gromyko told me they were "positively unsatisfactory." (An odd word.) Perhaps in stressing the enormous human and material damage which made major war unthinkable for Russia for years to come I had "over-exposed" her weakness, while in my suggestion that "revisionism" in Stalinist dogma was inevitable (and already in train) I had anticipated Titoism.

One day in Washington a secretary in the Soviet Embassy told me flatly that I would not be permitted to return to the U.S.S.R. At that time and for many years there was nothing more final and unalterable in human affairs than a Soviet visa rejection. As far as individuals kept "out" or kept "in" were concerned, Russia might as well have been a separate planet. On the day I learned that the Kremlin would not let me "in" again I cabled the news to Ilena.

I was not able to return to Russia, but not long ago I met an old colleague just back from there, who told me news of Ilena. She was well and had a good job—in Tamerlane's beautiful old city of Samarkand.

PART FOUR

LA GUERRE FROIDE

Why doth the Poxe so much affect to under-
mine the nose . . . that it provides that
one should not smell his own stinck?

JOHN DONNE

CHAPTER 1

A Lifetime Visa

IN THE AUTUMN of 1945 several members of the House Foreign Affairs Committee arrived in Russia in a special plane which turned out to be a magic carpet for me. Karl E. Mundt of South Dakota headed the group. Others were Congressmen Victor Wickersham of Oklahoma and Walter Horan of Washington, and Congresswoman Frances P. Bolton of Ohio. I toured around Moscow several days with them. As I was about to leave Russia for India they invited me to accompany them. We flew down the Volga and over Stalingrad, halting briefly at Baku, and then skirted the blue bowl of the Caspian, into Persia.

On the way Mr. Mundt dictated his impressions to a congressional secretary, "Tex" Convers, and kept me busy earning my fare by filling in names and spellings. They had already breezed through a half dozen countries in three weeks; Mr. Mundt was conscientiously determined to keep events and faces in the right places. Their remaining itinerary included, besides India, investigations in Iran, Iraq, Saudi Arabia, Pakistan, Burma, Siam, China and Japan. They did eventually get so confused that at Delhi it was agreed to call off the rest of the trip and fly straight home via Japan.

In fact the party was already thinking of omitting the scheduled visit to the Lord of Arabia.

"Skip any place but Saudi Arabia," I protested when I heard that. "You'd be the first congressmen in history to enter Riyadh! Practically Marco Polos!"

I was not speaking entirely disinterestedly. Only one other American reporter had been in Riyadh, up to that time.

The matter was still under debate when we reached Teheran. Our people were really getting homesick, and here was another country that would make them more so. At Teheran a fluttery State Department man met the plane, to shepherd the party to Riyadh. He was supposedly a Near Eastern specialist and he held the old King and the oil companies in such awe that he literally trembled at the audacious talk about excluding Riyadh. Elaborate plans had been made, he explained. A refusal now could cause an international incident.

When Mr. Mundt and the others agreed to go through with it the poor official still had two worries: how to dump Mrs. Bolton, and how to dump me. Mrs. Bolton had to be dropped, as he put it, because of the Arabs' contempt for naked-faced women. The King never, never received a woman outside the harem. The royal secretary, according to "State," had insisted that Mrs. Bolton excuse herself. He had not reckoned on the Bolton women of Ohio. Frances ridiculed him. If the Arabs had no conception of women as equals it was high time she began to teach them. The rest of the party stoutly supported her, insisting that all go or none. "State" then had no alternative but to take her at least as far as Dhahran, on the Gulf, while awaiting word from Riyadh. When the problem finally did reach Ibn Saud, we heard later, he laughed in kingly manner and ordered his wives to welcome Mrs. Bolton and show her around the harem.

She thus got the only really exclusive story. The rest of us never saw an Arab woman's face.

As for myself, "State" at first flatly forbade me to go along. Mr. Mundt then kindly made me the party's honorary press attaché (unpaid) for the trip, but nervous Nellie still demurred. It was highly irregular; no press attaché had been authorized from Washington. Now, especially, the monarch would be offended by the presence of a reporter; he had confidential matters to discuss. In any case, nobody could enter the country without a personal invitation from the King. That took long preparation; obviously the party couldn't be held up waiting for me.

"I don't think," I said, "you'll have to wait a minute." Reaching into my pocket I brought out an envelope bearing the royal coat-of-arms, and withdrew the royal letter within. Above the signature of King Abdul-Aziz Ibn Abdur-Rahman Al-Faisal Al Saud, Servant of Allah, otherwise, King Ibn Saud, was the one lifetime visa I ever received.

"Now, hear this," I said, sticking it under Nellie's nose. I read out the translation of the business part of that flowery Arabic communication as follows:

"In the name of the all-merciful God we thank you for your noble feelings toward our country and we welcome your visit at any time you may desire."

It was the only entirely satisfactory rejoinder I ever made to a self-important member of international beadledom.

The King's letter was dated May 21, 1942. The origin of it went back to April of that year, when in Cairo I met Karl Twitchell—the man who had first brought to King Saud the glad news that there was oil in his barren sands, fabulous underground oceans of it, enough to make him the richest man on earth. The King's letter had reached me when I was in India, and one war assignment after another had prevented me from using it. Now a chance was all set up for me. "State" withdrew his objections, finally pleading with me simply not to write anything "confidential" that I might learn, to embarrass him or the party. I didn't.

Like Mecca, Riyadh was a forbidden city out of bounds to infidels. Six days by camel from the Persian Gulf, it is only a half hour by plane. Flying in from Persia, across the Euphrates and the Tigris, we landed in the center of the great Dhahran oil concession which fringes the Gulf. Americans already had exclusive rights to the modest airport, since expanded into a great military base. When we arrived Ibn Saud's air force consisted of one Douglas C-47 given to him by President Roosevelt.

At Dhahran we found Main Street in the desert. Several hundred Americans, including two dozen American wives, were comfortably installed in California ranch cottages with air conditioning and electric refrigerators, around a swimming pool, kiddy playgrounds and homeside hospitality. It was like living on an island, as one of them put it; at the end of Main Street was a burning oil well and beyond it they had no place to go but desert. At another oasis down the Gulf, Qatif, more Americans were beginning to tap the immense vaults below the hot sands and helping to train 10,000 Arabs to extract and refine the Company's petroleum.

"Company" meant "Aramco," of course, the Arabian-American Oil Company, a fifty-fifty partnership of Standard Oil of California and the Texas Company. Together they held a concession, good till 1997, for the black gold inside all 400,000 square miles of Saudi Arabia. Floyd Ohliger, manager of the company, flatly said that all Arabia had "the richest undeveloped oil resources left in the world." He put it mildly. It is now believed that Arabia holds at least three times as much oil as all the reserves in the United States.

At the Riyadh airfield we were met by the King's cabinet, headed by Crown Prince Faisal, today King Ibn Saud II. The inevitable black coffee was served by skirted guards, and we inhaled glowing sandalwood. Then we got into new Ford cars with desert tires. Arabia may be roadless but the desert has natural roads of its own. Arab drivers, all mere boys, spread along a mile-long front and raced each other to the sprawling town, their accelerators flat on the floor, running at eighty miles an hour.

At Riyadh, the long, low, two-storeyed palace buildings, with their uneven whitewashed walls of mud brick, seemed part of the desert. We drew up inside a square lined with the King's courtiers, dressed in magnificent formal robes topped off with plaid and polka-dot *burnouses*. Then we were led up carpeted stairs to a large L-shaped room, a sea of Turkish and Persian rugs, and taken between rows of pillars hewn from the trunks of date palms. The whole effect was one of crude, barbaric splendor. In the heel of the L the walls were draped with fine brocades and dazzling cloth of gold.

There, in a gilded chair on a low dais, sat Ibn Saud, King of the Arabs.

CHAPTER 2

King Ibn Saud

IBN SAUD, six feet four, towered over all of us when he stood up to shake hands. Thick beard; long, flowing garments; grace of movement: he was a truly majestic figure. Part of the awesome first impression he made was a gaze which seemed fixed on some remote point in the back of your head, an illusion soon revealed to be due to a cast in his left eye.

Incense and rose water filled the air and bearded guards, their long swords dangling, ranged round the room. The business of confabulation got under way with the help of Ali Alirezeh, an Arab freshly milled from the University of California, whose colloquial Americanese seemed incongruous in that exotic setting. The conversation need not detain us now: honorifics, generalities, the exchange of mutual compliments between His Majesty and the party, all in preparation for the gentle touch for a loan which would come later and was in the King's eyes the big reason for the visit.

Eventually we were led off to detached quarters by the Crown Prince. He gave us part of his own palace overlooking the bathing pool and seraglio, through the lattices of which the congressmen, with their "press attaché" not far behind, periodically cast hopeful eyes. As it was not a Cecil B. De Mille production, languorous brown bathing nymphs were in strictest dearth. We did not glimpse an Arab woman all the time we were in the palace, and the few females we did encounter in the dusty lanes were hooded and all robed in black. Only their dark mocking eyes peered out, through slits in their heavy veils, before they turned and fled from the obscene sight of staring man.

Ali Alirezeh straightened me out on Ibn Saud's polygamy. He denied that the King had ever had more than four wives, which is the legal and moral limit permitted every pious Moslem. Four, that is, at a time. Moslems do, of course, sanction divorce, when the male finds it convenient. Ibn Saud had simply made generous use of the institution. Usually his harem had consisted of only three wives, one of whom was promptly divorced whenever the King took a new virgin as bride. According to Ali, Ibn Saud had a succession of more than 200 wives during his half century of virility. That meant an average of no more than four divorces a year.

With all this cornucopia of concupiscence, however, love had less to do than politics. The tribal sheiks who presented him with new brides would have been insulted had they been refused. The progeny gave them blood ties with the throne; the matches simply renewed or sealed political alliances. Since the king retained the male children, it was an improvement over the old system of holding chieftains' sons as hostages. Displaced wives generally stayed on in the palace to wait on their offspring. At the time I met Ibn Saud, he had thirty-nine sons, ranging from the Crown Prince down to a beautiful youngest boy, aged three. A number of royal daughters also survived, but Ibn Saud could not begin to remember how many. Nobody ever counted *them*. He illustrated the point with a story.

One day a young woman came into the harem with the King's sister, and warmly embraced him. Annoyed by the demonstration, the King said nothing till she had left; then he demanded to know who she was.

"What, you don't know your own child?" laughed his sister.

"It turned out," he told us, "that she was one of my younger daughters I had married off and hadn't seen for years. It's common enough for me to forget a girl's name, but this time I even forgot the face!"

I couldn't help wondering what Freud would make of all this. The father image here being as remote and collective as Santa Claus, presumably the child from infancy accepts as normal what in Christian society would be called "the broken home." However, for the average

bedouin who can afford no more than one wife, the system merely de-
prives him of the pleasure of mixed company. Where women are chat-
tels and slaves, men are slaves also. The Arab's "freedom" was strictly
limited, apart from his immediate family, to an all-male society.

Ibn Saud was proud of his paternal achievements and proud of his
sword: violence was the law of the desert; the loser got eaten and the
winner wore the eagle's wings. Zestfully King Saud related how he had
seized Riyadh, just before the turn of the century, with only forty followers, twenty of whom deserted. It took him until 1926 to conquer
Mecca and the Hejaz, overthrow King Hussein (backed by the Allies
in World War I), and finally restore Wahabi power over a unified
Arabian empire a quarter as large as the United States.

On a starlit roof, with a bright Southern Cross marking the purple
sky above the desert glory, the King seated us at a great U-shaped
table which supported two dozen tender lambs, roasted whole. Surrounding them were huge beehives of rice pilaff piled high in separate
bowls the size of small bathtubs. Stacks of curried fowl, fish, vegetables, fruit and fresh dates gleamed under the torches. There was
unleavened Arab bread, flattened out like pancakes, with baked-in
handles on one end, providing a convenient means of conveying food
to the mouth in a land where eating implements were abjured.

The King dipped in and broke off a leg of lamb with his fist, which
he proffered Mr. Mundt. Thirty princes sat alongside us, several to
help each guest. Eventually, stuffed like Peking ducks, we were led to
a large carpet-strewn terrace where court was held. Tobacco and wine
are forbidden to Moslems, but the ubiquitous coffee ranks as a close
substitute.

The King's Chief Coffee Pourer, Ibn Abdul Wahid, moved around
like a dancer, his dagger glittering, his brass pot flashing among the
cups like a serpent. A cup holds only a thimbleful of the molasses-
thick brew, as the Arabs drink it. Half of that was dregs, which Abdul
with an extravagant flourish repeatedly dumped on the expensive
Oriental rugs. Behind Abdul came the royal incense bearer, followed
by the royal perfume bearer. Bringing up the rear came the bearer
of the King's own bowl of water from Mecca and a huge silver loving
cup of buttermilk, a delicacy reserved only for the faithful, and happily
spared the guests.

The Arab monarch chatted along about the condition of man as it
looked from where he sat. One of the world's absolute rulers, undisputed lord, lawgiver and judge of all he surveyed, the old desert
warrior spoke in warm praise of "democracy," and "our common cause

in the war." (He had contrived to remain neutral until the very end.) There was, of course, little in his land which any American would recognize as "free enterprise"—except, of course, Aramco. The King and his tribal aristocracy simply owned the land and all the riches in and under it. Mecca's tribute was also his, and the Koran his law to protect it: a life for a life, an eye for an eye, and a severed hand for the thief. By a stern code unchanged for a thousand years, and by deft manipulation of tribal politics, Ibn Saud held together this nation of some six million turbulent illiterate nomads whose ancestors once ravaged Christendom and Asia with the conquering sword of the Prophet. Still almost completely isolated from science and the industrial world, these people were now about to be swept up by it, at last, with revolutionary results no man could yet foresee. A few more years, and a few billion American dollars, Cadillacs, and luxuries and corruption that money could buy for the few, and the old tribal brotherhood would be torn apart and never be the same again.

Now the old King spoke on of "fascism" and "nazism" and "communism." To him these were all godless creeds which had "nothing to do with us democracies." He had never seen a land ruled by any one of them, yet when he spoke of meeting Roosevelt in the Red Sea, in 1944, he was not acting a part. The President, as a fellow tribal chieftain, had deeply impressed him. With tears in his eyes he told us how he had put the whole palace in mourning for a week when he received news of Roosevelt's death.

Touched as I was by this display of Arab emotion, I could not be sure that the Republicans present, whom he apparently regarded as somehow attached to the President's court, fully appreciated his sentiments when he said tenderly: "I ordered his autographed portrait turned to the wall. I could not look at it without weeping."

Morally bound by discretion not to discuss the "confidential" nature of the King's remarks, what I can now reveal is not really earthshaking. The gist of Ibn Saud's "frank talk" was that he was broke! The war had cut off fees and donations from the pilgrimages to Mecca; his oil wells had not yet begun to make him the world's richest monarch.

"I'm in an embarrassing position," he said, his eyes wide, "of owning more than I possess! We are really a very rich country but it's all oil and it's still in the ground. The company pays me a royalty on the oil they take out, but production is too low. We need money today, not tomorrow."

Meat and rice had trebled in price. Cloth had doubled or more. He didn't need money for luxuries or nonsense, but to feed and clothe his people. Every day he found 2,000 hungry bedouins at his door, he said; and from what I saw he did not exaggerate. It was worse than Mecca. "If you don't believe me," he offered, "send your bookkeepers over here and we'll show them where the money goes."

That day each member of our party had been presented with an Arab robe and *burnouse,* tasseled with the royal gold thread, and a gold watch and bejewelled dagger. Now we shifted uneasily in our gilded chairs. State gifts, Ibn Saud explained, accounted for a big part of the royal budget. He fingered his own gold-embroidered *burnouse,* stretching it between his hands.

"We used to buy one of these for 40 *rials,*" said he to his interpreter; "now it costs nearer a hundred." Mrs. Bolton had now come up from the harem; the King, in an unprecedented gesture, had seated her on his left. She was dressed in her newly acquired Arab robe, the scarf draped gracefully over her shoulders. Suddenly the monarch reached over and tugged gently at it. "Take this," he said. "Before the war Indian merchants charged us only fifty *rials* for one of these. Today it costs 100 or more." Then he fingered her soft muslin robe. "Or take this. Formerly it cost maybe 150 *rials.* Now the robber merchants want 400 or 500 for one. That, gentlemen, is what inflation is doing to us!"

In due course the King got down to his request for hard cash. The U.S. was lavishing gifts, loans and lend-lease everywhere but here. Why? Wasn't Arabian oil supporting the democracies exclusively? We lost some face when our people's delegates had to admit we had no loans on hand. They offered the cold comfort that a request through the State Department would be sympathetically examined.

Ali Alirezeh, smelling pleasantly of rose water, took my arm. "The King will talk to you now," he announced. He led me to the sovereign. The congressmen and Mrs. Bolton moved away and the King seated me beside him. He took my hand in his, which I was surprised to find as soft as a woman's, and we remained thus throughout our talk. As I sat down there was a murmurous rustle as a hundred retainers, their stiff garments swishing, their arms clanking in unison, also sat. Their eyes never left me. Never had I had such an oddly unprivate "interview."

I asked about his own post-war hopes for the Middle East. The days of all colonies and mandates in Asia and Africa were almost over, he said. The promises of the Atlantic Charter meant that the entire system must soon be ended: complete and immediate independence for Egypt, Syria, Iraq and Libya, too.

"All Arabs," he said, "demand full sovereignty for all Moslem states, complete political and economic equality—and an end, of course, to immigration into Palestine!"

He talked at length about Palestine's importance as a holy place to 250 million Moslems all over the world. It was not fair for the Anglo-Americans to use Palestine as the sole dumping ground for Jewish refugees from Europe. It was not the Moslems who had sinned against the Jews, but Europeans themselves. Moslem and Jew had lived to-gether in peace in Palestine and could continue to do so, if given inde-pendence and self-government. But if one tried to drive out the other, or if a Jewish state were imposed on the Moslems, "there could never be peace."

"We Arabs were promised much and deceived much in the last war," the King wound up. "If we aren't heard this time there will be bloodshed. Not only over Palestine but over Africa; not only over the disposal of the Italian colonies and mandates, but over all remaining colonial territories in North Africa."

He pressed my hand in farewell and said: "Come and see us again. Come when you can stay longer. Tell your people of our friendship and our need."

Remembering this scene when Ibn Saud humbled himself to beg a few dollars from itinerant congressmen then reluctant to commit the U.S., I think how far we still were from understanding our deep involvement in these lands halfway round the world, by reason of American oil companies' claims on those cavernous oceans of treasure hidden in the sands of Araby. Before long we would discover in that backward monarchy a part of the "free world" crying for defense. Within the next decade the American oil barons would more than recoup their original investment in Arabia, and collect nearly a bil-lion dollars free of taxes to either the King or Uncle Sam. Yet if not the American oil barons, then who? The Communists? Perhaps. But even back in 1945 it seemed to me that in the old monarch's plea for largesse something else was foreshadowed: the new day when Arabia, like all the East, would call a plague on both the great houses of the infidels, and nationalize their resources for the profit of the Arabs alone. I was influenced by a talk I had at Riyadh with Harry St. John B. Philby, the Moslemized Englishman who was Ibn Saud's only for-eign adviser for many years.

"I give the oil companies twenty years," he said. "Then the Arabs will take over."

CHAPTER 3

Moment in Delhi

AT NEW DELHI's Willingdon airport I felt on familiar ground again. There I had left on flights to Calcutta, to the white villas and the palm-fringed shores of Bombay, to the lush valley of the Jhelum under Nanga Parbat's eternal snows, to the world's top story, at Darjeeling, and for wartime trips across the Hump into Yunnan. At Willingdon I had last seen General Stilwell when for an hour we sat in his plane while he gave me a horrendous account of his troubles with "the Peanut," as he called Generalissimo Chiang, "so that you can tell the American people the truth, when the time comes, about how their money was thrown away in China." And to Willingdon I would return later to an India newly independent.

I went on to Old Delhi and wrote and filed, without benefit of censors, some last words about Russia, from the comfort of the well-run Cecil, a paradise after the Metropole. My article was called "Russia Still Distrusts Us" and it summed up the results of four years of aid to Russia as George Kennan, then counsellor of our Moscow embassy, saw them. Kennan was in the process of evolving the thesis that would come to be known as the American "containment policy" toward the Soviet Union—later distorted by heavy American overemphasis on communist armed aggression as the primary menace to a political status quo visibly crumbling from other causes in many parts of the world.

Standing on the edge of Old Delhi in a large acreage of spacious lawns and gardens, the Cecil Hotel is shaded by great banyans and graced by tennis courts and a large pool, and up the lane there is, or used to be, a park of tame peacocks. As the sun waned the white-coated bearers at the Cecil would serve tea in the open, and the thing about that was that you had to be quick to get the wafery sandwiches into your mouth before the kites got there first. These large swift birds would hover motionless for hours, almost out of sight, until their sharp eyes sighted a crust of uncovered bread. Then they plunged like meteors. An unwary guest could easily lose both bread and a bit of skin 'twixt plate and lip. If you threw a scone into the seemingly empty sky a kite was sure to fall upon it before it hit the earth.

Years ago, when I first visited Delhi, there were monkeys all over the place and they used to raid ice boxes and vie with the kites for stray food. Despite such minor menaces without, and occasional lizards, chameleons and scorpions within, the Cecil usually had a waiting list. The motherly Swiss proprietress, Mrs. Hotz, always managed to find a place for a correspondent. She reserved a large round table for us which offered good fare featured by delicious curries and rice pilaff. On earlier trips I had shared the table with Herb Matthews of the *New York Times;* the gaunt and dour Bill Chaplin of N.B.C.; quiet and sensitive Bill Fisher of *Time-Life,* who was to walk into the sea one day and drown himself; unhappy John Morris, who took a similar way out when he jumped from a New York office of the United Press; Preston Grover of the Associated Press; Arch Steele, another old friend from China days, now of the *Herald Tribune;* irrepressible Darrell Berrigan (United Press), with his gift of friendship for all the strays of Asia; Ben Robertson, whose death on a Clipper I mentioned earlier; and the mad and gifted Jack Belden with whom I had covered war in China and loafed in a Kashmir houseboat.

Now the survivors were scattered East and West, but India was on the eve of the great transition and soon again to become and remain top news. Having held India against the Japanese, the British could no longer hold it against the Indians. Gandhi might not have been enough, but the mood of the new, well-equipped and well-trained Indian Army and its officers certainly was. In England the Labor party had come to power and Labor policy was independence, the sooner the better. In this the British were wiser than the French in Indo-China and North Africa, and wiser than the Dutch in Indonesia. By quitting India just in time they would save India from quitting the Empire—or Commonwealth, as it was now amended.

This time when I left I knew India would never be the same again: not for the British, and not for any white man. The era of privilege and pretensions to racial superiority that depended on the prestige of the white overlord was past. And one picture stayed in the back of my mind which quaintly symbolized the final anachronism of this time of the breaking of empire.

On a wartime visit to London I had gone to Downing Street to call on Mr. L. S. Amery, Secretary of State for India, an exalted position. He sat on a high carved chair behind an enormous carved old-fashioned desk and patiently explained to me why the British had been unable to prevent famine in India.

"Lack of shipping due to the war meant lack of food imports. Given the native Indian tendency to hoard, you naturally got a withdrawal of foodstuffs from the market, don't you see? Our central government simply didn't have the power to organize distribution on a national scale."

No, indeed it did not, I thought. As he spoke my eye wandered around the room, paneled in dark oak, poorly lighted, and bare except for a few fly-specked portraits of viceroys and their aides-de-camp. I could not help thinking of all the distinguished posteriors that must have sat here. Hastings himself, perhaps? Certainly Wellington, Minto, Kitchener, Curzon, the shadowy giants, the molders of empire.

When our interview ended I walked around Amery's desk to thank him and I reached up, so high was his chair, to shake hands. Only then I noticed, as I stood behind his desk, how short a man Amery was. I think he did not rise from his chair because to do so he would have had to use the footstool by means of which he had mounted to it, and on which his feet now rested high off the floor. It occurred to me that the British gentlemen who had sat here as overlords of India must have realized for years past that England could no longer prop herself up high enough to govern, from so small and distant a room, the world's second largest nation.

"Liberty does not descend to a people," said that inscription carved in the red stone of the Viceregal palace in India, "a people must rise to liberty." The English now heard and heeded the rising.

Today it seems hard to imagine an assembly of nations without India. Scarcely a decade ago none of India's neighbors could deal with her except by the grace of an English king. India was still a political cipher on the world stage, and during our whole history no Indian had ever been chosen by his people to represent them in the United States.

For two hundred years England held sway over the diverse population of this sprawling subcontinent by tactics of *divide et impera*. Now that it was ending, the English in India were having their last wry jest. "We divided and ruled," they said as they closed their clubs and prepared to leave, in two parts—Pakistan and the Indian Union—what was once united under British India. "And now we divide," they ended, "and *quit*."

Yet the bee fertilizes the flower it robs, and Britain was leaving behind her some lasting contributions to Asian civilization. In his brilliant historical study, *Asia and Western Dominance*,* K. M. Panikkar, one of India's ablest British-trained diplomatists, and a close

* John Day, N.Y., 1954.

friend of Nehru, listed a whole galaxy of benefits derived from the long European supremacy: the nineteenth and twentieth centuries' Asian reform movements (including a Hindu reformation), "policies of education, welfare schemes, political training" and the "first conception of the modern state to the Asian mind," as well as "the mechanism necessary to realize it in time." Panikkar further conceded that, along with its heavy impositions and exploitation, Western imperialism fostered republican ideals to supplant "Oriental despotism" and "a truly magnificent legal structure." Under it organized labor became a new social force, the status of women greatly improved, the whole universe of modern science was opened up and language and art were vastly enriched.

Communists in Asia would hardly concur in this generous appraisal. And yet it was under Western dominance, too, that Marxist Communism itself—that most disruptive and heretical but surely lineal descendant of Judeo-Christianity—arrived to continue that challenge to assumptions of Oriental faiths, and philosophies, which was begun by Christian missionaries centuries earlier.

CHAPTER 4

The New "Imperialisms"

IN THIS SYNTHESIS of private and public history a point of view had been gradually evolving. It underwent a sudden mutation at the time of the sunrise of the atomic age.

In Moscow we have already seen that the Russian Communists were under an inner compulsion to revise obsolete Stalinist dogma and doctrine in order to cope with vastly changed circumstances in Europe. Back in Asia I now saw the United States confronted by the need for equally swift transitions in thinking to meet on new high and equal ground the free states there which were emerging from the colonies and would in effect double the size of the political world.

In Russia I had left behind any illusions I may have had about the capacity of the Stalinists to help unify Europe peacefully under a Socialist form of society, although never before had the opportunity for this been greater. Preoccupied with their own grave wounds, living in constant dread that their weaknesses would be noticed and exploited by the Western Allies, and with a complex of guilt and inferiority fears brought to near-paranoia by America's surprise presentation of the atomic weapon, the Kremlin was from now on to omit few of the blunders most likely to injure Socialism's friends in Western Europe and to comfort its worst enemies. Cut off by hostile American policy (and their own diplomatic errors), from the capital goods imports desperately needed for their staggering reconstruction tasks, the Russian leaders resorted to the harsh alternative: remorseless squeezing of the occupied countries for reparations. This soon reduced their native allies in the satellite lands, the "local" Communists, to mere bill-collectors and policemen.

The early contradiction of Soviet policy in Eastern Europe lay in its dual roles as liberator and jailer, as revolutionary and exploiter, as generous comrade and Ivan the Terrible, the vengeful father-punisher. With Stalin's attempt to destroy Tito the paradoxes of Soviet policy toward fraternal Communist-run states reached their most dramatic point of irreconcilability. Tito's successful defiance of absolute Russian dictatorship, and of the principle of Kremlin infallibility, marked the dawn of a new heterodoxy in the world Communist movement—a process delayed by savage Stalinist repressions in Eastern Europe, but still going on today. When I wrote to the above effect,* soon after the Yugoslav-Stalin break, my prophecies earned me denunciations by party hacks as "an imperialist agent"—and permanently barred my way to any return to Stalin's Russia.

In Asia, the American dilemma had to be differently stated. It involved a split in national personality no less fundamental. The broad attraction of the American political ideal had always turned around the universal applicability of the American's revolutionary faith in every people's natural rights to national independence, sovereign equality, territorial integrity and self-determination: free choice of a government of, by, and for the people. Those principles had been reiterated in U.S. foreign policy from time to time, together with a corollary of non-interference in the internal affairs of other nations. Now a world victory presented America with unprecedented power and temptation to intervene to hasten self-determination by others, in ways favorable to the interests of the U.S.A.

Vacillating between historic neutralism ("no entangling alliances") and "manifest destiny," between support for Western Europe together

* "Can Tito's Heretics Halt Russia?" *Saturday Evening Post,* December 11, 1949.

with the status quo of its colonial system, and Tom Paine's sympathies for all unfree peoples, the United States verbalized for national freedom everywhere but followed practices which were now pro-independence and now pro-overlord, now liberator and now ally of dictators, now isolationist and now interventionist. This schizophrenia in our foreign policy would lead us on to acceptance of a new folklore in which the term "free world" came to mean "seventy-one countries outside the Iron Curtain which we erroneously refer to as the 'free world,' " according to Representative Thomas B. Curtis. With forty-one of them the U.S.A. would bind itself in military alliances. "Of these seventy-one nations," said Mr. Curtis, "forty-nine are . . . dictatorships or close oligarchies and the majority cannot even pass under the term 'benevolent' dictatorships. Of the remaining twenty-two nations most of them certainly have some claim to the adjective 'free' . . . but as far as the economic government of several of them is concerned, it is oligarchic and a small percentage of the nation is living off the backs of the other 99%." * And that statement left altogether out of consideration the still numerous colonial countries held by our "free" allies supported through NATO.

Between two world wars the term "imperialist" had largely meant Britain, France and the Netherlands. In Europe, the struggle between Titoism and Stalinism exposed the Tsarist atavisms behind Soviet Russia's "colonial" policy toward her European satellites. Now in the East it was disconcerting to watch America gradually become a new focus for accumulated racial hatred and national grievance and suspicion, while insurgent Asia groped toward a new equilibrium.

Revolutions as genuine and popular as the early American independence struggle were in ferment immediately after the war in China, India, Burma, Indo-China, Indonesia and Korea and Malaya. In few cases did the U.S.A. openly assist the revolutionists to power or show any notable comprehension of the fact that for colonial peoples their own liberation was the main objective of World War II. All these upheavals were essentially indigenous, anti-imperialist, and social revolutionary and nationalist in character. At the start not one was anti-American. They expected American moral if not material aid.

Not that the American behavior in Asia met the classical Marxist-Leninist definition of "imperialism," either. The essence of that was the exploitation of colonial monopolies in markets and raw materials for the super-profit of the foreign bourgeoisie. Actually, the queer

* U.S. Congressional Record, Feb. 18, 1955, q. in *A New Birth of Freedom,* by K. Zilliacus, N.Y., 1958.

thing about U.S. foreign policy was that often the profits made from its implementation derived almost entirely from exploitation of the domestic American market; the government collected from the American public the tens of billions which it passed on in profit-tribute to private industrialists and bankers who participated first in lend-lease and later in arms-aid programs. This "auto-imperialism" nevertheless developed its own bewildering paradoxes in the defense of democracy and freedom from fear of Communism.

Thus, within a short time after V-J Day Americans found themselves maneuvered into supporting France's playboy puppet emperor Bao Dai against a legitimate independence revolution in Indo-China; actively intervening in Chinese civil war to try to save the dictatorship which represented private ownership from destruction by the dictatorship for state ownership; suppressing an incipient Socialist (non-Communist) revolution already in power in Korea when our troops reached Seoul, and importing our long-exiled Mr. Rhee to set up a personal police state there; financing and arming the Dutch in their lost dream of overturning the independent native regime in Indonesia and putting their own queen in charge again; supporting, in Thailand, the Asian chieftain (Pibul Songrram) who had led his country to the Axis side in the war; and following policies in Spain and the Philippines which resulted in stabilizing the power of the political collaborators of the Axis.

In Saigon I watched the British army take over in a Trojan Horse maneuver for which General Douglas Gracey, an honorable soldier who hated political deceit, expressed personal distaste; he was merely obeying orders. The British promised the local Vietnamese revolutionists (mostly non-Reds then) that they would enter the country only to disarm the Japanese. After the natives allowed them to land without bloodshed the British let the French Vichyite officials and Foreign Legion officers out of jail. Then they helped the French attempt to beat the Vietnamese back into submission—the same Vietnamese whom the French had earlier surrendered to Japan without a struggle. For this purpose the Allies made extensive use of the Japanese troops whom they were supposed to disarm.

I reported in the *Post* that I had told those who complained about the doublecross: "If you Annamites really want your independence, don't wait for our help. You'll have to fight like hell for it, die by thousands, and make such a prolonged and bloody nuisance of yourselves that it will cost the French more than it is worth to reconquer you, and move public opinion in the United States. . . . And if you aren't prepared to make such sacrifices you would be better advised to bow your heads and reassume the yoke."

When I spoke of these things to General Douglas MacArthur during a Tokyo reunion he surprised me with the passion of his response. "If there is anything that makes my blood boil," he said, "it is to see our allies in Indo-China and Java deploying Japanese troops to reconquer those little people we promised to liberate. It is the most ignoble kind of betrayal, Snow, and it puts our cause in jeopardy everywhere in the Orient."

"Does that mean you're in favor of turning them all loose out here, General?" I asked.

"Most emphatically so!" Then MacArthur added, answering unvoiced criticisms: "Suppose their politics *are* corrupt and suppose they won't hold honest elections, as Paul McNutt was predicting to me would happen in the Philippines? 'Paul,' I said to him when he complained about that to me the other day, 'you're absolutely right. They *won't* hold an honest election; but I'll tell you something else. The Filipinos will hold as honest an election as you ever had in the state of Indiana!' After that Paul didn't say a word. How could he?"

All the same, we went on supplying the arms and ships without which France couldn't have held on for a year of that lost decade she threw away on civil war in Indo-China which killed hundreds of thousands of people who had done us no harm. Before the adventure was over France would have wasted in it the equivalent of all our Marshall Plan aid to her, and Mr. Dulles would be recklessly threatening to hurl hydrogen thunderbolts if China dared give "these little people we promised to liberate" equal help against the French.

In the end it was the French who left, the natives who stayed, and the Americans who paid—and are not through paying yet.

CHAPTER 5

Farther East

OVER IN the Philippines the Americans paid also, but with somewhat better results. Here at least the people liked us; they spoke English, they understood us, they trusted our guarantee of independence, and confidently waited for our help.

Help did come in abundance, billions in money and materials. Unfortunately it was featured by characteristic evils of our economy of "conspicuous waste" which made it a dubious model for underdeveloped countries. Generous though that aid was to the planter and the business man, little of it reached the ruined peasants and the have-not urban majority. The man with the cash (often the ex-collaborator) soon cornered the materials and siphoned off the inflationary dollars from the consumer. When independence came the Filipinos had not yet learned how to evolve a self-supporting economy from their fabulously rich and scarcely touched native resources.

One week-end Darrell Berrigan and I drove across the broken roads of Luzon and up to Baguio, to visit my old cottage amidst the scented pines hung with gorgeous mountain orchids. Outside, the place seemed intact. We stood on the edge of a precipitous ravine. From the house we looked into a valley 5,000 feet deep and caught a breath-taking view of the white beach on the Pacific, far below. When we stepped from that mile-high verandah into the cottage we found a whole Igorot village encamped in the house. Braves and squaws squatted in homespun and G-strings. Their hair in bands, their white-toothed smiles, their knives in braided belts, their lovely dark-eyed children underfoot, all made a picture of ordered chaos in that beautiful smoke-filled home which was built by Dean Worcester, America's first commissioner to the non-Christian tribes of Luzon.

All the fine Nara wood panels of the walls had been torn out, and most of the mahogany floors had been ripped up for firewood. Erected wholly within the place, in typical Igorot style, were six native huts, each complete with its own walls of bark and bamboo, its separate entrance just high enough to crawl through, and its own chimney spouting smoke into the outer domicile. These Igorots had been bombed or burned out of their misty, rainbow paradise at Bontoc and then had trekked down in terror to Baguio looking for shelter. Perhaps an old brave had remembered kindly Father Worcester and come looking for him. However they had found it, the old cottage, with its convenient panels and floors offering ready kindling for snapping fires over which to cook the delicious brown rice grown on their steep mountain terraces, must have seemed an answer to prayer. Thus the brown man rebuilds his home within the house the white man left behind . . .

As for Japan, it first seemed that the American success there would be a more lasting monument to the skilled hand of General MacArthur, acting in a role for which he might have been training all his life. It was ironic that MacArthur, at heart more of a Tory than Winston Churchill, was the man to enforce the really radical Potsdam directives. He did so, to the letter. In a matter of six months I saw Japan transformed. The nation was swiftly and totally disarmed, war industries were dismantled, principal war criminals were tried and punished, police repression was lifted, opposition parties were legalized, labor was organized, and began collective bargaining, totalitarian propaganda and education were banned in favor of our side, *zaibatsu* industrial monopolies were broken up, women attained equality of legal status with men, and a beginning was made toward agrarian reform. Finally, Proconsul MacArthur penned the Japanese a brand-new constitution which outdid Jefferson in guaranteeing all these innovations. It forever renounced armed force as an instrument of Japanese national policy.

"Why, I could be shot," MacArthur confided to Marty Sommers, Grove Patterson and me at luncheon one day, "if I tried to do some of the things at home that I am doing over here. They'd call me a Bolshevik if I pulverized Standard Oil or the U.S. Steel Corporation the way I have been pulverizing the *zaibatsu* monopolies here." He seemed awestruck by his own—or Potsdam's—audacity. "Of course I'm simply carrying out orders. But it's practically revolution, gentlemen, revolution!"

And so it was—but not quite, or MacArthur wouldn't have ended up chairman of Remington Rand. We saved the Emperor, and with him we saved the basic class structure and the economic structure. Before our occupation was over the reforms had been greatly modified by practice. MacArthur broke up the *zaibatsu* and made little ones out of big ones, but he wasn't told to make them into anything else. We wouldn't nationalize them; that wasn't authorized. We couldn't lend money to ordinary people to buy them—not even when they organized themselves into industrial co-operative associations, as I discovered when I was brought in as adviser to them. It turned out that nobody had the money to buy the industrial cast-offs of the *zaibatsu* families—except the friends, agents and relatives of the *zaibatsu* themselves. So back they came, the Mitsuis, the Sumimotos, the Mitsubishis and all the rest, even as the Krupps in Germany, and with them the old parties revived under new names.

Japan might well be grateful for the firm American stand which saved that land from joint Russo-American occupation, and the fate of a divided Germany. Yet the Japanese-American symbiosis was probably basically an "unnatural" one, in an economic sense. It would remain viable only as long as Japan was weak and dependent on American aid. Once Japan recovered from her wounds the contradiction between the pacifistic teachings of MacArthur's reign, which prepared the islands for a neutral role, and the later demands of American policy aimed at re-militarizing Japan as part of an anti-Communist bloc committed against America's former allies, China and Russia, would profoundly trouble Japan's internal as well as external life. Having lost one war and empire in a "crusade against Communism" in China, the prospect of being the advance base for another such conflict had little attraction for Japan, apart from the heavy American subsidy paid to her. Within a decade that would total many billions. Once that subsidy would be withdrawn or ceased to outweigh its disadvantages Japan might be expected to follow a policy like India's rather than serve as an instrument of either of the super-powers challenging each other across the straits of Formosa.

Wisdom also pointed toward neutrality as the best choice for the Korean people to whom the Russians and Americans had promised independence. Fate was to give them no freedom to exercise such discretion. Reasons for this were already clear in 1946 to an eyewitness of our attempts, and the Soviet attempts, to set up government there in our own mutually incompatible images.

CHAPTER 6

We Stop a Revolution

KOREA HAD almost as high a rate of literacy as the Philippines. She was rich in natural resources, and Japan left her with an industrial development ahead of China and India, little damaged by war. The essence of the Korean tragedy was that every condition except one seemed to favor an almost painless transition from a colony to a republic well started on the road to modernization. The exception was that Korea had to undergo an Allied occupation. And not just an American occupation or a Russian occupation, but occupation by both!

I remember a sad old gentleman who was our choice for mayor of Songdo. As his remarks came through to me by way of a Korean interpreter he sounded like this:

"There was one good thing about being occupied by Japan. We were one country and we were altogether, all being of hatred of Japan and all being of hope of freedom."

Songdo was a town on the thirty-eighth parallel where I spent New Year's Eve and the first week of 1946 with our troops who there faced the Russians during that winter of our early mutual discontent. The mayor went on:

"The best thing I think is no occupation at all. We could be sending home the Japanese by ourself after they quitting the war. That's all we like. Being free like Mr. Truman said. You know what he said?"

"Yes, I know. It's been quoted at me all the way from Saigon to Seoul," I replied. "He said: 'All people should have the right to choose their own form of government without interference from any foreign sources—in Asia as well as in the Western hemisphere.'"

"That's the right. But when we have *not* the right then we like only *one* army here—the American. But not two armies. Maybe the Russian army *only,* and Korea be *one* country. This way, we never be free." The mayor removed his odd hat and wiped his head with a cloth. Then he wiped his spectacles, wiped his eyes, and blew his nose. *"Sah, sah,"* he ended, "there will be weeping on both sides of us."

The mayor knew, as we all knew, that the U.S. had stopped a revolution in Korea—a revolution which might have dispossessed him as well as the Japanese.

The entire Korean underground movement was led by a left revolutionary coalition, dominated by the minority Korean Socialist and Communist parties within it. Even without Russian help it would quickly have won control of the whole country if we had not intervened. That victory looked inevitable for two reasons. The first reason was because there was no effective rival leadership inside the country. Socialists and Communists had organized and led all the groups of labor, youth, peasants and intellectuals who participated in wartime resistance activity inside Korea and in Manchuria. In Manchuria alone they controlled tens of thousands of armed guerrillas. They thus had the only nucleus of a Korean independence army.

There were, of course, cautious patriots among the Japanese-trained Korean officials, policemen and business associates and helpers of the Japanese. But these were "respectable" people who had obeyed Japanese law in order to protect their property. After liberation they would find their natural place in the conservative national parties. These were to be set up by elderly exiles like Syngman Rhee, whom we flew in from Washington, and Kim Koo and Kim Kyuh-sik, whom we flew in from Chungking, where they had lived under Chiang Kai-shek's patronage. Unfortunately, such people had but a negligible political organization inside Korea and could play no significant role at the time the underground independence movement first burst onto the streets of Seoul and elsewhere, just before Japan surrendered.

Early in August, 1945, the Japanese commander chose to forestall an uprising by releasing political prisoners in Korea and granting the people conditional freedom to organize. Self-governing bodies sprang up in many places in the course of a few weeks. Mass meetings were called in scores of towns. They chose "people's committees" which in turn elected delegates to a central conference held at Seoul. There the delegates proclaimed Korea's independence, set up a "People's Republic," and elected a "central commission" to prepare for national elections. The "commission's" constituent committees proceeded to spread over wide areas in the South, as well as all over the North, before General John L. Hodge arrived to establish American military government, a whole month after V-J Day.

By that time the parties supporting the "People's Republic" had already broadcast their "common program" to the nation and the world. They called for nationalization of Japanese lands, public ownership of Japanese mines, factories, industries, utilities, homes, shops and hotels, and for advanced laws affecting working hours and conditions, women, child labor and education.

The groups which participated in such activities were probably no larger an articulate fraction of the population than the American revolutionaries who supported George Washington. There was even less discernible opposition to them among the inert masses than in Washington's case. This brings up the second main reason why all Korea would have fallen peacefully to "people's committee" control if *both* the Americans and the Russians had kept out. Nationalization offered the most *practical* way for a nation whose main economic task was the prompt confiscation and operation of enormous wealth in enemy property. The extraordinary fact was that about 85 percent of all Korea's modern industry, and about 95 percent of modern urban enterprises of all kinds, were Japanese-owned. On the land, also, Japanese state and private capital had such a dominant place that about 80 percent of *all* Korea's wealth was controlled by Japanese.

Imagine a United States in which a foreign power owned all the great corporations: railways, telegraphs, telephones, shipping, mines, utilities, steel, iron, and other heavy industries, banks, insurance companies, distribution and service industries, and nearly all light industry of any size. That was Korea. How would the United States have gone about getting such wealth into the hands of non-existent native corporations or Rockefellers, Fords, Mellons, etcetera? There simply was no Korean bourgeoisie; the term was interchangeable with the Japanese, the foreign enemy. The aims of nationalism and social revolution thus coincided in a program of nationalization of industry and land. It seemed to observers on the spot far more difficult to dream up any equitable ways to squeeze Japan's multi-billion-dollar holding into private hands than to assume public ownership over it.

In North Korea the "People's Republic" promptly nationalized all Japanese property. In our zone General Hodge would not give the green light, however, to any further moves smacking of Socialism. He held that this decision should be made only after the Koreans had formed a new "representative government" chosen under our supervision. He did not think the "people's committees" really represented the majority. One of the first things General Hodge did was to authorize American-supervised, free, secret-ballot elections for district councils in some representative counties. To his surprise the "People's Republic" slate of candidates won an overwhelming majority; not one conservative was elected. These councils never took office and the experiment was not repeated. Gradually all the "people's committees" were dissolved in our zone, along with the "central commission." But that was not to be for several months.

Meanwhile we governed Korea through the Japanese-trained Korean assistants left in charge by Japan. Similarly, we had to use many Japanese-appointed Korean bureaucrats and policemen to enforce army orders. These people were the very persons whom the public thought of as "collaborators" and "puppets." General Hodge was not happy about that but it was not his fault. Our Army and State Department had been caught wholly unprepared to take over Korea. We had Japanese-speaking officers ready to run Japan but not *one* Korean-speaking officer. Hodge and his chief of military government, General Arnold, had no alternative but to tell our Japanese-speaking officers to pass on orders at first through the Japanese, and then through Korean "collaborators." We suffered the annoyance of being called "the interpreter's government."

Aside from the fact that Syngman Rhee's outspoken hatred of Russia and reverence for private property made him seem "safe" to a bothered and bewildered old-line infantryman like Hodge, who needed nobody to tell him that anything that looked like Socialism was against regulations, Rhee also had the advantage of knowing English and having an American wife. He was the lesser evil for us. When Hodge and Arnold let Rhee pack our "state advisory council" at Seoul with his own candidates Rhee cleverly made the most of it. Under him the council soon became a kind of *de facto* "provisional government."

It was not that General Hodge or our civilian officials in Korea deliberately planned it that way. They never had any coherent directives that I could discover, aside from getting everybody home by Christmas. Individual biases and tendencies we had, but no real policy. It was just that "by nature" we did not trust people who talked about nationalization and social reforms, and we brushed them entirely aside when it came to official appointments.

Yet it was not the Americans who finally defeated the social revolutionary forces in South Korea. What lost them their early popularity even among their close followers was not the "natural" favoritism which we showed to Syngman Rhee and his conservative associates on the "advisory council." Nor was it the fact that we helped Rhee and Co. build an alliance with the "respectables" among small business men, the get-rich-quick opportunists, and the "collaborator" bureaucracy and the police. What lost South Korea for Socialism was the egregious ignorance and miscalculations of the Russian advisers on whom the North Koreans had to depend and who imposed their tactics on their Southern allies. They could not learn any game but their own. They could not believe that the rules of parliamentary chess could here be played straight, to their own advantage. They lost because they would not understand that America wanted to leave, not to stay and build a colony. They insisted we were "imperialists," and they knew all about imperialists.

Russia's deliberate isolation of the North from the South, the Russians' refusal to take the smallest first step to reopen their zone to travel and trade, the early excesses of the Northern Korean leaders and the tales of woe brought south by tens of thousands of ruined refugees—all gradually cooled the ardor of their Southern sympathizers. This, as much as America's bungling, half-hearted and spasmodic attempts at suppression of the left, lost them support. In essence, the Communists failed because they were over-hasty and could not see any more modern ways to take power than the heavy-handed methods of Stalinism.

The obsolescence of Stalinist techniques of maneuver in a revolutionary situation were later to be blatantly revealed in Korea, in one crowning miscalculation. That was the supreme folly of North Korea's armed invasion of the South, on the gamble that America and the UN would not act. That war would result in a million casualties, three years of ruin, and finally a stalemate. It would return America to the continent with both feet, give Chiang Kai-shek an unexpected new lease on the life of a kept general in Formosa and make South Korea a U.S. protectorate. It would, by destroying the old economic bases of the country, make American-financed reconstruction on private capitalist lines inevitable. Finally it would reduce Soviet moral and political prestige to a new low from the full consequences of which it was saved only by our own mistake in attempting a counter-conquest of all North Korea, thereby provoking the armed intervention of China, to restore the previous equilibrium of forces. But Soviet policy in Korea could not, of course, be isolated from the fact that elsewhere in the world "the United States and the Soviet Union became ever more firmly committed to attitudes and policies of hostility," as Leland M. Goodrich points out in his admirable *Korea: A Study of U.S. Policy in the United Nations**—a book which shows clearly enough our own generous part in preventing the early unification of an independent Korea "free to choose its own government without interference from any foreign sources."

"But each problem," as Mao Tse-tung is fond of saying, "must be

* Council on Foreign Relations, N.Y., 1956.

examined in its entire complexity. Everything has two sides, a good side and a bad side."

Let us consider the Chinese revolution—a very different story—after another look at India.

CHAPTER 7

Death of a Giant

I WENT HOME from Korea and spent six months there and wrote a book in which I advocated a continuation of Roosevelt's "great design" in the development of our relations with Russia and China.* Then I worked for nearly a year in England, France and Italy. In December of 1947 I was assigned to India and Southeast Asia again. I reached New Delhi a few weeks before the Mahatma was violently hastened on his way.

The assassination of Mohandas Karamchand Gandhi moved and troubled me as much as any tragedy before or since. It was the only time I ever saw a whole nation lose a father and mourn with the contrition of a son who had done the killing. Once more I learned that great men are not slain by their peers but by young fools convinced that they are instruments of good, not evil, just as fine causes are lost for trivial, irrelevant reasons. The sad young fanatic from Poona who fired the fatal shots believed that Gandhi was evil incarnate because he had accepted Pakistan and partition rather than civil war. The assassin could not see that to martyr Gandhi would only increase his size and cause, just as nations cannot see that ideas cannot be killed by violence but can only be modified by time and betterment of the ideas.

Of course it was obvious enough after the event that Gandhi had to be killed. It was his "theophantic moment," as Jimmy Sheean put it; the precise time had arrived for him to enter the pantheon. But I know that I had no "premonition" whatever about it because my diary of the days before shows how completely out of touch I was with the dark angel.

I had dinner with Jimmy in New Delhi (it says here) after he arrived

* Stalin Must Have Peace, N.Y., 1947.

from Karachi on a hunch that Gandhi was soon going to fast to death.
I noted that Jimmy was "on the edge of getting religion and wants to
join Gandhi's *ashram*." I told him Gandhi had no intention of dying.
I had seen him survive too many fasts before; he knew exactly when
to stop. Then, such are the incongruities of life, the diary records an
anecdote Jimmy had brought over from Europe, to wit:

"Shinwell, minister of defense in the Labor Government, got into
a public phone booth in the House of Commons and discovered he
didn't have a two-penny piece for the box. He leaned out to borrow
from the first passerby, who happened to be Churchill, his critic and
adversary. 'I say, Winston,' Shinwell called, 'I've got a friend waiting
and I need tuppence to pay the operator. Would you be kind enough
to lend it to me?' Churchill fished in his waistcoat and slowly dragged
out four pence. 'Here you are, Shinwell,' said he, 'take two two-penny
bits and call up *both* your friends.' "

My chronicle continued:

"I paid off Jimmy Sheean with Mrs. Atkins' remark about her cocktail party. Not everybody is convinced Gandhi is a sacred person.
Mrs. Atkins, wife of an American attaché here, invited some officials
and correspondents to a Saturday cocktail party which coincided with
the climax of Gandhi's recent fast-to-the-death to end Hindu-Moslem
rioting. By Thursday she confided her worries to a friend. 'Dear me,'
she said, 'I do hope the Mahatma eats something today. If he dies before Saturday none of the Indians will come to my party and I shall
have to postpone it indefinitely!' "

Such was the dreadful stuff I was recording on the morning of
Gandhi's death. Jimmy Sheean was to have a talk with Gandhi that
afternoon and he asked me along. I said I would skip the prayer meeting but might later join him and his *guru*, as Jimmy now called Gandhi.
I was on my way to get a taxi at the Imperial Hotel when an Indian
newspaper man rushed up and shouted, "Gandhiji's just been shot!"

It was late afternoon when I reached Birla House and darkness
could not have fallen for hours afterward. Yet in my memory it was
all black there except for the lamp that shone in the room where the
Mahatma breathed his last. The garden soon filled but it seemed
empty as each man mourned in solitude for something in himself suddenly left friendless.

It was literally true that every Indian lost his father when Gandhi
died. Yet something larger happened. This small man so full of a great
love for all men reached beyond India and beyond time. He took the
world unto himself, or that part of it that felt his attraction psychically,

or rationally, or solely by the erosion of the years, as in my own case. There was a mirror in the Mahatma in which each person could see the best and worst about himself, and when the mirror broke men around him lost a bright image of the truth.

A few days earlier Gandhi had looked into me and reminded me of something critical I wrote about him early in the war. "You were not very kind to me in your last book," he said, wagging his head and threading a new spinning wheel. Never had I been more gently rebuked. I replied that I probably had not studied enough. "What you wrote was your honest point of view," he said. "We respect your honesty." Unexpectedly he took my hand and said, "You are more ready to listen to me now, I know." And I understood without words that he meant the atomic bombs and far worse things to come, which were the dusty answer the "freedom-loving allies" had got for victory in the war he had refused to fight, for which I had ridiculed him.

I didn't know Gandhi as a saint, as Sheean did, nor follow the metaphysics of his philosophy. It seemed to me that however he dressed it up with parables from the *Vedas* and *Upanishads* or Biblical allusions his teachings were essentially the Sermon on the Mount. He was as convinced of the existence of individual free will as Thomas Aquinas, but his idea of God, of whom he spoke as of an intimate friend, was not anthropomorphic. God was "an indefinable, mysterious power that pervades everything"; and it was more.

For Gandhi religion was no less than a "constant struggle for truth." In seeking God he simply sought to identify himself with "the highest truth," knowing that the goal was unattainable. In wishing to make men more godlike, Gandhi strove to make men understand that they were not Man as yet but only becoming so. "Life is becoming, and death is becoming; humanity is in a process of becoming God, but God is becoming, and also being, which is reflected in becoming." This is close to a definition, in words borrowed from Paul Cohen-Portheim (which also faithfully reflect the dialectics of Hinduism as well as Taoism), of the nature of Gandhi's grasp of truth. Gandhi's harmony with that "process" gave him a quality of "something unknown," as Nehru called it; something he tried to explain to us as he stood behind the still body at Birla House that dark night.

"The greatest prayer that we can offer is to dedicate ourselves to the truth," Nehru told the nation waiting to receive some consolation from him, "and to the cause for which this great countryman of ours has died."

In the narrowest sense the "cause" was Hindu-Moslem amity, but in a deep and universal sense Gandhi died for the theory and practice of reverence for life, or faith in "*ahimsa*-is-love-is-nonviolence-is-truth." From the moment we first met and I trudged with him over the hills of Simla to see Lord Irwin years ago, down to this night of sorrow, no more could be said about Gandhi than that. Many seek the truth; few leave behind them the masterpieces of civilized works consistent with good thoughts and good words that Gandhi did.

He made mistakes and was full of paradox. St. Simon truthfully said that "No man rules guiltlessly," and Gandhi was sovereign in a kingdom of Indian hearts. He used the power humbly, praying that others would follow in the same spirit. When suffering and bloodshed occurred he took the blame and was full of self-criticism and desire to atone for sins committed by people who misunderstood him. He welcomed his long imprisonments as beneficial penance and discipline, and he did not hate his jailers but praised them for adhering to their principles. An attempt on his life was made only a few weeks before he was killed. Gandhi was naturally a little indignant. "That young man should learn," he said of his would-be assassin, "that those with whom he disagrees are not necessarily evil." He knew he was not infallible and he raised no claims to a monopoly of the truth.

"The one thing I don't wish," he said, "is for anyone to start a cult about me when I am dead." Worship me not but go thou and do likewise.

His distrust of the machine and science seemed narrow and old-fashioned, but his spinning wheel and wearing the homespun taught all Indians that they had outgrown Britain's economic and intellectual dominance. Gandhi knew, as did his friend and fellow Socialist, the vegetarian George Bernard Shaw, that exaggeration is necessary in order to get a little attention for the simplest truths.

Nehru said that Gandhi had "straightened India's back." Gandhi said it was all an "experiment with truth." That was all he did in South Africa, where he first tried non-violent civil disobedience and broke the system of indentured Indian labor. When he showed the British in India that he could get a million Indian peasants to take salt from the sea non-violently and without paying the King a tribute, the truth became manifest that the days of the empire were numbered. In other experiments Gandhi laid the foundations of a national language to bring men together regardless of creed. Perhaps his greatest demonstration of the power of *ahimsa* was a lifelong campaign for equal rights for the Untouchables, whom the Republic eventually liberated from caste discriminations more than two thousand years old. And all this he did without hatred.

Gandhi did not win India's independence alone; he was simply foremost among those who led India to freedom without war, and among his followers he claimed the British too. "They need not have made us this great gift," he told me; he thought they had done so because finally "the British people had been deeply moved by India's firm adherence to the code of non-violence." When Britain abandoned force and India was free to leave the empire, she would, paradoxically, decide to stay. Gandhi said that both countries had "acquired some moral capital" in the transition, and could now enter a true partnership as equals.

You felt the whole world acknowledge that triumphant conversion of the strong by the weak on the day Gandhi was cremated beside the river Jumna. There in the middle of a flat open space called the Jumnaghat, a wide mile running below the massive old red sandstone Delhi Fort and the white marble palace of Shah Jehan, Gandhi was placed on a small brick platform where his eldest son stood waiting to crack his father's skull with a silver hammer to release his consciousness to heaven. Around him in an open square squatted the Indian cabinet and Gandhi's friends of the years. Close enough almost to touch the shrouded figure there I sat also, beside Ann Layard and Arthur Moore.

"Gandhi had a most surprising interest in people's personal lives," I heard myself reminiscing to Ann, "and a most disconcerting intelligence service. In the midst of our last talk about politics he suddenly asked me why Nym Wales and I had parted. Imagine him *caring* enough about that to ask!"

Nehru and the others stood above the body strewn with rose petals and tenderly laid sandalwood upon it and spread it with ghee and honey and almond paste and perfume. I reached for some chips of sandalwood and added them to the pyre and waited. Behind us two million Indians, their dark heads as close as grapes in a box, pressed on and on. I thought I had been swallowed and held physically and emotionally by crowds in China and Russia, but now I learned what human mass really is. The Indian police, newly on their own, had taken inadequate precautions to keep the people back and all at once their cordons gave way. A tidal wave of men and women and children surged up to the pyre, those in front thrown forward by the flood behind them.

At that moment I saw us as we must have looked from the air: at the center of the flower the Mahatma, ready to burst into flame; around him, inky petals of humanity closing in as if all India were about to engulf him and hold back his soul. Alarmed, Nehru stood up and motioned the crowd back. Lord Mountbatten joined him. Their shouts were heard only by those in front being slowly pushed forward, all powerless to stop. What a fitting end for the pyromaniacs of the press, I thought, if someone were now to ignite the oil-impregnated pyre and send us all up with the Mahatma.

Arthur agreed that it was time to leave. We had almost to crawl over the Mahatma to get out. As I slipped past Nehru he gave me a worried look and then turned again to chastize the frenzied mass. How we burrowed out of it, pulling Ann Layard behind us, I don't remember; but after minutes of suffocation in the heart of that dark flower it suddenly erupted us onto a kerchief of greenery and fresh air. The crowd had left plenty of space around some armed Gurkhas who sat quietly sipping tea, unaware of the panic a hundred yards beyond. When I reported the peril their admirably trained commander went into action at once; soon his short broad-hatted troops were beating their way into the human growth, their lathis swinging as wickedly as ever a British lancer moved against a Gandhi-led civil-disobedience movement. A few heads were cracked and cries of distress arose as the mass wavered, broke and opened a pathway to the pyre. Governor-General and Lady Mountbatten resumed their seats and Nehru's face relaxed. An orange flame rose up from Gandhi as sobbing women were dragged from the sputtering candle of his body. Smoke gathered in a faint stratus that drifted lazily over the Jumna. The Great Soul was on his way.

Thus I saw Gandhi depart in a paradox as he had lived in one, when in this last moment of irony his old adversary—force—had to clear a way so that this earth's gentlest apostle of loving kindness might ascend to nirvana in peace.

CHAPTER 8

The Essence of Gandhi

GANDHI'S TEACHINGS are written in monumental volume but in essence he became an avatar for three reasons. He demonstrated how to satisfy man's individual need to attain good internal government of body and mind; man's need for collective action to attain social reform and government good for all; and man's need for effective means to achieve both individual and collective planning for creative work and growth toward world unity without war.

We have had many teachers with answers to one or two of these needs. Gandhi was the only man I knew who reconciled all three in action. He made religion live in politics with highly positive results. He actually got God to work on the side of the little battalions. He was a modest man; in the end, he told me, he realized that much of the success attributed to his methods was "in reality no more than the passive resistance of the weak." But he did say firmly that he had done one new thing.

"My small contribution to the world," he claimed, "is that I have demonstrated that *ahimsa* (non-violence) and *satyagraha* (soul-force, or non-violent non-co-operation) are more than ethical principles. They can achieve tangible political results."

Of the three needs or truths about modern man which Gandhi personified it was the attainment of inner honesty which was his hardest task. "For me means and ends are practically identical," he repeatedly said. "We cannot attain right ends by way of falsehoods." One's inner truth must be made manifest to all. Knowing that he could not lead Indians to freedom until he had freed himself, Gandhi saw his personal disciplines as a necessary means to that end. Absolute control of bodily appetites and passions precedes certainty and precedes truth and all his asceticism was part of that unending search for truth: his preference for "innocent food," his rejection of wine and tobacco, his refusal to own anything, his *brahmacharya,* or non-violence or non-selfishness in sex (he was far from celibate!) and his many other abstentions.

Gandhi did not deny the first importance of man's simple physical

404

405 THE ESSENCE OF GANDHI

needs. "To a man with an empty stomach food is God," he said. But he put a large question mark behind the frenetic chase for money and possessions as a civilized end in life, while beneath masks of chrome and cosmetics the barbarian remained all unchanged. He denied that five thousand years of upward struggle, the whole galaxy of human greatness, all the Greeks, the ancient poets, the great philosophers, the long array of men of service who pierced some of the darkness, the billions of young soldiers sacrificed for the idea of men becoming Man, all added up to Cadillacs for desert sheiks, to atomic toys for medal-hung generals, to capitalism with million-a-day incomes for a few and hunger for myriads, or to Socialism with a knout but without love.

"Speak the truth," said Buddha, "and let a man overcome anger by love, let him overcome the liar by truth." Like Buddha, Gandhi had an urge to liberate man by truth that set him apart from the mass of mystics who seek only realization of Self in anti-social isolation and ascetic exhibitionism. He was no fakir. His asceticism was effective only because of his political action. He was a living synthesis of good means and good works. He was also a Socialist of a kind.

Gandhi said that he had "accepted the theory of Socialism even while in South Africa," before World War I. Communists then called him a muddled, confused sentimentalist: though he shared Marx's desire to eliminate the State, he rejected dictatorship, the antithesis of his philosophy, as a means to achieve it. But he was no Utopian and he resigned himself to the State as a necessary instrument for bringing about social justice.

"Strictly speaking," he said, "all amassing of wealth or hoarding of wealth above and beyond one's legitimate requirements is theft. There would be no occasion for theft and therefore no thieves if there were wise regulations of wealth and social justice." Yet Socialism no doubt was for him, like everything else, first of all an inward experience and he wished to see men self-persuaded and thus freed into Socialism, not bludgeoned into it. He said he would call no man evil because of his wealth; he would "invite all to co-operate in the conversion to state ownership." There could be "no pariahs in society, whether million-aires or paupers," for both were "sores of the same disease."

Nehru and other Indian Socialists were constantly irritated by Gandhi's apparent complacency about class distinctions; sometimes he even seemed to idealize them. But it was not always possible to know where the *sadhu* inwardly ended and the politician began. In Gandhi's "search for truth" he knew as well as Mao Tse-tung when "to take a curve" to achieve a goal. During the struggle for national freedom he wanted all Indians united; once independence was achieved, he led the others in demanding sweeping internal reforms. Jai Prakash Narain, India's Socialist party leader, told me a few days before the assassination that Gandhi was "the mightiest personal force we have against all the most backward elements in our society."

In a country with twenty percent of its population always starving, and another forty percent seriously undernourished, living beside some of the very richest men in the world, Gandhi knew that a day of wrath could not forever be postponed. But a great politician needs a perfect sense of timing and a knowledge of the capacities of his people at any given moment. Gandhi's country was not China, and not America.

"India is a peasant India," said Nehru, himself almost as puzzled by Gandhi as anyone, "and so he knows his India well, reacts to her slightest tremors, gauges a situation accurately and almost instinctively, and has a knack of acting at the psychological moment. India, even urban India, even the new industrial India, had the impress of the peasant upon her; and it was natural enough for her to make this son of hers [Gandhi], so like her and yet so unlike, an idol and a beloved leader. He revived ancient and half-forgotton memories and gave her glimpses of her own soul [until] the future became an alluring vision." *

Gandhi's asceticism not only gave him the prestige of a holy man in a country where religion is philosophy and philosophy is history; it established an unbreakable bond between him and the people. His voluntary fasts were little more severe than the "normal" diet which poverty alone imposed on hundreds of millions of Indians. Gandhi understood the masses by suffering with them, and through this they understood him. His great service was to make a bridge of himself between the intellectual and the root strength of the peasants. It has often occurred to me that Mao Tse-tung and Gandhi, though opposites in most things, were curiously alike in this respect. Mao also inured himself to extreme privations in youth and later led the Communist intellectuals to immerse themselves in the hardships of rural life, and equalize themselves with the peasants. He thereby established a genuine rapport with the people, largely peasants as in India, which the Generalissimo and other Kuomintang leaders never attempted.

In India the duel between the Communists and the Congress leadership would also finally be decided in the villages. Gandhi intuitively understood the imminence of that duel. "Thank God!" he exclaimed

* *Toward Freedom*, N.Y., 1941, p. 191.

at the end of his life, in exasperation with the delays in bringing about minimum reforms, "Congress is no longer the sole possessor of the field!" If Congress lost command of its bridge to the peasants, the Communists could yet take over and India would follow China.

Gandhi's methods did bring India freedom and some internal, economic, political and social changes of great importance. His moral influence also lay behind India's policy of neutrality and rejection of armed force in the settlement of disputes. It would be wrong to cite Kashmir to belie this or to assert that non-violent methods were a cult that died with the Mahatma. Gandhi himself deplored the use of force in Kashmir and without his influence India might be in far more serious trouble. She might have yielded to the temptation to use her superior numbers and resources to crush Pakistan's forces in Kashmir rather than merely tolerate the *status quo* imposed there by Pakistan.

It remains to be seen whether the legacy of Gandhi's methods in all India's policies, both external and internal, will suffice to save that great land from ultimate resort to violent social revolution. No one more clearly saw the nature of that test than Jawaharlal Nehru, on whose shoulders Gandhi and history now dropped the mantle of undisputed leadership. A few weeks after Gandhi's death, and just before I left Delhi, I spent a long evening alone with Nehru. And as I listened to him express his fears and hopes I understood that in him, and in the choice of him as a political heir, lay the Mahatma's last best gift to his countrymen and to the cause of peace.

CHAPTER 9

Dinner with Jawaharlal

NEHRU NEEDS no one to speak for him. No leader of international stature has expressed himself more lucidly nor explained the sources of his thought and action in more vivid English prose. But the record of a great man continues to grow, and this is true in Nehru's case, as in Gandhi's.

I had seen Nehru often and done a profile or two of him but on this last night before I left New Delhi we covered several topics of which I could not write before now. It was more than a month since Gandhi's death, and a fortnight after the *coup d'état* which put the Communists in power in Czecho-Slovakia. The cold war had begun its irrevocable course. Nehru, just at the start of his reign over free India, was deeply worried about the future, and now in retrospect some of his remarks help bring a meaning to the experiences I have been trying to share in these pages.

I remember that after a dinner of lamb chops (in his diet as in his agnosticism Jawaharlal was no disciple of Gandhi), we got into a discussion of—standing on one's head! This happened to be one piece of yoga that he took quite seriously; every morning at six he stood on his head for five minutes. He expertly demonstrated for me. When I attempted it myself he showed me the superiority of the chair, as opposed to the wall, to support the efforts of a novice.

"Being a complete reversal of the norm," Jawaharlal explained, "the headstand subjects the vertebrae and the abdominal muscles to completely different conditions in a sudden and highly beneficial way."

"I knew an old sinologue in Peking named L. C. Arlington," I said, "who used to tell me, 'Snow, you've got to stand on your head and think up, if you want to understand China.' I never believed he meant it literally, until now. Perhaps our Western politicians ought to begin practicing it if they want to understand what's happening in Asia—and Africa, too."

Nehru smiled. "Not a bad idea. There's nothing like it to prepare one both psychologically and physically for a tough day. It quickly clears the mind of fatigue and pessimism."

I myself later became a fairly regular head-stander and I learned to value one other yoga method with it: the deep-breathing exercise done lying prone and alternating between complete rigidity and complete relaxation. There is no more restful and refreshing respite from any kind of tension.

"How long will it take," Nehru asked while we were on the subject of China, "for the Communists to defeat Chiang Kai-shek?" Kuomintang victories were then daily being reported in the local press and I was surprised at the way he put the question.

"Two to three years," I said, expecting to be challenged. "What do you think?"

"Perhaps sooner. Chiang's regime is already spiritually defeated. One saw that even during the war."

"Does it worry you?"

"It's a pity the Kuomintang was so corrupt and incompetent. Evidently social revolution was inevitable. But *worry* us? We have too many internal problems to think of interfering with the course of history in China. We have to live with one Communist neighbor already. Now we'll have to learn to live with two." In Nehru's chambers then were photographs of two women. One was of his deceased and dearly beloved wife, Kamala. The other was of Mme. Sun Yat-sen. I wondered how much his talks with Mme. Sun, when he was in China, had helped him understand why revolution was "inevitable" there.

"Chiang probably wouldn't have lasted this long without American help," he went on. "Will America intervene again to save him now? That's what we wonder."

"I don't think so. I think we're through with Chiang Kai-shek."

"I hope you're right. Intervention would be bad for us, bad for the rest of Asia and bad for you, too."

"Meaning—war between Russia and the United States?"

He nodded. "India especially must have peace; at least five years of it. If there is a third world war India may be drawn in."

"I think there will be no major war in the near future."

"What makes you so sure? Things seem to me to be falling apart very fast. Russia is taking this very aggressive line everywhere since they set up the Cominform, and giving one provocation after another. Your people are talking more and more threateningly about using atom bombs on the Russians."

"Russia won't recover from her wounds in much less than a decade," I said. "Her present strategy is an offensive-defensive aimed at protecting what she already has, or at most picking up anything loose on the frontiers. But the Kremlin will be busy for a long time to come just consolidating Communisms's wartime gains without courting disaster in any kind of attack on America or her allies."

"I'm inclined to agree," said Nehru. "But what about your own country? Many feel it is even more unpredictable than Russia."

"Maybe a few individuals would like to try to wipe out Russia with some well-aimed bombs," I answered. "But our government won't initiate any aggressive war now, you may be sure of that."

"Of course I don't know your country. It seems to me there is danger that your capitalists may resort to militarism and war as the easiest way out if there is a serious depression."

"Militarism, perhaps, but not war. There are other ways out for American capitalism—other ways than war or Socialism right now."

"You mean the New Deal—back to the welfare state?"

"Not while American capitalism is feeling as confident as it is today. More likely we'll see a return to arms, on a big scale. The alternative is American subsidy for a kind of system of welfare states abroad —giving away capital to bankrupt countries to enable them to buy American products, thus exploiting the American taxpayer rather than any new colonial empire. We learned this technique from lend-lease during the war. It's no permanent solution for American capitalism, but it's better than relying entirely on state subsidy of the arms market. In fact I wrote a book last year, you know, arguing that while we held absolute superiority in the world, by means of our vast wealth, the atom bomb monopoly and Russia's weakness, we had this choice between leading everybody back onto the old dead-end road of the arms race or spending huge sums abroad, up to 100 billions over the next ten years, as an investment in peace, to help build up the war-devastated countries, including Russia, and to help finance the liberation and modernization of Asia and Africa."

"Wasn't that General Marshall's idea?"

"It was quite genuinely part of his hope. But the plan was advanced far too late. Russia and America had lost contact. There was between us only suspicion and hate. Instead of reassuring the Russians, it frightened them still more. Now we have their answer, born of their own fear and ignorance: that stupid Warsaw declaration that 'divides the world into two camps.' For our own ignorance, that was just what the doctor ordered. From now on we'll have little trouble turning the Marshall plan into a new race to re-arm, and the starving world take the hindmost."

Nehru sighed and shook his head. "It's a pity because the kind of economic help offered by Marshall to Europe is what nearly every country needs and is desperately needed here in India," he said. "But we aren't interested in this talk about 'two camps.' India will never sell her independence to join either 'camp.' We shall do our best to prevent any war between them, and we shall do everything to keep out of it when and if it comes. We simply cannot afford the luxury of having powerful enemies. Our one chance is to get five or ten years, *to build*."

"I'm afraid we are still as far from accepting Socialism as a third way or a third force as Russia is," I said. "And you're on the record as a Socialist. That's enough to scare off our congressmen."

I had just come from Burma, where a Socialist government was launching a novel and far more radical program than India's. Burma was nationalizing the land and some basic industries. That government was actually still fighting native Communists in a state of armed rebellion. Yet our American representatives on the spot viewed the Burmese government with the utmost distaste. They drew little distinction between Burmese Socialism and Communists tied to the Moscow "camp."

The program of Nehru and the Indian Congress at that time, as today, called for a "mixed economy" of state and private capitalism, including the most modest approach to land reform and state ownership only of large *new* basic industries, utilities and power and irrigation works. Would Nehru and his associates find the means to build that "skeleton" framework for a modern economy without resort to wholesale expropriations of capital from the native owning classes in a thoroughgoing social revolution? And if they failed to do it alone, to which "camp" would India then be obliged to turn for the best terms of needed outside aid?

On the answer to that question might hang the fate of the whole world. For if India's 350 millions joined the millions of the Chinese federation and the Soviet Union and its allies, the greater part of humanity would be dwelling within a Communist-led system of states. India's adherence would give such a system dominance in both Asia and Europe, if not before the councils of all nations.

"Wait for ten years" was again Nehru's answer to the question, "and we may know what can be done. In the meantime our program is very far from any 'sudden jump to Socialism,' as some have mistakenly described it. It is simply the continuation of a process of change going on all over the world, including the capitalists, excepting possibly the biggest of them all—that is, the U.S.A." But over the long view the Old Socialist remained unchanged in the convictions he had recorded about the general direction which the Asian nations, and ultimately all nations, were bound to take:

"Inevitably we are led to only one possible solution—the establishment of a Socialist order, first within national boundaries, and eventually in the world as a whole, with a controlled production and distribution of wealth for the public good. How this is to be brought about is another matter, but it is clear that the good of a nation or of mankind must not be held up because some people who profit by the existing order object to change. If political institutions or social institutions stand in the way of such a change, they have to be removed."

Asia's two foremost living political leaders, Nehru and Mao Tsetung, thus seemed to be in agreement on *ends;* it was only in the *means* toward those ends that they still strongly differed. Significantly, the Soviet Union also had no quarrel with Nehru's Socialist ends. It would eventually even resign itself to his Fabian means—for a time at least. As for the United States, our leaders clung doggedly to the belief that only under a system of production for private profit could democracy and freedom exist. Thus they could not wholeheartedly support either Nehru's means *or* his ends. In this predilection lay the greatest likelihood of America's ultimate isolation not only from most of Asia but from Europe as well.

In a time when men had cracked the secrets of matter and space itself, and when planned economies were already conquering the complexities of production and distribution for a third of mankind, few peoples outside the continental boundaries of the United States any longer believed that governments need stand by helpless before the old mystical "business cycle," complacently waiting for a "business upturn" as Micawber waited for "something to turn up," while millions went unemployed and billions in production were sacrificed to the god of *laissez-faire* sanctified above the public need and good.

I spoke of Gandhi to Nehru once more before I left Delhi.

Jimmy Sheean, my superstitious Irish friend, had been impressed with the fact that his wristwatch had stopped at an interview with Gandhi and had stopped again at the moment Gandhi was killed. One day at a press conference with Nehru we sat listening to him for some time when Sheean suddenly pointed to that same remarkable watch, which he had had repaired.

"Stopped again: at precisely the minute of our appointment with Nehru," he whispered.

Automatically I looked at my watch. It had also stopped.

I remembered then that Jimmy had waked up, the morning after the assassination, with "stigmata" on his fingers. It was true that they looked suspiciously like cigarette blisters; but I also recalled his odd prescience of Gandhi's death. Now the watch business was hard to explain. After the conference I found myself telling Nehru about the mystery. What did he make of it? Then this son of "occult" Asia, whom his people called Jewel of India, tilted his Gandhi hat to one side and smiled.

"What you need," he said, "are new watches."

CHAPTER 10

New Watches Needed

THERE HAS seldom been such successful demagoguery, conspired in by a responsible American political party, as the "twenty-years-of-treason" hoax which helped carry the Republican party to power in 1952. Nor was there in our history any campaign more costly to the American people, to our prestige abroad and to our internal unity and self-respect, than the triumph of lies and slander, spearheaded by McCarthy and Nixon, which charged Roosevelt, Marshall, Stilwell, Truman, Acheson and loyal men of the U.S. Foreign Service with betrayal of our country and "selling China to the Russians." It must remain a matter of national remorse to us that the honorable soldier who was to become our President for two terms was allowed by his advisers to lend support to the hucksters of these deceits by going to Wisconsin and touring there with Senator McCarthy, who had publicly called Eisenhower's wartime superior, General Marshall, "the greatest traitor in American history."

China was not, and could not have been, "sold out" by any Americans. China was never for a moment ours to sell. It was not ours to have and to hold in the 1940's any more than it is Russia's today. The Chinese revolution was not born in a vacuum unconnected with the outside world, but it was first and last a product of Chinese history, and only secondarily influenced by external phenomena.

It is too late now to debate the lost years when the deadly aberration of McCarthyism held the nation in thralldom; and it is much too late to fall before the great temptation to sentimentalize about what might have been if Congress had done more sober reflecting before Sputnik. In my own case it is especially impermissible to hind-think; what I thought is spread on the record. Almost a decade ago, as an associate editor of the *Saturday Evening Post,* I discussed our future problems with a revolutionary China for which I had, long before American intervention, predicted complete victory. I am sorry to have to quote my own authority at such length as follows, but I do not find elsewhere an analysis which contains this essence of the truth about

China and Russia as *I* saw it then and as I have seen it, for the most part, ever since.

"Will the Communist-led government inevitably mean that China must fall under the absolute domination of the Kremlin?" I asked.*
"Will Moscow be able to plant 'specialists' in the Chinese police force, the army, the party Politburo, the state apparatus, to constitute a government above government as in Eastern Europe? Will the Kremlin be able to dictate internal policy to Chinese Communists as well as control China's vote in the United Nations?"

These were the great "ethical" and "moral" questions which troubled our leaders in 1949, when we had not yet questioned the Chinese people's inalienable right, as Americans claimed the right in 1776, to choose their own form of government by revolution. And the answers? I continued:

"First, consider some geopolitical facts of fundamental significance. China is an immense country . . . and with two times Soviet Russia's population. It is rich in human and natural resources, with an ancient civilization which has survived 3,000 years of catastrophes to keep its basic values intact. China is the first country among all the colonies and semi-colonies in which Communists have won power.

"Second, China is the first *major* power outside Russia to fall into the hands of avowed Marxists.

"Third, the Chinese Red army fought its major battles for survival long before the recent war, and without any Soviet aid. Excepting Yugoslavia, China has the only Communists who actually came to power without the direct military intervention of Russian arms—or even the implied threat, as in the case of Prague.

"Fourth, the Chinese party alone in the world today is led by a Communist who remained in power despite a Comintern demand for his removal.

"Fifth, as a result of long isolation and independent development, the Chinese Communist party has acquired immense experience and self-confidence. A whole generation of civil war has trained great numbers of competent military and political leaders. . . . It is one thing for Russian generals to push around military or political bosses in the small, occupied states of Europe. It is quite another problem to manage a giant the size of China, run by a disciplined party in control of a great army which could make a good defense of its independence against any foreign power.

"Sixth, Mao Tse-tung's personality is reflected in the internal struc-

* See the *Saturday Evening Post*, April 9, 1949. Italics added here.

ture of a party that is deeply Chinese in character. The great majority have learned their Marxism from the history of the Chinese revolution and the textbooks and doctrines worked out in the writings of Mao Tse-tung and other native leaders.

"Seventh, the Chinese Communists were, until the Belgrade schism, the only non-Russian party which dared openly proclaim that it had made significant new contributions to the theory and revolutionary practice of Marxism . . . Mao Tse-tung and his followers were the first to prove that Communist-led revolutions in semi-colonial countries can conquer by combining the role of national liberation with anti-feudal social reform movements. In a setting quite unforeseen by the Kremlin hierarchy they proved that such revolutions can succeed without depending upon urban proletarian insurrections, without help from Russia or the world proletariat, and on the basis of the organized peasantry as a main force.

"As a result of the Communists' sovereign victory in China there already exists in East Asia a new set of circumstances with significant implications both inside and beyond the Marxist world. Moscow must deal with a major foreign power run by Communists possessing all the means of maintaining real equality and independence.

"If Russia were now to seek to deprive the Peking government of control over the economic, political and military life of Manchuria there would be a head-on collision of nationalisms within the Communist-run world. Chinese Communists could no more survive the loss of Manchuria to Russia than the latter could permit the annexation of the Ukraine by Communist Poland or its absorption into a Polish-German Communist federation.

"Far from accepting the role of satellites, either for Manchuria or China as a whole, the Chinese Communists look upon their country as the potential focus of a new federation of Eastern Socialist states* which can exist independently, on a plane of complete equality with the U.S.S.R. While the Kremlin cannot be much happier over such a prospect than it was about Tito's Balkan federation scheme, it would be highly illusory to imagine that the Russians will promptly repeat, in China, the mistakes which lost them effective control in Yugoslavia. They will proceed with extreme caution, hopefully waiting for the Americans to make the blunders on which their own success could be improvised.

"China now represents a long-range problem of 'management' for the Kremlin which can either be simplified or greatly complicated by

* China, Manchuria, Mongolia, Tibet and the non-Chinese tribes.

American policy. So long as it is true that the United States is the main support of the old regime in China, and of any or all anti-Communist parties, groups, politicians or war lords prepared to continue what is now clearly a lost war, Americans will easily hold their present positions as Foreign Enemy No. 1.

"The new Peking Communist regime has been established by a revolution which satisfied some urgent needs of the peasantry combined with the energy aroused by anti-foreign slogans of a nationalist movement. It can succeed only by continuing that same pattern—by redeeming the most important promises of internal progress, popular reform, and true national independence. It would be destroyed if it surrendered the interests of the Chinese people to any Russian demands which might make of China a colonial instrument or base for aggressive war against the United States.

"The new government's program envisages rapid industrialization, expanded public works and communications of all kinds, greatly increased and modernized agricultural output, enlarged facilities for mass education and public health work, and the training of thousands of new technicians capable of directing an economy co-ordinated by state planning. Yet it starts off with a nation that is bankrupt—its cities ruined, its railways wrecked, its machinery antiquated or useless, its river and canal systems broken down, its people hungry, weary and ragged, eager to work but lacking the tools and other means. Chinese Communists are not so stupid as to think, once they carry the full responsibility of power, that they can solve all those internal problems and simultaneously launch a war, against the United States.

"General MacArthur was quite right when he said recently that Chinese Red success did not endanger our security. As a market, China need not be missed; the balance of our trade there has been heavily unfavorable for many years. This is an excellent time for Uncle Sam to leave the initiative in our future relations entirely up to the Chinese, and give them plenty of time, years if necessary, to realize the main fact. That is, that Sino-American trade is at least as important to China as it is to the U.S.A.

"I have suggested that there are serious 'contradictions' between the aspirations of the Chinese Communists and Russian nationalist expansion under the guise of 'internationalism.' But such differences are a very minor matter compared to the 'contradictions' between the 'national aspirations of the Chinese Communists' and the aims of continued American intervention against them! If the purpose of American policy is to strengthen China's independence from Russia, then it is not likely to be achieved by forcing the Communists to resign themselves to the terms of Russian alliance, in self-defense. If it were demonstrated, however, that the United States does not intend to hold onto any part of China, nor to try to impose its will there in alliance with anti-Communists of all varieties, the factors I have discussed would then come into operation in establishing the character of Sino-Russian Communist relations.

"In any event in the long run the Chinese Communist party probably cannot and will not subordinate the national interests of China to the interests of the Kremlin. If our policy is washed clean of interventionism, history may evolve along lines for which all the necessary preconditions now exist. China will become the first Communist-run major power independent of Moscow's dictation.

"Peking might eventually become a kind of Asiatic Moscow, an Eastern Rome preaching a kind of 'Asiatic Marxism' out of Moscow's control. As such it would, of course, come to constitute the symbol of the overthrow of the European colonial system in Asia, as well as the denial of our own principles of democracy bound up with ideas of private property rights in the ownership of the means of production. On the other hand, it might also set up a frontier against the expansion of Communism *as an extension of Russian nationalism* in the East— a barrier as effective as that now erected at Belgrade in the West.

"People accustomed to thinking in terms of ideological absolutes may find it hard to understand how 'Communism' can be 'contained' by Communism, or how it could be checked by anything but its exact opposite, which they tend to see as 'capitalism.' But there are many shades and variations in meaning and growth in words of that type, and there will be more. Thus, it is likely that the threat of Soviet Russian world dictatorship will be checked by rival developments of Communist power as well as by social democracy and modified capitalism.

"There are risks involved in a policy of non-intervention in the internal affairs of China and other Asian states; there are perhaps even greater risks entailed by unqualified support for the status quo . . . The entire colonial system is close to an end. Any policy which denies that or aggressively attempts to revive imperialism—under whatever name—can only prolong the struggle for equality and independence at further frightful waste of human effort. It is much too late to restore any empires in this part of the world. Too late for Russia as well as for any other power."

End quote.

That was a year before we succumbed to McCarthyism, and we were still free to look for "mountains above tare-seeds" in Asia.

The Korean conflict created an emotional atmosphere which blurred our national vision about China for some time. Yet by 1958, few students would deny the validity of the foregoing analysis. Some years ago people as far apart as Dean Acheson, Senator Knowland, George Kennan and John Foster Dulles used to dismiss China as simply a puppet or "slave state" under the iron heel of Russia, ignoring the fact that a great revolution was occurring there. None of them would adhere to any such contention today. China manifestly has become not only Russia's political peer but is in her own right, and for the first time in modern history, one of the four major powers of the earth.

This phenomenal emergence of the Chinese republic, on a level quite different from the satellites of Eastern Europe, irrevocably changed the balance of power both inside the Communist-run world and between that world and the alliance system dominated by the United States. China's complete recovery of sovereignty in Manchuria and elsewhere on her continental frontiers, her extraordinarily rapid economic progress based on a "mixed economy" and a program of gradual, systematic transition toward Socialism, also became important ingredients of change in the whole structure of the Communist-held states. For when Stalin's successors did not, as many of their enemies hoped, repeat Stalin's mistakes in Yugoslavia in dealing with the Chinese, they had to begin to alter the rigid concept of absolute Kremlin dictatorship over all other national Communist parties.

While China thus proved to be the first major nation ruled by a Communist party that did not owe its ascendancy to Russian police power, and need not, therefore, depend upon it absolutely for survival, the United States not only continued to be the "main support of the old regime" but constantly improved "its position as Foreign Enemy No. 1" of the new republic. "Contradictions between the aspirations of the Chinese Communists and Russian nationalist expansion" did actually exist in 1949. But those "contradictions" became, as predicted, "a very minor matter compared to the contradictions between the national aspirations of the Chinese Communists and American intervention against them." Our reaction to the revolution stubbornly pushed China toward ever-closer collaboration with Russia.

So grotesquely did the Korean conflict distort our judgment that few of us could see ourselves as the Chinese and other Asians saw us. We seldom paused to think how our position would look if reversed. What if it were the Chinese who sat athwart *our* inner waters as a matter of security? Most of us quickly forgot how we put Chiang in possession of Formosa and tied down our country there in an alliance with a few hundred thousand refugees imposed upon the native majority. We forgot that it was on American initiative, and *not* as a result of demands by the revolutionary leaders, that we closed all our consulates, withdrew our diplomats from China and severed our contacts with the mainland. We forgot too quickly that we gave billions in arms and other supplies for the exclusive aid of Chiang Kai-shek which he used in a civil war that cost millions of casualties. We did not seem to remember that we gave another two billions in aid to Chiang Kai-shek and his exiled followers after 1949, and continued to subsidize them and their empty talk about a "reconquest" of China, in support of a position which was backed by no one else and exposed us to a possible conflict with the mainland republic in which we would be completely alone.

As far as most leaders among Asia's billion and a half people were concerned they saw America's Formosa protectorate solely in terms of power politics and as the fulcrum of an attempt to restore an old pre-war balance-of-power system. Thoroughly shattered by the collapse of colonialism, that system could not be rebuilt simply because the balance of forces now lay outside the true sphere of influence of both Russia and the U.S. It lay in the hands of nationalist or social revolutionary regimes which supplanted imperialist power, in what were now the neutral countries of Asia—particularly India, Burma and Indonesia, with Japan yearning to join them.

A strengthened system of neutral states might help to establish a more or less stable equilibrium of power in Eastern Asia. Yet any wholehearted support of that alternative was also excluded as long as we clung to the fiction that Chiang Kai-shek was China and insisted that nations with a different view were "morally" wrong and not worthy of the large-scale American aid which all of them needed.

It was America's pretensions to moral authority in its intervention in China's internal affairs which seemed most hypocritical to Asian eyes. Clearly the Formosan protectorate had been set up under the shelter of American armed force. Clearly it was that force which alone maintained the Chiang Kai-shek government. Yet our argument against recognition of the Chinese republic, and its claims to sovereignty in Formosa, rested solely on the contention that *we* could not countenance "changes brought about by force."

This paradox not only cut us off from all relations with the Chinese republic; it also created misunderstanding between America and India,

Indonesia, and other Asian powers. China and India together constitute two-fifths of the human race and most of Asia's peoples. Not only did we deny the right of the Chinese to overthrow and change a government by revolutionary means; American policy also made it clear that we looked upon India's refusal to join us in an armed pact against China as almost equally "morally" reprehensible. And yet it was in India, above all countries, that a new republic was established by non-violent means and whose foremost leader did more than any other individual in his time to try to bring civilized practices into use in relations between men and between nations.

Somehow, if the Western world was to avoid a cataclysm, it must learn to listen to and heed *both* these authentic voices rising clearly from resurgent and renascent Asia—the one appealing to tolerance and fraternal interest for understanding and generous help, before it was too late; the other arguing in the language of revolution, which Asians had now demonstrated their ability to employ more effectively than we could counteract it.

The old Asia was gone and a free Asia and a soon-to-be-free Africa were rising to take their place beside the nations of the West, just when atomic power might offer mankind rich promises of universal release from slavery and want. New and imaginative thinking was needed to measure the swift changes in time-space relationships between the societies and continents of men, just as for the control and use of the dreadful and marvelous services of mass and energy being freed by fission and fusion.

Not that the path of conflict between the Asians and ourselves was laid down by America alone. "God forbid that I should claim for our country the worth of perfect righteousness," said Harry S. Truman on October 15, 1957, in a modest assessment none could deny. "We have committed sins of omission and sins of commission, for which we stand in need of the mercy of the Lord. But I dare maintain before the world that we have done much that was right."

In the brief moment of twenty years the United States assumed world responsibility and extended military and non-military aid to others on an unprecedented scale. Some of its ultimate consequences might be questioned, but one impressive thing that could be said about our foreign policy was that we had nowhere used our immense power to initiate aggressive war, and that we had faithfully adhered to our obligations under the United Nations Charter.

No foreign policy ever attains all its aims. Even when given aims are achieved, and seem to be "right" at the time, the end result often turns out to be quite the opposite from that originally desired. Every power policy provokes an antithesis; the ensuing synthesis always reflects opposites and thus differs from both thesis and antithesis. We fought and won World War I to "make the world safe for democracy" —in alliance with Tsarist absolutism. Probably the most important single change brought about in that period was the Russian revolution. Winston Churchill boasted that he "did not become His Majesty's first minister in order to preside over the liquidation of the empire." Britain won the war—and liquidated most of the empire. Stalin opposed the Marshall Plan and arbitrarily "divided the world into two camps"; he frightened the "divided" West into a NATO alliance he wished to forestall. America imposed an embargo and economic blockade against China, hoping to hasten the end of the Peking regime. To this challenge China responded by mobilizing its vast human resources as never before, in a rapid industrialization and educational program which strengthened China's economic independence and by 1958 saw her graduating more doctors and more engineers than the United States, and three times as many teachers.

The more determined and dedicated our denial of the stability of the Soviet system became, the greater the impact it made on Western thought and practice. The very books we wrote to prove that the U.S.S.R. was "on the point of bankruptcy" (as John Foster Dulles asserted in 1956) testified to that. Conversely, the more stubbornly the Russians decried the evils of predatory American "imperialism" and "proved" our system a failure engaged in "digging its own grave," the more the Soviet elite copied American industrial techniques and envied American standards of comfort, and the more the ruling Soviet hierarchy recognized individual achievement in terms of differential material rewards. On our side, as Edmund Wilson said in *A Piece of My Mind,* "We have also been copying the Russians in less constructive ways such as our recent security purges and political heresy hunts."

America cannot, of course, do everything in the world—alone. America's "sins of omission and commission" may, indeed, more often be traced to a tendency to try to do too much abroad—and alone —rather than first doing the best possible at home. The awkward fact remains: fifteen out of sixteen persons on earth are not Americans and can never be expected to respond obediently to all the historical impulses which dictate our own policies. The rate of scientific discovery and overturn is so rapid now that within the next generation or so man is likely to advance, in an evolutionary sense, more than during the previous seven thousand years—if he can stay alive. In such a world radical social and political change and adaptation cannot be prevented. At most it can be slightly modified in the interest of general survival. Any policy which is not consciously designed to accommodate inevitable change, or which adheres strictly to nostalgic dreams of restoring the past, is necessarily doomed to failure.

Nationalism is not a particularly attractive phase of human development—especially somebody else's nationalism—but it is clearly an unavoidable transition toward regional organization, itself a step toward world order. The more every nation seeks to strengthen the United Nations organization, the more it focuses its means of communications with others (aid, investment, trade, cultural exchange, defense) in centralized planning, responsibility and accountability with and to other nations—the more realistic a foreign policy it will have, and the less likely it is to be upset by coming reform and revolution still foreseeable in many lands of an unevenly developed earth.

For two decades the U.S.S.R., attempting to "build socialism in one country," stood isolated and alone against the world. Today about two-thirds of the people of Europe and Asia live under state-planned economies, and challenge us with "competitive co-existence."

Behind the rivalry of the Soviet Union and the United States for dominance in the world market—with political ideas as well as things —there is one long-range question of first magnitude. Few speak openly of it but increasingly it troubles the best brains in all areas of leadership in the U.S.A., especially whenever there is any serious threat of a substantial withdrawal of the state subsidy to private industry, via defense spending, on which our economic stability has heavily depended for twenty years. That question is how much longer a still largely unplanned, unco-ordinated, private-profit motivated economy can compete successfully against wholly state-planned socialized economies which (in Russia and China) have moved forward over recent years at three to four times the rate of growth in gross national production of the United States, and are at present more than doubling that rate of growth in contrast to an American production in recessionary decline.

In this era, "competitive co-existence" is not just a matter of persuading coy Cambodians or Arab oil kings or dictators to take dollars rather than roubles or Chinese money. It is equally a matter of developing attractive alternatives in our domestic life which will not only arouse admiration but which can be emulated by nations in a hurry— and all backward nations are now, or soon will be, in a hurry. No foreign policy is greater than the success of the domestic system which inspires it, and during America's pursuit of cold war aims abroad grave questions have piled up in alarming proportions at home.

A seriously inadequate educational system; continued racial bigotry and discrimination; increasing thousands of derelict youths left unassimilated in the constructive life of society; antiquated public health, prison and court systems; a growing shortage of hospitals, doctors and funds for the support of non-military scientific and medical research; increasing billions of dollars worth of commodity surpluses accumulating in an economy where mounting billions were paid to subsidize farmers to grow less and less (while food cost more and more in unchecked inflation)—all pose problems which demand imaginative reform and modernization if our nation is not to lag behind in the world. Not the least of our unsolved dilemmas arises from a policy of apparently limitless nuclear weapons development, and a rapid poisoning of our atmosphere which may be preparing a sepulchre for ourselves and a world peopled by monsters unrecognizable as our children.

Meanwhile, our journey to the beginning had brought us to the crest of an altogether unexampled floodtide of human advance, ready to carry forward nearly two billion underfed and undereducated people who are awakening to new needs, new dimensions, new dreams of a future bright with hope and freedom. For all of us today it is a time for every nation to cast out the beam in its own eyes before seeking to cast out the mote in a neighbor's eyes, a parting time from our prehistory, a true childhood's end when men at last have to begin behaving like Man.

It is in this sense that Gandhi's truth and message of brotherhood imperatively has to be learned and put in practice. Otherwise all that I first set out to see, thirty years ago, all those

cities of men
And manners, councils, climates, governments

may altogether perish and leave no word behind of how they used their first full hour of freedom to turn the green earth into a dry and lifeless cinder.

Index

EDGAR SNOW, a native of Missouri, went to the Far East when he was twenty-two. He made his home in China for twelve years, studied the country and the language, and lectured at Yenching University in Peking, where he made friendships with students who are among China's leaders today. As a foreign correspondent in China, Burma, India and Indochina he worked successively for the *Chicago Tribune, New York Sun, New York Herald Tribune* and *London Daily Herald.* Then, as associate editor of the *Saturday Evening Post,* he reported wartime and postwar events in Asia and Europe, and became its widely quoted specialist on China, India and the U.S.S.R. He was the author of eleven books, including *Red Star Over China, The Battle for Asia, People on Our Side, Red China Today: The Other Side of the River,* and *The Long Revolution.* He died in 1972.